The Metaphor of Gender

The Metaphor of Gender

Identity in a Sacramental Universe

KATHERINE ABETZ

RESOURCE *Publications* · Eugene, Oregon

THE METAPHOR OF GENDER
Identity in a Sacramental Universe

Copyright © 2025 Katherine Abetz. All rights reserved. Except for brief quotations in critical publications or reviews, no part of this book may be reproduced in any manner without prior written permission from the publisher. Write: Permissions, Wipf and Stock Publishers, 199 W. 8th Ave., Suite 3, Eugene, OR 97401.

Resource Publications
An Imprint of Wipf and Stock Publishers
199 W. 8th Ave., Suite 3
Eugene, OR 97401

www.wipfandstock.com

PAPERBACK ISBN: 979-8-3852-2705-1
HARDCOVER ISBN: 979-8-3852-2706-8
EBOOK ISBN: 979-8-3852-2707-5
VERSION NUMBER 01/02/25

Scripture quotations are from the New Revised Standard Version of the Bible, copyright © 1989, National Council of the Churches of Christ in the United States of America. Used by permission. All rights reserved worldwide.

Contents

Acknowledgements | vii
Introduction | 1

1. **The Covenant of Language** | 16
   Verbiage or Meaning? | 18
   A Broken Contract | 21
   Airy Houses | 25
   The Symbol Speaks to Us | 29

2. **Renouncing the *Hubris*?** | 37
   Invented *Visibilia* | 39
   Allegory of the Masculine | 46
   An Allegorical Deity? | 54
   Green Glasses or Green Fingers? | 59

3. **A Biblical Motif** | 67
   Living In, Tasting Beyond | 70
   Wisdom and Humanity | 77
   The Divine Courtship | 84
   Allegory at Large | 87

4. **God's New Thing** | 94
   The Twofold Role of the Woman | 95
   A Protestant and an Anglican-Roman Catholic Interpretation | 97
   The Inversion Factor | 103
   An Allegorical Mary? | 109

5. *Hāʾādām* | 115
    God Alien Femaleness? | 118
    Non-Gendered *Imago Dei*? | 125
    Non-Gendered Origin? | 132
    The Resurrected Body | 139

6. **Gender as Metaphor** | 147
    Rethinking Sexual Difference | 150
    Patriarchy or Pseudo-Masculinity? | 156
    From Creation to New Covenant | 159
    Unity in Diversity | 166
    Postscript: Women, Men and the Dance | 172

7. **The Swamp of Ambiguity** | 175
    Poppy Field Identity | 177
    Exodus of Meaning | 181
    Swamp or Tehom? | 186
    Potential *Imago Dei*? | 188

8. **Writing the Body** | 201
    Maximizing the Difference | 202
    Next Steps | 208
    The Matriarchal Line | 217
    What is not assumed? | 223

9. **Inclusive Language** | 232
    Model as Weapon? | 234
    Discourse in the Churches | 238
    Authorship of Hebrews? | 244
    Born of Woman | 247
    An Exegetical Postscript | 257

10. **Narrative Identity** | 259
    Master or Disciple? | 261
    Contingent, Embodied and Different | 266
    Two Types of Self-Emptying | 271
    Concrete Universals | 280
    Postscript: The Mythic Way | 289

Conclusion | 292
Bibliography | 303
Index | 309

Acknowledgements

ELISABETH SCHÜSSLER FIORENZA LAMENTS the effect of the current neoliberal market on academic publishing, requiring feminists to "relinquish the analytic category 'wo/man' and replace it with the analytic category of gender." In Schüssler Fiorenza's words:

> Colleagues . . . told me that they were persuaded to drop the word 'feminist' from their titles and content descriptions in order to have their books published. It was no longer feminist or wo/men's but gender studies that were invited, published and promoted.[1]

Such a trend would look set to leave key questions of identity and sexual difference unanswered.

It would be too much to say that this book deals either with the analytic category of 'wo/man' (whatever that may be) or of gender *per se*. Its aim is to build on the frame of reference, argued in my earlier book, in which human beings are made in God's image, not the other way round. The journey may then begin of exploring what this means for women and the relationship between the sexes. In this endeavor, I stand on the shoulders of giants and giantesses (if I may be permitted to call them that). While not classing myself as a feminist as commonly understood by the term, I have found useful material in this field, much dating from

---

1. See Schüssler Fiorenza, "Feminist Remappings in Times of NeoLiberalism," 171; 177–79.

the late twentieth century. I would like to acknowledge the debt I owe to many women writers, among them Janet Martin Soskice in particular.

My journey began with my doctoral question: what does it mean for a woman to be created in God's image? In *The Wizard's Illusion*, I attempted to map the search for identity against a background of the history of Western thought. My aim was to answer the question behind the question: where do meaning and identity come from? In this, the second of my books on metaphor, I focus on identity and the *imago Dei*. As before, the map is sketched out and illustrated by characters and events from *The Wizard of Oz*.

Although I cannot claim to have literally walked the Land of Oz, I owe much to something of a similar nature. My thanks continue for support from my supervisor Dr Charles Sherlock, from my examiner Professor Benjamin Myers, from the Melbourne University of Divinity and the Dalton McCaughey Library staff. I am grateful to Revd. Anne Hibbard for being willing to read my work. I am grateful to Wipf and Stock for being willing to publish it. I am grateful to my husband Walter for many discussions. I am grateful for God's guidance into the unknown and undreamed of.

Lastly, I want to acknowledge future readers. A map is not much use without those who are interested enough to walk the country.

Introduction

'I am Oz, the Great and Terrible. Who are you, and why do you seek me?' . . .
 'I am Dorothy, the Small and Meek. I have come to you for help.'[1]

'I think you are a very bad man,' said Dorothy.
 'Oh, no, my dear; I'm really a very good man; but I'm a very bad Wizard, I must admit.'[2]

"ARE WOMEN HUMAN?" IS the title of an essay (in a book of the same name) by English writer and theologian Dorothy L. Sayers. That the question could be posed at all indicates a serious issue. The opening chapter of Genesis affirms the creation of gendered humanity in the divine image but what this means for women has received surprisingly little attention. Exploring the connection between the *imago Dei* and identity for women is the aim of this book.

Sayers writes about what she calls "sex-equality," which is "like all questions affecting human relationships, delicate and complicated."[3] To use a comparable term, I enter into the question of "sex-identity," equally

---

1. Baum, *Wizard of Oz*, chapter 11.
2. Baum, *Wizard of Oz*, chapter 15.
3. Sayers, *Are Women Human?*, 17.

affecting human relationships and equally, if not more, delicate and complicated. Sayers makes a plea for individual ability and interest to govern eligibility for work. The focus is on the differences between women, independent of gender. "Sex-identity" is on a different footing: the focus is on women as women.

That the question I wish to address is delicate and complicated will be evident in the title of this book. Other writers may have included "metaphor" and "gender" in their titles but none to my knowledge who have referred to the metaphor *of* gender. In my title I enter not one but two battlegrounds, since the meanings of "metaphor" and "gender" are highly contested. The nature and effect of "metaphor" is the focus of my first book, *The Wizard's Illusion*. In this, the companion book, I suggest that gender is a key to human relationships and that such relationships point beyond themselves, in the style of a metaphor, to a greater reality.

I have said that the focus is on women as women. The *imago Dei* does not isolate women's identity from humanity as a whole but establishes it, I maintain, in the social relationships which reflect the divine social relationships. I am not alone in this. In her chapter on the *imago Dei*, Janet Martin Soskice quotes Jewish writer, Tikva Frymer-Kensky:

> Whatever the precise interpretation, the plural nature of the creation of humanity applies to both the creator ("we") and the creature ("he created them male and female"). Social relationship is an indispensable part of both human nature and human purpose, and there can be no utterly single human being.[4]

If relationship is a key to the *imago Dei*, it is also relevant to the way metaphor works as I outline below.

Metaphor, Soskice points out, is a linguistic term, a form of figurative language.[5] Gender has a foot in the linguistic camp of many languages, but this is not my area here. "In a metaphor," says M. H. Abrams, "a word which in ordinary usage signifies one kind of thing, quality, or action is applied to another, without express indication of the relation between them."[6] Abrams draws attention to the terminology, introduced by I. A. Richards, of "vehicle" for the secondary subject of ordinary usage

---

4. Soskice, *Kindness of God*, 50–51 n. 25, citing Frymer-Kensky, *Studies in Bible and Feminist Criticism*, 101.

5. See Soskice, *Metaphor and Religious Language*, 16–17.

6. Abrams, *Glossary of Literary Terms*, 36–37, citing Richards, *Philosophy of Rhetoric*, chapters 5 and 6.

which points beyond itself to the "tenor" or principal subject. On these terms, I present gendered relationships at the human level as a *vehicle* pointing towards the *tenor*, divine relationships.

At this point things become delicate and complicated. In what sense does figurative language refer beyond itself, in particular in connection with the *imago Dei* in which direct observation of the tenor is unavailable? Soskice argues for a "critical realist" or "reality depicting" frame of reference for "metaphor" as a linguistic term, a frame applicable in theology and other areas.[7] But there are other possible ways of understanding metaphor. Soskice considers religious metaphor alongside scientific models, as does Sallie McFague. Soskice cites an idealist supposition that scientific models are necessary, but artificial, constructs which do not claim to describe external reality. Such models can then be classed as "heuristic" or "useful fictions." McFague employs the terms "heuristic" and "mostly fiction" as well as "functional" and "pragmatic" in relation to her usage of religious metaphor.[8]

In *The Wizard's Illusion* I considered McFague's "metaphorical theology" in some detail. McFague endorses an analogy in which the function of "metaphor" resembles the green glasses worn by the inhabitants of Oz which made the Emerald City look green.[9] She goes so far as to say: "What we *know* are the metaphors or projections of the self, the worlds it creates. The relativity of knowledge demands such a perspective."[10] If "metaphor" is no more than a projection of the self and the self creates the world or worlds, where does this leave social relationship?

McFague's work on "metaphor" and theological models has been influential in feminist analysis. Rosemary Ruether who claims to speak for feminist theology applies what might be called a "useful fiction" frame of reference to the *imago Dei*. She states:

> The definition of God as patriarchal male is presumed [in feminist theology] to be a projection by patriarchal males of their own self-image and roles, in relation to women and lower

---

7. See Soskice, *Metaphor and Religious Language*, chapter 7 "Metaphor, Reference and Realism."

8. See Soskice, *Metaphor and Religious Language*, 120–21. Cf. McFague, *Models of God*, xi–xii; 36; 192 n 37.

9. See McFague, *Metaphorical Theology*, 41; cf. 150.

10. McFague, *Speaking in Parables*, 147. McFague's italics.

nature, upon God. Thus it is not 'man' who is made in God's image, but God who has been made in man's image.[11]

A feminist critique, she continues, "constructs images of God that will better manifest and promote the full realization of human potential for women and men." The projection is seen as useful or beneficial. The assumption of a "useful fiction" frame of reference is contrary to tradition, as Ruether points out: "This ideological critique of the image of God idea in Scripture and Christian tradition changes fundamentally the nature of the discussion."

The nature of the discussion is, as I say, complex. Dorothy's encounters with the Wizard of Oz may serve to illustrate this complexity. At her first meeting, Dorothy asks for the Wizard's help in the belief that he actually can perform magical acts. At her second meeting, Dorothy discovers that his magical acts are no more than a "useful fiction." One might say that this discovery changes fundamentally the nature of the discussion. At the first meeting, Dorothy adopts the role of "Small and Meek" in response to the Wizard's claim to be "Great and Terrible." At the second meeting, her disillusionment becomes indignation: "I think you are a very bad man." This change in attitude is reflected in Ruether's analysis of the "image of God idea in Scripture and Christian tradition." But there is a difference between Dorothy and Ruether in the way in which the change of attitude comes about. Dorothy describes the Wizard as "a very bad man" because she finds out that his wizardry is only a "useful fiction." For Ruether, the "patriarchal" projection is "very bad" from the outset because of its negative effect on women. On this ground she wishes to change the nature of the discussion. Dorothy's frame of reference might be termed "reality depicting": she expects a wizard to be able to perform real magical acts. Ruether has no parallel expectation. Her presentation assumes that the *imago Dei* is a "useful fiction," with the corollary that women can benefit from it as well as men.

I stated above that what it means for women to be created in God's image has received surprisingly little attention. A perceived imbalance in the *imago Dei* may account for this. The focus has been on lack of sex-equality rather than on sex-identity. Sayers goes so far as to ask: "Are women human?" Kim Power reports that in 585 the ecclesiastical Council of Mâcon voted on whether women were "*homo*," i.e., human or not. The

---

11. See Ruether, "Christian Tradition and Feminist Hermeneutics," 286–87. Cf. n 42. Ruether cites McFague's *Metaphorical Theology* and *Models of God*.

humanity of women is said to have been affirmed.[12] Earlier, says Power, Augustine of Hippo had "wrestled with the concept of women as the *imago Dei*" in a climate in which other patristic writers denied it.[13] This kind of history lends some color to claims that Christianity has favored a "patriarchal" way of thinking that puts women's equality in doubt.

McFague writes of "patriarchalism" as the "superior-subordinate paradigm" of men over women:

> Feminists who have analyzed the patriarchal model have only brought into sharp relief the pattern that, from at least the time of Augustine, has been the dominant one in the Christian understanding of relations between God and humanity, as well as people with each other.[14]

In this "patriarchal" climate of thinking, as discerned through feminist analysis, "women do not model God," says McFague, while "men have a 'role-model' in God for defining their self-identity."[15] The feminist remedy for this is for women to be said to model God. Feminist psychoanalyst Luce Irigaray states that "monotheistic religions cannot claim to be ethical unless they submit themselves to a radical interrogation relative to the sexual attribution ... of their paradigms." She goes on to ask: "are the peoples of monotheism ready to assert that their God is a woman?"[16]

Feminist analysis declares that Christian tradition has excluded women from the *imago Dei*. But how wholesale was this exclusion? Augustine of Hippo dissented from other patristic views, reports Kim Power. Further, the consensus of thought at Mâcon was not so overriding as to decide against the humanity of women. Far from reflecting the dominant pattern of a "patriarchal" culture, the Council is said to have been *divided* about the status of women. Something else was operating besides a pattern of patriarchy. Nuances along these lines, however, tend to be overlooked in a "useful fiction" frame of reference.

12. See Power, *Veiled Desire*, 58. Power cites Ranke-Heinemann, *Eunuchs for the kingdom of heaven*, 168. Cf. Børresen, "God's image. Is woman excluded?," 210. Citing Gregory of Tours, *Historia Francorum*, Børresen reports that the issue was resolved on the basis of Genesis 1:27 and also the term "Son of man" applied to the son of the Virgin.

13. See Power, *Veiled Desire*, 56–58.

14. See McFague, *Metaphorical Theology*, 145–49. Among feminist works, McFague cites Daly, *Beyond God the Father* and Ruether, ed., *Religion and Sexism*.

15. McFague, *Metaphorical Theology*, 149–50.

16. *Irigaray Reader*, 185.

The feminist critique of "the image of God idea in Scripture and Christian tradition changes fundamentally the nature of the discussion," states Ruether. But is it a discussion on equal terms? Irigaray asks whether the peoples of monotheism are ready to *assert* that their God is a woman. She writes of the "upheaval in the symbolic order" that such an (ethically necessary) substitution would occasion.[17] Grace M. Jantzen goes so far as to canvas the notion of "a deliberate replacement of the traditional masculinist projection of God with a feminist pantheist projection."[18] But a "symbolic order" in which the notion of God relies on assertion or projection is a different conception to that in which humanity is said to be made in God's image. C. S. Lewis writes that in "the Church . . . we are dealing with male and female not merely as facts of nature but as the live and awful shadows of realities utterly beyond our control and largely beyond our direct knowledge."[19] The notion that we are at liberty to *assert* that God is a woman (or a man) is foreign to Lewis's way of thinking. It is the other way round. God determines what humanity is like, not vice versa. Lewis states: "We have no authority to take the living and seminal figures which God has painted on the canvas of our nature and shift them about as if they were mere geometrical figures."[20] Gender is understood here to be a "mystical" reflection of transcendent realities, something to be received, not asserted.

As depicted by Lewis, the *modus operandi* of the *imago Dei* is not *intended* to arise from masculine projection. Key feminist writers have unmasked it as such, not without reason but perhaps with less than justice. This book takes issue both with a "symbolic order" that is no more than a "patriarchal" construct and also with the recommended feminist cure. If a method of human projection was employed by "patriarchy" at its worst, it would be ironic for feminists to copy it. Rather than perpetuating a method of projection on feminist terms, this book recommends correcting an aberration in thinking about the *imago Dei*.

Projection as a method in religious thinking is not without difficulty. Jantzen notes that Freudian and Marxist theory considered religion an *illusion* on this very account: "Atheism has, indeed, regularly been seen as

---

17. *Irigaray Reader*, 185.
18. Jantzen, *Becoming Divine*, 265.
19. Lewis, "Priestesses in the Church," 93–94.
20. Lewis, "Priestesses in the Church," 92.

the logical conclusion of projection theories of religion."[21] Such a history, however, does not deter Jantzen from using projection as a method. She goes on to say:

> I suggest, however, that projection can be understood in a much more interesting and positive way. Though it is not my main concern . . . it would be entirely possible that there actually was a divine being with just those attributes which (some) humans projected from their own traits: indeed it might be argued that the Christian teaching that human beings are made in the divine image would have exactly that consequence.[22]

Jantzen favors a "useful fiction" frame of reference. While the fiction might depict reality it is not her main concern to consider whether it actually does. Actuality is, however, a matter of concern in traditional understanding of the *imago Dei*.

I agree with many feminist writers in taking the *imago Dei* as a premise. But what is meant by the *imago Dei*? My primary reason for resisting a method of projecting male attributes to portray a notion of God is that such a *method* is in conflict with what it means to be created in God's image. The same goes for projecting female attributes. The kind of thinking that would posit "projection" as a legitimate means in religious discussion alters the meaning of metaphorical language, symbolic reference and sacramental identity as will be seen. Further, such thinking weakens the premise, as in the case of Jantzen, for whom the divine image is not the main concern.[23]

In order to explore what it means for a woman to be created in God's image it is necessary to first ask whether gendered humanity *is* thought to be created in the divine likeness. Secondly, it is necessary to be clear that the claim to be made in the image of God means to be made like God as a copy is to an original. Thirdly, one must be consistent about where this information comes from. It then becomes possible to ask what this means, for women in particular. Such questions engage with what is meant by a "symbolic order" in terms of gendered identity as well as epistemology: how do we know that we know?

21. Jantzen, *Becoming Divine*, 88–89.
22. Jantzen, *Becoming Divine*, 89.
23. Cf. Rees, "Sarah Coakley: Systematic Theology and the Future of Feminism," 307. Rees contrasts Coakley's "doctrine of creaturehood" with "autonomous models typical of feminism." Rees states that Coakley "points to the *imagio dei* as the fundamental point of enquiry regarding both gender and difference" (303).

Given the biblical source for knowledge of the *imago Dei*, I argue for the reliability of the biblical narrative, anchored in a concept of covenant and communication between God and humanity. While the information that gendered humanity is made in God's image comes from Genesis 1:26–27, details relevant to women about the nature of the gendered *imago Dei* can be found, I maintain, in Genesis 2–3. Such details are assumed and developed in the New Testament, in particular by the apostle Paul.

In this context the book explores biblical typology expressed in gendered terms. Such typology is based on the concept that the biblical writings, diverse as they are and presenting as they do a developing divine revelation through human agency nevertheless have an overarching coherence.[24] The assumption of biblical coherence is currently under dispute, not least in relation to women's leadership in the churches and the possibility of using feminine language for God. Doubt about biblical coherence, however, may itself be open to question.

Willard M. Swartley traces questions about coherence in some detail, in the context of questions about women. He begins by contrasting biblical interpretation that functions like a mirror with that which functions like a window: "some method must be used which gives the text distance from the interpreter's ideology, a method which allows the text to speak its piece, to function as a window."[25] The assumption of unity and consistency in the biblical writings, in which scripture interprets scripture leads too easily in Swartley's view to what he calls "the mirror game," the text reflecting back "what we want it to say."[26] He goes on to claim: "liberationist writers (at least some of them) concede that not all of the texts say the same thing. This vulnerability becomes a strength

---

24. The 2004 Seattle Statement of the Anglican-Roman Catholic International Commission (ARCIC), *Mary: Grace and Hope in Christ*, paragraph 7 n. 1 states: "By typology we mean a reading which accepts that certain things in Scripture (persons, places, and events) foreshadow or illuminate other things, or reflect patterns of faith in imaginative ways (e.g. Adam is a type of Christ: Romans 5:14; Isaiah 7:14 points towards the virgin birth of Jesus: Matthew 1:23). This typological sense was considered to be a meaning that goes beyond the literal sense. This approach assumes the unity and consistency of the divine revelation."

25. See Swartley, *Slavery, Sabbath, War and Women*, 185–87. Regarding the liberationist position, he remarks: "the very coherency difficulty of the position testifies to a breakthrough in overcoming the tyranny of the mirror game played by the interpreter's ideology. The interpretation represents a wounded, but not despairing, position in coherency."

26. Swartley, *Slavery, Sabbath, War and Women*, 185–86.

because it shows that the projection of the interpreters' ideology onto the text has been broken."

Liberationist writers, according to Swartley, are less likely than traditionalists to use biblical texts to mirror their own ideology because liberationists "*see something that doesn't say exactly what they would like the text to say.*"[27] What he does not acknowledge is that, for liberationists, unpalatable texts are not necessarily *required* to be authoritative. Such texts can be judged from an extra-biblical perspective, once again a matter of the interpreter's ideology.[28] Put in terms of Swartley's analogy, even if texts do function as windows, as far as authority goes the blinds can be drawn on some of them. Once biblical coherence is open to doubt, the debate soon widens into the reality-depicting efficacy, or otherwise, of biblical language. One need not stop at *biblical* language. McFague reports on "the contemporary crisis of language" in general: "As Iris Murdoch says, 'We can no longer take language for granted as a medium of communication. Its transparency is gone. We are like people who for a long time looked out of a window without noticing the glass—and then one day began to notice this too.'"[29]

Focus on the window glass rather than on the view; modification of the glass so that the Emerald City looks green; projection as a positive method irrespective of truth claims; projection as a means to promote the full realization of human potential—this kind of thinking has formed the background to much feminist theology. This is not to say that traditional interpretation of the *imago Dei* has been guiltless of what Swartley calls the "mirror game." It is to cast doubt on the proposed remedy.

This book attempts to look through biblical texts as "windows," providing access, however limited, to external truth. Broadly speaking it divides into two parts, chapters 1–6 concerned with the symbolic reference of religious language, chapters 7–10 with the source and nature of identity for women. Chapter 1 challenges presuppositions behind the "contemporary crisis of language." Chapter 2 compares a traditional (Augustine's)

---

27. Swartley, *Slavery, Sabbath, War and Women*, 185–86. Swartley's italics.

28. Cf. Swartley, *Slavery, Sabbath, War and Women*, 189–91. He refers to "Nestorian hermeneutics" in which readings deemed to have human authority only would be non-normative, and attempts to overcome the "Nestorian" factor by using "faithfulness to the gospel" as the perspective to measure and accommodate diversity. He does not comment on the role of ideology in assessing what "faithfulness to the gospel" entails.

29. McFague, *Speaking in Parables*, 27; 35. McFague takes this citation from Dallas High, *Language, Persons and Belief*, 27. McFague does not give a direct citation of Murdoch's work.

and feminist (Elizabeth A. Johnson's) interpretation of the *imago Dei* and asks whether both are an exercise of the "mirror game." Chapters 3 and 4 look for narrative clues relevant to women as the *imago Dei*, on the assumption that different texts give access to a coherent, if moving, panorama. Chapters 5 and 6 focus on exegesis of key texts. Chapter 7 returns to the "crisis of language" and the effect on identity. Chapter 8 explores a feminist quest for embodiment, including the link made by psychoanalysis with the subconscious mind. Chapter 9 appraises a feminist aspiration for "inclusive language" while Chapter 10 contrasts constructed identity with that which is received from an outside source. It is suggested here that the textual vista regarding the *imago Dei*, more pleasant than sometimes surmised, is in fact well worth looking at, in particular without some traditional perspectives which have impeded such viewing.

Some further observations may help to explain terms as I use them. I have already touched on language of a "symbolic order." C. S. Lewis writes of "male and female not merely as facts of nature but as the live and awful shadows of realities utterly beyond our control and largely beyond our direct knowledge." I contrasted this understanding with Irigaray's remark about the "upheaval in the symbolic order" which would arise if God was asserted to be a woman. My point was that Lewis and Irigaray present different frames of reference. Irigaray relies on an assertion about "God," apparently invoked as a *useful fiction* to underwrite a feminist ethic. Lewis describes a situation in which male and female as *facts* of nature offer a clue to greater *realities*. This book follows Lewis's understanding of "symbol" as primarily to do with something visible. We can see male and female as facts of nature. We cannot see God directly but the "live and awful shadows" help us to gain some idea of what God is like.

While male and female are shadows (or symbols) of higher realities, I add that gendered human relationships function more like a metaphor than a symbol. Alongside the symbolic significance of male and female, I propose that the meaning of the *imago Dei* is to be discerned in *relations* between the sexes. I have said that the claim to be made in the image of God means to be made like God as a copy is to an original. Our direct knowledge of the Godhead is limited; yet we know something of the trinitarian inter-relations. We also know something of what I call the divine-humn level, the relations between Christ and the Church. There is more to be said at this level, I believe, in the relationship between Mary and Jesus.

I have stated that chapters 1–6 engage with the symbolic reference of religious language. M. H. Abrams writes:

> A symbol, in the broadest use of the term, is anything which signifies something else; in this sense, all words are symbols. As commonly used in [literary] criticism, however, 'symbol' is applied only to a word or phrase signifying an object which itself has significance; that is, the object referred to has a range of meaning beyond itself.[30]

Abrams cites the Good Shepherd as an example of "symbol" used in the second sense. We may compare his definition of "symbol" with what he says about "metaphor": "a word which in ordinary usage signifies one kind of thing, quality, or action is applied to another, without express indication of the relation between them."[31] While the meanings of "metaphor" and "symbol" overlap, "symbol" is used in a broad sense (the signifying efficacy of words in general) as well as a specific sense (an object pointing beyond itself in a pictorial way as in the Good Shepherd or male and female, signifying higher realities). "Metaphor" is more evocative than pictorial, with ordinary words modified to suggest subtle analogies. "Symbol" (in both senses) and "metaphor" are assumed to have signifying efficacy in relation to external reality.

Two more modes of expression warrant attention. The first is "allegory," the second "model." Allegory may be described as a projected symbol. It is a literary device in which a concept generates its own imagined picture. In *Pilgrim's Progress*, for instance, the emotion of despair is projected as the figure of a giant. The apostle Paul makes use of allegory in presenting the figures of Hagar and Sarah as illustrations of the old and new covenants (Galatians 4:21–31). One may compare this *allegorical* portrayal of the old and new covenants with the statement in Hebrews 10:1 that the law offers "a shadow of the good things to come." In Hebrews, the old covenant is said to be a symbol (or typological foreshadowing) of the new covenant. In Galatians, the allegorical figure of "Hagar" does not point to the allegorical figure of "Sarah." Rather, both figures are material representations of the two covenants, presented as alternatives. We may note, however, that the distinction between symbol and allegory is somewhat lost in a projected universe.

---

30. Abrams, *Glossary of Literary Terms*, 95.

31. Abrams, *Glossary of Literary Terms*, 36–37. Abrams cites I. A. Richards, *Philosophy of Rhetoric*, 1936, chapters 5 and 6.

"Model" is a term favored by McFague and used by her in more than one way. As seen above, she writes of "the patriarchal model" in which "women do not model God" while "men have a 'role-model' in God for defining their self-identity."[32] She identifies some metaphors as "models" or metaphors with "staying power." A "model" in this sense is a "metaphor that has gained sufficient stability and scope so as to present a pattern of relatively comprehensive and coherent explanation," as in the case of the metaphor of "God the father."[33] In other words, in a "model" (construct or way of thinking) established by means of a "model" (metaphor with "staying power")[34] women do not "model" (are not said to be like) God. For McFague, as already seen, religious metaphor offers no more than a "useful fiction" frame of reference. On these assumptions, "God" and "image of God" amount to no more than useful fictions.

All matters involving human relationships are delicate and complicated, says Dorothy Sayers. One can add that they are even more delicate and complicated if the efficacy of language as a means of communication is under dispute. As indicated above, one must begin with the significance of ordinary language before going on to what is meant by "metaphor" and "symbol." Such linguistic usage does not operate in an epistemological vacuum. McFague offers a helpful explication of the classical "metaphor of association or transference" which, she states, is "the transference of a word from what it usually means to some other object," as in "the milk of human kindness" or "God the Father." She continues:

> The ability to employ this sort of metaphor . . . seems to rest on a confidence that things really *are* associated, that the center holds, that the web is not broken—that, in other words, the universe is in some sense sacramental, that God is somehow the true and original father, that all things are connected among themselves because they are connected in God . . . as Paul Ricoeur puts it, "it is an index of the situation of man at the heart of the being in which he moves, exists and wills, that the symbol speaks to us."[35]

---

32. McFague, *Metaphorical Theology*, 149–50.
33. See McFague, *Models of God*, 34.
34. McFague, *Models of God*, 34.
35. McFague, *Speaking in Parables*, 106. McFague's italics. She cites Ricoeur, *The Symbolism of Evil*, 356.

Here McFague outlines *why* "classical" metaphor operates as it does: "the universe is in some sense sacramental"; "the symbol [at the heart of being in which man moves] speaks to us."

McFague herself disclaims this kind of confidence. She goes on to say that "the Christian symbolic universe does *not* hold together for most of us." In spite of this she continues to invoke the imprimatur of Paul Ricoeur, inappropriately I maintain, since her kind of metaphor is on a new footing, connected with the feminist desire to challenge the "patriarchal model." In relation to the metaphor "God the father," McFague writes that the problem "does not lie with the model itself . . . for it is a profound metaphor and as true as any religious model available, but it has established a hegemony over the Western religious consciousness which it is the task of metaphorical theology to break."[36] In other words, the model, "God the father," spelled here with a lower case "f," can function as a "profound metaphor" *independent* of "the web . . . [in which] God is somehow the true and original father, [where] all things are connected among themselves because they are connected in God." This is the useful fiction frame of reference where the web is broken. Language itself, metaphorical or otherwise, is not exempt from this exercise.

Symbol, metaphor, sacramental universe, symbolic order: these modes of understanding are integral to Christian experience. The feminist critique bears witness to this while seeking to reissue such modes from an epistemology of projection. But there is a price to pay. Meaning is no longer received; it is asserted. Identity becomes self-focused, strident and competitive. Whatever the rhetoric, there is a loss of the "other" in favor of the self, a loss of actuality and relationship. I do not believe that the price is worth paying, nor do I believe that it is in any way necessary, in order to establish identity for women.

While I offer a positive reading for the way in which women participate in the *imago Dei*, much of this book could be described as a conversation with various feminist writers in terms of their methods and conclusions. The book engages with aspects of linguistic, epistemological and historical enquiry, as well as thinking in the social sciences, including a "symbolic" deriving from psychoanalysis. The broad-ranging nature of enquiry has the effect of producing an argument that proceeds in overlapping circles rather than in a linear fashion.

---

36. McFague, *Metaphorical Theology*, 29.

As noted above, psychoanalyst Luce Irigaray asks whether the peoples of monotheism are ready to assert that their God is a woman, a response which would substitute one form of monotheism for another. But is Christianity "monotheistic" in the sense implied? Janet Martin Soskice cites Jürgen Moltmann: "The patriarchal ordering of the world . . . is a monotheistic ordering, not a Trinitarian one."[37] In a series of essays, Soskice contrasts a tendency towards "patriarchal" monotheism (as in "sloppy eighteenth-century rhetoric of the 'fatherhood of God and the brotherhood of man'")[38] with "the great efforts made by theologians and philosophers to give account of God's Being as *to-be-related*."[39] This book attempts to apply this relational account of God's Being to an account of the *imago Dei*.

Soskice goes so far as to state: "We may now stand at a moment of evangelical opportunity in the West, a time in which Christians not only need to hear a fully relational account of the Trinitarian life of God, but may also be receptive of it."[40] I believe that the *imago Dei*, viewed in symbolic and sacramental terms, has a key role to play in this. The term "symbolic" accords with the notion that humanity as male and female provides a glimpse of the Godhead. The term "sacramental" accords with the notion that humanity as male and female in some sense offers an embodied representation of the Trinitarian God. Broadly speaking, the term "symbolic" is concerned with visible reference, as of a copy to an original. The term "sacramental" is concerned with the reception of meaning and identity. Both aspects are relevant to what it means for a woman to be made in God's image.

One further word must be said with regard to the likeness between the Godhead and humanity. While Irigaray asks whether "God" can be characterized, apparently in literal terms, as a woman, Lewis writes of male and female as "shadows of realities" which are "largely beyond our direct knowledge." The indirect nature of the correspondence should not be underestimated. Lewis considers that the "language in which we express our religious beliefs and other religious experiences, is not a special language, but something that ranges between the Ordinary

---

37. Soskice, *Kindness of God*, 82. Soskice quotes Moltmann, "The Motherly Father: Is Trinitarian Patripassianism Replacing Theological Patriarchalism?"

38. Soskice, *Kindness of God*, 83. Italics in the text.

39. See Soskice, *Kindness of God*, 119–20.

40. Soskice, *Kindness of God*, 119.

[i.e., everyday language] and the Poetical."⁴¹ He attempts to capture the nature of poetic language:

> Burns tells us that a woman is like a red, red rose and Wordsworth that another woman is like a violet by a mossy stone half hidden from the eye. Now of course the one woman resembles a rose, and the other a half-hidden violet, not in size, weight, shape, colour, anatomy or intelligence, but by arousing emotions in some way analogous to those which flowers would arouse. But then we know quite well what sort of women (and how different from each other) they must have been to do so. The two statements . . . are even, in their own proper way, verifiable or falsifiable: having seen the two women we might say 'I see what he meant in comparing her to a rose' and 'I see what he meant in comparing her to a violet', or might decide that the comparisons were bad.⁴²

There is an elusive likeness between the women and the respective flowers. One would need to see the women to judge whether the comparisons were apt or not. On the other hand, if one lived in a country in which roses (or violets) did not grow the descriptions would not perhaps mean very much. And if one lived in such a country, one might assume that the comparison had something to do with the size, weight, shape, color, anatomy or intelligence of the women. But one would be wrong.

There is a similar poetical element in the concept of the *imago Dei*. The likeness is symbolic. There is something elusive about it. It is not predictable. In this sense anthropomorphic projection is in the same case as trying to predict the rose-like quality of a woman without knowing anything about roses. Size, weight, shape, color, anatomy or intelligence might be projected but the result would be an illusion. By contrast, to continue the analogy, the *imago Dei* in its symbolic aspect would claim to know something of the divine rose-likeness even without direct access to it. The *imago Dei* lays claim to glimpses of, and messages from, a far country.

---

41. Lewis, "Language of Religion," 171–72. Lewis makes a distinction between religious language that borders on the poetical and more abstract theological language, which, he says is often necessary but "is not the language religion naturally speaks."

42. Lewis, "Language of Religion," 168. Lewis alludes to Robert Burns, "A red, red Rose," line 1 and William Wordsworth, "She dwelt among the untrodden ways," line 5.

1

The Covenant of Language

When Dorothy and her companions attempt to find their way in the Land of Oz they follow the Yellow Brick Road. When they leave the Road they become lost or in grave peril. This is not to say that there are no dangers to encounter on the Yellow Brick Road. There is nevertheless a degree of safety and purpose in remaining on it.[1] In my earlier book, *The Wizard's Illusion*, I suggested that the efficacy of language in depicting the external world rests on something of a "Yellow Brick Road" which enables the navigation of the universe. While it applies to language in general, the well-trodden way of the Road is of particular relevance to metaphor.

In the Introduction, I made reference to what McFague calls "classical" metaphor, as in "the milk of human kindness" and "God the Father." McFague's comment on the underlying assumption is worth repeating:

> The ability to employ this sort of metaphor . . . seems to rest on a confidence that things really *are* associated, that the center holds, that the web is not broken—that, in other words, the universe is in some sense sacramental, that God is somehow the true and original father, that all things are connected among themselves because they are connected in God . . . as Paul Ricoeur puts it, "it is an index of the situation of man at the heart of the being in which he moves, exists and wills, that the symbol speaks to us."[2]

---

1. See Baum, *Wizard of Oz*, chapter 7 for example.
2. McFague, *Speaking in Parables*, 106.

The Covenant of Language

To depart from this confidence, as McFague herself does, is to lose touch with the safety of the known way. It is to lose touch with the universe and what it has to say to us. In terms of my illustration from *The Wizard of Oz* it is to deviate from the Yellow Brick Road.

McFague reports on a new awareness of the importance of metaphor: "The voices insisting on the primacy of metaphor are legion, coming from philosophy, the sciences, religion, the arts and the social sciences."[3] But if her kind of metaphor disowns the confidence on which metaphor rests, what is the result? In acknowledging the voices which insist on metaphor's primacy, McFague is less than clear about possible disruption in the discussion. Are all the voices talking about the same thing? Are all the travelers on the same road?

Among the many arguing for of the primacy of metaphor, McFague cites C. S. Lewis: "All our truth, or all but a few fragments, is won by metaphor." McFague takes this remark from the frontispiece of a bibliography on metaphor.[4] She supplies a "sprinkling of quotations" from this frontispiece, with the result that her citation of Lewis appears cheek by jowl with one from Friedrich Nietzsche: "To know is merely to work with one's favorite metaphors." This might give the impression that Nietzsche and Lewis are talking about the same thing, which is far from the case.

Elsewhere McFague cites "a famous passage from Nietzsche":

> What then is truth? A mobile army of metaphors, metonymics, anthropomorphisms: in short a sum of human relations which become poetically and rhetorically intensified, metamorphosed, adorned, and after long usage, seem to a nation fixed, canonic and binding; truths are illusions of which one has forgotten that they *are* illusions; worn-out metaphors which have become powerless to affect the senses, coins which have their obverse effaced and now are no longer of account as coins but merely as metal.[5]

For Nietzsche, metaphor is a means, not to truth, but to illusion.

Nietzsche and Lewis may be at one in upholding the prevalence of metaphor. They are directly opposed about its reality-depicting efficacy.

---

3. McFague, *Metaphorical Theology*, 32.

4. See McFague, *Metaphorical Theology*, 201, n. 2. McFague takes her "sprinkling of quotations" from Warren A. Shibles, *Metaphor: An Annotated Bibliography and History*.

5. See McFague, *Models of God*, 5, citing Friedrich Nietzsche, "On Truth and Falsity in Their Ultramoral Sense." The italics are in the text as cited.

For Nietzsche, illusion is produced through the agency of "worn-out metaphors." The original "metaphor" was an acknowledged "anthropomorphism," making no claim to point to truth. Truth was never at issue. "Metaphor" never claimed that it was, but long usage has given "metaphor" a currency that was never warranted. By contrast, Lewis states: "All our truth, or all but a few fragments, is won by metaphor."

VERBIAGE OR MEANING?

To explore this further, I turn to Lewis direct. The quotation cited by McFague comes from his essay, "Bluspels and Flalansferes."[6] Like Nietzsche, Lewis is writing about worn-out or dead metaphors. His point, however, is that forgetting the original meaning of the metaphor may lead not so much to illusion but to nonsense. For Lewis, the vehicle behind the metaphor was originally employed to point to a truth. To forget this process is to run the risk of using words without the meaning behind them. To illustrate this danger, Lewis invents the words "bluspels" and "flalansferes" as meaningless contractions of the original metaphors, "blue spectacles" and "Flatlander sphere." The Flatlander sphere, for instance, supplies an analogy to explicate how space which seems infinite in three dimensions might be finite in four: a Flatlander with only two dimensions might have a similar difficulty understanding how a sphere could be finite. The contraction "flalansfere," on the other hand, would not be likely to convey anything.

Lewis warns against mere verbiage as opposed to meaningful use of language:

> We shall find . . . that real meaning, judged by this standard, does not come always where we have learned to expect. *Flalansferes* and *bluspels* will clearly be most prevalent in certain types of writers. The percentage of mere syntax masquerading as meaning may vary from something like 100 per cent in political writers, journalists, psychologists, and economists, to something like forty per cent in the writers of children's stories.[7]

Lewis is not arguing that all metaphors are equally meaningful but rather that "good metaphors" are a means of access to truth while "mere syntax" is not.

6. See Lewis, "Bluspels and Flalansferes," 36–50.
7. See Lewis, "Bluspels and Flalansferes," 48–49.

McFague's citation of Lewis comes from the conclusion of Lewis's essay. Here is what he says in context:

> I said at the outset that the truth we won by metaphor could not be greater than the truth of the metaphor itself; and we have seen since that all our truth, or all but a few fragments, is won by metaphor. And thence, I confess, it does follow that if our thinking is ever true, then the metaphors by which we think must have been good metaphors. It does follow that if those original equations, between good and light, or evil and dark, between breath and soul and all the others, were from the beginning arbitrary and fanciful—if there is not, in fact, a kind of psycho-physical parallelism (or more) in the universe—then all our thinking is nonsensical.[8]

Nietzsche would no doubt presume that such equations *were* from the beginning arbitrary and fanciful (and never meant to be anything else). There is a consequence to that assumption, as Lewis points out.

Let us now return to McFague's observation about "classical" metaphor seeming "to rest on a confidence that things really *are* associated." Lewis evidently subscribes to this confidence. He indicates that writers of children's stories are also inclined to share it. My use of illustrations from *The Wizard of Oz* is in line with this confidence: while the story is a fantasy, there are truths to be found in it. McFague, on the other hand, dissociates herself from such thinking: "the Christian symbolic universe does *not* hold together for most of us." She posits what she calls "metaphor by juxtaposition" in which the "connections are not spelled out; two images are simply juxtaposed and the reader is left to make his or her own connections."[9] In effect this is to share Nietzsche's estimation of metaphors as "anthropomorphisms." But McFague does not stop there as will be seen.

What have these remarks to do with gender and the *imago Dei*? We have McFague's assurance that "classical" metaphor is underwritten by a confidence that "God is somehow the true and original father, that all things are connected among themselves because they are connected in God." She writes this in a prequel to a series of four books on what she calls "metaphorical theology" although, on her terms, neither "metaphor" nor "theology" claims to offer access to external truth. In her series, McFague aligns herself with feminist theologians, concerned about "the

---

8. See Lewis, "Bluspels and Flalansferes," 50.
9. See McFague, *Speaking in Parables*, 106–8.

profound structural implications" of the metaphor (or model) of "God the father," which "has established a hegemony over the Western religious consciousness." The task of "metaphorical theology" is, she says, to break this hegemony.[10]

What McFague does not say directly is that to break the "hegemony" of the metaphor "God the Father" is to break the web in which "all things are connected among themselves because they are connected in God," with the result that the confidence which underlies "classical" metaphor is no longer present. That is to say, to break the hegemony of the metaphor "God the Father" is to disallow "classical" metaphor with its possible access to truth. One is left with "metaphor of juxtaposition," if there is such a thing, a mere association of ideas. It is on these revised terms that McFague retains the model of "God the father," stating that it is "a profound metaphor and as true as any religious model available." For McFague, this metaphor is "true" in a relativized sense. It does not rest on the way in which things hold together. In short, McFague abandons the Yellow Brick Road.

I have said that McFague appears to share Nietzsche's estimation of metaphors as "anthropomorphisms." But she does not share his pessimistic attitude towards them. Having demythologized the ground on which Christianity rests, McFague wishes to "remythologize Christian faith."[11] She intends, for example, to "look at new religious images and models being suggested by women"[12] even though, in her method, religious images and models no longer operate in the old way. One may observe the demythologizing/ re-mythologizing process in a feminist approach to the *imago Dei*. Rosemary Ruether reports that the feminist critique "changes fundamentally the nature of the discussion" about "the image of God idea in Scripture and Christian tradition."[13] In other words, the *imago Dei* is demythologized, assumed to constitute a human idea or anthropomorphism. Feminism is then said to construct "images of God that will better manifest and promote the full realization of human potential for women and men."

In support of the alleged feminist method, Ruether cites McFague's understanding of metaphor as outlined in the first two books of her

---

10. McFague, *Metaphorical Theology*, 29.
11. McFague, *Models of God*, 40.
12. McFague, *Metaphorical Theology*, 29.
13. See Ruether, "Christian Tradition and Feminist Hermeneutics," 286–87.

series.[14] According to Ruether, a feminist reconstruction "assumes all of our images of God are human projections."[15] McFague applies this approach more broadly. In her estimation, access to the world is a matter of human projection:

> What we *know* are the metaphors or projections of the self, the worlds it creates. The relativity of knowledge demands such a perspective. Without assuming an idealistic perspective (the world out there is only what subjects say it is), a moderate Kantianism (and we are all one way or another, Kantians) insists that in a sense . . . all theology, philosophy, physics, and art is autobiography.[16]

Despite the disclaimer implied in "moderate" Kantianism or idealism, McFague goes so far as to describe "all theology, philosophy, physics and art" as "autobiography" or projection of the self. Similarly, a change in the nature of theological discussion on feminist terms reduces the *imago Dei* to an idea, not a reality. McFague states that such thinking is premised on "the relativity of knowledge." On this basis one might ask how much room is left for meaning as opposed to verbiage.

A BROKEN CONTRACT

The primacy of metaphor, says McFague, is being asserted in "philosophy, the sciences, religion, the arts and the social sciences."[17] If these disciplines operate as projections of the self, what does this say about the nature of metaphor and the disciplines themselves? There is much at stake, as I attempt to outline in *The Wizard's Illusion*. It is not my purpose here to revisit these matters in detail. But a sketch is necessary, insofar as it is relevant to various feminist positions.

I have given this chapter the title "The covenant of language." This is in line with McFague's association of classical metaphor with a sacramental universe, all things connected among themselves because they are connected in God. We have seen it again in Lewis's remark that without some sort of psycho-physical parallelism in the universe all our thinking is nonsensical. This assumption has underwritten thought and language

14. See Ruether, "Christian Tradition and Feminist Hermeneutics," 287; 291 n. 42.
15. Ruether, "Christian Tradition and Feminist Hermeneutics," 287.
16. McFague, *Speaking in Parables*, 147–48.
17. McFague, *Metaphorical Theology*, 32.

within the Judeo-Christian and classical tradition. It is an assumption, however, that is currently under question.

As seen above, McFague draws attention to Nietzsche's unmasking of metaphors in their claim to offer access to truth. George Steiner locates "Nietzsche's subversion of 'truth'"[18] in a movement, dating from the late nineteenth century, which had the effect of dissociating language from access to the external world.

> It is my belief that this contract is broken for the first time, in any thorough and consequent sense, in European, Central European and Russian culture and speculative consciousness during the decades from the 1870s to the 1930s. *It is this break of the covenant between word and world which constitutes one of the very few genuine revolutions of spirit in Western history and which defines modernity itself.*[19]

Steiner finds this linguistic parting of the ways in the loss of the "covenant between word and object," a denial that external "being is, to a workable degree, 'sayable.'"[20] The breach in linguistic reference can be viewed negatively, as in Nietzsche's disavowal of truth. But some early exponents viewed it positively, as releasing language from utilitarian servitude.

The denial of truth and access to truth finds early expression, according to Steiner, in the work of two nineteenth century French poet-philosophers, Stéphane Mallarmé and Arthur Rimbaud. Mallarmé repudiates "the covenant of reference":

> To ascribe to words a correspondence to 'things out there', to see and use them as somehow representational of 'reality' in the world, is not only a vulgar illusion. It makes of language a lie. To use the word *rose* as if it was, in any way, like what we conceive to be some botanical phenomenon, to ask of any word that it stand in lieu of, as a surrogate for, the perfectly inaccessible 'truths' of substance, is to abuse and demean it.[21]

On these terms, representation is servitude while true freedom is the realization "that what words refer to are other words," a realization which

---

18. Steiner, *Real Presences*, 132.
19. Steiner, *Real Presences*, 93. Italics in the text.
20. Steiner, *Real Presences*, 90–91.
21. Steiner, *Real Presences*, 95.

"can recuperate for human discourse . . . the unlimited creativity of metaphor which is inherent in the origins of all speech."[22]

For Rimbaud, loss of access to the outside world leads to focus on the inner world. But this is not the Cartesian thinking self. Rimbaud detects "the splintered images of other and momentary 'selves'" in ways, says Steiner, that appear "radically subversive of order and creation."[23] As with Mallarmé, the intention is positive as well as negative. Douglas Parmée reports on this engagement:

> This supreme revolt, not only against the organisation of society but against any normal conception of life, is being undertaken not as a mere destruction but as a destruction that will lead to a new and better conception of mankind, in which due weight will be given to all the fresh findings of the poet on the nature of man and his relation with his fellows and the surrounding world. Rimbaud's purpose is not only artistic but moral: if and when we can recognise and understand all the hitherto unknown and neglected aspects of humanity, . . . if we can accept all the monstrous discoveries of the poet as something natural, then the poet will have become a *multiplicateur de progrès*.[24]

The theory for which Rimbaud is known derives from letters written "to two friends in May 1871 . . . : *On a tort de dire; je pense. On devrait dire; on me pense. Car Je est un autre.*" Parmée suggests that his encounter with this "other" ("the non-rational, sensorial aspect of the poet's imagination") resembles the "unconscious of psychologists."[25] The aim is a fresh start, including "a more equitable and natural society" for the benefit of women.

Words do not refer to "things out there"; words are liberated to refer to their own inner world, indicates Mallarmé. The "other" of one's inner world has the potential to rethink humanity, claims Rimbaud. Encounter with the universe (and what lies behind) has no apparent say in these matters. By contrast, Steiner describes the anchor point for "the covenant between word and object":

> Western theology and the metaphysics, epistemology and aesthetics which have been its major footnotes, are 'logocentric'. This is to say that they axiomatize as fundamental and pre-eminent the concept of a 'presence'. It can be that of God (ultimately,

---

22. Steiner, *Real Presences*, 97–98.
23. Steiner, *Real Presences*, 99.
24. Parmée, *Twelve French Poets*, lv.
25. Parmée, *Twelve French Poets*, lii–liv.

it *must* be); of Platonic 'Ideas'; of Aristotelian and Thomist essence. It can be that of Cartesian self-consciousness; of Kant's transcendent logic or of Heidegger's 'Being'. It is to these pivots that the spokes of meaning finally lead. They insure its plenitude. That presence, theological, ontological or metaphysical, makes credible the assertion that there 'is something *in* what we say'.[26]

Linguistic efficacy has traditionally drawn its cogency from the outside; language is said to be underwritten by a "presence," a process which Steiner terms "logocentric." To break the contract between word and world, to deny a sense of authenticating "presence" in language, marks a radical change in the history of thought.

The difference between traditional and deconstructionist thinking might be summed up as that between covenantal and non-covenantal linguistics. As Steiner reports, deconstructionist writer, Jacques Derrida confirms the distinction:

> Derrida's formulation is beautifully incisive: "the intelligible face of the sign remains turned to the world and the face of God". A semantics, a poetics of correspondence, of decipherability and truth-values arrived at across time and consensus, are strictly inseparable from the postulate of theological-metaphysical transcendence. Thus the origin of the axiom of meaning and of the God-concept is a shared one. The semantic sign, where it is held to be meaningful, and divinity "have the same place and time of birth" (Derrida). They constitute the Hebraic-Hellenic copula on which our *Logos*-history and practice have been founded. "The age of the sign," says Derrida, "is essentially theological."[27]

Grace Jantzen says something similar:

> In the terminology of Jacques Derrida . . . it is the assumption of the divine presence (even when that presence is held to be absent, as in secularism) that ultimately grounds the system of signs, and brings to rest the ceaselessly shifting signifiers, holding them all together in an onto-theological unity.[28]

It is this onto-theological unity which Derrida wishes to disown. Steiner states: "The issue is, quite simply, that of the meaning of meaning as it

---

26. Steiner, *Real Presences*, 121. Italics in the text.
27. Steiner, *Real Presences*, 119–20.
28. Jantzen, *Becoming Divine*, 10, citing Derrida, *Margins of Philosophy*: 1–27.

is re-insured by the postulate of the existence of God. 'In the beginning was the Word.' There was no such beginning, says deconstruction, only the play of sounds and markers and the mutations of time."[29] At this extreme, Lewis's distinction between verbiage and meaning would seem in itself meaningless.

If the covenant between word and object was broken, as Steiner suggests, in the decades from the 1870s to the 1930s, a break representing dissociation from God as "presence" in an onto-theological unity, the task of McFague's "metaphorical theology" to break the hegemony of the metaphor "God the father" might seem a work of supererogation. McFague began her series on "metaphorical theology" in the 1980s. Was the hegemony of the "*Logos*-history" not by then already broken? However that may be, McFague particularizes her project in two ways. Firstly, she applies it to, and distances herself from, the Christian symbolic universe. Secondly her wish to demythologize the metaphor "God the father" has a feminist impetus. For many feminists, opposition to a "logocentric" (or Word-centered) source of meaning accords with dissociation from the *masculine* Father and Son.

AIRY HOUSES

I have used the Yellow Brick Road as a device to illustrate what Steiner calls "presence." As I read her work, McFague does not stray from the Road to the extent of some feminist writers. But, to my mind, her attempt to retain some solidity in her project only makes it more equivocal. She writes:

> I agree with the deconstructionists that all constructions are metaphorical and hence miss the mark; I nevertheless disagree with them when they say that language (writing) is only about itself and that no construction is any better than any other. To claim that all constructions are metaphorical is to insist that one never experiences reality "raw"; it does not follow from this, however, that there is nothing outside language. All that follows is that our access to reality is in every case mediated and hence partial and relative.[30]

---

29. Steiner, *Real Presences*, 120.
30. McFague, *Models of God*, 26.

This attempt to straddle the divide underestimates the extent of the rift. It is one thing to insist that one never experiences reality "raw." It is another to deny a representational function to words. McFague disagrees with the contention that no construction is better than any other. Deconstruction, in its full rigor, would repudiate the notion of "better" as meaningless.

In McFague's citation of "a famous passage from Nietzsche," truth is represented as stemming from a "mobile army of metaphors" or "anthropomorphisms" which become "fixed" by long usage.[31] For Nietzsche, unlike Lewis, metaphor is a means, not to truth, but to illusion. As I judge, McFague tries to steer a course between these two positions. Her theory of metaphor does not go beyond human projections or what Nietzsche calls "anthropomorphisms." McFague claims that these projections are "productive of reality."[32] In other words, McFague draws back from what Janet Martin Soskice terms "reality depicting" language while stopping short of admitting that the kind of reality produced by her constructions is illusory.[33] McFague cautions against allowing metaphors to become "fixed." Such constructions are "'houses' to live in for a while, with windows partly open and doors ajar; they become prisons when they no longer allow us to come and go, to add a room or take one way— or if necessary, to move out and build a new house."[34] In these kinds of "houses" the contrast between truth and illusion is sidestepped. "Truth" is relativistic and movable in order to remain contemporary.

McFague describes her project to "remythologize Christian faith" as an "exercise of the deconstruction and reconstruction of metaphors in which we imagine the saving power of God in our contemporary world."[35] The component of deconstruction removes the foundation of a claim to truth. The component of reconstruction builds what I call "airy houses." McFague's method begins with an unsubstantiated picturing (an "as-if") which looks for a measure of truth to support it. But such "truth" is always provisional. It can be displaced by a "better" construction. When the notion of "better" enters the moral sphere, the detachment of relativism would seem less than sustainable: at this point detachment tends to

---

31. See McFague, *Models of God*, 5.
32. McFague, *Models of God*, 26.
33. See Soskice, *Metaphor and Religious Language*, 140–41.
34. McFague, *Models of God*, 27.
35. McFague, *Models of God*, 63. See also section "The World as God's Body," 69–78.

give way to impassioned belief. The feminist critique of "patriarchy" is particularly open to challenge on this methodological ground.

Unlike Nietzsche, McFague places a positive value on human constructions or anthropomorphisms. Like Nietzsche, she disclaims pointing to external truth: "theology, at any rate my kind of theology . . . is, as it were, painting a picture. The picture may be full and rich, but it *is* a picture. What this sort of enterprise makes very clear is that theology is *mostly* fiction."[36] In saying this, McFague does not regard "fiction" in the same light as Lewis's estimation of children's stories. As seen above, Lewis contrasts the proportion of meaningful language use in children's stories with that of "mere syntax masquerading as meaning" in the work of "political writers, journalists, psychologists, and economists." Lewis situates meaningful use of language in the understanding that there is "a kind of psycho-physical parallelism (or more) in the universe," another way of referring to what Steiner calls "presence" in language.[37] McFague, however, disowns this "presence."

If one departs from the Yellow Brick Road it is well to be familiar with the topography of the country. In *The Wizard's Illusion*, I take the liberty of inventing features, unvisited by Dorothy and her companions, but relevant to an exposé of thinking about language. At one point in the story, the travelers come to a river without a bridge. When they attempt to cross the river, they are carried some distance downstream. On their way back to the Yellow Brick Road, they come to the Deadly Poppy Field. In *The Wizard's Illusion*, I liken the narcotic effect of the poppies to the deceptive potential of McFague's theological method. This is what I call the "Land of the As If." I stated above that McFague stops short of admitting that the kind of reality produced by her constructions is illusory, but she does warn against staying too long in any one construction. In consequence, her method vacillates between fragile yet fruitful "fictions" and a more Nietzschean disavowal of their claim to truth.[38]

If one cannot place reliance in the reality-depicting potential of theological metaphor where does one stand? In *The Wizard's Illusion*, I liken the river to the trajectory of deconstruction. In deconstruction there is nowhere to stand; in the long run the river will flow on to a nihilistic sea. In this book I take the further liberty of inventing a feature downstream

---

36. McFague, *Models of God*, xi. McFague's italics.
37. See Lewis, "Bluspels and Flalansferes," 50.
38. See McFague, *Models of God*, 27–28.

from the "Land of the As If," which I call the "Swamp of Ambiguity." I will suggest that feminist writers, Luce Irigaray and Catherine Keller inhabit this land. While disavowing the more pessimistic aspects of deconstruction, McFague's method shares some of its assumptions. There is traffic between the Land of the As If and the Swamp of Ambiguity.

In the Introduction I referred to the mooted "upheaval in the symbolic order" arising from Luce Irigaray's challenge to the peoples of monotheism, that God should be declared a woman.[39] Irigary was a pupil of Freudian psychoanalyst, Jacques Lacan. Grace Jantzen offers this context for Irigaray's assertion:

> To begin to understand Irigaray's answer [to Freud and Lacan] . . . and to see what religion has to do with it, it helps to see that according to Freudian theory modified by Lacan, the achievement of subjectivity . . . takes place according to what Lacan, in a deliberate echo of Catholic liturgy, calls the Law or Name of the Father. This thinly disguised religious formula indicates the authoritative nature of social demand, its patriarchal character, and also its religious structure. Indeed the obverse of the boy's repression of his desire for his mother is his entry into the language and civilization and social world of the fathers, which after Lacan can be referred to as 'the symbolic'. The 'symbolic' in French thought . . . includes all of language . . . and . . . can be used to designate the broad conceptual patterns of civilization.[40]

One can see here a possible source for an alleged onto-theological unity in an overly masculine guise, said to originate in the inner world of psychoanalysis, the boy's repression of his desire for his mother. Despite the echo of Catholic liturgy, this is to relocate the "symbolic." Irigaray responds:

> [Women] want to seize that which already exists so as to bring it back to an invisible source—their source?—a place from whence they might create, create themselves *ex nihilo*? Has not history forced this impossibility upon them? They must continue to live, cut off from their beginning and from their end.[41]

---

39. *Irigaray Reader*, 185.
40. Jantzen, *Becoming Divine*, 9–10.
41. *Irigaray Reader*, 109.

The Covenant of Language 29

Does her proposed "upheaval in the symbolic order" follow Arthur Rimbaud's new and better conception of mankind, projected from the inner world?

What Irigaray does not say is that religions should abandon a symbolic order. Similarly, Ruether does not argue that the image of God idea in Scripture and Christian tradition should be discarded. McFague retains theological "metaphor" but places it on a new footing. There is, Ruether acknowledges, a fundamental change in the discussion. I stated in the Introduction that assertion, rather than reception, of a symbolic order, leads to focus on the self rather than the "other." McFague's "airy houses" are, as she admits, "the metaphors or projections of the self, the worlds it creates."[42] Psychoanalysis delves deeper into the self, positing a projected "symbolic" which encompasses the broad conceptual patterns of civilization. Irigaray offers a feminist version of this. I will return to these matters in later chapters.

Let us pause here. This chapter has highlighted what I have called the Yellow Brick Road which has to do with the source of meaning and the words which carry it. To depart from the Road is to depart from words carrying meaning. The words may persist; the meaning is weakened or denied, depending on how far away one travels. In terms of words carrying meaning, "metaphor" is a key tool in the box. Away from the Road "metaphor" functions differently; in effect it stays in its box.

I come now to what Paul Ricoeur means by "symbols." I have said that "metaphor" is a tool to navigate the universe, to uncover its truth as Lewis remarks. For Ricoeur, metaphors uncover "symbols" embedded in the cosmos. Augustine says something similar: the world is a "sign" of its maker. But one can easily lose sight of this, even while ostensibly keeping to the Road. Ricoeur does not exempt Christian theology from this practice.

THE SYMBOL SPEAKS TO US

Nowhere is the equivocal nature of McFague's project more evident, to my mind, than in her appeal to the work of Paul Ricoeur. In her extended discussion of the operation of "metaphor," McFague claims to be influenced by Ricoeur. She states: "The relationship between image and concept which I support is articulated by Ricoeur, whose well-known phrase

---

42. McFague, *Speaking in Parables*, 147.

'The symbol gives rise to thought' is balanced by an equal emphasis on thought's need to return to its rich base in symbol."[43] But here McFague omits her earlier departure from the "classical" metaphor of transference and what lies behind it: "a confidence that things really *are* associated, that the center holds, that the web is not broken." McFague cites Ricoeur on this point: "it is an index of the situation of man at the heart of the being in which he moves, exists and wills, that the symbol speaks to us."[44] In this understanding, "symbol" is anchored in the cosmos. To turn away from this understanding is to turn away from the rich base of "symbol" as primary source.

"The symbol speaks to us," says Ricoeur. There is "a kind of psycho-physical parallelism (or more) in the universe," says Lewis. Steiner describes a "covenant between word and world" in which a transcendent "presence" forms the center to which "the spokes of meaning finally lead." These various expressions have in common what I call the Yellow Brick Road. As Steiner puts it: "That presence, theological, ontological or metaphysical, makes credible the assertion that there 'is something *in* what we say."[45] Among the various philosophical systems which "axiomatize as fundamental and pre-eminent the concept of a presence" Steiner includes Cartesian self-consciousness. But this is self-consciousness not yet divorced from the "face of God" (in deconstructionist terms), or party to a break in the hegemony of the metaphor "God the father" (in feminist terms). Ultimately God must be there, says Steiner. But this is not where McFague and many feminists sit.

I made a distinction above between covenantal and non-covenantal linguistics. These are my terms for the assumption (or denial) of an external agency which communicates with us and authenticates our thinking. Even our *Logos*-history, to use Steiner's word for it, has, according to Ricoeur, been insufficiently attentive to this "other." Cartesian self-consciousness would seem a turning-point in this respect. Soskice reports the feminist charge that the "God" of the "Cartesian period" functions as "the divine guarantor of the veracity of the insights of the [male] Cartesian subject."[46]

---

43. McFague, *Models of God*, 197, citing Paul Ricoeur "Biblical Hermeneutics," *Semeia* 4 (1975); and *The Rule of Metaphor*, study 8.

44. McFague, *Speaking in Parables*, 106. McFague's italics. She cites Ricoeur, *The Symbolism of Evil*, 356.

45. Steiner, *Real Presences*, 121.

46. Soskice, *Kindness of God*, 121–22.

There are earlier aberrations.[47] Ricoeur makes a distinction between philosophical thinking and the non-philosophical sources of philosophy. What he calls the non-philosophical source of philosophy is the "symbol" which speaks to us. He writes:

> Philosophy has attempted in various ways to colonize this outside entirely for its own benefit and to make it its own. Renouncing this *hubris* seems to me the first stage in a philosophy that is at once responsible for its arguments and prepared to recognize its Other and to be instructed by it.[48]

It is the symbol which gives rise to thought, says Ricoeur, not the other way round. McFague disowns this "outside": "the Christian symbolic universe does *not* hold together for most of us." Her kind of "symbol" or "metaphor" is on a new footing. Her constructions are "productive of reality." For Ricoeur, the "symbol" is a messenger for reality.

"What our time lacks . . . is an imaginative construal of the God-world relationship that is credible to us," says McFague. She continues: "The theologian ought not merely interpret biblical and traditional metaphors and models but ought to remythologize, to search in contemporary life and its sensibility for images more appropriate to the expression of Christian faith in our time."[49] Her "metaphorical theology" builds on what Nietzsche calls anthropomorphisms, a far cry from Ricoeur's requirement that philosophy should be instructed by its "Other." McFague borrows a positive approach to "symbol" from Ricoeur, but not on Ricoeur's terms. For Ricoeur, the re-mythologizing component of McFague's project would be an exercise in *hubris*. Something similar could be said about Ruether's description of the feminist project, constructing "images of God that will better manifest and promote the full realization of human potential for women and men."[50] For McFague and Ruether, thought comes first. What is credible to us, says McFague. What is beneficial for us, indicates Ruether.

I believe that McFague's kind of re-mythologizing opens the door to what Ricoeur calls "dogmatic mythology" which is the "temptation

---

47. Cf. an ancient tradition of Western metaphysics in which the Logos, as seed of generation, is symbolically male on the grounds that only males are truly generative (*Kindness of God*, 108–9, 110 n. 24.)

48. Ricoeur, "Reply to Stephen T. Tyman," 472.

49. McFague, *Models of God*, 32–33.

50. See Ruether, "Christian Tradition and Feminist Hermeneutics," 286–87.

of gnosis."[51] This is what happens if thought gives rise to symbol (as in the search for appropriate contemporary images) rather than the other way round. Speculative thought, says Ricoeur, is in danger of "rationalizing symbols as such, and thereby fixing them on the imaginative plane where they are born and take shape." But McFague and other feminists are not alone in the "temptation of gnosis." Ricoeur goes so far as to place Augustine's "pseudo-concept of original sin" under this heading, "the very claim to resolve the problem of evil by means of knowledge."[52] For Ricoeur, the first step is to renounce this kind of thinking: "In this sense, confronting gnosis and that which resembles it in the Christian sphere of theology, I assign to hermeneutics a *reductive* function." The *method* must be abandoned, says Ricoeur. He goes on to say, "And yet we must not simply stop with the failure of successive gnoses . . . The challenge has to be taken up as a provocation to think more and to think anew."[53]

Philosophy needs to be instructed by its "Other," states Ricoeur. The method of allowing thought to give rise to "symbol" must be abandoned. By contrast, feminism seeks to *modify* the method in favor of women. As represented by Ruether, feminism assumes that the *imago Dei* has always been the image of God *idea*. Far from abandoning the idea, feminism wishes to promote it on its own terms. This runs directly counter to Ricoeur's reductive approach towards the method. But it is not only the method but the assumption behind it which is at issue. If the *imago Dei* is not "symbol" in Ricoeur's sense, there is nothing to anchor it. It becomes an "anthropomorphism" in Nietzsche's sense. All that is said about it ultimately lacks meaning.

Let us return to the Christian symbolic universe along with Ricoeur's endorsement of it. Let us be clear that this is not the "symbolic order" of psychoanalysis, despite the claimed association with the "Law or Name of the Father."[54] Let us also be clear that it is not a deistic guarantor of the Cartesian subject. The extent to which the *imago Dei* is a human idea or projection is the extent to which Ricoeur assigns "a *reductive* function" to hermeneutics. For Ricoeur, it is not the starting-point of the "outside" which is at fault. What is at fault is the departure from it.

---

51. Reagan and Stewart, *Philosophy of Paul Ricoeur*, 46.
52. Ricoeur, "Reply to Stephen T. Tyman," 473. Ricoeur's italics.
53. Ricoeur, "Reply to Stephen T. Tyman," 475.
54. Cf. Jantzen, *Becoming Divine*, 9–10.

I believe Ruether and others oversimplify what is at stake. The Christian tradition they reject has left a legacy of mixed messages. Ricoeur detects successive "gnoses" in the Christian sphere of theology, among them Augustine's "pseudo-concept of original sin." But Augustine does not always espouse this kind of hermeneutic. Rowan Williams makes the intriguing comment that Augustine "is most philosophically interesting when not being self-consciously philosophical."[55]

Williams says this in the context of Augustine's dissertation on language and doctrine in which Augustine moves beyond a Platonic system of representation:

> Augustine is . . . obliged by his commitment to the incarnate Christ to *deny* that the incorruptible and immaterial can ever as such be an object for the cognition of material, historical and 'desirous' beings. Only in the non-finality of historical relationships . . . and in the consequent restlessness . . . is unchanging truth to be touched.[56]

There is some hint of deconstruction in this. Williams continues:

> It is possible to see Augustine's treatment of reality and representation as moving in [the] direction [of] . . . the popular notion that everything is language, everything is interpretation . . .

This, however, is not the full sum of Augustine's treatment. As Williams observes earlier:

> The Word's taking of flesh . . . manifests the essential quality of the world itself as 'sign' or trace of its maker. It instructs us once and for all that we have our identity within the shifting, mobile realm of representation, non-finality, growing and learning, because it reveals what the spiritual eye ought to perceive generally—that the whole creation is uttered and 'meant' by God, and therefore has no meaning in itself.[57]

Augustine's description of the world as "sign" has affinities with Ricoeur's description of "symbols" which speak *to* us. What the spiritual eye ought to perceive generally is relevant to Augustine's theory of the *imago Dei*. I will return to this in the next chapter.

---

55. Williams, "Language, Reality and Desire in Augustine's *De Doctrina*," 138.

56. Williams, "Language, Reality and Desire in Augustine's *De Doctrina*," 145–46. His italics.

57. Williams, "Language, Reality and Desire in Augustine's *De Doctrina*," 141.

Ricoeur claims that philosophy needs to be instructed by "symbol." Augustine claims that we need assistance in this respect: we understand the world as "sign" (and language as a system of representation or sign) through recognizing that the Wisdom of God has *become* a sign. Here is Augustine direct:

> Since therefore, we must enjoy to the full that truth which lives unchangeably, and since, within it, God the Trinity, the author and creator of everything, takes thought for the things that he has created, our minds must be purified so that they are able to perceive that light and then hold fast to it. Let us consider this process of cleansing as a trek, or a voyage, to our homeland . . . This we would be unable to do, if wisdom itself had not deigned to adapt itself to our great weakness and offered us a pattern for living; and it has actually done so in human form because we too are human . . . So although it is actually our homeland, it has also made itself the road to our homeland. And although wisdom is everywhere present to the inner eye that is healthy and pure, it deigned to appear even to the carnal eyes of those whose inner eye was weak or impure.[58]

One might ask what the effect would be for a feminist perception of the "*Logos*-history" if Wisdom were to be capitalized and acknowledged as feminine.

In Augustine's eyes, says Williams, the symbolic order of the Old Testament "looks forward to the point at which it is *shown* to be such, when it is finally revealed to be *signum*" of "the definitive sign," i.e., Christ."[59] He continues:

> To . . . deliberately go on inhabiting a symbolic structure . . . in the old way . . . is to turn the old order of signs into something different . . . The sign chosen for itself as against the liberation towards the one true *res* offered by the final sign of Christ is being turned into a pseudo-*res*: symbolic practice has lost its innocence.

This description would appear to reflect the old covenant as it appears in Hebrews 10:1 as opposed to Galatians 4:21–31. As noted in my Introduction, in Hebrews the old covenant foreshadows (functions as *signum* of) the new covenant. In Galatians, the old covenant, chosen for itself, becomes a figure of slavery.

58. See Augustine, *On Christian Teaching*, Book One, X–XIII.

59. See Williams, "Language, Reality and Desire in Augustine's *De Doctrina*," 146–47.

The possibility that a symbolic practice could be turned into a pseudo-*res* or thing in itself is, I believe, what Ricoeur means by the temptation of gnosis or rationalizing symbols as such. In this kind of practice, thought gives rise to symbol (and vice versa in a closed system) which is the reverse of what Ricoeur argues for. Ricoeur goes so far as to suggest that Augustine himself is not immune to this kind of wrong thinking. One might ask whether Augustine is prone to this sort of thing when he *is* being self-consciously philosophical.

I shall not attempt to "think more" along these lines, beyond relating it to the feminist quest for women's identity and the feminist practice of projected symbolism or "re-mythologizing." I believe here that aim and practice are at odds with each other. The quest for identity or meaning belongs to the realm of world as "sign" of God the true *res*, the world in receipt of "presence." To "re-mythologize" is to enter the realm of the pseudo *res*, the realm of illusion in other words.

One must add to this the feminist motive for "re-mythologizing," born of dissatisfaction with the current "symbolic order." One must ask in how far the symbolic order espoused by the churches has been prepared to recognize its "Other" and to be instructed by it. Augustine's centering of meaning in the Wisdom of God made flesh is a further footnote to the "*Logos*-history" outlined by Steiner. I would add that even before the Word becomes flesh, there is a solid covenant between word and world: this *Word* is the One through whom the *world* was made. Over against what appears a solely *masculine* representation of Father and Son stands the biblical tradition that the Word was with the Father *before* the world was made and that, prior to the Incarnation, the Word is depicted as the *feminine* Wisdom (Proverbs 8).

One can travel only so far from the Yellow Brick Road before losing a sense of meaning. "What if the loans of belief in transcendence, made to us since Plato and Augustine in reference to signifying form, were called in?" asks Steiner.[60] The purpose of this book is to ask what it means for a woman to be created in the image of God. If meaning itself is no longer a meaningful term, the question will have no answer. Various departures from the Yellow Brick Road by feminist writers are of no assistance here. This is not to say that our *Logos*-history is above critique. It is to situate the critique differently.

---

60. Steiner, *Real Presences*, 134.

This book is a modest attempt to think more and think anew about the *imago Dei*. It is an exercise in thinking anew about the biblical sources. But before embarking on this venture, some attention must be paid to existing theories. The next chapter considers two key theories of the *imago Dei*, Augustine's and Elizabeth A. Johnson's.

2

Renouncing the *Hubris*?

IN DOROTHY'S FIRST ENCOUNTER with the Wizard of Oz, he presents himself as "Oz, the Great and Terrible." On her return to the Emerald City, the Wizard reveals himself as a little old man, with a bald head and wrinkled face, who admits that he has been "making believe." One might describe this admission as "renouncing the *hubris*" of his former persona. The little man had presented himself as a great and terrible Wizard in order to make the wicked Witches of the East and the West think that he was more powerful than they were. Once the wicked witches were destroyed, the little man was able to reveal his stratagems to Dorothy and her companions.[1]

We may compare the means used by the Wizard of Oz to confront evil with the means used by Dorothy. The little old man masquerades in accord with the concept of wizardry. The purpose of the deception is to instill fear in order to keep the wicked witches at bay. In the land of the Wicked Witch of the West, Dorothy is protected from evil by the mark on her forehead, the kiss from the good Witch of the North. The mark of the kiss represents the Power of Good, and that, says the leader of the Winged Monkeys, is greater than the Power of Evil. The Wizard's masquerade accords with the *concept* of wizardry but not its actuality. The mark of the kiss represents the real thing.

---

1. See Baum, *Wizard of Oz*, chapters 11 and 15.

The previous chapter introduced a claim by Paul Ricoeur that Augustine's "pseudo-concept of original sin" is a form of gnosis: "the very claim to resolve the problem of evil by means of knowledge."[2] Ricoeur rejects this kind of thinking: "In this sense, confronting gnosis and that which resembles it in the Christian sphere of theology, I assign to hermeneutics a *reductive* function." A comparison of approaches to evil by the Wizard of Oz and Augustine might appear far-fetched but they have this in common: the attempt to resolve (or confront) the problem of evil by means of a conception. By contrast, Ricoeur wants the concept or philosophy of evil to be instructed by its "Other," the primal symbols of stain and wandering. This is not the place to consider such symbols of evil or further symbols representing the power of good. It is the method, as outlined by Ricoeur, which concerns us here.

For Ricoeur, the method of beginning with a concept is philosophical *hubris* which must be renounced. Instead, one must begin with "symbol." In the parallel terms of *The Wizard of Oz*, one must begin with the kiss on the forehead. In terms of this book, one must begin with the *imago Dei*. This chapter considers two attempts to uncover the meaning of the *imago Dei*, one by Augustine, the other by feminist writer, Elizabeth A. Johnson. I will argue that both attempts are flawed in Ricoeur's sense, and that philosophical *hubris* is compounded in Johnson's approach by the presuppositions of the feminist method. My critique of Augustine's theory of the *imago Dei* draws attention to an alternative suggestion from his translator, Edmund Hill. It is Hill's approach, based on direct resemblance between the Godhead and humanity, which forms the kernel of my proposal for the *imago Dei* presented in chapter 6.

This book makes use of analogies. Before going any further, let us consider an analogy of artificial flowers. Early attempts at making them were recognizably artificial because the flowers were too regular in shape. More recent attempts are harder to distinguish from real flowers when viewed from a distance. This is because the shape of real flowers is copied with more care. Earlier attempts involved an assumption about what flowers *ought* to be like. Later attempts have paid attention to what flowers *are* like.

Makers of artificial flowers have direct access to real flowers. This makes the comparison clear if one wishes to make it. Some artificial flowers are not intended to be exact copies of the real thing. Even an

---

2. Ricoeur, "Reply to Stephen T. Tyman," 473. Ricoeur's italics.

intentional copy is never the same as the real thing. But it is in line with Ricoeur's recommendation: the concept is instructed by its "other." By contrast, feminist theology which "assumes that all our images of God are human projections" rules out the possibility of being instructed by an "other."[3]

If one applies all this to the *imago Dei*, one may say that human beings are an image of the "Other". In this case human beings are not the makers. The "Other" is the Maker. If we want to know what it means to be *imago Dei*, we can either look towards the "Other" as a starting-point or make some assumptions about what the "Other" ought to be like and proceed accordingly. "It is not 'man' who is made in God's image, but God who has been made in man's image," says Ruether.[4] This is to assume that the "Other" has always been nothing more than a human projection, a surmise which turns God as a knowable entity into a useful fiction. One can then take issue with the kind of use the fiction has been put to and replace it with supposedly better alternatives. One might wonder what effect this method would have if applied to artificial flowers. Would they still merit the name "flowers"?

This book argues that key traditional views of the *imago Dei* have been rather like early attempts at making artificial flowers. This does not mean that the "Other" has played no part in these views. It does mean that human assumptions have got in the way and that the result has had a stiffening effect, much like the stiffness of early artificial flowers. As I say in my Introduction, human likeness to God is subtle and elusive. Divine likeness should not be overstated any more than the flower-likeness of artificial flowers should be overstated. Coming to grips with the *imago Dei* is a complex and delicate matter. Grasping too strongly has led us astray.

INVENTED *VISIBILIA*

This section considers a kind of thinking that has led us astray in the past and looks set to lead us even further astray in the future. The previous chapter drew attention to a traditional belief in a message-bearing universe, the kind of universe that assures us that we have access to something beyond ourselves. Traditionally, this "Other" has validated the efficacy of language. McFague locates the classic metaphor of transference in

---

3. See Ruether, "Christian Tradition and Feminist Hermeneutics," 286–87.
4. Ruether, "Christian Tradition and Feminist Hermeneutics," 287.

this context. Her "metaphorical theology" disowns this kind of universe but does not completely abandon it. McFague retains the *concepts* of "metaphor" and "theology" but not their substance. One might surmise that this kind of approach is a modern innovation. But this is not the case. There is a precedent in Western history for the *method* of reducing religious belief to an underlying concept.

A philosophical movement towards monotheism in late antiquity led to departure from belief in the Greco-Roman gods. The moral depravity of the old gods had become a source of embarrassment in academia.[5] But the gods were not completely abandoned. Rather, they were reinterpreted as personifications, material projections of human qualities or of abstractions. Lewis writes:

> During a period of religious controversy it is, indeed, the most obvious way of tuning primitive documents to meet the ethical or polemical demands of the moment. The Stoics, apart from their general doctrine of the gods as manifestations of the One, were always ready to explain particular myths by allegory. Saturn eating his children could be harmlessly interpreted as Time 'bearing all his sons away'.[6]

In the academia of late antiquity, pagan myths were explained allegorically. Hence allegory and philosophy were connected.

The method did not stop there. Lewis notes: "the habit of applying allegorical interpretation to ancient texts naturally encouraged fresh allegorical constructions, and this method was freely practiced by both pagans and Christians."[7] Patristic writers were philosophically educated. Robert M. Grant states that Clement of Alexandria's fourth or "philosophical" method of interpreting Scripture "owes much to the Stoics and to Philo" and that Origen "sets forth most thoroughly and adequately the principles of Christian allegorization."[8] While Jerome and Augustine attacked Origen's use of the allegorical method, Grant reports that "even those who attacked him most vigorously were often influenced by his thought." Augustine comments on the early chapters of Genesis in this regard: "There is no prohibition against . . . [allegorical] exegesis,

---

5. See Augustine, *City of God*, II.
6. Lewis, *Allegory of Love*, 62.
7. Lewis, *Allegory of Love*, 61–62.
8. See Grant, *Short History of the Interpretation of the Bible*, 55–60.

Renouncing the Hubris?

provided that we also believe in the truth of the [Eden] story as a faithful record of historical fact."[9]

What Lewis calls "a profound change in the mind of antiquity" was accompanied by introspection and awareness of internal moral conflict,[10] seen in terms of "contending forces which [could not] be described at all except by allegory."[11] Consequently, allegory and a subjective element in literature go hand in hand from late antiquity onwards. This genre is still evident in *Pilgrim's Progress* published in 1678.

From a literary point of view, the old gods did not die even when allegory was no longer a popular genre. Lewis describes their revival in the Romantic period. While no longer worshipped or employed to personify a moral struggle, the gods were enjoyed for their aesthetic qualities. By this stage, reports Lewis: "The gods must be, as it were, disinfected of belief; the last taint of the sacrifice, and of the urgent practical interest, the selfish prayer, must be washed away from them, before that other divinity can come to light in the imagination."[12]

This brief history has traced what might be called variations on an allegorical theme. Allegory as a literary method predates late antiquity but its demythologizing aspect, reducing religious belief to the concept behind it, gives it a new slant. The old gods then resurface in various guises. Carl Jung describes their reappearance in the archetypes of the subconscious mind.[13] Both Romantic and Jungian trajectories would seem influential in some current feminist writing, as is considered below.

I turn now to a closer look at the method of allegory, in particular when the method becomes a predominant feature, as in a projected universe. The Introduction drew attention to various literary terms: "symbol," "allegory," "metaphor," "model." I will come to the term "model" in McFague's sense below. Lewis makes a clear distinction between "symbol" and "allegory." He writes of "the fundamental equivalence between the immaterial and the material [which] may be used by the mind in two ways":

> On the one hand you can start with an immaterial fact, such as the passions which you actually experience, and can then invent *visibilia* to express them. If you are hesitating between

---

9. *City of God*, XIII, 21.
10. Lewis, *Allegory of Love*, 58.
11. Lewis, *Allegory of Love*, 113.
12. Lewis, *Allegory of Love*, 83.
13. Jung, *Aspects of the Feminine*, 122.

an angry retort and a soft answer, you can express your state of mind by inventing a person called *Ira* with a torch and letting her contend with another invented person called *Patientia*. This is allegory.[14]

Allegory does not point to a greater reality. It is a construct that generates its own picture, which reduces back to the immaterial fact, concept or emotion that gave it birth.

On the other hand, access to a higher reality beyond the world of our senses can be obtained through "symbol." Lewis goes on to say:

> But there is another way of using the equivalence, which is almost the opposite of allegory, and which I would call sacramentalism or symbolism. If our passions, being immaterial, can be copied by material inventions, then it is possible that our material world in its turn is the copy of an invisible world. As the god Amor and his figurative garden are to the actual passions of men, so perhaps we ourselves and our 'real' world are to something else. The attempt to read that something else through its sensible imitations, to see the archetype in the copy, is what I mean by symbolism or sacramentalism.[15]

Lewis differentiates between "symbol" and "allegory" in terms of the relation of each to the viewer: "The allegorist leaves the given—his own passions—to talk of that which is confessedly less real, which is fiction. The symbolist leaves the given to find that which is more real."

"Symbolism," continues Lewis, "makes its first effective appearance in European thought with the dialogues of Plato." He notes Platonic examples: "The Sun is the copy of the Good. Time is the moving image of eternity."[16] In *City of God* Augustine writes about the *imago Dei* in somewhat similar terms:

> We do indeed recognize in ourselves an image of God, that is of the Supreme Trinity. It is not an adequate image, but a very distant parallel. It is not co-eternal and, in brief, it is not of the same substance as God. For all that, there is nothing in the whole of God's creation so near to him in nature.[17]

---

14. Lewis, *Allegory of Love*, 44–45.
15. Lewis, *Allegory of Love*, 45.
16. Lewis, *Allegory of Love*, 45.
17. *City of God*, XI, 26.

But Augustine goes on to discern likeness to God, not in human beings as such but in an activity of the human *mind*: "We resemble the divine Trinity in that we exist; we know that we exist, and we are glad of this existence and this knowledge." In locating the *imago Dei* in the *mind*, Augustine parts company with symbolism in the sense of a *material* copy of an invisible world. The pictorial aspect of Augustine's theory is one step removed from symbolic representation. Allegorical *visibilia* express aspects of the human mind as will be seen.

In Western history, key aspects of former religious belief are interpreted as *visibilia* representing an alleged prior concept. One can see this process in Lewis's example of Saturn eating his children interpreted as Time "bearing all his sons away." In other words, religious belief is unmasked or *demythologized*. The myth is no longer believed to reflect a higher reality. If one continues to make use of the myth, one does so in full awareness of its allegorical status. As noted, use of the method in relation to ancient texts promoted fresh allegorical constructions. Patristic writers made use of these in the new religious context. The danger of this method was that it gave free reign to religious speculation, as was the case with Origen's allegorical formulations.

In the light of these factors, let us now consider the feminist approach to the *imago Dei* as represented by Ruether. She goes so far as to claim that traditional interpretation of the *imago Dei* has always been allegorical: "it is not 'man' who is made in God's image, but God who has been made in man's image."[18] The method, unmasked as the product of patriarchal projection, is then reissued by feminist theologians from the premise of "a just and truthful anthropology." This opens the door to fresh allegorical constructions. Whether feminists remain aware of the allegorical nature of their projections may be less than clear. I find the term "symbol" used freely, but not in Ricoeur's or Lewis's sense.

As an example, Ruether poses a question about the representative role of women in Catholicism. She questions why men are allowed to be priests in the Roman Catholic Church while women are offered partnership with men in the ministry of the laity and are said to share in the general priesthood of the church.[19] "If men can be 'brides,' symbolically,"

---

18. Ruether, "Christian Tradition and Feminist Hermeneutics," 287.
19. Ruether, "Christian Tradition and Feminist Hermeneutics," 268–69.

asks Ruether, "why can't women be symbolic 'bridegrooms'?"[20] The pivotal word in her question is "symbolic."

"Only one wearing the masculine uniform can (provisionally, and till the *Parousia*) represent the Lord to the Church," writes Lewis, speaking as an Anglo-Catholic.[21] In other words, the male priest is to Christ as a copy to an original. In a feminist reconstruction, the old idea of copy in relation to an original is no longer relevant. The feminist "critique of the image of God idea in Scripture and Christian tradition changes fundamentally the nature of the discussion," says Ruether.[22] But if symbolic likeness is said to function as an illustrated concept, and if "bridegroom" is the imaginary picture generated from the concept, women could, in this revised sense, be regarded as "bridegrooms." This would be allegory.

I draw attention to Ruether's question in order to illustrate the ways in which different kinds of representation can become confused. If applied elsewhere, her question might sound something like this: if lions can represent the cat family, why can't cats represent courage? Men and women can equally represent the Church just as cats and lions can equally represent the cat family. It does not follow that women represent reality beyond the social institution *in the same way* as men. Further to the analogy, lions represent courage while cats in their "nine lives" represent indestructibility: in this case, symbolic representation between cats and lions is not interchangeable. Symbolic likenesses are, as I say, a complex and delicate matter.

I come now to what Sallie McFague means by "model." As seen in chapter 1, her "metaphorical theology" rejects the dominance of the model-metaphor "God the father." The sacramental universe is consequently undermined, along with access to an "outside." McFague is then at liberty to detach theological formulations (including biblical ones) from reference to an "outside." The sacramental universe is demythologized, reduced to allegorical status in other words. "Metaphorical theology" continues on the basis of fresh allegorical constructions.

For McFague, Scripture and Christian tradition offer no more than a human construction for their time:

> On my view, what we have in Paul's letters and in the Gospel of John are two highly imaginative (and very different) attempts to

---

20. Ruether, "Christian Tradition and Feminist Hermeneutics," 270.
21. Lewis, "Priestesses in the Church?," 93.
22. Ruether, "Christian Tradition and Feminist Hermeneutics," 287.

express the salvific love of God in metaphors and concepts appropriate to their time . . . The question we must ask is, . . . What should we be doing for our time that would be comparable to what Paul and John did for theirs? Does Christian theology involve, either through translation or through interpretation, using the metaphors and concepts of Scripture (and the tradition), or does it involve taking scriptural texts as a model of how to do it, that is, of how to do it in the language of one's own time? I believe the second option is the necessary and appropriate one.[23]

In this description, biblical writers begin with a prior concept (the "salvific love of God") and express it in "highly imaginative" ways. McFague advocates following this "model" (or method) with the aim of producing further "highly imaginative" expressions (or "models" as she calls them elsewhere).

McFague states that her second option is radical in the sense that it is a self-conscious recommendation. She adds: "For examples of relatively unselfconscious radical theological recontextualizing, we need only think of Augustine's Neoplatonism or Thomas's Aristotelianism, both of which are considered nonetheless to be in continuity with the very different theologies of Paul and John." Johnson has something to say about Thomas's Aristotelianism in this respect:

> One of the most influential androcentric syntheses in the Catholic tradition is that of Aquinas . . . [who] accepted, as part of the Aristotelian heritage . . . the notion of ancient Greek biology that the male seed carried all the potency for new life . . . From woman's natural inferiority in the order of creation Aquinas reasonably deduces a host of consequences, such as that . . . women may not be ordained priests since priesthood signifies the eminence of Christ and women do not signify what pertains to eminence; women should not preach since this is an exercise of wisdom and authority of which they are not capable.[24]

From a feminist perspective, Thomas's Aristotelian "recontextualizing" would seem less than happy.

Whether this kind of "recontextualizing" is really in continuity with Scripture may be open to doubt. Johnson cites Elizabeth Clark and Herbert Richardson, "The Man Who Should Have Known Better":

> Some commentators have observed that there are elements in Aquinas's theology that could have led him to a more positive

---

23. See McFague, *Models of God*, 30–31.
24. Johnson, *She Who Is*, 24–25.

evaluation of women's nature . . . his belief that in one sense women were indeed created in the image of God.[25]

But the possibility of Aquinas's "recontextualizing" being open to correction by Scripture is precisely what the feminist critique of Scripture and tradition rules out.

How do these various ways of thinking accord with my illustration of artificial flowers? In parallel to a sacramental universe, artificial flowers are known to be copies of real flowers. Versions recognized as stiff and ugly have led to more careful copying of the real thing. Let us assume, however, that defective versions from the past have led to doubt about the whole copying process. Consequently, all artificial flowers are deemed to be projections from human presuppositions. The proposed way forward is to rethink the presuppositions in order to improve the projections. McFague's project broadens the application to suggest that theology past and present has represented, and can continue to represent, whole garden schemes of invented *visibilia*.

ALLEGORY OF THE MASCULINE

Augustine is often portrayed as a misogynist. Uta Ranke-Heinemann sums him up as follows:

> This illustrious saint shaped the ideal of Christian piety more than anyone before or after him, and his negative attitude to women proved especially fatal . . . Possidius, for many years his friend and fellow lodger reports of him that, "No woman ever set foot inside his house, he never spoke with a woman except in the presence of a third person . . . He made no exceptions, not even for his own elder sister and his nieces, all three of them nuns."[26]

"Such behaviour," comments Ranke-Heinemann, "would suggest the man was psychically disturbed."

---

25. See Johnson, *She Who Is*, 25; 280, citing *Women and Religion: a Feminist Source-book of Christian Thought*.

26. Ranke-Heinemann, *Eunuchs For the Kingdom Of Heaven*, 121–22 citing Possidius, *Vita 26*. But cf. Brown, *Augustine of Hippo*, 194: "Augustine maintained to the last the natural clannishness of the Africans. His widowed sister would settle at Hippo to take charge of the women 'servants of God'; as did his niece." Augustine's "absolute prohibition on female visitors" was due to his "austere monastic routine."

Sister Prudence Allen's assessment is more positive. She maintains that Augustine, standing "in a watershed in the history of the concept of woman in relation to man," was influenced in various, sometimes conflicting ways, by the Stoics, Neoplatonists and early church fathers. She points out, however, that his meditations on the original creation and the final resurrection led him to conclude "that women and men are eternally distinguished by sex and that neither sex is naturally superior to the other."[27]

As seen above, Sallie McFague draws attention to Augustine's Neoplatonism and Thomas Aquinas's Aristotelianism. She states that both examples of "theological recontextualizing" are considered to be "in continuity with the very different theologies of Paul and John."[28] What McFague does not say is that Augustinian Neoplatonism and Thomistic Aristotelianism may be problematic in this respect. The next section will return to Thomas Aquinas. This section engages with Neoplatonic input in Augustine's theory of the *imago Dei*.

Augustine's understanding of the gendered *imago Dei* may be said to arise from an attempt to reconcile a seeming discrepancy between Genesis 1:26–27 (in which both male and female are said to be made in God's image) and 1 Corinthians 11:7 (which states that the man is the image and glory of God while the woman is the glory of man). His solution draws on philosophical thinking of his day. Michael Azkoul describes Augustine's understanding of "mind" as "Platonic." He outlines Augustine's perception as follows:

> The intellect, unlike the senses, is fed by two streams: from the soul and indirectly, from the world of phenomena. The intellect, stamped or 'impressed' with Divine Ideas, beckons us to contemplate the soul and the heavenly realm to which it is akin. When the intellect or reason concerns itself with the physical world, it produces 'science' (*scientia*); but when it searches the realm of the spirit, it uncovers 'wisdom' (*sapientia*). Inasmuch as both *scientia* and *sapientia* comprehend some aspect of the truth, they both, to some degree, require illumination. The higher we ascend on the scale of being, the greater the 'light' given to the soul.[29]

---

27. Allen, *The Concept of Woman*, 222.
28. McFague, *Models of God*, 30–31.
29. Azkoul, *Influence of Augustine of Hippo on the Orthodox Church*, 155.

Augustine applies this understanding of the human mind to his interpretation of the gendered *imago Dei*.

At the time of the Christological debates and increasing devotion to Mary as *Theotokos*, ecclesiological attention began to center on anthropology, including the question of whether women are in the image of God. Kim Power reports that the "problem of women" stems from the ancient model of "masculine and feminine as symbols for superior and inferior capacity for rationality, morality, power and strength."[30] Philo had accepted this model, excluding women from his concept of full humanity. Power describes how Augustine inheriting this tradition, from Origen and Ambrose as well as philosophical sources, used the word *sapientia* for the masculine principle and *scientia* for the feminine principle. Augustine understood both men and women to have *both* principles of mind. The masculine principle allowed direct contemplation of, and eventual eternal union with, God. The feminine principle, being concerned with temporal matters, would pass away. Consequently, women were understood to be in God's image in having a lasting "manly mind" in a woman's body.[31]

In the *City of God*, Augustine writes: "some people suppose that women will not keep their sex at the resurrection . . . For my part, I feel that theirs is the more sensible opinion who have no doubt that there will be both sexes in the resurrection."[32] But a controversial passage in *The Trinity* would appear to indicate that women *per se* are not made in God's image:

> But we must see how what the apostle says about the man and not the woman being in the image of God avoids contradicting what is written in . . . Genesis 1:27. It says that what was made to the image of God is the human nature that is realized in each sex, and it does not exclude the female from the image of God . . . So how are we to take what we have heard from the apostle, that man is the image of God, and so he is forbidden to cover his head, but the woman is not and so she is told to do so? In the same way, I believe, as what I said when I was dealing with the nature of the human mind, namely that the woman with her husband is the image of God in such a way that the whole of that substance is one image, but when she is assigned her function

---

30. Power, *Veiled Desire*, 132–33.
31. See Power, *Veiled Desire*, 133–49.
32. Augustine, *City of God*, XII, 17.

of being an assistant, which is her concern alone, she is not the image of God; whereas in what concerns the man alone he is the image of God as fully and completely as when the woman is joined to him in one whole.[33]

Read as excluding woman from the *imago Dei*, except insofar as she accompanies her husband, Augustine has been discredited in the eyes of many feminist writers.[34] Standing against this perception, Kim Power and Augustine's translator, Edmund Hill contend that "the woman" and "the man" are not meant here to be taken literally, but refer to functions of the mind.[35] Augustine goes on to say: "there can be no doubt that man was not made to the image of him who created him as regards his body . . . but as regards the rational mind, which is capable of recognizing God."[36]

For Augustine, the mind or inner "man," common to men and women, constitutes the theatre for the *imago Dei*.[37] He argues from Colossians 3:10 that the renewal of the mind "according to the image of him who created him" applies to both man and woman. ("Is there anyone then who would exclude females from this association, seeing that together with us men they are fellow heirs of grace?"). But Corinthians 11:7 appears to suggest that the man (and not the woman) is the image of God. At this point the divisions of the mind (the masculine *sapientia* and feminine *scientia*) come into play:

> It is only because she differs from the man in the sex of her body that [the woman's] bodily covering could suitably be used to symbolize that part of the reason which is diverted to the management of temporal things, signifying that the mind of man does not remain the image of God except in the part which

---

33. Augustine, *The Trinity*, XII, 10: 327–28.

34. For example, see Doyle and Paludi, *Sex and Gender*, 252 citing Ruether, "Misogynism and virginal feminism in the fathers of the church," *Religion and Sexism*.

35. Cf. Power, *Veiled Desire*, 138–39 and Hill, n. 27 in Augustine, *The Trinity*, XII, 12: 339. In his "Foreword to Books IX –XIV," Hill notes that "mind" as his translation of *mens* "means more than 'mind' commonly means in English; it is the subject of the highest psychic functions, volitional and affective as well as cognitive."

36. Augustine, *The Trinity*, XII, 12.

37. Augustine did not invent this idea. Origen had written, "We do not understand . . . this man . . . whom Scripture says was made 'according to the image of God' to be corporeal . . . But it is our inner man, invisible, incorporeal, incorruptible, and immortal which is made 'according to the image of God.'" (See Genesis Homily 1, 63.)

adheres to the eternal ideas to contemplate or consult them: and it is clear that females have this as well as males.[38]

Gendered differences are said to refer back to mental functions. In this interpretation, neither male nor female are said to be directly in God's image but rather the male body functions as a projected "symbol" or allegory of the "masculine" part of the human mind.

There are specific difficulties with this theory as well as with the allegorical approach in general. Firstly, as Power points out, identifying *sapientia* (wisdom) with the *masculine* principle had more in common with the "*vir sapiens* of the philosophic tradition" than with the Hebrew tradition. Philo had represented Wisdom "as the mother of creation, as God is the Father of the universe."[39] Philo had also asserted that "as woman is to man, and Sense-perception is to Mind, so man is to God . . . He must be obedient to God as woman is to man."[40] Philo's language, at this point, is reminiscent of Augustine's own insistence (in *City of God*) on Adam's need for submission: "it is to man's advantage to be in subjection to God, and it is calamitous for him to act according to his own will, and not to obey the will of his Creator."[41] Had Augustine allowed his own understanding of man's submission of the will to parallel his understanding of man's contemplation of God, he could have allowed *sapientia* to remain feminine, resulting in a feminine principle of mind (in both men and women) surviving in eternity.[42] Is the "Platonic" propensity in line with Swartley's "mirror game"?[43]

Secondly, Augustine's theory of the *imago Dei* is less about likeness to God, as in a copy to an original, and more about journey towards (or away from) God. While the allegorical "he" and "she" have a pagan philosophical origin, they reappear in biblical guise in the following passage from *The Trinity*:

> As we climb inward then through the parts of the soul by certain steps of reflection, we begin to come upon something that is not

---

38. Augustine, *The Trinity*, XII, 12.
39. Power, *Veiled Desire*, 136.
40. Power, *Veiled Desire*, 133.
41. Augustine, *City of God*, XIV, 12.
42. For Augustine, *sapientia* is masculine, not in relation to God but to *scientia* which is not party to the *imago Dei* except via *sapientia*. The nature of gendered language in covenantal relationship is explored further in chapter 3.
43. See Swartley, *Slavery, Sabbath, War and Women*, 185–86.

common to us and the beasts, and that is where reason begins, and where we can now recognize the inner man. But through that reason which has been delegated to administer temporal affairs he may slide too much into outer things... that is to say the reason which presides as the masculine portion in the control tower of counsel may fail to curb her. In such a case... the sight of eternal things is withdrawn from the head himself as he eats the forbidden fruit with his consort.[44]

The journey towards (or away from) God is spelled out in Hill's comment:

> The whole virtue of Augustine's structure of the *psyche* is that it is pregnant with dynamic possibilities; it is in constant movement, either in the right or the wrong direction. That is why in Book XII [of *The Trinity*] he casts it into the dramatic form of a paradise story in microcosm... In this way he graphically suggests the defacement of the divine image.[45]

Hill goes so far as to draw a diagram of Augustine's representation of the *imago Dei*. The diagram shows *sapientia* (cast as Adam), always in danger of moving away from God through the agency of *scientia* (cast as Eve) but also restored to contemplation of the eternal Word through the agency of faith in Christ incarnate and virtue (cast as Mary). Hill admits his use of Mary to illustrate faith in Christ is not explicit in Augustine's theory. I will have more to say about allegorical use of the mother of Jesus in chapter 4.

The *imago Dei*, portrayed as a paradise story and its reversal, may owe something to Augustine's appeal to Colossians 3:10 on the renewal of the mind. But the mind's need for renewal does not accord with the Platonic hierarchy in which the intellect, impressed with Divine Ideas, contemplates the heavenly realm to which it is akin. One may compare Augustine's theory of language as sign, in which unchanging truth is not available to the spiritual eye except through the agency of the Word or Wisdom of God becoming flesh as sign of the creator. Here *sapientia* in the Platonic sense is already dethroned.

I have said that Augustine's proposal is less about likeness than journey towards God. His appeal to the renewal of the mind does not directly explicate the gendered *imago Dei*. It is the "masculinity" associated with it

---

44. Augustine, *The Trinity*, XII, 13. Cf. Origen, Genesis Homily 1 15.
45. Hill, "Foreword to Books IX–XIV," in Augustine, *The Trinity*, 261–62.

which supplies the gendered aspect of likeness. C. S. Lewis distinguishes between two kinds of nearness to God:

> One is likeness to God . . . But, secondly, there is what we may call nearness of approach. If this is what we mean, the states in which a man is 'nearest' to God are those in which he is most surely and swiftly approaching his final union with God, vision of God and enjoyment of God. And as soon as we distinguish nearness-by-likeness and nearness-of-approach, we see that they do not necessarily coincide.[46]

On these terms Augustine depicts the *imago Dei* in the sense of "nearness-of-approach". While the renewal process will increase likeness to God, it is not, in itself, likeness to God.

The allegorical relation of body to mind raises the problem of dualism between mind and body, a disembodying tendency applying more generally in allegory as a philosophical method. It should be recalled that Augustine resorted to allegory in order to *include* women in the *imago Dei*, although not their physical sex.[47] Whether allegory is the only way to reconcile 1 Corinthians 11:1–16 with Genesis 1:26–27 is another matter. Hill offers an alternative interpretation based on direct symbolic likeness between humanity and the Godhead:

> I think [Augustine] has missed a genuine suggestion of Paul's in this same chapter that interpersonal human relationships can to some extent be regarded as a reflection of the interpersonal divine relationships.
>
> In 1 Cor 11:3 the apostle writes, *I want you to know that the head of every man is the Christ, and the head of woman is the man, and the head of the Christ is God.* The relationship signified by "head of" is not merely one of dominion or priority, but of origin, as is clear from what he later says, *The man is not from the woman, but the woman from the man* (verse 8). So here we have a chain of relationships or origin, God–Christ–man–woman; for God and Christ we can read Father and Son; and so we can set up a proportion: as the Son is to the Father, so is the woman to the man; as the Son is from the Father, so is the woman from the man. The man and the woman are of course Adam and Eve; in the case of that pair the woman is from the substance of the

---

46. Lewis, *The Four Loves*, 4.

47. Cf. Chrysostom, whose interpretation of 1 Cor 11:7–10 excluded women from the *imago Dei* on the basis that the *imago Dei* has to do with male authority. See *Discourse 2 on Genesis*, quoted in Clark, *Women in the Early Church*, 35.

man in equality of nature just as the Son is from the substance of the Father in equality of nature.[48]

The key to the *imago Dei*, suggests Hill, is interpersonal relationship. This is in line with the observation by Jewish writer, Tikva Frymer-Kensky, cited in the Introduction, that social relationship is a common factor between creator and creature male and female.[49]

It is noteworthy that the lack of reference to the *imago Dei* for women in 1 Corinthians 11:7 is an omission, not a denial.[50] Nevertheless, Lewis writes:

> In verse 3 [Paul] has given us a very remarkable proportion sum: that God is to Christ as Christ is to man and man is to woman, and the relation between each term and the next is that of Head. And in verse 7 we are told that man is God's image and glory, and woman is man's glory. He does not repeat 'image', but I question whether the omission is intentional, and I suggest that we shall have a fairly Pauline picture of this whole series . . . if we picture each term as 'the image and glory' of the preceding term.[51]

In one way Lewis is right; from a logical linguistic point of view, the sequence requires a repetition of "image and glory." That is why I think the omission significant. If "image" had been repeated, woman would have been the "image" of man. As it is, she is the "glory" of man but not the "image." The reason, I suggest, is that she is *not* the image of man but of God.

Chapter 6 offers a more detailed exploration of 1 Corinthians 11:1–16, in comparison with Genesis 1:26–27 and Colossians 3:10. These passages raised a genuine exegetical question for the early church, a question that has not gone away. Augustine's solution may perhaps help to convince moderns that the motive of including women does not always justify the method of biblical interpretation. That he was not a misogynist is demonstrated, I think, by the following exhortation: "Do not despise yourselves, you men: the son of God assumed manhood. Do not despise yourselves, you women: God's son was born of woman."[52]

---

48. See Augustine, *The Trinity*, XII, 338 n. 22.

49. See Soskice, *Kindness of God*, 50–51.

50. Cf. 1 Corinthians 11:11–12.

51. Lewis, "Christianity and Literature," 19. Lewis only claims to make a literary, not a theological point here.

52. See Bettenson, *Later Christian Fathers*, 218, citing Augustine, *de agone Christiano*, 12.

AN ALLEGORICAL DEITY?

Elizabeth A. Johnson bases her proposal of SHE WHO IS to signify God on Thomas Aquinas's He Who Is.[53] She refers to the biblical ground for such naming:

> Near the start of the biblical story of deliverance and covenant stands an enigmatic encounter. A bush is burning in the wilderness without being consumed. In respect for the presence of the holy, Moses removes his shoes . . . In this context the exiled shepherd asks the ancestral God for a self-identifying name. It is graciously given: I AM WHO I AM (Ex 3:14), *'ehyeh 'asher 'ehyeh*, safeguarded in the sacred tetragrammaton YHWH.[54]

Johnson states that philosophical interpretation of this incident has colored its reception:

> Of all the interpretations of the name given at the burning bush . . . the one with the strongest impact on subsequent theological tradition links the name with the metaphysical notion of being. YHWH means "I am who I am" or simply "I am" in a sense that identifies divine mystery with being itself.

She claims that this kind of metaphysical nuance, Hellenistic rather than Hebraic, is evident in the Thomist "He Who Is."[55]

"From the Septuagint translation onward the idea that the name YHWH discloses the ontological nature of God gained precedence in Jewish circles and was widely used in early Christian theology,"[56] says Johnson. She continues:

> Aquinas fills this name with all the transcendent significance that accrues to pure, absolute being in his system. God whose proper name is HE WHO IS is sheer, unimaginable livingness in whose being the whole created universe participates.

This is to attribute to Aquinas a method (similar, as will be seen, to Johnson's own method) of treating the name of God as a receptacle for the content of a projected idea, rather than as a means of encounter with the living God, as described in Exodus 3:13–14.

---

53. Augustine also refers to God as "HE WHO IS." See *City of God* VIII, 11 and XII, 2.
54. Johnson, *She Who Is*, 241.
55. Johnson, *She Who Is*, 241–42, citing Walter Kasper, *God of Jesus Christ*, 147–52.
56. Johnson, *She Who Is*, 242.

Johnson cites the Thomist name for God in the original Latin, "*Ergo hoc nomen, "qui est," est maxime proprium nomen Dei.*" She comments:

> The androcentric character of the standard English translation of God's name as HE WHO IS is piercingly evident. That character is not accidental but coheres with the androcentric nature of Aquinas's thought as a whole, expressed most infamously in his assessment of women as deficient males. The original Latin, however, could be rendered differently.[57]

Johnson responds with a feminist alternative. One must ask, however, whether the "is" of SHE WHO IS signifies what it does in the Thomist "He Who Is."

The meaning of "is" as applied to God, and to creation in relation to God, appears in the Thomist doctrine of analogy. Johnson touches on it:

> Analogical predication rests on an interpretation of the doctrine of creation that sees all things brought into being and sustained by God who is cause of the world . . . All creatures participate to some degree in "being". . . Thanks to this ontology of participation, every creature in some way shares in divine perfection, although in no way does God resemble creatures. Looking at creatures we can glean clues about the characteristics of that primordial fire which is their origin and sustenance . . . Thanks to the relationship of creation, words are but pointers to the origin and source of all.[58]

E. L. Mascall elaborates on the presupposition behind the doctrine of analogy:

> We are not merely concerned with the question "How can an infinite, necessary and immutable Being be described in terms that are derived from the finite, contingent and mutable world?" but with a question that is anterior to this and without which this cannot be properly discussed at all, namely "How is the possibility of our applying to the infinite Being terms that are derived from the finite order conditioned by the fact that the

---

57. Johnson, *She Who Is*, 242. Cf. Soskice, *Kindness of God*, 85 n. 3. Soskice cites J. Gibson "Could Christ have been born a woman?" in a claim that Albert the Great introduced the Aristotelian argument that "a woman is a defective man, and . . .since Christ ought to represent perfection . . . He should be incarnate as a man."

58. Johnson, *She Who Is*, 113–14.

finite order is dependent for its very existence on the fiat of the infinite and self-existing Being?"⁵⁹

For Johnson, analogical predication depends on "an interpretation of the doctrine of creation." Mascall states that analogical predication depends on the fiat of self-existing Being. The encounter of the burning bush allows access to the primordial "Is." I do not find this encounter in SHE WHO IS.

Despite admitting that, for Aquinas, "words are but pointers to the origin and source of all," Johnson does not engage with "He Who Is" on these terms. She writes: "Aquinas fills this name [He Who Is] with all the transcendent significance that accrues to pure, absolute being in his system." This is like turning artificial flowers into a system of their own. The system might acknowledge the derivative status of artificial flowers, endowing "real flowers" with "transcendent significance." The impetus would nevertheless come from the system, not from actuality.

As seen above, Sallie McFague finds in Augustine's Neoplatonism and Thomas's Aristotelianism a reflection of an alleged biblical method in which "the salvific love of God" is expressed in "metaphors and concepts appropriate to their time."⁶⁰ She recommends this surmised method as a model for contemporary theology. The proposal of SHE WHO IS would seem to follow this kind of procedure. Johnson suggests that the name "He Who Is" could be translated as "who is" or "the one who is," with the understanding that the antecedent of *qui* is grammatically masculine to agree with its intended referent *Deus*."⁶¹ Taking the Thomist *qui* as a conceptual springboard, Johnson proposes "a feminist gloss on this highly influential text":

> If God is not intrinsically male, if women are truly created in the image of God, if being female is an excellence, if what makes women exist as women in all difference is participation in divine being, then there is cogent reason to name toward Sophia-God, "the one who is," with implicit reference to an antecedent of the grammatically and symbolically feminine gender. SHE WHO IS can be spoken as a robust, appropriate name for God. With this name we bring to bear in a female metaphor all the power

---

59. Mascall, *Existence and Analogy* 116.
60. McFague, *Models of God*, 30–31.
61. Johnson, *She Who Is*, 242.

carried in the ontological symbol of absolute, relational liveliness that energizes the world.[62]

The surmised Thomist method becomes, in McFague's words, a model for contemporary (feminist) theology.

The feminist gloss proposed by Johnson hinges on a change of gender in the antecedent of "who." She outlines her method: "In English the 'who' of *qui est* is open to inclusive interpretation, and this indicates a way to proceed." On this basis, Johnson argues the legitimacy of an implicitly feminine antecedent. But the change of gender is not the only change at issue. The assumption behind it has changed. In the Thomist doctrine of analogy, as Johnson attests, words are said to point to the origin and source of all. In her proposed alternative, words point not to the origin and source of all but to an "ontological symbol" which is said to derive its cogency from below. The feminist "we" supplying "all the power" of the female metaphor would seem a long way from the Christian sphere of theology, open to being instructed by its "Other," as advocated by Ricoeur.

For McFague and Johnson, the system is self-contained, as in a world of artificial flowers in which "real flowers" are no more than a philosophical concept. In this context, one must ask about the role of imagination. Johnson cites a Thomist remark in this respect: "We can acquire the knowledge of divine things by natural reason only through the imagination."[63] Johnson adds a significant rider: "Without necessarily adopting Aquinas's epistemology, we can hear the truth of his observation." But in the absence of a Thomist epistemology, where does one arrive? McFague endorses the "highly imaginative" approaches in Paul's letters and John's gospel but does not claim knowledge of divine things in a Thomist sense.

Johnson offers a fuller description of these factors in a discussion of "women's religious experience":

> According to Tillich's well-known analysis, symbols point beyond themselves to something else, something moreover in which they participate. They open up levels of reality, which otherwise are closed, for us, and concomitantly open up depths of our own being, which otherwise would remain untouched. They cannot be produced intentionally but grow from a deep level that Tillich identifies as the collective unconscious ... Women's

---

62. Johnson, *She Who Is*, 242–43.
63. Johnson, *She Who Is*, 46, citing Aquinas, *Summa Theologiae* 1, q.12, a.13.

> religious experience is a generating force for these symbols, a clear instance of how great symbols of the divine always come into being not simply as a projection of the imagination, but as an awakening from the deep abyss of human existence in real encounter with divine being.[64]

Here Johnson does talk about encounter, at the level of the collective unconscious. Imagination is said to be projected from this level in order to generate "symbols of the divine". I will return to this process in chapter 8.

I have said that the procedure adopted in Johnson's proposal of SHE WHO IS departs from the method espoused by Ricoeur. Nevertheless, Johnson cites Ricoeur in support of her method of producing "symbols for divine mystery." She writes:

> The symbol gives rise to thought. With this axiom Paul Ricoeur points to the dynamism inherent in a true symbol that participates in the reality it signifies . . . It gives its gift of fullest meaning when a thinker risks critical interpretation in sympathy with the reality to which it points. So it is when the concrete, historical reality of women, affirmed as blessed by God, functions as symbol in speech about the mystery of God. Language is informed by the particularity of women's experience carried in the symbol.[65]

Johnson's departure from the Thomist epistemology, however, changes the nature of the reality in which the "symbol" is said to participate.

In proposing SHE WHO IS, Johnson parts company with Aquinas in terms of epistemology. In another sense, there may be a similarity. For Aquinas, as represented by Johnson, the emphasis is on participation in divine perfection. Likeness to God is a matter of inference. Johnson's feminist gloss follows this lead. She states: "If what makes women exist as women in all difference is participation in divine being, then there is cogent reason to name toward 'Sophia-God' . . . with implicit reference to an antecedent of the . . . feminine gender." For Johnson, the nature of women's divine likeness may be inferred from women's existential experience interpreted as participation in what she terms "the ontological symbol of absolute, relational liveliness that energizes the world."

Elsewhere this process is spelled out in terms of empowerment for women. Johnson writes:

---

64. Johnson, *She Who Is*, 46–47,
65. Johnson, *She Who Is*, 47.

Renouncing the Hubris?

> Women's experience of self, interpreted as experience of God, fleshed out with values characteristic of women's ways of being in the world, comes to a theological flashpoint when women begin to articulate and act in accord with their dignity as *imago Dei, imago Christi.*[66]

Experience of self is *interpreted* as experience of God. Likeness is intrinsic to the interpretation which is "fleshed out" in female terms. The *imago Dei* then becomes a formula which determines the theological flashpoint. There is a circularity here, reminiscent perhaps of Swartley's "mirror game."[67]

Associating the *imago Dei* with empowerment or participation in divine perfection has more to do with what Lewis would call "nearness-of-approach" rather than "nearness-by-likeness." Something of the sort appears in Augustine's *sapientia*, with access to the heavenly realm operating as the determinative factor. The tendency is for the gendered aspect to become an attachment, rather than intrinsic to the *imago Dei*. Such thinking paves the way for projection or allegory as in SHE WHO IS. The previous section noted that Augustine's use of allegory raises the problem of dualism between mind and body. I find a somewhat similar dualism in Johnson's approach, in particular for women said to be *imago Christi* in which the embodied aspect is, of necessity, downplayed.

GREEN GLASSES OR GREEN FINGERS?

This chapter has considered two things: the *imago Dei* and how we know about it. In Scripture, the *imago Dei* is a given. Human beings are *created* in the image of God, as artificial flowers are created in the image of real flowers. Knowing about the *imago Dei* implies some degree of human agency. But it is the kind of knowing which recognizes its "Other," renouncing the philosophical *hubris* of beginning with its own preconception. In this section I use the term Green Fingers to depict this kind of knowing, in contrast with a Green Glasses orientation which begins with its own preconceptions and then projects them onto external reality. While not green or flower-like in themselves, Green Fingers are in touch with things green and growing.

---

66. Johnson, *She Who Is*, 69.
67. See Swartley, *Slavery, Sabbath, War and Women*, 185–86.

The artificial flower analogy may serve to remind us that we are a copy of an original. This is what Lewis calls "nearness-by-likeness." Lewis distinguishes "nearness-by-likeness" from "nearness-of-approach." Green Fingers, open to the messages from a sacramental universe, constitute the first step towards "nearness-of-approach." A Green Fingers method allows for knowledge of the *imago Dei*. It is not the *imago Dei* itself. One must be very clear about these distinctions. For Augustine, nearness-of-approach, said to be masculine, is then classed as the *imago Dei*. Put simply, this is to confuse the Green Fingers method with the artificial flower analogy, to the detriment of both. There are consequences in this, not only in traditional apprehension of the *imago Dei* but also in the feminist response to it.

I have said that we need to be clear about distinctions. We also need to be clear about interconnections. *Mary: Grace and Hope in Christ*, paragraph 8 states: "The Old Testament bears witness to God's creation of men and women in the divine image, and God's loving call to covenant relationship with himself." As a given status, the *imago Dei* is independent of the call to covenant relationship. In another sense, the *imago Dei* is dependent upon, and symbolic of, that covenant relationship. A fresh appraisal of these interconnections would be timely.

There are mixed messages in Western philosophy and religion, a situation which impinges on the *imago Dei* in particular. The Green Fingers understanding of access to a message-bearing universe is an ancient one, affirmed by Christianity, but known beyond it. This is one strand of the Western heritage. Paul Ricoeur calls on philosophy and Christian theology to renounce any attempts to "colonize this outside."[68] I have suggested that a colonizing or Green Glasses method makes its debut with the demythologizing and reinterpretation of the Greco-Roman gods. The effects of this method are widespread, not least in traditional interpretation of the *imago Dei*.

Key modern feminists are quick to denounce the result of a colonizing method. But far from renouncing the method itself, feminist theology diverts it to its own purposes, on the assumption that "all of our images of God are human projections."[69] Unlike the little old man who renounces the *hubris* of his alter ego, Elizabeth Johnson offers a feminist alternative to "Oz the Great and Terrible." SHE WHO IS never gets beyond "Oz the Great and Terrible" as a *method*, even in rejecting him.

68. See Ricoeur, "Reply to Stephen T. Tyman," 472.
69. Ruether, "Christian Tradition and Feminist Hermeneutics," 287.

This book critiques traditional interpretation of the *imago Dei* insofar as it represents a Green Glasses method while upholding the sacramental universe which validates the critique. I submit that SHE WHO IS operates at a disadvantage in this respect. Even at its most patriarchal, traditional interpretation of the *imago Dei* retains some validity from the "Other" of a sacramental universe and also the possibility of self-correction. In abandoning the sacramental universe, SHE WHO IS undermines her own validity and is not open to self-correction except in a relativist way, dependent on the sensibility of the time. McFague and others depart from the Yellow Brick Road for unstable and volatile territory, as I explore further in chapter 7. At the same time women seek to be treated as "other" by men. I will return to this below.

The complexity of the feminist response to "Oz the Great and Terrible" ought not to be underestimated. On the one hand, "Oz" is unmasked or demythologized. On the other hand, the surmised method is sustained in fresh allegorical formulations. I said earlier that McFague detects and advocates whole garden schemes of invented *visibilia*. At the same time, she espouses "an 'in touch' model of being and knowing" with the world as "neighborhood."[70] While this might sound like being in contact with external reality, this is a *model* which, on McFague's terms, belongs *within* a Green Glasses understanding. Nevertheless, an aspiration to be "in touch," with the natural world in particular, is by no means abandoned. Similarly, the wish to be treated as "other" by men does not belong within a Green Glasses understanding.

I find a similar ambivalence in feminist religious aspiration. Johnson acknowledges "divine mystery," the God beyond all knowing:

> Prophets and religious thinkers have long insisted on the need to break down false idols and escape out of their embrace toward the living God, speech about whom becomes in its own turn a candidate for critique whenever it is held too tightly. The process never ends, for divine mystery is fathomless.[71]

She goes so far as to quote C. S. Lewis in this context:

> My idea of God is not a divine idea. It has to be shattered time after time. He shatters it Himself. He is the great iconoclast. Could we not almost say that this shattering is one of the marks

---

70. McFague, *Super, Natural Christians*, 95.
71. Johnson, *She Who Is*, 39, citing Lewis, *A Grief Observed*, 52.

of His presence? . . . And most are offended by the iconoclasm; and blessed are those who are not.

Johnson comments: "What needs to be shattered according to feminist theological critique is the stranglehold on religious language of God-He." This is to equate the iconoclastic effect of the feminist theological critique with that of encounter with the living God.

For Johnson and others, encounter is not at issue. God remains out of reach while the idea of God persists on its own terms. McFague sums up the tendency: "I do not *know* who God is, but I find some models better than others for constructing an image of God commensurate with my trust in a God as on the side of life. God is and remains a mystery."[72] Here the "image of God" functions as a projected illustration of the concept that God is on the side of life. Meanwhile "mystery" hovers in the wings. SHE WHO IS displays a similar ambivalence. On simple allegorical terms, she functions as a projection of women's experience. As a "symbol" of "divine mystery" she aspires to higher things.

At this point I return to the fate of the Greco-Roman gods. The first section of this chapter traced their history in Western literature. In the Romantic period, says Lewis, the gods were enjoyed for their aesthetic qualities. For this to happen "the gods must be, as it were, disinfected of belief; the last taint of the sacrifice, and of the urgent practical interest, the selfish prayer, must be washed away from them, before that other divinity can come to light in the imagination."[73] Despite the disinfecting process, something is retained. I believe that Johnson and others *demythologize* the Green Fingers approach but do not discard it. Stripped of its covenantal context, the fathomless aspect of the *via negativa* is retained as a concept. One is then free to project one's approximations or ideas of God as "symbols" while acknowledging their religious limitations. "Divine mystery" is thus reborn in the sphere of the imagination.

In one sense, a Romantic writer might treat the old gods lightly. But religious nostalgia may not be far away. "That other divinity" appears in Keats's "Ode on a Grecian Urn":

> What leaf-fring'd legend haunts about thy shape
> Of deities or mortals, or of both,
> In Tempe or the dales of Arcady? . . .

---

72. McFague, *Models of God*, 192, n 37. McFague's italics.
73. Lewis, *Allegory of Love*, 83.

Thou, silent form, dost tease us out of thought
As doth eternity.[74]

One can read this as aspiration for an unattainable "beyond." Such a "beyond" could function as a precursor to "divine mystery" coming to light in the sphere of imagination.

Religious thinking along these lines will tend to "tease us out of thought." One can compare Luce Irigaray's depiction a visionary future:

> And so, those who renounce their own will go towards one another. Calling on one another beneath all saying [*dire*] already said, all words already uttered, all speech [*parole*] already exchanged, all rhythms already hammered out . . . Giving, receiving themselves/one another in the as yet unfelt/beyond reason . . . So as to be reborn of it, invested with the telling [*dire*] of a forgotten inspiration. Buried beneath all logic. Surplus to any existing language . . . The abeyance of all signification, unveiling the trade that underlies it, and venturing beyond . . . In this opacity, this night of the world, they discover traces of the gods who have fled, at the very moment when they have given up ensuring their salvation. Their radiance comes of their consenting that nothing shall ensure their keeping. Not even being—that perimeter of man's narrative. Nor God—that guarantee of the meaning or non-meaning of the whole.[75]

Here is both *demythologizing* and *re-mythologizing* of a most radical kind. Demythologizing is applied to all linguistic signification, to God as "that guarantee of the meaning or non-meaning of the whole" and even to "being—that perimeter of man's narrative." Giving up ensuring one's salvation could be on a par with disinfecting religious belief of urgent practical interest. But it is precisely at this point, says Irigaray, that one discovers traces of the gods who have fled.

Margaret Whitford, Irigaray's editor, comments:

> One of the horizons evoked by this text is the *parousia*, the second coming, or the advent of the divine . . . This horizon—the horizon of sexual difference—would open up the possibility of an undreamed-of fertility: a kind of re-creation of the world. *Parousia* should not simply be a utopian future, but the construction by men and women in the present of a bridge between past and future: '*we would be* the bridges' . . . This horizon is also

---

74. See Keats, "Ode on a Grecian Urn" in Smyth, *Book of Poetry*, 177–79.
75. *Irigaray Reader*, 218.

described in *Ethique* as the third era: the age of the Spirit and the Bride, beyond the Old Testament (the reign of the Father) and the New Testament (the reign of the Son).[76]

Irigaray is not referring to these "ages" in a Christian sense, since she demythologizes God as the guarantor of meaning. Rather the Christian terminology of "Father," "Son," "Spirit" and "Bride" reappears, it seems, as "that other divinity" which comes to light in the imagination.

I have suggested that Irigaray's visionary utopia demonstrates aspects of demythologizing and re-mythologizing. I have also suggested a possible sphere of overlap between religious demythologizing and religious aspiration, detectable perhaps in terms of Romantic yearning. One can take this to an extreme of deconstruction and this is what I think Irigaray's utopia does. At one level there is a difference between demythologizing and deconstruction in that, unlike deconstruction, demythologizing reduces to the concept behind it. Deconstruction of language would, in its full sense, reject the concept as well. But a yearning for an absolute remains a pole of deconstruction. Somewhere, suggests Irigaray, beyond the night of the world, beyond the abeyance of all signification, beyond all logic and coherence, a harmonious humanity is reborn.

The revolutionary utopia espoused by Irigaray is charged with a deconstructionist denial of signification. At the same time, it demonstrates a Romantic yearning for liberation. There is a further element here. Irigaray writes as a feminist psychoanalyst. There are "traces of the gods who have fled" in Carl Jung's archetypes of the sub-conscious mind. Jung writes:

> Significantly enough, it is Kant's doctrine of categories, more than anything else, that destroys in embryo every attempt to revive metaphysics in the old sense of the word but at the same way paves the way for a rebirth of the Platonic sprit.[77]

Metaphysics in the old sense is abandoned. The memory of metaphysics is not. That is to say, the old versions of metaphysics are *demythologized* and then reborn in the "living dispositions" in the unconscious psyche.[78] Irigaray has her own slant on this rebirth. I will come to this in chapter 8.

Deconstruction in its full sense would reject God, even the concept of God. By definition, feminist theology does not go as far as this. As seen, Johnson espouses an alleged connection between religious symbols, the

---

76. See *Irigaray Reader*, 164. Italics in the text.
77. Jung, *Aspects of the Feminine*, 119.
78. Jung, *Aspects of the Feminine*, 122.

subconscious mind and the imagination.[79] Irigaray's Utopia stretches this kind of imagining to its limit, stripping the sacramental universe of its last vestige of coherence in order for an unlikely harmony between the sexes to be reborn. Such thinking is a long way from the Green Fingers approach which acknowledges God as "Other."

While sidelining God as "Other," many feminists denounce "Oz the Great and Terrible" for his failure to recognize woman as "other." Irigaray calls this failure "a specular economy" in which a woman's bodily surface reflects the male back to himself.[80] She suggests that we need to "rethink sexual difference."[81] Her proposal goes so far as to reject male-formed patterns of thought, hence the "abeyance of all signification" seen above. Few theologians take this step but "Oz the Great and Terrible" continues to rankle. Soskice cites Mary Daly: "if God is male, then male is God."[82] "'Woman' may ever be that which is 'not God,'" continues Soskice. She adds: "Often the female is associated with the negative of a balanced pair, a tendency inherited from Greek thought."

I ask whether it is possible to recognize woman as "other" in a frame of thinking in which God does not operate as "Other." Paul Ricoeur calls on theologians to renounce the method of beginning with preconception and to return to "symbol" or primary "other". This is a call, not to renounce all signification but rather all philosophical *hubris*. To take this journey is to come hard up against religious language of God-He. One might do so in the confidence that God as "Other" is quite capable of shattering preconceptions in this area, and perhaps further afield. Key feminist writers claim that pride is not a woman's sin.[83] What then of philosophical *hubris*?

In relation to preconception, Soskice vividly contrasts the life of a new mother with that of "religious contemplatives" who are usually male.[84] "Is the busy new mother a sort of Christian 'on idle'?" she asks. We will recall that Augustine's *sapientia* is considered akin to God because able to contemplate God. For Augustine, *scientia*, focused on worldly matters, does not qualify as the *imago Dei*. The question posed by Soskice presents

---

79. See Johnson, *She Who Is*, 46–47.
80. See McFague, *Super, Natural Christians*, 189 n. 22.
81. Soskice, *Kindness of God*, 108.
82. See Soskice, *Kindness of God*, 71–72, citing Daly, *beyond God the Father*, 19.
83. See Hampson, *Theology and Feminism*, 146. Cf. Johnson, *SHE WHO IS*, 64–65.
84. See Soskice, *Kindness of God*, 13–14.

a similar contrast. But let us not forget that considering the female as the negative of a balanced pair is inherited from *Greek* thought. The biblical writings can speak for themselves in this matter. Religious contemplation could perhaps be at risk of "dogmatic mythology," from which Augustine himself may not be immune.[85] Does not the busy new mother, getting her hands dirty, have something in common with Green Fingers? If so, in terms of nearness-of-approach at least, *scientia* will come into her own.

---

85. See Reagan and Stewart, *Philosophy of Paul Ricoeur*, 46 and Ricoeur, "Reply to Stephen T Tyman," 473.

3

A Biblical Motif

ONE OF THE PLACES visited by Dorothy and her companions is a country in which everyone is made of china. The travelers must cross it on their way to the country of the good Witch of the South. The inhabitants of the china country are small and easily broken but recognizable as replicas of people.[1] In *The Wizard's Illusion* I compare the distinction between flesh and blood humanity and its china replicas to the distinction between the Godhead and humanity made in God's image. If one was familiar only with people made of china it might be hard to imagine what it would be like to be flesh and blood. One might leap to the wrong conclusion about the nature of the similarity.

I argue that incorrect surmise in this respect has bedeviled proposals regarding the *imago Dei* from the outset. The previous chapter considered proposals from Augustine and Elizabeth Johnson. Augustine contends that divine likeness resides in a masculine operation of the mind. For Johnson, women's experience of themselves functions as a key to the *imago Dei*. Both proposals begin with an assumption about the nature of the similarity between humanity and the Godhead. This is not the procedure recommended by Ricoeur who wants hermeneutics to steer away from preconception. A reading of 1 Corinthians 11:1–16, offered by Augustine's translator, Edmund Hill, is anchored in biblical story in terms of gender and divine likeness, in a way commensurate, I believe,

---

1. See Baum, *Wizard of Oz*, chapter 20.

with Ricoeur's method. In a similar attempt to avoid extra-biblical assumptions, this chapter and the next will follow the motif of gender in relation to the Godhead as it appears in biblical writings. My intention at this point is to largely favor a literary approach. Chapters 5 and 6 will revisit some texts along with exegetical concerns raised by them.

Before beginning an appraisal of gendered biblical language in relation to the Godhead, it is necessary to be clear about literary methods. C. S. Lewis describes the method of "symbolism" or "sacramentalism" as the attempt to see the archetype in the copy.[2] He distinguishes this method from that of allegory. "If you are hesitating between an angry retort and a soft answer, you can express your state of mind by inventing a person called *Ira* . . . and letting her contend with another invented person called *Patientia*. This is allegory," writes Lewis. One can see this kind of thinking in Elizabeth Johnson's projection of women's experience. For Johnson, "language generated by women's experience" interweaving with other "ancient symbols" can offer "an alternative to dominant patriarchal language about God."[3] On such terms, the figure SHE WHO IS could contend with "Oz the Great and Terrible," which is my name for a patriarchal figure reflecting what Johnson calls "the stranglehold on religious language of God-He."[4]

In my china country analogy, humanity is a copy of the Godhead as the figurines are a copy of humanity. To speak of the Godhead in gendered human language is to attempt to see the archetype through the language of the human copy. This is what Lewis calls symbolism. While encountering an allegorical direction in some feminist interpretation, this chapter attempts to see the archetype through the lens of gender, the familiar terms of human relationships understood to point to something beyond themselves. Two things must be borne in mind. While the *aim* is to discern likeness between copy and archetype, the *method* entails apprehension of the difference between them.

The previous chapter made a distinction between a Green Glasses and a Green Fingers approach to external reality, in particular to transcendent reality. In a Green Glasses approach, the greenness is in the Glasses: aim and method come together here. In a Green Fingers approach, the greenness is not in the Fingers but in what they are in touch

2. Lewis, *Allegory of Love*, 45.
3. See Johnson, *She Who Is*, 103.
4. Johnson, *She Who Is*, 39.

A Biblical Motif

with. There is nothing elusive in a Green Glasses approach. Either one wears the Glasses or one does not. A Green Fingers approach requires more sensitivity.

In a section of *C. S. Lewis on Scripture* entitled "We see through a glass darkly," Michael J. Christensen writes:

> The great medieval theologian Thomas Aquinas related to ultimate reality in the intuitive as well as in the rational sense, and concluded that human beings can know what God *is* and that he is his own essence, but we cannot know in any precise, affirmative sense *what* God's essence is. The attributes of the Infinite cannot be contained in finite language or thought. Aquinas also asserted, however, that mankind was not destined to silence about the Source of his religious experience. We can speak of God in two ways. We can say what God is not (*via negativa*) . . . We can also approximate the nature of God by employing useful analogies (what can be termed *via analogia*).[5]

Here we have what I term a Green Fingers approach. Even the *via negativa* tells us something about God, albeit in a negative way. The *via analogia* draws one near to God through approximations.

A rationale for the *via analogia* appears in the Thomist doctrine of analogy but the method itself reaches beyond rational explanation. Christensen cites Lewis:

> The human predicament, on the deepest level, is man trying to rationally understand . . . a Reality which can only be imaginatively envisioned or spiritually tasted. We experience transcendent Reality only in precious moments of mystical encounter. Reality quickly vanishes "when we try to grasp it with discursive reason," as Lewis recognizes. When we attempt to translate Reality into descriptive knowledge (i.e., propositional truth), we get abstraction. "This is our dilemma," he concludes, "either to taste and not to know or to know and not to taste." "Of this tragic dilemma," Lewis says, "myth is the partial solution. In the enjoyment of a great myth we come nearest to experiencing as a concrete what can otherwise be understood only as abstraction."[6]

"Myth" in this sense means narrative about transcendent reality which facilitates intuitive and imaginative encounter.

---

5. Christensen, *C. S. Lewis on Scripture*, 57–58.
6. Christensen, *C. S. Lewis on Scripture*, 56, citing Lewis, "Myth Became Fact."

Intuitive apprehension of transcendent reality via "myth" or "symbol" is very different from McFague's kind of re-mythologizing. She writes:

> Theology, at any rate my kind of theology, is principally an elaboration of a few basic metaphors and models in an attempt to express the claim of Christianity in a powerful, comprehensive and contemporary way. As remythologization, such theology acknowledges that it is, as it were, painting a picture. The picture may be full and rich but it *is* a picture. What this sort of enterprise makes very clear is that theology is *mostly* fiction: it is the elaboration of key metaphors and models.[7]

McFague's kind of theology projects Christianity in self-contained pictures, as in the allegorical figures, *Ira* and *Patientia*. She goes on to emphasize the projected nature of her method: "It insists that we do not know very much and that we should not camouflage our ignorance by either petrifying our metaphors or forgetting that our concepts derive from metaphors." That is to say, one must be very conscious of the Glasses.

Let us return to the china figurines. Let us suppose that contact with flesh and blood humanity is of that elusive nature which parallels the Thomist description of humanity's relation to God. Speech about humanity on the part of the figurines could either try to reflect that elusive encounter or could redirect the discussion towards a picture of humanity independent of any claim to encounter. Such a picture might express contemporary aspirations of the china variety. At the same time the old idea of encounter might persist in some vague transferred sense. Otherwise, one might wonder why the notion of humanity would be relevant at all.

LIVING IN, TASTING BEYOND

This chapter maintains that there are messages to be received from the transcendent world and that Scripture is a literary means for the reception of such messages. The meaning of the *imago Dei* is not conveyed in a propositional way but rather in the context of story. "In the enjoyment of a great myth," says Lewis, "we come nearest to experiencing as a concrete what can otherwise be understood only as abstraction."[8] For Lewis, the

---

7. McFague, *Models of God*, xi–xii.
8. Christensen, *C. S. Lewis on Scripture*, 56.

great story of the Bible is "myth" in this sense: spiritual truths and ideas can also be tasted, experienced as concrete.[9]

Ricoeur says something similar about the sense of participation that accompanies figurative apprehension:

> Analogy is a non-conclusive reasoning that proceeds through a fourth propositional term (A is to B as C is to D). But in symbol I cannot objectivize the analogous relation that binds the second meaning to the first. By living in the first meaning I am drawn by it beyond itself: the symbolic meaning is constituted in and through the literal meaning, which brings about the analogy by giving the analogue. Unlike a comparison that we *look at* from the outside, symbol is the very movement of the primary meaning that makes us share in the latent meaning and thereby assimilates us to the symbolized, without our being able intellectually to dominate the similarity. This is the sense in which symbol "gives"; it gives because it is a primary intentionality that gives the second meaning.[10]

This is to contrast clinical analogy (A is to B as C is to D) with a more intuitive approach.

This chapter attempts to follow the *via analogia*, not, as Ricoeur would term it, from the outside but from the inside, beyond rational explanation. At the same time, one must be clear about the method. McFague writes that her theological constructions are "'houses' to live in for a while."[11] Such "houses" can be modified or abandoned in accord with the "pressing issues of one's day." This kind of "living in" stops short of the symbolic trajectory outlined by Ricoeur. Lewis writes about "symbolism" or "sacramentalism." So does McFague, as will be seen below. This does not mean that they are talking about the same thing.

I have discussed McFague's "metaphorical theology" at length in *The Wizard's Illusion*. While not specifically feminist in content, McFague's project expounds a method also found in key feminist interpretation, as in Elizabeth Johnson's SHE WHO IS. As such, it merits attention here. Grace Jantzen explores the "positive" potential of the method, undeterred by the argument that projection theories prove that religion is

---

9. Something of tasting Reality by entering into it as "myth" may be found in the scriptures themselves, e.g. in the Song of Moses: Exodus 15, notably verses 8–11.

10. Reagan and Stewart, *Philosophy of Paul Ricoeur*, 38–39. Ricoeur's italics.

11. McFague, *Models of God*, 27.

an illusion.¹² While not admitting that her theology leads to illusion, McFague keeps half an eye on the non-referential aspect. "The picture may be full and rich but it *is* a picture," she says. How full and rich will be seen below.

This chapter attempts a literary exploration of the *imago Dei*. This is to move away from intellectual domination. McFague also distances her method from a clinical approach which she describes as "the attempt to denude religious language of its concrete, poetic, imagistic, and hence inevitably anthropomorphic, character, in the search for presumably more enlightened (and usually more abstract) terminology."¹³ Her theology "does not 'demythologize' but 'remythologizes,'" she says. But one cannot *re-mythologize* without a prior *demythologizing* component. McFague writes: "I do not *know* who God is, but I find some models better than others for constructing an image of God commensurate with my trust in a God as on the side of life."¹⁴ In other words, abstraction is there from the beginning. Christianity is reduced to the concept that God is on the side of life. The models are projected from the prior concept. McFague denies, in this context, that her method is allegorical in direction. Despite the denial, this is allegory.

For McFague, the Bible itself is a "poetic classic or classic model" which can be appropriated but which is also open to correction.¹⁵ This is to bring one's prior assumptions to biblical interpretation. Here is a fuller description of her assumptions in this respect:

> Christian faith is, it seems to me, most basically a claim that the universe is neither indifferent nor malevolent but that there is a power (and a personal power at that) which is on the side of life and its fulfillment. Moreover, the Christian believes that we have some clues for fleshing out this claim in the life, death and appearances of Jesus of Nazareth. Nevertheless, each generation must venture, through an analysis of what fulfillment could and must mean for its own time, the best way to express that claim. A critical dimension of this expression is the imaginative picture, the metaphors and models, that underlie the conceptual systems of theology.¹⁶

---

12. Jantzen, *Becoming Divine*, 88–89.
13. McFague, *Models of God*, 32.
14. McFague, *Models of God*, 192 n. 37.
15. See McFague, *Metaphorical Theology*, 62–65.
16. McFague, *Models of God*, x–xi.

Here "the life, death and appearances of Jesus of Nazareth" function as raw material to flesh out a prior claim about God. Such material can then be modified at will. McFague offers the following example:

> We are letting the metaphor of the world as God's body try its chance. We are experimenting with a bit of nonsense to see if it can make a claim to truth. What if, we are asking, the "resurrection of the body" were not seen as the resurrection of particular bodies that ascend, beginning with Jesus of Nazareth, into another world . . . What if God's promise of permanent presence to all space and time were imagined as a worldly reality, a palpable, bodily presence?[17]

In this method, the resurrection of the body is demythologized. The "myth" or story is taken out of it. It can then be reissued or re-mythologized in another guise.

The experiment has two parts to it. The "bit of nonsense" accords with the "mostly fiction" aspect of McFague's method. Nevertheless, the imagined picture can "make a claim to truth," taking on a life of its own. McFague continues:

> What this experiment with the world as God's body comes to, finally, is an awareness, both chilling and breathtaking, that we as worldly, bodily beings are in God's presence. It is the basis for a revived sacramentalism, that is, a perception of the divine as visible, as present, palpably present in our world . . . We meet the world as a Thou, as the body of God where God is present to us always in all times and in all places. In the metaphor of the world as the body of God, the resurrection becomes a worldly, present, inclusive reality, for this body is offered to all: "This is my body."[18]

At this stage McFague is "living in" her own model. It may be a temporary "house." Its chilling and breathtaking nature might tell another tale.

The imagined picture can make a claim to "truth," says McFague. She goes so far as to propose a "sacred world order," reflecting the wish for "connection, continuity and coherence" despite "the disjunctive, divided, skeptical, postmodern mind-set."[19] McFague labels these opposing

---

17. McFague, *Models of God*, 69–70.
18. McFague, *Models of God*, 77.
19. See McFague, *Super, Natural Christians*, 52–53. McFague adds the disclaimer: "Needless to say, either of these mind-sets can exist in actual Catholics and Protestants; and both can exist in the same person or culture—and I believe they should."

tendencies "Catholic" and "Protestant" respectively, and factors both into her "functional cosmology." To my mind, the "Protestant" tendency accords with the "mostly fiction" aspect of her method, the "Catholic" tendency with its sacramental flavor. The proposal does not signal a return to a classical view that "the universe is in some sense sacramental, that God is somehow the true and original father, that all things are connected among themselves because they are connected in God."[20] Chapter 1 noted McFague's dissociation from this view: "the Christian symbolic universe does *not* hold together for most of us."

I believe that McFague's claim to "truth" mimics the *via analogia* in language but not in method. In other words, she reissues "sacramentalism" within her Green Glasses orientation. She also says that her kind of theology is "in the tradition of the *via negativa*: finding little to say of God with certainty, it boldly makes its case hypothetically and lets it rest."[21] She states that her theology "says much" but "means little."[22] One may contrast her approach with that of the traditional *via negativa* which says little but means much.

Let us return once more to the china figurines and their attempt to speak about human beings. I suggested above that this discussion might continue independent of any claim to encounter with humans. If I take this analogy to a feminist discussion of God, I find that Johnson expresses her distance from the "very word God, given the history of its use in androcentric theology."[23] She concludes:

> Acknowledging the poverty and idolatry connected with the term [God], it may yet be transformed in a different semantic context generated by women's experience. Ultimately this strategy may be superseded, for old wineskins cannot forever hold new wine.[24]

There is a progression here. In some sense the wineskins have already changed. In terms of my analogy, a "china" experience now dominates the discussion. The next step for the figurines would be to abandon the term "humanity."

---

20. McFague, *Speaking in Parables*, 106.
21. McFague, *Models of God*, 40.
22. McFague, *Models of God*, xii.
23. Johnson, *She Who Is*, 42.
24. See Johnson, *She Who Is*, 42–44.

I draw attention to the progression outlined by Johnson because it appears in various ways in feminist commentary on the biblical writings. Johnson does not go so far as to abandon the word "God." She hopes to redeem it, at least for the time being, by "pouring the new wine of women's hope of flourishing into the old word."[25] This is to modify the tradition in McFague's sense. In stepping back from the Thomist epistemology, Johnson steps away from the *via analogia*. Grace Jantzen openly rejects the doctrine of analogy on the grounds that it privileges men and men's minds which are "held to be nearest in likeness to God of anything in human experience."[26] But if the *via analogia* is classed as a wineskin, the fault may not lie with the skin but with contamination in the beverage.

"What both Ricoeur and Gadamer do very well," states McFague, "is show us how we can become integrated into a tradition, appropriate it as our own, overcome our initial alienation to it, allow its poetic universality to speak to us and our concerns."[27] She comments: "The difficulty with this view, of course, is that many *do* experience tradition as alien and here we must part company with Gadamer." Both McFague and Johnson claim in some sense to follow Ricoeur but there is a sticking point. McFague goes so far as to detect a qualifying note in Ricoeur's method: "for what religious language as metaphor does is to insist on the 'is not' as well as on the 'is.'" Here the question of orientation comes to a head. For McFague, the "is not" of religious metaphor accords with a disavowal of external reference. Her kind of theology is "*mostly* fiction."[28] In describing the operation of metaphor, Ricoeur admittedly uses the terms "is" and "is not."[29] For Ricoeur, the literal "is not" gives way to the symbolic meaning.

"By living in the first meaning I am drawn by it beyond itself," says Ricoeur.[30] This is how I read biblical usage of gendered metaphor for God. One can live in the literal meaning only to be drawn by it beyond itself. The *via analogia* goes beyond rationality in engaging sensory aspects of the imagination, the appeal, it is argued here, not to male imagination alone. This chapter and the next attempt to let biblical language, in McFague's parlance, "try its chance" on its own terms. They attempt to

25. Johnson, *She Who Is*, 44.
26. See Johnson, *She Who Is*, 46 and Jantzen, *Becoming Divine*, 174–77.
27. See McFague, *Metaphorical Theology*, 63–64.
28. See McFague, *Models of God*, xi–xii.
29. See McFague, *Metaphorical Theology*, 214 n. 45. McFague cites *The Rule of Metaphor*, 255–56.
30. Reagan and Stewart, *Philosophy of Paul Ricoeur*, 38–39.

integrate us into a tradition, to allow its poetic universality to speak to us and our concerns.

The next two sections explore biblical parallels, expressed in gendered terms, between the human and divine levels of existence, in particular in their relevance to women. The *via analogia* assumes the possibility of such parallels. Biblical metaphor is understood to point beyond its literal meaning or "vehicle" to a non-literal meaning or "tenor" as a china figurine points to its flesh and blood equivalent. To read such language correctly is to engage one's literary sensibility. In one sense the focus is on the tenor: this is symbolic reference. In another sense the focus is on the vehicle: this is sacramental reference.

As noted, Lewis refers to "sacramentalism" or "symbolism" as the attempt to see the archetype in the copy.[31] The *imago Dei* may be said to be something of a test case for the reception of biblical language in Lewis's sense. The *imago Dei* both points to God and bears messages about God. It depends on the point of view. If one is looking at visible human beings in order to understand what God is like, one will be regarding humanity symbolically. The perspective moves from the thing seen to what is unseen. If one is concentrating on the visible and wondering what significance humanity has, and if God is understood to give humanity significance, this can be described as a sacramental understanding. The perspective moves from what is unseen to what is seen. If humanity as male and female is made in the image of God, gender becomes sacramental. The attempt to read the messages, to see the archetype in the copy, does not mean that the archetype is male and female, but that male and female provide correspondences to some far higher reality.

The next two sections seek to taste the meaning of biblical texts, but the very word "texts" is a distancing one. If the story is to be experienced as "myth" in Lewis's sense, it requires empathetic reading with the understanding of continuity despite the chronological breadth of biblical writings, varieties of genre and movement between Old and New Testament. My focus is on biblical pairs: on the human level, Adam and Eve; on the divine level, "the Lord" and Wisdom. There is also a level which I class as divine-human: "the Lord" as husband to Israel as wife and the corresponding motif of bridegroom and bride in the New Testament. The next chapter considers a further pair: Mary and Word-Wisdom incarnate. As the story-like character of interaction is apprehended, care is needed to

---

31. Lewis, *Allegory of Love*, 45.

interpret any clues the appropriate way round. The use of the familiar to portray the unfamiliar may mislead in terms of which is the original and which the copy.

WISDOM AND HUMANITY

"Ultimately, whether theological vocabulary is masculine or feminine is of little consequence," states Mary Hayter. She continues:

> The masculine terminology does not denote a male deity; the feminine terminology does not denote a female deity; nor does the mixture of masculine and feminine terminology denote an androgynous God/ess. Rather the indications are that the God of the Bible uniquely incorporates and transcends all sexuality.[32]

The difficulty with such a statement is that the significance of masculine or feminine language for God is not addressed by the assertion that the God of the Bible uniquely incorporates and transcends all sexuality.

While it is undoubtedly true that God is in some sense above and beyond both sexes, this observation is an expression of the *via negativa* rather than the *via analogia*. It involves taking metaphors and removing the analogical content from them: it is to say what God is *not* like, not what God *is* like. Hayter applies the *via negativa* to gendered language for God with the intention, it seems, of discounting its significance. But this is not the only way of detaching gendered language from God as referent. Mayer I Gruber agrees that the "LORD is neither specifically male nor specifically female."[33] Unlike Hayter, she does not appear to think that gendered language for God is of little consequence. She continues: "Hence to the very same extent that the God of Israel can be compared to a father the God of Israel can and should be compared also to a mother."

In this vein, she draws attention to explicit references to God as mother in the book of Isaiah:

> It appears that the presupposition that Isa.56–66 is the work of Trito-Isaiah rather than the continuation of Second Isaiah may have prevented sensitive scholars from asking why it is that one anonymous prophet used an entire series of explicitly maternal

---

32. Hayter, *New Eve in Christ*, 41.
33. Gruber, "The Motherhood of God," 8.

expressions for the LORD, the like of which do not occur anywhere else in the Hebrew Bible.[34]

Gruber offers her own explanation of these expressions:

> Perhaps ... the anonymous prophet understood that the women were especially attracted to idolatrous cults because of the insensitivity of his predecessors such as Jeremiah and Ezekiel who had intimated that in the religion of Israel maleness is a positive value with which divinity chooses to identify itself while femaleness is a negative value with which divinity refuses to identify itself. Perhaps, as a result of this realization our prophet deliberately made use of both masculine and feminine similes for God.[35]

The view that paternal and maternal comparisons can and should apply equally is extended to the surmised method employed by the author of Isaiah 40–66. This interpretation would imply that the gendered language for God is an ideological projection. (But if biblical writers depicted the God of Israel by means of ideological projection, it would seem arbitrary to describe non-Hebraic religions as *idolatrous* cults.)

In support of gender-inclusive terms for God, Gruber cites Phyllis Trible, "Depatriarchalizing in Biblical Interpretation."[36] Elsewhere, Trible detects biblical "counter-voices" in "neglected traditions" within "a patriarchal document."[37] There is some suggestion of the *via analogia* in her comment on Genesis 1:27:

> If "male and female" gives the clue for interpreting "the image of God," the phrase "image of God" gives the clue for understanding "God." In both instances, the tenor is not defined by the vehicle. It is the moon that can be seen but not possessed.[38]

This kind of symbolic glimpsing, however, is somewhat offset by her detection of a contrast between "the basic metaphor" of "the image of God male *and* female" and what she calls "partial metaphors":

> Metaphors such as God the father (Ps. 103:13), the husband (Hos. 2:16), the king (Ps. 98:6), and the warrior (Exod. 15:3) are

---

34. Gruber, "The Motherhood of God," 7.
35. Gruber, "The Motherhood of God," 14.
36. See Gruber, "The Motherhood of God," 7–8.
37. Trible, *Rhetoric of Sexuality*, 202.
38. Trible, *Rhetoric of Sexuality*, 21.

> diverse and partial expressions of the image of God male. By the same token, metaphors such as God the pregnant woman (Isa. 42:14), the mother (Isa. 66:13), the midwife (Ps 22:9) and the mistress (Ps. 123:2) are diverse and partial expressions of the image of God female. All these partial metaphors involve societal roles and relationships which the basic metaphor organizes without necessarily promoting. In fact, the basic metaphor contrasts with the imbalance of these partial metaphors. It presents an equality in the image of God male *and* female, although the Bible overwhelmingly favors male metaphors for deity.[39]

Trible discerns a *disparity* between the equality of the "basic" metaphor and the inequality of the "partial" metaphors. Here the so-called basic metaphor does seem to operate as vehicle defining or at least critiquing specific language for God.

This section and the next are an attempt to follow the *via analogia* regarding gendered language for God without preconceived judgments about equality. It is an attempt, in Trible's words, to apprehend the moon that can be seen but not possessed. Two distinct traditions of correspondence are considered: the human pair, male and female, in parallel with a pair presented as masculine and feminine at the divine level, and the human pair, male and female, in parallel with a divine masculine figure and human feminine figure. (I use the terms "masculine and feminine" with regard to the divine and divine-human relationships rather than "male and female" but the biblical presentation is more directly anthropomorphic.)

Leonard Swidler seems to follow the *via analogia* in detecting a link between Wisdom and the myth of Genesis 2–3:

> Wisdom is the "good and evil" which the *Ishah* of Genesis 2 desired to know but never learned. It is the image of *Ishah* as transformed by the true knowledge of benediction and malediction, the divine antitype of *Ishah*. "It shows what *Ishah* would have been had she waited for God's self-unveiling instead of attempting to grasp the secrets of God herself."[40]

In Swidler's depiction, the woman of Genesis 2 corresponds with Wisdom as her divine antitype.

---

39. Trible, *Rhetoric of Sexuality*, 22. Trible's italics.

40. Swidler, *Women in Judaism*, 29, citing George Tavard, *Women in Christian Tradition*.

In terms of correspondence, one needs to attend closely. In support of Swidler's observation, the divine antitype plays the feminine role in relation to God in biblical and apocryphal wisdom literature. Here is a sample:

> With you [i.e., God] is wisdom, she who knows your works,
> and was present when you made the world;
> she understands what is pleasing in your sight
> and what is right according to your commandments (Wisdom of Solomon 9:9).

Elsewhere correspondences can be traced in key passages. On the human level, the woman is brought forth from the man and is welcomed by him with delight (Genesis 2: 21–23); on the divine level, her divine antitype is said to come forth "from the mouth of" (Sirach 24:3) "the Lord" and to be "beside the Lord" in a relationship of delight (Proverbs 8:30). The woman and her divine antitype are depicted as relationally feminine to the respective masculine figures; the masculine figures supply the origin for the feminine figures while the feminine figures bring delight and rejoicing to the relationship.[41]

Nevertheless, Wisdom, depicted as the feminine consort of God's throne (Wisdom 9:4), takes on the authority of God in relation to humanity:

> "Who has learned your counsel, unless you had given wisdom
> and sent your holy spirit from on high?
> And thus the paths of those on earth were set right
> and people were taught what pleases you,
> and saved, by wisdom." (Wisdom 9:17–18)

When the Word-Wisdom "pitches camp" in Jacob (Sirach 24:8; cf. John 1:14), the focus is her relationship with humanity; in this relationship she plays the masculine role in terms of priority.[42]

---

41. Cf. McKane, *Proverbs*, 357. Regarding Proverbs 8:30–31 McKane writes that "the picture is thought to be that of the child Wisdom who is the 'darling'... of Yahweh... 'I was delights daily' can be taken to mean that Wisdom experienced pleasure without alloy or that she gave delight to Yahweh... Wisdom is a child without a care, her brow unfurrowed by anxiety, the vivacious playmate of God and man, with heaven and earth as her playground. I have already indicated that this interpretation... could contribute to a precise hypostasis—Wisdom as the child of Yahweh, begotten not made."

42. There are literary parallels between the figure of Wisdom as presented in Proverbs 8: 22–30 and the Logos incarnate (John 1:1–5; John 17:5, Colossians 1: 15–17)

"I came forth from the mouth of the Most High [says Wisdom]
and I covered the earth like a mist.
I dwelt in the highest heavens,
and my throne was in a pillar of cloud.
Alone I compassed the vault of heaven,
and traversed the depths of the abyss.
Over waves of the sea, over all the earth,
and over every people and nation I have held sway.
Among all these I sought a resting place;
in whose territory should I abide?

Then the Creator of all things gave me a command,
and my Creator chose the place for my tent.
He said, 'Make your dwelling in Jacob,
and in Israel receive your inheritance.'" (Sirach 24:3–8)[43]

The verb "to pitch camp" (*skēnoō*) occurs in the Johannine prologue: "the Word became flesh and lived [pitched camp] among us" (John 1:14). But the delight to be expected in the relationship does not eventuate. The poignancy of "he came to what was his own and his own people did not accept him" (John 1:11) deepens in the light of the prior literary context.

Carol A. Newsom points out that, in general, the implied speaker of Proverbs 1–9 is the father while the implied listener with which the reader identifies is a son. She writes that the speeches about, or attributed to, Wisdom, "belong to the same cultural voice that speaks through the father . . . Where the father is the authoritative voice in the family, *Hokmot* is the corresponding public voice."[44] Put differently, it could be said that two levels are operating simultaneously: on the human level, a human father talking to a grown up son ("Hear, my child, your father's instruction," Proverbs 1:8); on the divine level, Wisdom in relation *to* "the Lord" ("The Lord by wisdom founded the earth," Proverbs 3:19), and also as public voice *for* "the Lord" (Proverbs 8:32–36). The correspondence between divine and human of Genesis 1:26–27 is picked up as correspondence of voices in the Proverbs prologue. But in Proverbs, instead of the human pair, male and female, the human level is represented by

---

43. Augustine writes of Wisdom being "begotten or made by God." Edmund Hill comments: "a reference probably to Prv 8:22, which reads in the Greek and Latin versions from it, 'The Lord created me at the beginning of his ways', a very embarrassing text for the Fathers embattled with the Arians. Hebrew has 'possessed me.'" (Augustine, *The Trinity*, VII, 4, see note 20, 233.) Cf. use of *qānâ* in Genesis 4:1.

44. Newsom, "Woman and the Discourse of Patriarchal Wisdom," 142–46. Her emphasis appears to be a sociological, rather than a specifically literary point.

the father addressing the son. From a literary point of view the wisdom tradition supplies an interesting precedent for the Godhead portrayed as masculine and feminine translating to a father-son relationship when the Word is made flesh.

This biblical survey demonstrates the overarching possibilities of gendered language. Not only does Proverbs 8:22–31 provide a detailed description of the divine relationship in masculine and feminine terms, but Wisdom herself, in the wider biblical context, is depicted as both feminine and masculine: feminine in the Proverbs prologue, whereas Jesus is traditionally understood to be the Incarnation of the pre-existent eternal Word or Wisdom.[45] Depicted as feminine at the divine level in relation to "the Lord," Wisdom becomes flesh as male, in line with Wisdom's masculine persona in relation to humanity. Rather than "equality," as suggested by Trible,[46] the interpretive clue of male and female in the image of God would appear to be "relationship," as proposed by Hill.[47] In spite of this insight, Hill does not apparently consider that gender itself is relational. In a passage about the Son's equality, consubstantiality and co-eternity with the Father, Augustine writes: "The Son of course is the Father's Word, which is also called his Wisdom."[48] Translator Hill remarks: "And Wisdom is feminine. This is going to involve me in some changes of gender, which I ask the reader to excuse."[49]

For Hill, Wisdom's change of gender from the divine feminine to the human masculine appears problematic.[50] Augustine goes on to write (as translated by Hill): "when the fullness of time came she was sent . . . in

---

45. See Augustine, *City of God*, XX,26: "Christ himself is prophetically called 'the tree of life' [cf. Proverbs 3:18] because he is himself the Wisdom of God of which Solomon says, 'Wisdom is a tree of life to those who embrace her.'"

46. Trible, *Rhetoric of Sexuality*, 22.

47. See Hill, 338 n. 22 on Augustine, *The Trinity*, XII.

48. Augustine, *The Trinity*, IV, 27.

49. Hill, n. 87 on Augustine, *The Trinity*, IV, 27, 184. Cf. Ruether ("*Imago Dei*, Christian Tradition and Feminist Hermeneutics," 269) who writes on the September 30, 1988 Papal statement on the "Dignity and Vocation of Women": "The Pope . . . boldly claims that God . . . can be said to have both male and female qualities, and that mutuality between men and women in the image of God mirrors the mutual love within the Persons of the trinitarian God." Ruether then poses the question: "Has one of the three Persons changed gender?"

50. Cf. McFague who writes: "Current research on the relationship of Sophia to the Logos claims that their roles were similar and eventually became competitive, with the female, subordinate one giving over to the male, equal one: Sophia was absorbed by the Logos, the Son who is equal to the Father.' (*Models of God*, 208, n. 33).

order that the Word might become flesh, that is become man."[51] Augustine maintains that the grammatical feminine applied to Wisdom does not imply that Wisdom is female in sex. He says this in a passage that refers to the appropriateness of interpreting the language of human relationship in reference to the Godhead in a spiritual and symbolic sense.[52] Hayter states: "it is highly doubtful that feminine Wisdom, Torah, Spirit, Righteousness, or any other 'feminine figure', actually tell us anything about sexuality in God."[53] This would appear to miss the point that human sexuality is the vehicle, in Trible's terminology, of "the moon that can be seen but not possessed."[54] God is not to be seen in terms of human sexuality; rather, gendered human relationship is to be seen as a unique clue in offering a glimpse of God.

The wisdom tradition contains echoes of Genesis 2–3. Swidler states that the feminine character at the divine level supplies a depiction of the reality that Eden was intended to mirror. On the human level, the harmonious relationship of male and female is tragically severed almost from the beginning.[55] Nevertheless, Trible finds some echo of the lost bond between male and female in the Song of Songs:

> In many ways . . . Song of Songs is a midrash on Genesis 2–3. By variations and reversals it creatively actualizes major motifs and themes of the primeval myth. Female and male are born to mutuality and love. They are naked without shame; they are equal without duplication. They live in gardens where nature joins in celebrating their oneness . . . Paradise Lost is Paradise Regained.[56]

The Song of Songs has also been interpreted as an allegory of the love story between God and the people of God.[57] The theory draws attention

---

51. Augustine, *The Trinity*, IV, 27.

52. See Augustine, *The Trinity*, XII, 5: "anyone of sober good sense . . . must get accustomed to discovering the traces of spiritual things in bodies in such a way that when he turns upward from here and starts climbing with reason as his guide in order to reach the unchanging truth itself *through* which these *things were made* (Jn 1:3), he does not drag along with him to the top anything that he puts little value on at the bottom." (Hill's italics)

53. Hayter, *New Eve in Christ*, 24.

54. Trible, *Rhetoric of Sexuality*, 21.

55. See Trible, *Rhetoric of Sexuality*, chapter 4 "A Love Story Gone Awry."

56. See Swidler, *Women in Judaism*, 31 citing Trible, "Depatriarchalizing in Biblical Interpretation."

57. See the Introduction to the Song of Solomon in the HarperCollins Study Bible

to another biblical relationship depicted in terms of male and female. Divine and human levels run parallel in the wisdom tradition but are brought together in the prophetic tradition in a relationship described in marital terms. The parallel is no longer between the divine and human levels but between the divine-human and human levels.

THE DIVINE COURTSHIP

Correspondences between earthly marital discord and discord between God and the people of God are not only described but also acted out in the book of Hosea. On the positive side, the marital relationship is a strong expression of the rapprochement between the divine and human. On the negative side the feminine character plays the part of a harlot.

Hosea's prophetic task requires him to marry a harlot in order to symbolize the unfaithful behavior of Israel towards Yahweh. The two levels (human and divine-human) appear as two parallel marriages. The two levels are distinguished by literary style. The description of the human level takes the form of bare narrative (Hosea 1:1–3; 3:1–3). By contrast the description of the marital relationship between God and Israel takes the form of a dramatic poem with a graphic depiction of the fate Israel must suffer for her infidelity (Hosea 2).

The picture of the wife held up to public shame in being stripped naked for her infidelity (Hosea 2:3) alters a motif in the primal depiction of relationship between husband and wife. Nakedness is no longer associated with the relationship of delight (as in Genesis 2:23–25) but with shame and misery (as in Genesis 3). Israel's husband has the power to highlight this shame, the power of exposing his wife's behavior by stripping her naked. It must be remembered, however, that the husband in this case is God, and that Israel as wife is an inclusive term for the people of Israel. On the human level there is no suggestion that Gomer physically suffers the fate figuratively threatened for Israel. The worst she appears to undergo is being bought back "for fifteen shekels of silver and a homer of barley" after an adulterous affair.[58]

On the divine-human level, intensity of shame is the reverse of intensity of delight restored:

> Therefore I will now allure her,

(NRSV).

58. See Hosea 3:1–2.

and bring her into the wilderness,
and speak tenderly to her.
From there I will give her her vineyards,
and make the Valley of Achor [or Misery] a door of hope.
There she shall respond as in the days of her youth (Hosea 2:14–15).

Derek Kidner comments on the two-sided nature of being brought into the wilderness:

> This is the positive and creative side of [God's] severity, for 'the wilderness' could mean either of two things for Israel: either her life in ruins or her pilgrim spirit and youthful promise recaptured. Here it offers the second, by way of the first. The thought of setting out with God is picked up by a later prophet, who sang of that short-lived honeymoon:
> 'I remember the devotion of your youth,
> your love as a bride,
> how you followed me in the wilderness,
> in a land not sown.'[59]

Isaiah 62:1–4 offers a prophetic picture of "Jerusalem's salvation" in terms of marriage:

> For Zion's sake I will not keep silent,
> and for Jerusalem's sake I will not rest,
> until her vindication shines out like the dawn,
> and her salvation like a burning torch.
> The nations shall see your vindication,
> and all the kings your glory;
> and you shall be called by a new name
> that the mouth of the Lord will give.
> You shall be a crown of beauty in the hand of the Lord,
> and a royal diadem in the hand of your God.
> You shall no more be termed Forsaken
> and your land shall no more be termed Desolate;
> but you shall be called My Delight is in Her,
> and your land Married;
> for the Lord delights in you,
> and your land shall be married.[60]

---

59. See Kidner, *Love to the Loveless*, 32 on Je. 2:2.

60. Strictly speaking, the land, not the people, is described as married. This would appear to be metonymy, i.e., the name of one thing applied to another with which it is closely associated as in "crown" for king.

The theme of delight is resumed in this marriage. God the husband reaches out to the people of God with joy. (It is, in fact, "the mouth of Yahweh" who confers the new name on Jerusalem.) God's delight in the divine-human intimacy is highlighted: "as the bridegroom rejoices over the bride so shall your God rejoice over you" (Isaiah 62:5b).

The response of humanity as bride is expressed in terms of clothing in Revelation 19:7–8:

> "... Let us rejoice and exult and give [God] the glory!
> for the marriage of the Lamb has come,
> and his bride has made herself ready
> to her it has been granted to be clothed
> with fine linen, bright and pure"—
> for the fine linen is the righteous deeds of the saints.[61]

Far from being stripped naked for her infidelity, the bride has been clothed in her good deeds, to the glory of God.

Biblical parallels, expressed in terms of masculine and feminine, are traced in summary form in *Mary: Grace and Hope in Christ*, paragraph 9:

> The covenant between the Lord and his people is several times described as a love affair between God and Israel, the virgin daughter of Zion, bride and mother: "I gave you my solemn oath and entered into a covenant with you, declares the Sovereign Lord, and you became mine" (Ezekiel 16:8; cf. Isaiah 54:1 and Galatians 4:27). Even in punishing faithlessness, God remains forever faithful, promising to restore the covenant relationship and to draw together the scattered people (Hosea 1–2; Jeremiah 2:2, 31:3; Isaiah 62:4–5). Nuptial imagery is also used within the New Testament to describe the relationship between Christ and the Church (Ephesians 5:21–33; Revelation 21:9). In parallel to the prophetic image of Israel as the bride of the Lord, the Solomonic literature of the Old Testament characterizes Holy Wisdom as the handmaid of the Lord ... In the New Testament these prophetic and wisdom motifs are combined (Luke 11:49) and fulfilled in the coming of Christ.

In looking for what it means to be human as male and female, biblical correspondences point to the understanding that gendered humanity reflects the divine-human relationship of God-with-us and us-with-God presented as masculine and feminine and, as was seen earlier, the divine relationship of "the Lord" and Wisdom presented as masculine

---

61. Cf. the nakedness referred to in Revelation 3:17–18.

and feminine. To this point, correspondences observed between human and divine as well as human and divine-human levels use the analogy of masculine and feminine in keeping with a ruler and consort style of relationship. That this is not the only way that feminine and masculine operate together will become apparent in the next chapter.

ALLEGORY AT LARGE

"We can speak of God in two ways," writes Christensen, citing Thomas Aquinas. "We can say what God is not (*via negativa*) . . . We can also approximate the nature of God by employing useful analogies (what can be termed *via analogia*)."[62] We can taste or catch glimpses of what God is like. Phyllis Trible likens this kind of access to that of a finger pointing to the moon which can be seen but not possessed.[63] This chapter has attempted to speak of God on these terms. Gendered language tells us something about the nature of God. It allows us to see the moon, no more but also no less.

For Trible, however, the moon presented in the biblical writings is not the moon she wishes to see. She detects gendered equality in what she calls "the basic metaphor of the image of God male and female," albeit at odds with the overwhelming balance of male references for deity. In her approach it is the image of God, perceived as equally male and female, which is determinative. This is to divert language away from the God which it points to. The danger is that the moon will no longer be the moon but rather a pie which can be divided up on equal terms. Gruber moves towards this in suggesting that the anonymous writer of Isaiah 40–66 wished to redress the gender balance and, on this account, presented a God who identified with women. One can go further. Grace Jantzen promotes a "divine horizon for women" on a radically subjectivist basis, undeterred by the argument that a non-ontological approach reduces the moon to an illusion, as it were pie in the sky.

Much hangs on the approach to language. Paul Ricoeur says one must live in the literal meaning of figurative language in order to be

---

62. Christensen, *C. S. Lewis on Scripture*, 57–58.

63. Trible, *Rhetoric of Sexuality*, 21. (McFague cites Trible's statement in *Metaphorical Theology*, 7 in support of her "metaphorical way." But cf. Johnson on C. S. Lewis in chapter 2, "Green Glasses or Green Fingers".)

drawn beyond it.[64] Despite some similarity of terms, McFague does not attempt to see the moon. Her model-metaphors are "'houses' to live in" but there is no beyond for them to be drawn into. She finds certainty only in the assertion of "a God as on the side of life."[65] Based on this, her project "boldly makes its case hypothetically and lets it rest."[66] Her method only goes so far as to present a "picture which may be full and rich but *is* a picture."[67] Despite her mooted "sacramentalism," McFague's "functional cosmology" is not the outworking of "seeing the moon," but it might look like it.[68]

While this chapter has focused on biblical correspondences and their possible relevance to the *imago Dei*, traditional understanding of the *imago Dei* has been beset by something which resembles McFague's "sacramentalism" rather too closely. This comes to the fore in the approach to Mary, mother of Jesus. Something of importance is missed in the process. Before moving on to this, I will return once again to a history of allegorical interpretation in relation to the *imago Dei*, along with the feminist response to it.

Allegory as a method is not in itself antithetical to "seeing the moon." Ricoeur observes: "The Old Testament has an allegorical relation to the New, as when St. Paul compares Hagar and Sarah to the two alliances of servitude and freedom (Gal 4:24–27)."[69] Nevertheless, there is a point at which allegory moves from literary device to a philosophical approach which reduces language to a subjectivist projection. Ricoeur writes further: "Origen only expanded and systematized a Pauline reading of the Old Testament." Chapter 2 noted that Jerome and Augustine attacked Origen on this account.

Expanding and systematizing a method, even a biblical method, can turn it into something else. G. Lloyd Carr differentiates between an allegorical method of biblical interpretation in which historicity is ignored and a deeper, hidden or spiritual meaning imposed on the text and typology which "recognizes the validity of the Old Testament account in its own right, but then finds . . . a clear parallel link with some event or teaching

---

64. Reagan and Stewart, *Philosophy of Paul Ricoeur*, 38–39.
65. McFague, *Models of God*, 192 n. 37.
66. McFague, *Models of God*, 40.
67. McFague, *Models of God*, xi–xii.
68. See McFague, *Models of God*, 77 and *Super, Natural Christians*, 52–53.
69. See Reagan and Stewart, *Philosophy of Paul Ricoeur*, 221, 254 n. 1.

in the New Testament which the Old Testament account foreshadows."[70] Typology—looking forward from Old to New Testament—is the reverse of reading the Old Testament allegorically—seeing the Old Testament in the light of the New. Once redirected towards a hidden meaning, the allegorical method can take on a life of its own.

Jerome and Augustine attacked Origen on his approach to the allegorical method but "even those who attacked him most vigorously were often influenced by his thought," states historian Robert Grant.[71] Augustine's theory of the *imago Dei* would seem a case in point. Elsewhere Augustine argues against interpreters who detect hidden meanings in the paradise story, who "take it for granted that [its fruit-bearing trees] were not visible and material objects, but were thus described in speech or writing to stand for spiritual and moral truths." Augustine takes the middle ground: "There is no prohibition against [allegorical] exegesis, provided that we also believe in the truth of the [Eden] story as a faithful record of historical fact."[72]

Translator Edmund Hill says that Augustine casts his theory of the *imago Dei* "into the dramatic form of a paradise story in microcosm."[73] As noted in chapter 2, Hill goes so far as to produce a diagram of Augustine's theory, illustrated by allegorical figures. At the same time Hill admits the limitations of a diagram: "the whole virtue of Augustine's structure of the *psyche* is that it is pregnant with dynamic possibilities; it is in constant movement, either in the right or the wrong direction." Hill describes the theory in the following terms. (The figures—indicated by my square brackets—belong to Hill's diagram):

> In sin the highest or sapiential function of the human *psyche* [identified with Adam] falls down from its lofty contemplation of spiritual truth, by consenting to the lower sciential function's lust for material power [identified with Eve], into the depths of carnal enslavement [identified with the serpent]. In redemption the right order is restored by a movement in the opposite direction, initiated by the Word made *flesh* [Christ]. It is only when the sciential function has consented to this divine condescension by *faith*, and begun to control the appetites of the outer man by *virtue* [a process identified with Mary], that the highest

70. See Carr, *Song of Solomon*, 24.
71. Grant, *Short History of the Interpretation of the Bible*, 60.
72. *City of God*, XIII, 21.
73. See Augustine, *The Trinity*: Hill's "Foreword to Books IX–XIV," 258–69.

sapiential function can begin to be released once more for the loving contemplation of the divine.[74]

Augustine overtly associates the man and the woman of the paradise story with the two-tiered human *psyche*. Translator Hill admits that Augustine does not in so many words "allegorize or parabolize this redemptive process for the *psyche* in terms of Christ and Mary." Hill comments: "Perhaps he felt it would be taking too great a liberty with the historical objectiveness of the gospel narrative. But the possibility of such a counter-allegory is there in Augustine's account of redemption in Book XIII."

A middle ground with regard to the allegorical method might have cautioned against depicting the redemptive process in terms of Christ and Mary. Nevertheless, the trajectory of the theory suggests what Hill calls a counter-allegory. Augustine would not have been alone in treating Mary, mother of Jesus as an allegorical figure. Elizabeth Johnson offers a useful summary of historical developments in this respect.

"A deep ambiguity has afflicted the *imago* doctrine throughout the Christian tradition," writes Johnson:

> While affirming that human beings generically are created in the image and likeness of God, theology also adopted the hardy form of gender dualism found in Hellenistic thought. It was not a long step from the identification of men with mind, reason, and spirit and concomitantly of women with bodiliness and passion in a metaphorical sense, to a stance that cast actual men alone in the representative role of headship, the primary image of all superior qualities and therefore of God, while women were relegated to secondary status in nature and grace. This dichotomization of humanity proceeded to the point where women were even projected to be the symbol of evil, the anti-image of God, the representative of evil tendencies in the sin-prone part of the male self.[75]

To this negative tradition about women, Johnson opposes her positive alternative: "Women's experience of self interpreted as experience of God, fleshed out with values characteristic of women's ways of being in the world, comes to a theological flashpoint when women begin to articulate

---

74. See Hill's Foreword, 262. Hill's italics.
75. Johnson, *She Who Is*, 70.

and act in accord with their dignity as *imago Dei, imago Christi*."[76] I will return to this.

I turn now to the figure of Mary. Johnson describes maternal imagery for the Holy Spirit in early Syriac Christianity:

> The Spirit's image was consistently that of the brooding or hovering mother bird. Among other maternal activities, the Spirit mothers Jesus into life at his conception in Mary's womb, empowers him into mission at his baptism, and brings believers to birth out of the watery womb of the baptismal font...[77]

This early usage was later redirected towards new objects:

> In time most of this maternal imagery migrated away from the Spirit and accrued to the church, called holy mother the church, and to Mary the mother of Jesus, venerated as mother of the faithful as well. The symbol of the maternity of the Spirit was virtually forgotten...

The effect of this transition is a shift of orientation. Traditional language for the Holy Spirit becomes a source for an alternative religious purpose. Other sources, reports Johnson, contribute to Mary presented as "a powerful mother figure":

> Starting with the transfer to her of the iconography and devotional practices originally directed toward the Great Mother in the Mediterranean region, she is addressed as the mother par excellence, Mother of God, Mother of Mercy, Mother of Divine Consolation, our Mother.[78]

On these terms, religious language becomes a commodity, open to redirection on the part of the worshipper.

A process of redirection is also discerned in the history of the biblical figure of Wisdom. Johnson writes:

> The Hellenized cult of Isis was experienced as a temptation to Jews of the diaspora to turn from the traditional faith of their

---

76. See Johnson, *She Who Is*, 69–70.

77. See Johnson, *She Who Is*, 86.

78. See Johnson, *She Who Is*, 102. Citing Elaine Pagels "God the Father/ God the Mother," *The Gnostic Gospels*, Johnson also notes "discourse about God the Mother in various gnostic communities, some of whom describe the divine Mother as part of an original couple, others of whom write about her as prior to and creative of the male creator God."

ancestors ... Personified Wisdom was the answer of Orthodox Judaism to this threat.[79]

Wisdom's later trajectory is quite complex, influencing Christian pneumatology, Christology and Mariology ... First century Christians, in their effort to express the experience of the saving significance of Jesus, ransacked the Jewish religious tradition and the surrounding Hellenistic culture for interpretive elements. Along with Son of God, Son of Man, Messiah and Logos, the tradition of personified Wisdom was ready to hand.[80]

Far from objecting to a process of redirection, Johnson proposes a continuation of the method. "Discourse about holy mystery in the symbols of spirit, *sophia*, and mother provides glimpses of an alternative to dominant patriarchal language about God," she says, adding that such ancient symbols must pass through "the fire of critical feminist principles" in order to free them from a "complementary" status of remaining "subordinate and stereotyped within a dualistic framework."[81]

Due to her preoccupation with negative and positive approaches to women, Johnson does not detect a deep ambiguity in her own depiction of the *imago Dei*. This is the ambiguity of orientation. Here I return to points I made earlier. The traditional *via negativa* and *via analogia* attempt to look towards the face of God, albeit very imperfectly. Taken too far, the allegorical method diverts attention towards its own constructions. Associating a Hellenistic division of the human psyche with Adam and Eve is a form of allegory, with ongoing consequences from the constructions as Johnson points out. Johnson counters this allegorical usage with her own allegory of women's experience, SHE WHO IS. In the process, experience of self and God are fleshed out not only with "values characteristic of women's ways of being in the world" but also "their dignity as *imago Dei, imago Christi*." The context divests the tradition of its orientation towards God. In McFague's parlance, the tradition becomes a classic model which can be drawn upon and revised as needed.[82]

First century Christians "ransacked" Jewish and Hellenistic sources for interpretive elements in relation to the saving significance of Jesus, claims Johnson. She advocates a continuation of the method:

---

79. Johnson, *She Who Is*, 92.
80. Johnson, *She Who Is*, 94.
81. Johnson, *She Who Is*, 103.
82. See McFague, *Metaphorical Theology*, 60–64.

> In summary there are Jewish and Christian biblical texts that, with their trajectories, bear potent female images of the living God present and active throughout the world. When within a feminist perspective the clearly personified figure of Sophia is linked with the hints half guessed in spirit and *shekinah* and the power of the mother symbol, both the aptness of speaking in female terms of the mystery of God and a modicum of material content for doing so come to light.[83]

The process of discovering material content for speaking in female terms of the mystery of God is particularly apt, indicates Johnson, in relation to the figure of Mary due to her role in popular Catholic Christianity. For many, Mary connotes a "concrete expression" for the biblical description of "God's unbreakable love for the people of the covenant," she says: "In devotion to her as a compassionate mother who will not let one of her children be lost, what is actually being mediated is a most appealing experience of God."[84] Elsewhere Johnson writes: "the Marian tradition is a golden motherlode which can be 'mined' in order to retrieve female imagery and language about the holy mystery of God."[85] This is to allow the process of "mining" to come full circle: what is already borrowed may be borrowed back again. Johnson does not consider whether the process itself, of "mining" or "ransacking," might have contributed to the problems she discerns in the first place.

"Each generation must venture, through an analysis of what fulfillment could and must mean for its own time, the best way to express [the Christian] claim," says Sallie McFague. "A critical dimension of this expression is the imaginative picture, the metaphors and models, that underlie the conceptual systems of theology."[86] On these terms, there is no particular reason why the Marian tradition should not have borrowed from other sources. But the method has not necessarily been a happy one. The next chapter will attempt to divest the mother of Jesus of non-biblical accretions and to rediscover her unique role.

---

83. See Johnson, *She Who Is*, 103.
84. Johnson, *She Who Is*, 102–3.
85. Johnson, "Mary and the Image of God," 27.
86. McFague, *Models of God*, x–xi.

4

God's New Thing

In *The Wizard of Oz* the Wicked Witch of the West captures the four companions but does not dare to physically attack Dorothy. The girl is protected by the mark of the kiss on her forehead, placed there by the good Witch of the North. She also wears the Silver Shoes which give her a power of which she is unaware until the end of the book. The Wicked Witch of the West makes use of Dorothy's ignorance of this power by enslaving her and putting her to work.[1]

Chapter 3 drew attention to Phyllis Trible's detection of biblical "counter-voices within a patriarchal document."[2] Trible indicates that recovering neglected traditions may have the effect of restoring some balance in the "patriarchal stamp of scripture." While reclaiming these traditions may offer a biblical source for women's identity, I suggest that the term "counter-voices" does not quite do justice to development regarding gender in Scripture as a literary whole. This chapter outlines what could be described as something of a counterplot in terms of male and female and their symbolic significance.

Uncovering a biblical counterplot is a method which bears little resemblance to that of Jantzen's feminist religious symbolic or Johnson's SHE WHO IS. Jantzen disengages from ontological realism and metaphysical truth in favor of a "divine horizon," projected from what

---

1. See Baum, *Wizard of Oz*, chapter 12.
2. Trible, *Rhetoric of Sexuality*, 202.

feminists "consider most worthy and to be valued."³ Similarly, SHE WHO IS draws content from women's experience of themselves. By contrast, this chapter explores the scriptural account of God's novel configuring of gendered relationships. Women's experience of themselves is not absent in this process but it is God's action which initiates the experience, not the experience which generates the perception of God. This is the difference between reception and projection as interpretive methods. In the parallel terms of *The Wizard of Oz* Dorothy receives the kiss and the Silver Shoes. It is not her doing.

In her adventure with the Wicked Witch of the West, Dorothy does not know how to use the power of the Silver Shoes. Somewhat similarly, I argue that inadequate appreciation of a biblical counterplot has impeded apprehension of the gendered *imago Dei*. Some longstanding cultural influences would seem at work. The Western tradition of linguistic efficacy—in my shorthand, The Yellow Brick Road—is broader than the Judeo-Christian tradition. Even the medieval symbolic universe included syncretistic elements. Influences from such fellow travelers have not always been happy ones for women's identity, as will be seen.

THE TWOFOLD ROLE OF THE WOMAN

There is a relationship of male and female which is described in the New Testament as "a great mystery." Ephesians 5:31–32 harks back to the original purpose of marriage. Verse 31 is a quotation of Genesis 2:24: "For this reason a man will leave his father and mother and be joined to his wife, and the two will become one flesh." But man and woman on the human level are not chiefly in view in the Ephesians passage as verse 32 makes plain: the great mystery is said to apply to Christ and the Church. The terms of human relationship of verse 33 are enjoined because of the correspondence to the divine-human relationship of delight. This correspondence gives an added dimension to "the reason" given in the book of Genesis.

Genesis 2 prefigures this relationship at the divine-human level. But this is not a complete picture because there is another biblical pair that presents a rather different view of woman and man at the divine-human level, as is also prefigured in Genesis. To understand this biblical pair as woman and man, it is necessary to go back to the beginning of the story:

---

3. See Jantzen, *Becoming Divine*, 89; 258.

> The LORD God said to the serpent, "Because you have done this ... I will put enmity between you and the woman, and between your offspring and hers; he will strike your head, and you will strike his heel (Genesis 3:14–15).[4]

The judgment meted out to the man has to do with the ground from which he was taken. The judgment meted out to the woman is more complex. Beside her own penalty, she is also a party in the judgment meted out to the serpent. The woman is involved in terms of enmity placed by God between her and the serpent and as ancestral mother of the descendant who will be the enemy of the serpent's descendant. The man in the Garden is not said to have any part in these matters.

Genesis 2 describes, at some length, the process of producing a suitable companion for the man, finally pronounced to be bone of his bone and flesh of his flesh and suitable, prophetically, to detach the man from father and mother so that he may cleave to her and the two will become one flesh. Genesis 3 describes the loss of spontaneous delight in the primal relationship.[5] Birth-giving then takes on a prominent role, not only because of the disagreeable aspects for the woman but also because of the promise of redemption that comes through it. The purpose of redemption is the restoration of the relationship of delight at a new level. It could be said that whereas marriage is originally given for the purpose (among others) of birth, birth takes on the purpose of preparing for the divine-human marriage.

A preview of the *nature* of the divine-human marriage appears in the celebratory poem of Genesis 2:23. In this preview the woman (*ishah*) is the companion-consort of the man (*ish*) as the corresponding "woman" (the Church) is companion-consort of Christ, as revealed in Ephesians

---

4. *Mary: Grace and Hope in Christ* paragraph 28, n. 4 refers to a problematic variant translation in the Latin Church: "The Hebrew text of Genesis 3:15 speaks about enmity between the serpent and the woman, and between the offspring of both. The personal pronoun ... in the words addressed to the serpent, 'He will strike at your head,' is masculine. In the Greek translation used by the early Church (LXX), however, the personal pronoun *autos* (he) cannot refer to the offspring (neuter: *to sperma*), but must refer to a masculine individual who could then be the Messiah, born of a woman. The Vulgate (mis)translates the clause as *ipsa conteret caput tuum* ('she will strike at your head'). This feminine pronoun supported a reading of this passage as referring to Mary, which has become traditional in the Latin Church. The Neo-Vulgate (1986), however, returns to the neuter *ipsum* ..."

5. Cf. Trible, *Rhetoric of Sexuality*, 131: "In creating Eros, Yahweh caused joy and nourishment to come from the earth. But since disobedience has disrupted creation, the earth itself (not the deity) will now produce pain and famine."

5:31–32. A preview of the *means of accomplishing* this divine-human marriage appears in the poem of judgment (Genesis 3:14–15). Regarding Genesis 3:15, Kidner writes:

> There is good New Testament authority for seeing here the *protoevangelium*, the first glimmer of the gospel. Remarkably, it makes its début as a sentence passed on the enemy . . . only the New Testament will . . . show how significant was the passing over of Adam for *the woman* and *her seed* (*cf.* Mt. 1:23; Gal. 4:4; 1 Timothy 2:15).[6]

In the former case the woman is at the side of the man. In the latter case the man is *passed over* in favor of the woman and her seed. For this reason, typology associated with the woman needs to be discerned with some care.

Chapter 3 considered the biblical motif of male and female which culminates in the "great mystery" of Ephesians 5. The chapter traced parallels, expressed in gendered terms, at the human, divine and also divine-human levels. The counterplot, foreshadowed in Genesis 3:15, is perhaps less about symbolism and more about biology. Divine and human come together here in an unprecedented way.

A PROTESTANT AND AN ANGLICAN-ROMAN CATHOLIC INTERPRETATION

Typology in connection with the woman in the paradise story needs careful attention. Key traditions in this regard, while differing from each other, fail to do justice, I believe, to the complex nature of her roles. Barth's interpretation of the role of Mary and the *imago Dei*, and the Anglican-Roman Catholic International Commission statement, *Mary: Grace and Hope in Christ* offer examples of variant approaches. Feminist writers single out Barth's theology as extreme in its negative effect on women. This is not to say that Barth is necessarily representative of Protestant interpretation which, in general, may tend to ignore gendered typology. I will return to some Protestant tendencies with regard to gender in later chapters.

I begin with Barth's comments upon "born of the Virgin Mary" in the Apostles' Creed. It is difficult to do justice to Barth's theological method in a short space, but I suggest that Barth's comments on the Virgin Birth are revealing in this respect. Significantly, Barth tends to anchor

---

6. Kidner, *Genesis: An Introduction and Commentary*, 70–71.

his theology in "the second article, that it pleased God to become man."[7] This places the second article in an ahistorical relation to the first article on creation in a way which is symptomatic of Barth's approach to biblical history. In a letter to Bultmann (Basel, 24 December 1952), Barth writes:

> As I see it, one can and should read all theology in some sense backwards from [the one central figure in the NT]: down to anthropology, ethics and then methodology . . . I have not become "orthodox" for this reason. I could list for you the points at which I have diverted a good deal from the paths of what can meaningfully be called "orthodoxy" and will continue to diverge on the stretches that are before me.[8]

If theology is to be read backwards from "the one central figure in the NT" in what sense can the Word be said to *become* flesh? Elsewhere Barth goes so far as to say that, while it has shown itself necessary to the Christological and Trinitarian reflections of the Church, "the whole concept of the *logos asarkos*, the 'second person' of the Trinity, as such, is an abstraction":

> The New Testament speaks plainly enough about the Jesus Christ who existed before the world was but . . . it does not speak of the eternal Son or Word as such, but of the Mediator, *the One who in the eternal sight of God has already taken upon Himself our human nature*, i.e., not of a formless Christ who might well be a Christ principle.[9]

If Christ is to be understood as already having taken on our human nature from all eternity, one might wonder about the role of Mary.

In commenting on "born of the Virgin Mary" in the Apostles' Creed, Barth writes: "The male has nothing to do with this birth."[10] This might sound reminiscent of Kidner's statement about the *protoevangelium* of Genesis 3:15, in which the man is passed over. But Barth observes further:

> What is involved here is, if you like, a divine act of judgment. To what is to begin here man is to contribute nothing by his action and initiative. Man is not simply excluded, for the Virgin is there. But the male, as the specific agent of human action and

---

7. Barth, *Dogmatics in Outline*, 53.

8. *Letters*, 107.

9. Barth, *CD*, III/1, 54. My italics. (For ease of reading, I have consistently taken the liberty of transliterating Barth's Greek lettering.)

10. Barth, *Dogmatics in Outline*, 99.

history, with his responsibility for directing the human species, must now retire into the background, as the powerless figure of Joseph. That is the Christian reply to the question of woman: here the woman stands absolutely in the foreground, moreover the *virgo*, the Virgin Mary. God did not choose man in his pride and in his defiance, but man in his weakness and humility, not man in his historical rôle, but man in the weakness of his nature as represented by the woman, the human creature who can confront God only with the words, 'Behold, the handmaid of the Lord; be it unto me according as Thou hast said'.

On these terms, the male of the human species is powerless in being absent. The woman is powerless in being present. Humanity is represented by the woman as the agent of human weakness. This, says Barth, is "the Christian reply to the question of woman." Barth says nothing of "the passing over of Adam for *the woman* and *her seed*."[11]

For Barth, the nativity appears illustrative rather than biologically significant. This would seem the consequence of his retrospective method in relation to biblical history. He continues: "The miracle of Christmas is the actual form of the mystery of the personal union of God and man, the *unio hypostatica*." He arrives at the "actual form of the miracle" through the agency of the mystery:

> One thing may be definitely said, that every time people want to fly from this miracle, a theology is at work, which has ceased to understand and honour the mystery as well, and has rather essayed to conjure away the mystery of the unity of God and man in Jesus Christ, the mystery of God's free grace. And on the other hand, where this mystery has been understood and men have avoided any attempt at natural theology, because they had no need of it, the miracle came to be thankfully and joyously recognised. It became, we might say, an inward necessity at this point.[12]

An inward necessity is a far cry from a ground-breaking historical pregnancy.

The extent to which the "miracle of Christmas" (as actual event) becomes no more than an illustration of the *unio hypostatica* (as inward necessity) is a measure of its loss of actuality in world history. Chapter 3 reported Ricoeur's observation: "The Old Testament has an allegorical

---

11. Kidner, *Genesis*, 70–71.
12. Barth, *Dogmatics in Outline*, 100.

relation to the New, as when St. Paul compares Hagar and Sarah to the two alliances of servitude and freedom (Gal 4:24–27)."[13] Here historical figures and events are used as illustrations. Barth could be said to be arguing an allegorical relation between the "miracle of Christmas" and the *unio hypostatica*. In this case, failing the "miracle of Christmas," the *unio hypostatica* is no more than a philosophical concept. Barth admits his departure from orthodoxy: his philosophical method is primary; the figures and events secondary. I will have more to say about this in chapter 7.

I find confirmation of this ahistorical approach in Barth's presentation of the *imago Dei*:

> According to 1 Corinthians 11:7 there is a man who actually *is* the *eikōn kai doxa theou* and from this standpoint the same can be said of every man. And side by side with this man there is a woman who is his *doxa* as He (the Head of the woman but not without her) is the *doxa* of God, and from the standpoint of this woman, or rather of her Husband, the same could be said of every woman. This man together with this woman is the man who is the image of God [*Dieser Mann mit dieser Frau ist der Mensch, der das Ebenbild Gottes ist*], who *is* it and does not merely indicate it or establish its physical possibility, like Adam and Seth and all the subsequent members of the genealogical tree.[14]

This is to read anthropology backwards. The primal relationship of man and woman merely establishes the physical possibility of mirroring the divine level. Typology has become potentiality. This would mean that there has been only one male and no actual physical female directly in God's image. Barth writes further:

> There is no need for us to pursue at this point the anthropological equation in respect of this relationship between man and wife as Paul develops it in 1 Corinthians 11 . . . It is obvious that all that he had to say about man and woman was seen from this angle, in the light of the relationship between Jesus Christ and His community, and therefore of His divine likeness, and that it is only in this way that it is presented as an 'order of creation'. We must be content merely to assert that the agreement of Paul's teaching with Genesis 1:26 f. must not be underestimated in this respect (where it is often overlooked).[15]

---

13. See Reagan and Stewart, *Philosophy of Paul Ricoeur*, 221, 254 n. 1.
14. Barth, *CD* III/I, 203. See discussion: 195–205.
15. Barth, *CD* III/I, 205.

Barth does not refer here to 1 Corinthians 11:11–12 which states that man is also dependent on woman.

In the absence of typological correspondence, it is not clear why the Church is called a woman. The man (Christ), albeit not without the woman (the Church) constitutes the *imago Dei*, says Barth. But while this "woman" is an essential component in the *imago Dei*, she receives her status from the standpoint of her husband. Once again, the "woman" would seem to represent the weakness of the human condition. Whether openly conflated or not, the roles of Mary and the Church would seem linked: the weakness of humanity, represented by Mary, the Christian reply to the question of woman, and the woman who is the Church fully dependent for her status as *imago Dei* on the man, Christ.

I now turn to paragraphs 26–27 of *Mary: Grace and Hope in Christ*. Here multiple correspondences are discerned in terms of Church and "Mary-Eve typology." These are summed up in the following statement about the relationship between Mary and the disciple John, initiated by Jesus on the cross (John 19:25–27):

> These last commands of Jesus before he dies reveal an understanding beyond their primary reference to Mary and "the beloved disciple" as individuals. The reciprocal roles of the 'woman' and the 'disciple' are related to the identity of the Church . . . A corporate understanding of 'woman' . . . calls the Church constantly to behold Christ crucified, and calls each disciple to care for the Church as mother. Implicit here perhaps is a Mary-Eve typology: just as the first 'woman' was taken from Adam's 'rib' (Genesis 2:22, *pleura* LXX) and became the mother of all the living (Genesis 3:20), so the 'woman' Mary is, on a spiritual level, the mother of all who gain true life from the water and blood that flow from the side (Greek *pleura*, literally 'rib') of Christ (19:34) and from the Spirit that is breathed out from his triumphant sacrifice (19:30, 20:22, cf. 1 John 5:8). In such symbolic and corporate readings, images for the Church, Mary and discipleship interact with one another. Mary is seen as the personification of Israel, now giving birth to the Christian community (cf. Isaiah 54:1, 66:7–8), just as she had given birth earlier to the Messiah (cf. Isaiah 7:14).

One of the references cited here is Isaiah 54:1 which is about a barren woman who will bear children. The apostle Paul cites this verse in his allegorical portrayal of Hagar and Sarah as figures of the old and new covenants. It is not clear to me what this verse has to do with Mary, mother of Jesus. Mary was not barren.

The correspondences discerned here are complex. By associating with John, other disciples might share the call to adopt Mary as mother, but the link to the Church is through John (as disciple) not Mary. Further, this associative approach with John and, through the association, to Mary, is not the same as the typological approach, a point recognized in the words "implicit here perhaps is a Mary-Eve typology." Typologically, the "woman" can be understood corporately as Church in the sense that the Church is the antitype of *ishah* who gains life from the side of Adam. If Mary is seen as the mother or source of the Church, she will correspond typologically not with Eve but with Adam. The first "woman," in being taken from Adam's rib, corresponds to "all who gain true life" from Christ's side. This is the companion-consort role. The mother role of *ishah* is not paralleled by Mary (as a personification of Israel) giving birth to the Christian community, but by the historical Mary giving birth to the Messiah (since she is the mother of the descendant who crushes the serpent's head).

Kim Power reports that Augustine developed the figure of Mary as "a feminine meta-symbol . . . who could exemplify the ideal *Scientia*."[16] This might imply a companion-consort motif in connection with Mary as an allegorical figure. But Augustine does not mention Mary in connection with companion-consort typology in the following passage:

> Now in creating woman at the outset of the human race, by taking a rib from the side of the sleeping man, the Creator must have intended, by this act, a prophecy of Christ and the Church.[17]

Augustine goes on to draw out the parallel between the woman and the Church in terms of origin:

> The sleep of that man clearly stood for the death of Christ; and Christ's side, as he hung lifeless on the cross, was pierced by a lance. And from the wound there flowed blood and water, which we recognize as the sacraments by which the Church is built up. This, in fact, is the precise word used in Scripture of woman's creation; it says not that God 'formed' or 'fashioned' a woman but that 'he built it (the rib) up into a woman'. Hence the Apostle

---

16. See Power, *Veiled Desire*, 171–72.
17. Augustine, *City of God* XXII, 17.

also speaks of the 'building up' of the Body of Christ, which is the Church.

Finally, he suggests a parallel between the nature of relationship between the man and woman in the Garden and between Christ and the Church:

> The woman, then, is the creation of God, just as is the man; but her creation out of man emphasizes the idea of unity between them; and in the manner of that creation there is, as I have said, a foreshadowing of Christ and his Church.

The companion-consort of Christ is the Christian community of which Mary is a part.[18] Power cites Augustine on this point: "Mary is more blessed in receiving the faith of Christ than in conceiving the flesh of Christ."[19] The different degrees of blessedness bear witness to the distinction between Mary as the antitype of Eve in her physical relationship with Christ and Mary as a member of the metaphorical body of Christ.

New Testament parallels between *ishah* and the Church (Ephesians 5:31–32, cf. 2 Corinthians 11:1–3) do not allude to the mother of Jesus.[20] But Mary is nevertheless the archetypal mother in the sense of giving birth to the Messiah. These literary distinctions are important, in particular if the role of Mary as human mother of Christ is to be apprehended in its uniqueness and not subsumed into the role of the Church.

THE INVERSION FACTOR

The typologies indicated in Genesis 2–3 need to be carefully discerned, as noted above. The man in the Garden and the descendant (of the woman)

---

18. Cf. Matthew 12:46–50; Mark 3:31–35; Luke 8:19–21. Cf. also *Mary: Grace and Hope in Christ* paragraph 25 with regard to John 2:1–11.

19. Augustine, *De virginitate*, 3, quoted in Power, *Veiled Desire*, 179.

20. *Mary: Grace and Hope in Christ* paragraphs 28–29 draw attention to the woman who gives birth to a male child in Revelation 12 and suggests that while "most scholars accept that the primary reading of the woman is corporate" there may be a secondary reference to Mary. In this regard, Robert H. Mounce writes: "The woman is not Mary the mother of Jesus but the messianic community, the ideal Israel." See *The Book of Revelation*, 236–39. Mounce notes "the interesting suggestion" of G. B. Caird (*A Commentary on the Revelation of St. John the Divine*) on this point. Verse 5 depicts the ascension immediately following "nativity." Caird suggests that this is "an anomaly . . . only in the fancy of the modern critics because for John 'the birth of the Messiah . . . means not the Nativity but the Cross.' Following the [parallel passage] of Psalm 2, the birthday of a king is the day of his accession."

who crushes the serpent's head are both individual males. Besides the two men, there are also two women, the woman in the Garden and the mother of the descendant who crushes the serpent's head. There is a third "woman" who is not an individual. In this latter case, the name "woman" arises solely from the correspondence made with one of the functions of the woman in the Garden, sustained as a term for the people of God in relation to God. While it may be natural to identify her *individual* counterpart with both functions attributed prophetically to the woman in the Garden, the consequence is that the particular function of the mother of the descendant tends to be underestimated.

Mary is the antitype of Eve in the function of birth-giving. She is not, historically, the bride of Jesus. Her relationship to the "man" is different. On the human level it is the relationship of mother to son, which is not radically new. The revolutionary aspect of this relationship is not on the merely human level. Mary's role as mother of the Redeemer is unique because it reverses the relationship not only between male and female but also between divine and human. Instead of the divine being the source of the human it is the other way around. Albeit a human mother, Mary is *theotokos*, God-bearer.

Prefiguring of the descendant in his humanness includes, and is highlighted by, prefiguring of the descendant's mother.[21] In this regard, the most striking of Old Testament passages is the somewhat obscure text of Jeremiah 31:21–22:

> Set up road markers for yourself,
> make yourself guideposts;
> consider well the highway,
> the road by which you went.
> Return, O virgin Israel,
> return to these your cities.
> How long will you waver,
> O faithless daughter?
> For the LORD has created a new thing on the earth:
> a woman encompasses a man.

This translation comes from the New Revised Standard Version. The second half of Jeremiah 31:22b (*nᵉqēbâ tᵉšōbēb geber*) is subject to various translations, including "the woman sets out to find her husband again."[22]

---

21. Cf. the mother of Immanuel (Isaiah 7:14) and of the Servant (Isaiah 49:1) and a similar allusion in Micah 5:3.

22. See footnote on Jeremiah 31:22 in the HarperCollins Study Bible (NRSV).

If the latter is the meaning of those lines it would imply that the faithless daughter of Jeremiah 31:22a is also the woman of Jeremiah 31:22b, that is, that the faithless daughter (i.e., Israel), by Yahweh's contrivance, will set out to find her husband (i.e., Yahweh) again. But if this were envisaged, it would be more natural to address Israel as "O faithless wife," rather than as a daughter.[23]

The motif of "a new thing" is repeated in verses 31–34:

> The days are surely coming, says the Lord, when I will make a new covenant with the house of Israel and the house of Judah. It will not be like the covenant that I made with their ancestors when I took them by the hand to bring them out of the land of Egypt—a covenant which they broke, though I was their husband, says the Lord . . . they shall all know me, from the least of them to the greatest, says the Lord; for I will forgive their iniquity, and remember their sin no more.

The new covenant will not be like the old, although Yahweh was the husband of Israel under the old covenant. In this context there is a suggestion that a woman is going to relate to a man in a radically new way.

Trible detects poetic links throughout Jeremiah 31:15–22 that resonate with the notion of womb, with woman enclosing man.[24] She translates *t^ešōbēb* of Jeremiah 33:22b as "surrounds":

> In the last line of the poem, the word *female* (*n^eqē bâ*) resonates with all these [feminine] images [in Jeremiah 31:15–22] . . . this word occurred in Genesis 1:27 as a generic term to include all females. Moreover, it was used there in poetic parallelism to the phrase "image of God," a parallelism approximated in Jeremiah 31:22b. In both these passages this noun is object of the verb *create* (*bārā*) with *God* (or *Yahweh*) as subject. Thus, the text of Genesis 1:27 . . . provides an external witness to the kind of internal function the noun *n^eqēbâ* has here in Jeremiah.[25]

---

23. Cf. Gerald L. Keown et al, *Jeremiah 26–52*, 122–23: "The three-word saying at the end of v. 22 . . . uses vocabulary not found elsewhere in the Book of Consolation . . . 'Female will encircle he-man' is more likely about giving birth than about finding a husband, since being without a husband is not a problem raised in chapters 30–31 . . . Wordplay connects the current situation represented by the daughter . . . 'who turns away' and the new thing created by God, a female who . . . 'encircles.'"

24. See Trible, *Rhetoric of Sexuality*, 40–50.

25. Trible, *Rhetoric of Sexuality*, 48.

By poetic analysis, Trible discerns that the meanings of "virile male, child to adult" are associated with man [*geber*] who is surrounded by *nᵉqēbâ*.²⁶ She writes:

> After calling Israel a "turnabout [*haššōbēbā,* v. 22a] daughter," the poet juxtaposes immediately the description of female surrounding [*tᵉšōbēb,* v. 22b] man. Two very different portraits of the female are thus associated through assonance; yet this association yields a radical transformation with the positive superseding the negative in Yahweh's new creation.

Here is a radical change in the relationship of male and female, with the implication that this is to be understood generically. But the exegesis stems from an appraisal of poetic nuances in the passage. Trible does not suggest the second meaning that has been discerned in this text in terms of fulfillment in the New Testament.

William L. Holladay notes that "Roman Catholic exegesis till modern times has been dominated by Jerome's view that the clause [Jeremiah 31:22b] refers to the Virgin enfolding Christ in her womb."²⁷ While not apparently sharing this view, Holladay goes on to acknowledge:

> [Jeremiah] here indicates two convictions: first, that the situation is far worse than people could imagine, so that Yahweh must move all the way back to Genesis 1 to make it right; and second, that Yahweh will make it right even so. The reassignment of sexual roles is innovative past all conventional belief, but it is not inconceivable to Yahweh. (One may also add that it is no more inconceivable than the assumption behind the notion of a new covenant, vv 31–34.)

The reassignment of sexual roles reverses the order of creation in a novel way because it occurs on the divine-human level. In this relationship the woman is the origin, the God-man born from her.

As human mother of the God-man, Mary presents a new twist in rapprochement of heaven and earth in terms of gender. This very fact in all its importance is weakened if Mary is identified with the antitypes of Israel to "the Lord" (or the bride to the bridegroom) on the divine-human level, and Wisdom to "the Lord" on the divine level, because these relationships parallel the creational assignment of sexual roles, not the reassignment of sexual roles. Something of what this reassignment of

---

26. Trible, *Rhetoric of Sexuality,* 48–49.
27. Holladay, *Jeremiah 2,* 195.

sexual roles might mean for women is expressed by Mary's kinswoman Elizabeth: "Blessed are you among women, and blessed is the fruit of your womb. And why has this happened to me that the mother of my Lord comes to me?" (Luke 1:42–43) There is also some hint in John's gospel that Mary and Jesus are to be regarded as generic woman and man. Jesus addresses his mother as "woman," never as "mother."[28] Pilate presents Jesus to the Jewish crowd: "Here is the man" (John 19:5).[29]

In further distinction from the bride role of the new messianic community, the birth of Jesus from a human mother occurs under the old covenant. Paul writes: "But when the fullness of time had come, God sent his Son, born of a woman, born under the law, in order to redeem those who were under the law, so that we might receive adoption as children" (Galatians 4:4). Hermann N. Ridderbos remarks:

> He was the Son of the Father, who stood by His Father's side already before the sending (cf. 1 Cor. 8:6, 2 Cor. 8:9, Phil 2:6 and Col. 1:15). The Sonship designates not merely an official but also an ontological relationship (*cf.* Phil. 2:6). The words *born of a woman*, do not refer to the beginning of His existence as Son, but as the child of a woman . . . The woman was not only the medium of His coming into the flesh, but from her He took all that belongs to the human. She was in the full sense His mother. That Paul in these words is also reflecting on the virgin birth is, as we see it, extremely doubtful.[30]

The virgin birth, if in view at all, is not the primary focus; rather the human birth of Jesus (born under the law) is contrasted with the spiritual adoption of the redeemed (who were under the law). Alan Cole writes: "Christ was born under law-conditions so that He might ransom those who were themselves under such conditions."[31] The nature of the ransomed state is pictured in the allegorical development of Sarah, summed up in the quotation from Isaiah 54:1, as it appears in Galatians 4:27. Cole comments:

> The quotation from Isaiah liv is appropriate for many reasons, although there is no direct evidence in the original that it was

---

28. John 2:4; 19:26. But Jesus addresses the Samaritan woman similarly (John 4:21), perhaps because she represents non-Jews who regard Jesus as the Savior of the world.

29. Like the original *hāʾādām*, the word for Jesus is *anthrōpos* here.

30. Ridderbos, *Epistle of Paul to the Churches of Galatia*, 155.

31. Cole, *Epistle of Paul to the Galatians*, 116.

> ever applied to the barren Sarah. Its direct reference is to desolate Israel, and secondarily to Jerusalem ... Since in this passage Israel is seen as the 'bride' of God, the thought of Revelation finds a ready echo. And because the Christian Church is also seen as the 'bride of Christ' (see 2 Cor xi. 2 for the Pauline use), a whole system of identifications comes into operation at once.[32]

A whole system of identifications with the allegorical Jerusalem does not entail the birth of Jesus and Mary, his mother. Jesus is born under the law, by allegorical association, under Hagar.

The church that is the bride is not made up of those "born of woman" but of those adopted by God, as attested in John 1:12–13 and 3:1–10. *Mary: Grace and Hope in Christ* paragraph 11 states:

> Paul speaks of the Son of God being born "in the fullness of time" and "born of a woman, born under the law" (Galatians 4:4). The birth of Mary's son is the fulfilment of God's will for Israel, and Mary's part in that fulfilment is that of free and unqualified consent.

I would reiterate that Mary's free and unqualified assent occurs under the old covenant. Paragraph 18 of *Mary: Grace and Hope in Christ* goes on to suggest a connection between the birth of Jesus and Christian birth and adoption: "The virginal conception ... points to the new birth of every Christian, as an adopted child of God. Each is 'born again (from above) by water and the Spirit' (John 3:3–5)."[33] The point being made here is that both births are a "sign of the presence and work of the Spirit." If the miraculous nature of Jesus's birth is highlighted, the similarity between the birth of Jesus and the new birth of every Christian is highlighted, as both are births from above. Otherwise, they belong to different covenants. Mary herself must enter the new covenant.[34]

As noted above, Mary is not the antitype of *ishah* in the companion-consort relationship, except insofar as she is part of the Church. But to say that is to put the matter negatively. Surprisingly perhaps, the most detailed interchange between Jesus and his mother occurs at a wedding.[35]

---

32. Cole, *Galatians*, 134–35.

33. It might be asked whether the suggestion that Christ's birth *points to* Christian rebirth is typology in reverse, pointing from Christ rather than towards Christ.

34. Matthew 12:46–50; Mark 3:31–35; Luke 8:19–21; Luke 11:27 cf. Acts 1:14. Cf. *Mary: Grace and Hope in Christ* paragraph 25.

35. John 2:1–12. In John's gospel, roles at a wedding are theologically significant. See Schneiders, *Written That You May Believe*, 135 on Jesus as the true Bridegroom in

In alerting Jesus to the problem ("they have no wine") Mary obviously expects Jesus to be able to do something about it. Jesus does not query this. He responds: "Woman, what concern is that to you and to me? My hour has not yet come." Mary does not argue but in effect ignores this response. ("His mother said to the servants, 'Do whatever he tells you.'") Does she take it upon herself to determine that his hour *has* come?[36] If so, Jesus tacitly submits. Mary is not the bride, but she plays an active role behind the scenes at the wedding.[37]

AN ALLEGORICAL MARY?

The role of the first woman is twofold: she is both wife of the first man and ancestral mother of the descendant who will crush the serpent's head. Typology associated with the mother of Jesus has tended to combine the two, a tendency which dates from the time of the early church. I argue that this step has obscured the role of the historical Mary to the detriment of women's identity.

The previous chapter cited Elizabeth Johnson on the migration of religious language. Maternal imagery addressed to the Holy Spirit was redirected toward the Church and also Mary who was "venerated as the mother of the faithful."[38] The ARCIC statement, *Mary: Grace and Hope in Christ*, confirms this tendency, stating that early exegetes "delighted in drawing feminine imagery from the Scriptures to contemplate the significance both of the Church and Mary" (36) while popular devotion endowed Mary with a special place in the communion of saints (35).

John 2:9–10 and 3:27–30.

36. Cf. Tasker, *The Gospel According to St. John, An Introduction and Commentary*, 56: "it is impossible to interpret the words *mine hour* on the lips of Jesus without reference to other passages in the gospel where 'the hour' invariably refers to the hour of the passion."

37. *Mary: Hope and Grace in Christ*, paragraph 25 observes: "Jesus begins by calling into question his former relationship with his mother ("What is there between you and me?"), implying that a change has to take place. He does not address Mary as 'mother', but as 'woman' (cf. John 19:26). Jesus no longer sees his relation to Mary as simply one of earthly kinship. Mary's response, to instruct the servants to 'Do whatever he tells you' (2:5), is unexpected; she is not in charge of the feast (cf. 2:8). Her initial role as the mother of Jesus has radically changed. She herself is now seen as a believer within the messianic community."

38. Johnson, *She Who Is*, 86.

This kind of migration was fueled by further speculation about Mary. "Fathers as early as Justin Martyr . . . and Irenaeus . . . reflecting on texts like Genesis 3 and Luke 1:26–38, developed, alongside the antithesis of Adam/New Adam, that of Eve/New Eve," records the ARCIC statement (36). Mary as the New Eve was said to share in the New Adam's victory over sin and death. Both "Eve" figures were credited with "virginity," the "virgin" Eve's disobedience resulting in death, the virgin Mary's obedience opening the way to salvation (36). In patristic reflection, virginity came to be understood "not only as physical integrity, but as an interior disposition of openness, obedience, and single-hearted fidelity to Christ which models Christian discipleship and issues in spiritual fruitfulness (37)."[39]

A link was forged between Mary's obedience and her virginity. Could a parallel link have been forged between Eve's disobedience and loss of virginity? Janet Martin Soskice reports: "Gregory of Nyssa believed that the acquisition of genitalia was implied in the first couple's post-lapsarian 'clothing with skins,' and that the resurrected body would be sexless."[40] She acknowledges that Augustine "to his lasting credit" disagreed with this view. The nature of the resurrected body was a vexed question in the early church, as will be considered in the next chapter.

The ARCIC statement outlines further historical linking of the roles of the Church and Mary.[41] But Catholic writer Sandra M. Schneiders wishes to disown stereotypes associated with the various depictions of Mary, mother of Jesus. She writes: "The historical Judas was male, but this does not imply that men are more typically the locus of the mystery of unbelief and betrayal than women. The same must be said of Mary as model of conversion and discipleship."[42] Schneiders goes further here in disowning associative roles in relation to other depictions of Mary:

> If [Mary] is understood as the new Eve in relation to the new Adam, or as Sion giving birth to the Messiah, her role is unique and is not shared by other Christians, women or men. Just as men do not participate any more than women in Jesus' unique role as Savior of the World, new Adam, or Messiah, so women

---

39. The statement adds: "The Fathers presented Mary the Virgin Mother as a model of holiness for consecrated virgins, and increasingly taught that she had remained 'Ever-Virgin,' (37)."

40. See Soskice, *Kindness of God*, 44–45 and 45 n. 15.

41. See paragraphs 38–51.

42. Schneiders, *Written That You May Believe*, 97.

do not participate any more than do men in Mary's unique role as new Eve or Lady Sion.

These latter examples add a further factor. Unlike the depiction of Judas as the locus of the mystery of unbelief and betrayal, Jesus's role as Savior of the World is not an allegorical one. Nevertheless, the allegorical "Lady Sion" is said to interact with the narrative details about Jesus. On patristic terms, this is to mix "literal" and "allegorical" exegesis.

Something of a smorgasbord of roles is at issue. Mary, says Schneiders, can be seen as model of conversion and discipleship; Mary can be seen as the new Eve in relation to the new Adam; Mary can be seen as Sion giving birth to the Messiah. Such a selection attributed to one figure tends easily towards a conflation of roles. Mary becomes allegorical bride as well as historical mother of Christ. Schneiders points out that this interpretation runs counter to the narrative: Jesus's mother is not the key figure representing the new people of God. I would add that Mary regarded as Lady Sion giving birth to the Messiah is similarly out of tune with the narrative. In Jesus's work of salvation, Sion does not give birth to the Messiah but, rather, the Messiah gives birth to the new Sion. Schneiders disclaims any significance in these portrayals for women's (or men's) identity. I will come to my own view of the significance of Mary, mother of Jesus, in terms of women's identity, in chapter 6.

In disclaiming the mother of Jesus as the representative figure for the people of God, Schneiders turns to another figure for this purpose. She finds her in the woman who meets the resurrected Jesus. This encounter is said to parallel "the creation account, where God walks and talks with the first couple in the garden . . . and promises salvation through a woman":

> In this garden of new creation and new covenant, Jesus, who is both the promised liberator of the new creation and the spouse of the new Israel, encounters the woman who is, symbolically, the Johannine community, the church, the new people of God.[43]

Spouse of the new Israel *and* salvation promised through a woman! These associations would suggest that *both* functions of the woman in the Garden apply to an individual antitype. Unlike the "Mary-Eve" typology suggested in the ARCIC statement (26–27; 33), the proposed individual antitype is not Mary, mother of Jesus, but Mary Magdalene.[44]

---

43. Schneiders, *Written That You May Believe*, 217.
44. Cf. chapter 3.

Chapter 3 noted Elizabeth Johnson's appraisal of the Marian tradition, along with her response. Johnson reports that the figure of Mary, as a "concrete expression" drawn from the biblical description of "God's unbreakable love for the people of the covenant," has come to be regarded "as a compassionate mother who will not let one of her children be lost."[45] She also says that the Marian tradition "is a golden motherlode which can be 'mined' in order to retrieve female imagery and language about the holy mystery of God."[46] These complex associations and suggested re-associations may be contrasted with Karl Barth's assertion: "The true Godhead and the true humanity of Jesus Christ in their unity do not depend on the fact that Christ was conceived by the Holy Spirit and born of the Virgin Mary."[47] While the methods detected by Johnson and promoted by Barth may differ, the effect on the historical Mary would appear similar. In either case the historical Mary has little part to play.

This chapter has attempted to uncover a biblical counterplot in terms of the symbolic relations between male and female. The plot centers on the historical mother of Jesus in her specific role as mother of the descendant who crushes the serpent's head. To pinpoint the typological role of Mary is not to deny that she can function in other ways. While Mary is not the type of Wisdom in companion-consort relation to "the Lord," this is not necessarily to deny her capacity to function representatively on the human level in terms of wisdom.

In the book of Proverbs, the figure of Wisdom has a counterpart on the human level in the alphabetical poem at the end of chapter 31, the somewhat daunting description of the perfect wife. The description is of woman, not as romantic sexual partner, as appears in the Song of Songs, but as mistress of a household. This woman is wise: "she opens her mouth with wisdom." Like Wisdom she has a public voice: "let her works praise her in the city gates."[48] In this idealized picture, her sons call her blessed and her husband sings her praises: "Many women have done excellently, but you surpass them all." In real life Elizabeth says to Mary: "Blessed are you among women, and blessed is the fruit of your womb."[49] This can be compared with the remark made by an unknown woman

---

45. Johnson, *She Who Is*, 102–3.
46. Johnson, "Mary and the Image of God," 27.
47. Barth, *Dogmatics in Outline*, 100. Cf. chapter 7, "*Potential* imago Dei?"
48. Proverbs 31:26; 29–31. Cf. Proverbs 1:20–21.
49. Luke 1:42.

to Jesus: "Blessed is the womb that bore you and the breasts that nursed you," to which Jesus replies: "Blessed rather are those who hear the word of God and obey it."[50] It is clear that biological relationship is not enough for the degree of blessedness that Jesus has in mind. But Mary spans both degrees of blessedness. The biological mother of Wisdom may be said in some sense to encompass all women in her unique experience.[51]

In summary, if the woman of the Garden is seen as a type of Wisdom in relation to "the Lord" or a type of the Church in relation to Christ, the typological association has to do with the relationship of delight. If the woman is seen as a type of Mary, the typological association has to do with the pronouncement of judgment and with what Kidner terms "the first glimmer of the gospel."[52] In the former cases, the primal woman and her antitypes play the companion-consort role in relation to the masculine figure; in the latter case, the source and priority of masculine and feminine are reversed. To appreciate this reversal, Mary's role as antitype of Eve needs to be distinguished from other devotional or allegorical associations.

Mary of Nazareth proclaims: "Surely, from now on all generations will call me blessed."[53] Nevertheless, Catholic writer Schneiders wishes to disown the Mary as a representative figure for women. Tina Beattie writes:

> It may be easier for a woman who has a non-Catholic upbringing to enjoy and celebrate Mary than for a woman who has always been taught to see Mary as a rebuke to her own sexual desires.[54]

Some clarification in this area would seem desirable. Taken to an extreme, the New Eve as model of holiness and obedience, as well as compassionate mother who will not let one of her children be lost, might almost make the role of the New Adam redundant.

My Introduction depicted "patriarchal language about God" in terms of a contrast between "Oz the Great and Terrible" and "Dorothy the Small and Meek." This chapter has identified a figure which could be termed "Mary the Small and Meek" or, as it might be, "Mary the Pure and

---

50. Luke 11:27–28.

51. Cf. Swidler's observation that Wisdom "shows what *Ishah* would have been had she waited for God's self-unveiling." (*Women in Judaism*, 29.)

52. Kidner, *Genesis*, 70–71.

53. Luke 1:48b.

54. Beattie, *Rediscovering Mary*, 11. Cf. Ranke-Heinemann, *Eunuchs For the Kingdom Of Heaven*, chapter XXX, "Notes on Mariology."

Virginal." To take this further, the contra-figure for "Mary the Pure and Virginal" might not be "Oz the Great and Terrible" but "Eve the Sinful and Sexually Active." In this context would SHE WHO IS function as an antidote, or as a counter-irritant or distraction without treating the root cause of the problem?

5

Hā'ādām

TOWARDS THE END OF *The Wizard of Oz*, Dorothy and her friends travel south to consult with the good witch Glinda about Dorothy's wish to return to Kansas. En route they come to a steep rock-strewn hill and attempt to climb it in order to reach the country of the Quadlings which is Glinda's territory. Progress, however, is impeded by strange creatures with flat heads, necks composed of compressed flaps and no arms. When the Scarecrow attempts to climb the hill one of the creatures shoots out with the flat head, knocking him over and sending him tumbling backwards downhill. Dorothy and her friends are unable to proceed on foot and have to call on the Winged Monkeys to carry them over the hill.[1]

Creatures with flat heads appear from a rocky hillside and dispute right of passage to all comers. What exactly are these Hammer-Heads? The first one encountered by the travelers is said to be the strangest "man" they had ever seen. If it is a man it is not a man in the ordinary sense. It does not take a large stretch of the imagination to conclude that such creatures would be basically genderless.

Phyllis Trible depicts the original "earth creature" of Genesis 2 in somewhat similar terms. She presents *hā'ādām*, the creature from *hā'ādāmâ* (the earth), as sexually undifferentiated until the creation of "the woman."[2] Trible writes:

---

1. See Baum, *Wizard of Oz*, chapter 22.
2. See Trible, *Rhetoric of Sexuality*, chapter 4, "A Love Story Gone Awry."

> Elsewhere I have proposed an interpretation of *hā'ādām* as androgynous until the differentiation of female and male in Gen 2:21–24 ... I now consider that description incorrect because the word *androgyny* assumes sexuality, whereas the earth creature is sexually undifferentiated. To understand the earth creature as either humanity or proto-humanity is, I think, legitimate.[3]

For Trible, the original "earth creature" is non-male and non-sexual. She presents the earth creature as a staging-post in a creative process which eventually produces sexuality and gender, as will be seen below.

What then is the relevance of a genderless earth creature to the *imago Dei*? Trible does not address this question directly. She acknowledges "the dominance of male language in scripture" but also finds alternative language in "female imagery and motifs," claiming that Genesis 1:27 offers a clue in this respect. But the alleged clue is not a direct one. She sums up her position:

> Focusing upon the phrases "male and female" and "in the image of God," we discovered that the formal parallelism between them indicates a semantic correspondence between a better known and a lesser known element. Thus the parallelism yields a metaphor. "Male and female" is its vehicle; "the image of God," its tenor. At the same time, this tenor becomes itself a vehicle pointing to "God". The repetition of the word *God* establishes similarity between the Creator and human creatures while the addition of the word *the-image-of* connotes their difference. Here the lack of any formal parallelism between the two components suggests a semantic disparity. Thus, this latter metaphor saves the former from idolatry by witnessing to the transcendent Creator who is neither male nor female nor a combination of the two. Only in the context of this Otherness can we truly perceive the image of God male *and* female.[4]

Trible detects a parallel between "male and female" and "the image of God" and another parallel between "the image of God" and God. She does not, however, find "any formal parallelism" between the Creator and human beings. In other words, she finds a double metaphor in Genesis 1:27 with the result that "the image of God male *and* female" only

---

3. Trible, *Rhetoric of Sexuality*, 141 n. 17. Trible's italics. Phyllis Bird comments: "I do not think one can eradicate the male image of *hā'ādām* from this passage as Trible attempts to do." ("Sexual Differentiation and Divine Image in the Genesis Creation Texts," 25 n. 30.)

4. See Trible, *Rhetoric of Sexuality*, 200–201.

functions as the first stage in a process pointing to the "transcendent Creator who is neither male nor female nor a combination of the two." At some point in this process sexual differentiation is no longer relevant. Is there an echo here in reverse of a genderless earth creature giving way to sexual differentiation?

While my two previous chapters attempted a broad-ranging literary appraisal of gendered biblical themes, this chapter and the next are more analytical in flavor, assessing exegesis of key passages. This chapter considers feminist theories in relation to the early chapters of Genesis. Chapter 6 engages with the Pauline commentary on the *imago Dei* as it is taken up in redemption. Edmund Hill's discernment that interpersonal human relationships mirror divine relationships is premised on a *unity* of substance (or equality of nature) that is also *diversity* of priority: "as the Son is from the Father, so is the woman from the man."[5] This premise is disputed in various ways in the interpretations of feminist writers, Kari Elisabeth Børresen, Phyllis A. Bird, Phyllis Trible and Lone Fatum.

Hill's interpretation of the *imago Dei* assumes that the first three chapters of Genesis function as a literary whole. I follow him in this. Historian of religion, Anders Hultgård writes:

> With the acceptance of the Pentateuch in the Persian period as the basic religious document of Judaism, the creation texts in Genesis 1:1—2:4a and 2:4b–3:24 set the guidelines for nearly all subsequent accounts on the origin of man in early Jewish religion. Being part of the sacred *tōrāh* both Genesis stories were in equal degree considered divine revelation and could not be opposed as conflicting accounts.[6]

Overarching divine revelation in the creation texts is not, however, determinative in the arguments presented by Trible and others.

It is a "fundamental mistake," states Hultgård "to equate the modern western concept of 'God' with that of the biblical texts."[7] Mistake or not, Hultgård adds that "much work done in the field of feminist theology" projects "the modern image of a genderless and sublimated God back into biblical times." By this means, he continues, "it becomes possible to reinterpret a massively patriarchal body of texts in more 'favorable directions.'" Such interpretation is a two-stage process. The first step

---

5. See Hill on Augustine, *The Trinity*, XII, 338 n. 22.
6. Hultgård, "God and Image of Woman in Early Jewish Religion," 32.
7. Hultgård, "God and Image of Woman in Early Jewish Religion," 29.

(projecting a genderless God back into biblical texts) is followed by the further step (reinterpreting texts to favor the inclusion of women). Modern feminist writers may not be quite alone in this kind of convoluted thinking. This chapter considers and assesses interpretation by Børresen, Bird and Trible alongside Augustine's theory of the *imago Dei* as well as his remarks on the resurrected body.

GOD ALIEN FEMALENESS?

"The idea of *imago Dei*," says Kari Elisabeth Børresen, "is fundamental in theological anthropology, being a primary example of interaction between the concept of God and the definition of humanity."[8] But what is meant by the concept of God and how is humanity defined? Historian of religion, Anders Hultgård distinguishes the term "God" in its "general sense as a concept of modern western civilization" from "God as a personal name of the supreme deity of Judaism, Christianity and Islam."[9] He states further that in order "to preserve his character as a personal god YHWH had to be spoken of in either of the grammatical genders masculine and feminine." Hultgård comments: "The male-centered worldview of the Israelite-Jewish tradition did not leave room for any hesitation in the choice."[10] This comment would suggest that a method of projection was already at work in the sacred *tōrāh*, the male-centered definition of humanity determining the concept of God.

In an alleged history of projection as an interpretive method, Børresen adds a further step. She claims that women were originally excluded from the *imago Dei* and that key church fathers included women in the creation texts by "backdating" their genderless baptismal identity.[11] Nevertheless, says Børresen, this genderless identity was and continues to be in conflict with "God-alien femaleness" stemming from the religious culture of monotheistic patriarchy.[12] I will consider Børresen's remarks on the *imago Dei* in Christian tradition below. But first I will turn to the creation texts as they stand on the assumption that the Genesis stories have an overarching continuity and are not to be opposed as conflicting accounts.

---

8. Børresen, "Introduction: *Imago Dei* as Inculturated Doctrine," 1.
9. Hultgård, "God and Image of Woman in Early Jewish Religion," 30.
10. Hultgård, "God and Image of Woman in Early Jewish Religion," 31.
11. See Børresen, "Introduction: *Imago Dei* as Inculturated Doctrine," 2.
12. Børresen, "Patristic Interpretation of Gen 1,27 and 1 Cor 11,7," 187.

Genesis 1:26–28 gives the significant information that humanity (*ādām*) made in God's image is both singular and plural: "in the image of God he created him" (singular); "male and female he created them" (plural).[13] Humanity is like God in the sense that God is also presented as both singular and plural. God says, "Let us [plural] make *ādām* in our [plural] image"; "so God created *hā'ādām* in his [singular] image." Humanity as singular is termed *ādām* or *hā'ādām*. Humanity as plural is termed "male and female" (*zākār ûn^eqēbâ*) The blessing and the task of being fruitful and multiplying and having dominion are given to them, (humanity as plural). Genesis 2 describes how *hā'ādām* (singular) becomes man and woman or husband and wife (plural). But Genesis 2 concludes not with the plural but with the singular. "Therefore a man leaves his father and his mother and clings to his wife, and they become one [singular] flesh."

Despite the similar play on singular and plural, the phrase "image of God" does not occur in Genesis 2. But Genesis 3 gives an ironic twist to the idea of humanity being made in God's likeness, ironic that is if humanity is already in the likeness of God. The serpent tells the woman that if she eats the fruit she will become "like God." This is a different kind of likeness, not a given likeness but an acquired likeness (since the woman must first eat the fruit), and yet the story of Genesis 3 reveals that this acquired likeness is not "nearness-of-approach" but the reverse. God admits that "the man" (*hā'ādām*) has become "like one of us" in one respect, knowing good and evil. In consequence, God drives out "the man" and guards the way to the tree of life, in order that "the man" should not become like God, it can be inferred, in the other respect of living forever. There is a bar in the way of nearness-of-approach, an angel with a flaming sword.

In spite of this setback, the creational status is still intact, according to Genesis 9:6: "Whoever sheds the blood of a human [*hā'ādām*], by a human shall that person's blood be shed; for in his own image God made humankind." Genesis 5:1–2 makes it clear that *ādām* is to be understood as male and female (*zākār ûn^eqēbâ*), and God is even said to name male and female *ādām*. The early chapters of Genesis thus reveal a high degree of literary development of what it means for humanity to be like God, yet the picture has overarching consistency. The unauthorized attempt to acquire likeness to God leads to a loss of access to God. Nevertheless, the creational status of being like God as gendered unity in diversity remains.

---

13. See footnotes in NRSV translation.

At this point I return to Børresen's remark that the idea of the *imago Dei* is a primary example of interaction between the concept of God and the definition of humanity. Børresen and Hultgård seem to be at one in thinking that the male-centered religious culture determined the masculine depiction of God. But what if God is not monotheistic in the sense assumed by modern Western civilization? This book has already noted the remark by Jewish writer, Tikva Frymer-Kensky that "the plural nature of the creation of humanity applies to both the creator ('we') and the creature ('he created them male and female')."[14] Edmund Hill's reading of 1 Corinthians 11 also highlights unity in diversity at both the divine and human levels. In biblical terms, an assertion of "God-alien femaleness" leaves out the importance attached to the creation of the woman and the delight of the man in her arrival, along with Jesus's endorsement of the primal relationship connecting Genesis 1 and 2 (Matthew 19:3–5; Mark 10:5–9).

Let us now consider what Børresen has to say, firstly about patristic interpretation of the "creational image of God" and secondly about later interpretation in the Christian tradition. Børresen begins with the assumption that Christianity inherited a legacy from Judaism of a male-centered *imago Dei*. "As a patriarchally inculturated, monotheistic religion," she writes, "Christianity excludes femaleness at the divine level. It follows that women cannot be God-like *qua* females, with corresponding lack of fully human status, i.e. full religious capacity *qua* women."[15] But there is another element in this. Børresen maintains that alleged "God-alien femaleness" was to some extent redressed by the patristic method. She continues:

> Traditional Christian anthropology starts with two contrasting tenets: 1. Androcentric gender hierarchy or female subordination is established by God's creative order. 2. Human equivalence in the sense of woman's parity with men is realised though Christ in redemption. The ensuing asymmetry between women's creational inferiority and their salvational equality is affronted by 'feminist' church Fathers, in order to include women in human God-likeness *already* from creation, *in spite of* their God-alien femaleness.

---

14. See Soskice, *Kindness of God*, 50–51, citing Frymer-Kensky, *Studies in Bible and Feminist Criticism*, 101.

15. See Børresen, "Patristic Interpretation of Gen 1,27 and 1 Cor 11,7," 187.

This reinterpretation did not, she adds, affect women's "God-given subservience *qua* females, a split which has been upheld in theological anthropology until this century."

Børresen draws attention to a "classic stratagem, initiated by Clement of Alexandria . . . and elaborated by Augustine," which "defines God's image, *imago Dei*, as an incorporeal and consequently sexless quality, linked to human capacity of virtue and intellect." She adds that this "gender-free privilege in man-like disguise permits *backdating* women's redemptive Christ-likeness to the creational level."[16] As noted in chapter 2, Augustine included women in the *imago Dei* through an alleged "masculine" operation of mind, common to both sexes. In this sense Børresen's contention that Augustine and others fail to offer full religious status for women *as female* would seem borne out.

What is not borne out, however, is the reason given by Børresen for Augustine's "stratagem." As seen in chapter 2, Augustine's interpretation did not arise because he thought that women were inferior by creation or "equal" due to salvation. Rather he had an exegetical problem. As he read it, Genesis 1 said that both male and female were made in the image of God. But some New Testament passages appeared to cast doubt on this creational status. Augustine therefore resorted to a contemporary philosophical theory in his exegesis of 1 Corinthians 11:1–16 in order to support his belief in the inclusiveness of Genesis 1:26–27 *against* other church fathers who said that women were not made in the image of God. His "feminist" tendency was fuelled at this point not by the New Testament but by the Old.

Børresen admits the exegetical difficulty posed by 1 Corinthians 11:7: "all patristic exegesis understands this text as literally affirming men's *exclusive* God-likeness."[17] She states that Augustine "affronts 1 Cor 11,7 by stating that women *too* are created in God's image." She also states that Augustine "strives to combine the two creation accounts":

> Augustine distinguishes between two modes of God's *unique* creation act: the instant, seminal *informatio* expressed in Gen. 1, and the successive *conformatio* described in Gen 2. By this exegetical device, Augustine is able to connect the sexual differentiation according to Gen.1,27b–28 with the preceding image

---

16. See Børresen, "Patristic Interpretation of Gen 1,27 and 1 Cor 11,7," 187. Børresen's italics.

17. Børresen, "Patristic Interpretation of Gen 1,27 and 1 Cor 11,7," 199. Børresen's italics.

text of Gen. 1,26–27a. It follows that the formation of Adam *and* his woman in Gen. 2,7,18,21–32 is linked to the creation of theomorphic humanity.[18]

In consequence, "the female human being, *femina/mulier*" is included "in the God-like human prototype, *homo*," continues Børresen. What is not clear in this account is Augustine's exegetical motivation for linking Genesis 1:27b–28 with 1:26–27a. Given the assumption that Genesis 1:27b ("male and female he created them") was not originally connected with the *imago Dei*, why could not Genesis 2, which does not mention the *imago Dei*, be read in harmony with Genesis 1:27b on its own? A God-like male-centered prototype of Genesis 1:26–27a could then more readily be harmonized with a God-like male only reading of 1 Corinthians 11:7.

In Børresen's view, Christian tradition has retained the notion of male-centered hierarchy in the creative order due to its "patriarchal inculturation." Despite the surmised tradition of back-dating women's redemptive Christ-likeness to the creational order, traditional typology excludes femaleness from reflecting the divine level:

> Surviving from the early thought of *imago Dei* as exclusively male, traditional typology transposes God-willed gender hierarchy from creation to the redemptive order. In nuptial imagery God-like Adam prefigures Christ, who as new Adam and divine Redeemer is incarnated in perfect manhood. The ancillary role of *non-*theomorphic Eve is here re-enacted by the church or Mary as new Eve, representing dependent and consequently womanlike humanity.[19]

This is to allege that the method of projection functions in two directions. In terms of likeness to God, women's inclusion in the redemptive order is projected backwards to enable women's inclusion in the *imago Dei*. In terms of traditional typology, women's exclusion from the *imago Dei* is projected forwards to enable "God-willed gender hierarchy" in the redemptive order.

Janet Martin Soskice contrasts modern critical methods with the patristic approach to the creation texts:

---

18. See Børresen, "Patristic Interpretation of Gen 1,27 and 1 Cor 11,7," 197–99. Børresen's italics. Cf. Børresen's discussion of Gregory of Nyssa's "two-stage theory" of creation, Genesis 1:26–27a (purely spiritual) and Genesis 1:27b–28 (sexually differentiated).

19. Børresen, "Introduction: *Imago Dei* as Inculturated Doctrine," 3.

> Biblical critics now believe that the stories of the creation of humankind in Genesis 1 and 2 arise from two sources, Yahwist and Priestly, which fed into the final text of the book, and they do not spend much time trying to resolve apparent contradictions. It was not so for the early Christian theologians, for whom any apparent inconsistencies had to be resolved . . . Early exegetes puzzled as to what to do with 1 Cor. 11:7: 'For a man ought not to have his head veiled, since he is the image and reflection of God; but woman is the reflection of man.' Did this mean that women were not fully in the image of God, a reading that would put Paul at variance with Genesis 1?[20]

Unlike Børresen, Soskice would here confirm that it was the New Testament, rather than the Old Testament text which seemed to cast doubt on women's "theomorphic" status.

Børresen alleges that key patristic writers imposed women's baptismal identity on the creation texts. Soskice states that early Christian writers attempted to resolve apparent contradictions. There is a difference of temper but not necessarily of detail here. As noted, Børresen states that Augustine links the formation of Adam and his woman in Genesis 2 with the creation of theomorphic humanity in Genesis 1. Soskice agrees that patristic writers interpreted Genesis 1 in terms of Genesis 2:

> One might have thought that the Fathers with their biblical conservatism would have given priority to the narrative of Genesis 1 if only because it is the first; but overwhelmingly they preferred to discuss the second creation narrative where Eve is made from Adam's side. Gen 1:27 on its own is certainly puzzling. What can it mean that God created man (*Ha'adam*, the Hebrew male collective) in his own image, male and female? Early theologians canvassed the idea of a primal androgyne which, or who, was subsequently supplanted by the later creation of two persons of different sexes; but this reading was generally dropped in favour of concentration on the second story where *Ha'adam* (which seems in Genesis 2 to be the single male human) is made first, and Eve from his side. This was the story of Genesis 2 read in a particular way—a way which fitted better the accepted order of things—man (the male) was alone at first, and God created Eve *for him* as a companion and a helper.[21]

---

20. See Soskice, *Kindness of God*, 42–44. Soskice's italics.

21. Soskice, *Kindness of God*, 42–43. Soskice draws attention to Augustine's famous surmise that a man would have been a better helper for Adam except in capacity to reproduce.

The puzzle of the *imago Dei*, says Soskice, was resolved by reading Genesis 2 in a particular way, fitting the accepted order of the day. One might add that this reading of Genesis 2 also better fitted 1 Corinthians 11:7 read in a particular way.

How does one judge a form of exegesis which fits the order of the day? Børresen alleges that "God-alien femaleness" derives from the patriarchal era of the biblical writings. We have seen that Augustine harmonizes 1 Corinthians 11:7 with Genesis 1 by an appeal to a "masculine" operation of mind, a recourse seemingly fitting the accepted order of his day. Judged by feminist standards, however, this modification of "God-alien femaleness" was not a happy one. Børresen writes:

> Androcentric bio-sociology and Neoplatonic anthropology are here exegetically twisted in order to insert deviant femaleness as fully human in terms of religious capacity, thereby dismantling male God-likeness through asexual device. Nevertheless, women's *imago Dei* persists in man-like disguise, thus sharpening the conflict between rational privilege and subordinate female humanity. In fact, Augustine's holistic combination of *informatio* and *conformatio* as describing God's unique creative act, strengthens the mancentered identification of patriarchal sex roles and God-willed gender hierarchy.[22]

On the other hand, Børresen traces what she calls the "gradual *humanization* of *imago Dei*," noting approvingly an "updated definition of God's image" in the "present accommodation to post-patriarchal culture" in which "both women and men are created God-like *qua* male and female human beings."[23] This latter definition appears to fit the order of the day without lament.

In a shifting process of "theological inculturation," theological anthropology no longer defines gender hierarchy as divinely ordained, says Børresen.[24] Current insights, however, are said to bear the hallmark of earlier "inculturation":

> It is important to note that this *aggiornamento* builds upon the church Fathers' efforts to insert women as God-like and therefore fully human, their *sub-male* femaleness notwithstanding. In

---

22. Børresen, "Patristic Interpretation of Gen 1,27 and 1 Cor 11,7," 201.

23. See Børresen, "Introduction, *Imago Dei* as Inculturated Doctrine," 3; Børresen, "Patristic Interpretation of Gen 1,27 and 1 Cor 11,7," 188.

24. Børresen, "Introduction: *Imago Dei* as Inculturated Doctrine," 4.

fact, contemporary biblical interpretation utilises three equality strategies, all of which are inherited from patristic exegesis.[25]

I will return to these "equality strategies" in the last section of this chapter. Børresen proposes describing God "by both male and female metaphors" on the grounds that "both women and men are understood to be theomorphic."[26] But can such issues be resolved by means of "theological inculturation"?

Soskice brings the question back to biblical exegesis:

> We find ourselves to this very day torn between two positions which are each compelling but seem at the same time incompatible. We must say that, Christologically speaking, women and men cannot be different, for 'all will bear the image of the man of heaven'. But we must also say that sexual difference is not, or should not be, a matter of theological indifference. Genesis 1 suggests that sexual difference has something to tell us, not just about human beings, but about God in whose image they are made, male and female. The unresolved question then is: where, why, and how does sexual difference make a difference?[27]

I believe the question is not beyond an exegetical resolution. I will come to this in chapter 6. Meanwhile I turn to two Old Testament exegetes, Phyllis Bird and Phyllis Trible.

NON-GENDERED *IMAGO DEI*?

"Genesis 1 suggests that sexual difference has something to tell us, not just about human beings, but about God in whose image they are made, male and female," says Soskice. This is to assume that the *imago Dei*, described in the first chapter of Genesis, is intended to include sexual difference. By contrast, Børresen maintains that the *imago Dei* of Genesis 1 originally applied to the God-like male and that the understanding that women were included, albeit in a largely subservient way, was instituted through patristic exegesis. The assumption that Genesis 1:27b ("male and female he created them") was originally meant to be read separately from

---

25. Børresen, "Patristic Interpretation of Gen 1,27 and 1 Cor 11,7," 188.

26. Børresen, "Introduction: *Imago Dei* as Inculturated Doctrine," 4; cf. "Patristic Interpretation of Gen 1,27 and 1 Cor 11,7," 204.

27. Soskice, *Kindness of God*, 45.

Genesis 1:27a ("So God created man in his own image, in the image of God he created him") is spelled out more fully by Phyllis A. Bird.

Soskice reports: "Biblical critics now believe that the stories of the creation of humankind in Genesis 1 and 2 arise from two sources, Yahwist and Priestly, which fed into the final text of the book." Phyllis Bird follows this line, attributing Genesis 1 to a Priestly source (which includes later genealogies) and Genesis 2–3 to a Yahwist source. Further, Bird believes that two separate sources fed into the final text of Genesis 1: the Wortbericht (account of God's words) and the Tatbericht (account of God's deeds).

Based on the theory of two separate sources, Bird claims that, in Genesis 1, human status as the image of God is to be read separately from sexual differentiation. She states: "According to Gen 1:26, humans are in some unspecified but essential way 'like' God, and this is related to their position or function within the created order, as exercising dominion over their fellow creatures." In sexual function, on the other hand, humans are like the animals, "living creatures . . . designed as sexual pairs (implied by the blessing) and enjoined to 'be fruitful and multiply and fill the earth' (vv.22, 28)":

> This word of blessing and command applies to humans as well as other creatures. Like them, but unlike God, humans are sexual beings. That is the meaning of the statement that is added in v.27 to the report of the final act of creation; *ādām* is created in the image of God, but *also* male and female.[28]

Bird discerns the likeness of humanity to God in terms of humanity's representative task as outlined in the second command of Genesis 1:28, to have dominion over other creatures. She claims that the first command, "to be fruitful and multiply" underscores the *unlikeness* of humanity to God.

The distinction between the *imago Dei* of Genesis 1:26–27a and sexual differentiation in verse 27b is argued in terms of "Wortbericht" (announcement) and "Tatbericht" (execution report):[29]

> The parallel clauses of vs 27 . . . form a bridging couplet between the primary . . . statement concerning the divine likeness, introduced in the Wortbericht (26) and repeated as the lead sentence of the Tatbericht . . . and the pronouncement of

---

28. Bird, *Faith, Feminism and the Forum of Scripture*, 51–52.

29. See Bird, "Sexual Differentiation and Divine Image in the Genesis Creation Texts," 6; 20 n. 4.

Hāʾādām

the blessing of fertility (vs 28)—a new theme found only in the Tatbericht . . . The two parallel cola contain two essential and distinct statements about the nature of humanity: *adam* is created *like* (i.e., resembling) God, but *as* creature—and hence male and female. The parallelism of the two cola is progressive, not synonymous. The second statement adds to the first; it does not explicate it.[30]

The assumption that the "Wortbericht" and "Tatbericht" represent separate sources for the final text of Genesis 1 is pivotal in the conclusion that the "second statement adds to the first; it does not explicate it."

Soskice states that Genesis 1 tells us something, not just about human beings, but about God in whose image they are made, male and female." Bird disputes this reading:

In our analysis the meaning and function of the statement, "male and female he created them," is considerably more limited than is commonly assumed. It says nothing about the image which relates *adam* to God nor about God as the referent of the image. Nor does it qualify *adam*'s dominion over the creatures or subjugation of the earth. It relates only to the blessing of fertility.[31]

Bird admits that appearances might belie her analysis:

In the expanded execution report, the word that conveys dominion is joined directly to the preceding words of blessing, creating an extended series of imperatives, all apparently governed by the rubric of blessing . . . and all apparently conditioned by the dual qualification of bi-sexual nature and divine resemblance.[32]

She continues, however, that appearances may mislead:

Such a reading of vss. 27–28, however, which treats the series of words addressed to *adam* as homogeneous and relates both statements of nature (God-like and bi-sexual) to the whole series without discrimination, ignores the interpretive clues contained in the Wortbericht and in the parallel construction of vs. 22. Fertility and dominion belong to two separate themes or concerns: one the theme of nature with is sub-theme of

---

30. Bird, "Sexual Differentiation and Divine Image in the Genesis Creation Texts," 11. Bird's italics.

31. Bird, "Sexual Differentiation and Divine Image in the Genesis Creation Texts," 12–13.

32. Bird, "Sexual Differentiation and Divine Image in the Genesis Creation Texts," 12.

sustainability (fertility), the other, the theme of order with its interest in position and function.

While appearing connected in the *imago Dei*, nature and order are two separate themes, says Bird.

Bird rules out the suggestion that sexual difference in Genesis 27b has something to tell us about God. She adds a further argument. This time the method is attributed to the Priestly editor:

> The idea that God might possess any form of sexuality, or any differentiation analogous to it, would have been for P an utterly foreign and repugnant notion. For this author/editor, above all others in the Pentateuch, guards the distance between God and humanity, avoiding anthropomorphic description and employing specialized terminology (e.g. *bārā*) to distinguish divine activity from analogous human action.[33]

Utter aversion to anthropomorphic description of God on the part of the Priestly writer, does not, in Bird's view, preclude "thinking" in male terms. Bird adds: "For P, as for J, the representative and determining image of the species was certainly male, as 5:1–3, 9:1, and the genealogies which structure the continuing account make clear. Though the Priestly writer speaks of the species, he thinks of the male, just as the author of Psalm 8."[34]

What can be said here? While it is true that God would not have been understood to be like humanity in terms of biological gender, the reciprocal notion (that male and female reflect something of what God is like) is not ruled out. Soskice notes:

> Whatever meaning we give it, the startling divine plural of Gen 1:26, 'Let us make humankind in our image, according to our likeness' is no accident. The Church Fathers saw in it a reference to the Trinity . . . but however we construe it, some connection is being made between the sociality of the Godhead and the sociality of the human race which is more than one, male and female. The point is not an androgynous God, or even a God who is both male and female—such notions would have been abhorrent to the Priestly writer. The point, rather, is difference, and from within difference creativity, reciprocity and

---

33. Bird, "Sexual Differentiation and Divine Image in the Genesis Creation Texts," 11.

34. Bird, "Sexual Differentiation and Divine Image in the Genesis Creation Texts," 12.

generation, not as of God, but as of the creature made in the image of God.[35]

As Bird concedes, the command "to be fruitful and multiply" is immediately followed, in verse 28, by the command to have dominion over it. As it stands, there is an added dimension of purpose to human procreation that is not given to other creatures. In further distinction from earlier acts of creation, this is also the first time that God communicates with a named third party. Significantly, God said *to them*, "be fruitful and multiply."

The distinction between Priestly and Yahwist authorship does not, for Bird, preclude similarities between the creation accounts:

> The author [of Genesis 2] has personified humankind in a single representative, to whom he has given the name of the species; as in Genesis 1, his model is male—here a peasant farmer . . . the Yahwist's account . . . makes the same essential points about human nature as Genesis 1, but it does so through narrated actions rather than declarations.[36]

For Bird, the creation accounts differ in genre but not in message, which she says is "essentially the same." But if the distinction consists in narrated actions in Genesis 2–3 as opposed to declarations in Genesis 1, what becomes of the so-called Tatbericht (account of God's deeds) in Genesis 1?

The model for the human species is male in both the Priestly and Yahwist accounts, says Bird. She writes of the "conspicuous androcentrism" of the Yahwist account,[37] but notes further nuances:

> The theme of sexual differentiation is here too, but the way in which it is introduced gives unique attention to the relationship between the sexes—in the "original" order and in the "fallen" state that describes life as we know it, "outside the garden" . . . Human life, in this account, is characterized by interactions—with other creatures, with others of the same species, and with God (elaborated as the story continues). Humans are relational beings in their fundamental nature. And these relationships have both social and psychological dimensions . . . The story is told from the man's point of view, reflecting the male-centered society in which it arose; but the message is one of mutuality, of

---

35. Soskice, *Kindness of God*, 50–51.
36. Bird, "Theological Anthropology in the Hebrew Bible," 58.
37. Bird, "Sexual Differentiation and Divine Image in the Genesis Creation Texts," 20.

man and woman made for each other and bound together, in joy and (in the next episode) pain.³⁸

Bird states that the story is told from the man's point of view, but she concedes a key qualifying factor:

> One of the most remarkable features of this account is its view of the male domination that characterized the world of ancient Israel. For the Yahwist, this "given" order is the primary sign of disordered relationships in a creation estranged from God.³⁹

Nature and order belong to separate themes in Genesis 1, says Bird. In Genesis 2–3, however, nature (the mutuality of man and woman) is said to give way to a new order (of male domination in creation estranged from God).

Bird distinguishes the Yahwist from the Priestly account in terms of linguistic usage. The use, in Genesis 1, of *ādām* is contrasted with the use, in Genesis 2, of *hā'ādām* (which she translates "the human"). Such a linguistic contrast between Genesis 1 and 2 cannot be sustained because the term *hā'ādām* appears in Genesis 1:27. The term "the human" for *hā'ādām* in Genesis 2 is qualified: *hā'ādām* "bears the appellation of the species but does not fully represent it." For this reason, Genesis 2–3 is said to be told from the man's point of view. Bird does not allow for the possibility that the narrative is told from God's point of view.⁴⁰

While her method appears exegetical, Bird places it in a broader theological context. She "identifies the Bible as a site of debate, where readers overhear the conversations of an ancient community and are drawn into its debate to continue it in their own time and place":

> This understanding involves an historical-critical approach to the text that sets the biblical writings in the social and religious contexts of their origins, enabling dialogue with the text that honors the integrity of the ancient writers and the "cross-cultural" nature of the encounter.⁴¹

---

38. See Bird, *Faith, Feminism and the Forum of Scripture*, 58–59.

39. Bird, *Faith Feminism and the Forum of Scripture*, 62.

40. See discussion in Bird, "Sexual Differentiation and Divine Image in the Genesis Creation Texts," 13–18.

41. See Bird on her method in the Preface to *Faith, Feminism and the Forum of Scripture*, vii.

The ancient text "is located within a conversation that has both ancient (canonical and post-canonical) and contemporary partners," Bird says elsewhere, adding that, in her view, "the revelatory content of the word and its contemporary meaning are apprehended only through this conversation and may not be identified with any particular text or locution nor with the author's imputed intention." This stated restriction does not prevent her taking issue with "the traditional interpretation of the *imago*-bearing *adam* as male (an interpretation which rests on conflation . . . with Genesis 2)" on the grounds that it fails "to observe the writer's intention . . . expressed primarily by the structure of the argument, rather than the culturally captive language that serves as its vehicle."[42]

What Bird means by the writer's intention would seem to owe much to what Børresen calls "the continuous revelatory interplay between God and humanity, acted out in shifting historical contexts."[43] Bird states:

> Genesis 1 invites, and demands, renewed reflection on the meaning of sexual differentiation as a constitutive mark of our humanity and the meaning of God-likeness (image) as the defining attribute of humankind. And it contributes to this constructive task by its silences as well as its assertions. Genesis 1, in contrast to most interpreters, does not link its two fundamental statements about *adam*, but juxtaposes them as parallel holistic assertions, ordering them, however, so that the *imago*-dominion statement is prior and encompassing. Nor does the text establish any hierarchy within the species either of gender or function; all its statements pertain to the species as a whole. Thus it may serve as a foundation text for a feminist egalitarian anthropology, since it recognizes no hierarchy of gender in the created order.[44]

The structural implications of the text are spelled out in a footnote:

> The text itself permits an egalitarian reading, I would argue, despite the fact that it must be viewed as unintended and unforseen by the ancient author. It not only permits such a reading, it encourages it, by the "emptiness" of its key terms, the structure of its pronouncements, and its restraint from specifying social roles and responsibilities. An egalitarian reading, however, belongs to a new context of interpretation, in answer to a new

---

42. See Bird, "Sexual Differentiation and Divine Image in the Genesis Creation Texts," 19–20.

43. Børresen, "Introduction: *Imago Dei* as Inculturated Doctrine," 4.

44. Bird, "Sexual Differentiation and Divine Image," 19.

question beyond the horizon of the ancient author—but no less valid for its novelty.[45]

Bird would seem to allow more positive potential in an ancient text than the "God-alien femaleness" detected by Børresen. Nevertheless, egalitarian anthropology does not supply any detail about the meaning of sexual differentiation. I turn now to the rather different approach of Phyllis Trible.

NON-GENDERED ORIGIN?

As noted in chapter 3, Phyllis Trible focuses on equality of male and female as the clue pointing to the image of God.[46] By contrast, she claims that traditional interpretations of Genesis 2–3 are "misogynous." In support of this claim, the reader is referred to feminist surveys.[47] Trible outlines the principles governing her alternative approach:

> Within scripture, my topical clue is a text: the image of God male and female. To interpret this topic, my methodological clue is rhetorical criticism. Outside scripture, my hermeneutical clue is an issue, feminism as a critique of culture. These clues meet now as the Bible . . . wanders through history to merge past and present.[48]

Trible's method of "rhetorical criticism" is said to investigate "the individual characteristics of a literary unit."[49] On such terms, Genesis 1 and Genesis 2–3 are distinct units: Genesis 1 is described as a poem,[50] Genesis 2–3 as a story.[51] "A literary study of Genesis 2–3 may offer insights that traditional perspectives dream not of," states Trible.[52] At the same time Trible's hermeneutical clue of feminism as a critique of culture wanders through alleged literary boundaries.

---

45. See Bird, "Sexual Differentiation and Divine Image," 24 n. 22.
46. See Trible, *Rhetoric of Sexuality*, 22.
47. See Trible, *Rhetoric of Sexuality*, 72–73. See also 139 n. 1. For "recent expositions of misogynous readings," Trible cites Merlin Stone, *When God Was a Woman*, 5–8, 198–233; June Singer, *Androgyny: Toward a New Theory of Sexuality*, 85–100."
48. Trible, *Rhetoric of Sexuality*, 23.
49. Trible, *Rhetoric of Sexuality*, 11. See section "The Methodological Clue."
50. Trible, *Rhetoric of Sexuality*, 12.
51. Trible, *Rhetoric of Sexuality*, 72.
52. Trible, *Rhetoric of Sexuality*, 74.

While they are both Old Testament scholars, I have stated that Trible has a rather different approach to Bird. Trible differentiates between Genesis 1 and Genesis 2–3 but her focus is less on surmised authorship and more on actual content of the chapters. On the other hand, her combination of interpretative "clues" does not always lend itself to close attention to the text. Trible's analysis of Genesis 1 does not detach the *imago Dei* from sexual differentiation in terms of separate sources of "Wortbericht" and "Tatbericht." Nevertheless, Trible distinguishes between the image of God male and female and the image of God as it points to the transcendent Creator ("who is neither male nor female nor a combination of the two").[53]

At the beginning of this chapter, I drew attention to Trible's double metaphor in relation to Genesis 1:26–27 and also to Trible's depiction of the so-called earth creature of Genesis 2. The Hebrew word *hā'ādām* appears in both Genesis 1 and Genesis 2. According to Trible, however, the word means different things in different contexts. Trible states that, in Genesis 1, *hā'ādām* refers to two creatures comprising the one humanity: "Hā-'ādām is not an original unity that is subsequently split apart by sexual division. Instead, it is the original unity that is at the same time the original differentiation."[54] By contrast, her interpretation of Genesis 2 presents *hā'ādām* as an original humanity or proto-humanity, a unity which subsequently becomes differentiated.

For Trible, *hā'ādām* of Genesis 2, the creature from *hā'ādāmâ* (the earth), is sexually undifferentiated until the creation of "the woman."[55] She makes a distinction between "derivation" and "differentiation":

> Woman is not derived from man, even as the earth creature is not derived from the earth . . . Dust of the earth and rib of the earth creature are but raw materials for God's creative activity . . . Differentiation from the earth, on the other hand, and from the man, on the other, implies neither derivation from them nor subordination to them.[56]

Trible proposes an original unity (earth creature) which *becomes* diversity (male and female). She calls this progression "differentiation." She goes on, however, to state that "differentiation" is also unity: "Sexuality is the recognition not of division but of the oneness that is wholeness, bone

---

53. See Trible, *Rhetoric of Sexuality*, 200–201.
54. Trible, *Rhetoric of Sexuality*, 18.
55. See Trible, *Rhetoric of Sexuality*, chapter 4, "A Love Story Gone Awry."
56. Trible, *Rhetoric of Sexuality*, 102.

of bone and flesh of flesh."⁵⁷ Beyond acting as shared raw material, it is not clear why "bone of bone and flesh of flesh" should "produce oneness that is wholeness."

One may compare Trible's interpretation with the idea put forward by Hill that interpersonal human relationships reflect their *unity* of substance (or equality of nature) that is also *diversity* of priority.⁵⁸ The prior period in which it is "not good" for *hā'ādām* to be alone (Genesis 2:18) allows for the diversity of priority. Hill's addition that relations between male and female mirror divine interpersonal relations brings Genesis 2 into line with Genesis 1:26–27. A compartmentalized approach, as in the literary units of Trible's rhetorical criticism, does not lend itself to this kind of integration. Trible's discussion of Genesis 2–3 does not refer to the image of God, except in a closing comment:

> Life has lost to Death, harmony to hostility, unity and fulfillment to fragmentation and dispersion. The divine, human, animal, and plant worlds are all adversely affected. Indeed, the image of God male and female has participated in a tragedy of disobedience.⁵⁹

Reference to the image of God male and female in this context does not derive directly from Genesis 2–3 but rather, it would seem, from her broad "hermeneutical clue."

Variation in the meaning of *hā'ādām* is not conducive to a clear theory of *imago Dei*, at least at first sight. Let us return, however, to Trible's double metaphor. At the beginning of this chapter, I asked whether an allegedly genderless earth creature said to give way to sexual differentiation is a reflection in reverse of an alleged metaphor in process from the image of God male and female to the image of the "transcendent Creator who is neither male nor female nor a combination of the two." At one point, Trible's describes the earth creature in words that parallel the description of the transcendent Creator. She writes that, in Genesis 2:7–20, the word *hā'ādām* "designated one creature who was sexually undifferentiated (neither male nor female nor a combination of both)."⁶⁰ While she does not

---

57. Trible, *Rhetoric of Sexuality*, 103.
58. Hill in Augustine, *The Trinity*, XII, 338 n. 22.
59. Trible, *Rhetoric of Sexuality*, 139.
60. Trible, *Rhetoric of Sexuality*, 98. One may compare Trible's theory of a genderless earth creature in Genesis 2 with the report by Soskice (*Kindness of God*, 42) that some early exegesis of Genesis 1 "canvassed the idea of a primal androgyne which, or who, was subsequently supplanted by the later creation of two persons of different sexes."

say so directly, the genderless earth creature could, on Trible's hermeneutical terms, be seen to function as a genderless image of God mirroring the genderless Creator. In other words, varied meanings of *hā'ādām* could be said to mark the transition between the image of God male and female and the genderless image of the transcendent Creator.

I have suggested that Trible's rhetorical criticism which confines itself to alleged literary units is somewhat at odds with her broad feminist hermeneutic. Her reading of Genesis 2-3 warrants further scrutiny in this respect. She divides the text into scenes:

> ... the plot unfolds by two opposite movements with an intermediate turning point. Entrance into a garden (scene one) opposes expulsion from a garden (scene three). Life opposes Death. Between these two opposite movements occurs disobedience, the turning point of the story (scene two) ... .[61]

Scene one is further divided into episodes: creation of the earth creature (Genesis 2:7-8); creation of plants (Genesis 2:9-17); creation of animals (Genesis 2:18-20); creation of human sexuality (Genesis 2:21-24). Trible states that such a study "fits the text," unlike traditional perspectives which "fail to respect the integrity of this work as an interlocking structure of words and motifs with its own intrinsic value and meaning."[62]

It is difficult, however, to sustain Trible's tracing of the development of unity (earth creature as proto-humanity) to diversity (sexual differentiation), and back to unity (oneness that is wholeness), in terms of Hebrew usage. When, in Genesis 2:22, God brings *'iššâ* ("the woman") to "the man," he brings her not to *'îš* as might be expected after alleged differentiation but to *hā'ādām* (supposedly sexually undifferentiated). And in the man's poetic greeting in verse 23, it is *hā'ādām* who speaks and who makes the confusing announcement that *'iššâ* was taken out of (the supposedly sexually differentiated) *'îš*. It should be noted that *'îš* and *'iššâ*, while they can be translated "man" and "woman," can also mean "husband" and "wife." Usage of the term *'îš* may simply refer to the fact that "the man" is now "the husband," rather than implying that he was not previously male.

Trible explains some of these anomalies on her own terms:

> After the creation of *'iššâ* and *'îš*, the sexually undifferentiated earth creature exists no longer. Accordingly, the word *hā'ādām*

---

61. Trible, *Rhetoric of Sexuality*, 74.
62. See Trible, *Rhetoric of Sexuality*, 79-105.

has now acquired a second usage in the story: it designates the male character. A third usage is yet to come.[63]

In episodes one, two and three of scene one the term *hā'ādām* described the sexually undifferentiated creature from the earth. But after the creation of *'iššâ* and *'îš* in episode four, the earth creature no longer existed, and *hā'ādām* designated the male character. This usage persisted throughout scene two and has continued in scene three until the closing paragraph where *hā'ādām* now becomes a generic term that keeps the man visible and renders the woman invisible (3:22–24).[64]

On purely literary terms one might ask why a word for a now extinct earth creature should become a word firstly for the male character and secondly an inclusive generic term. The parallel between the earth creature differentiated from the earth and human sexuality differentiated from the earth creature is not echoed in this development. The arrival of the earth creature does not signal the earth's disappearance, nor does "earth" become an inclusive term for something else.

To my mind Trible's literary judgment is also open to question in her distinction between "differentiation" and "derivation." As noted above, "derivation" as such is not seen to play a part in God's creative activity and "differentiation from the earth" does not imply derivation from it.[65] But a denial of derivation would weaken the significance of the judgment on the man. "Formed from the earth as the first act of creation (2:7), *'ādām* returns to *hā'-ªdāmâ*," states Trible.[66] How so if, when judgment is pronounced, the earth creature no longer exists? Further, what distinction is made here between "formed from the earth" and derivation?

Elsewhere Trible appears to admit derivation. She writes: "As *'iššâ* is taken from *'îš*, so *hā-'ādām* is taken from *hā-ªdāmâ*. Yet *hā-'ādām* is never portrayed as subordinate to the earth. On the contrary, the creature is given power over the earth so that what is taken from becomes superior to."[67] Here, it is the conclusion of subordination rather than the fact of derivation that Trible denies. She goes so far as to add: "By strict analogy, then, the line 'this shall be called *'iššâ* because from *'îš* was taken this' would mean

---

63. Trible, *Rhetoric of Sexuality*, 107.
64. Trible, *Rhetoric of Sexuality*, 134.
65. Trible, *Rhetoric of Sexuality*, 102.
66. Trible, *Rhetoric of Sexuality*, 132.
67. Trible, *Rhetoric of Sexuality*, 101.

not the subordination of the woman to the man but rather her superiority to him." Truer to the text, I would add, is the recognition that it is not the creative process *per se* but God's determination which establishes the relations between man and creation and between man and woman.

Trible amends her strict analogy: "Since the context for this statement concerning *'iššâ* and *'îš* is the preceding line, 'bone of my bones and flesh of my flesh,' the connotation of woman's superiority is inappropriate. The relationship of this couple is one of mutuality and equality, not one of female superiority and certainly not one of female subordination."[68] In other words, derivation *per se* implies neither inferiority nor superiority. But, as Trible goes on to attest, this situation of mutuality and equality does not last. As a consequence of disobedience, "union is no more; one flesh is split. The man will not reciprocate the woman's desire; instead he will rule over her."[69] I will return to this.

In Trible's theory of the *imago Dei*, "male and female" is the vehicle for "the image of God," while "the image of God" is in turn the vehicle for the transcendent Creator. As I understand her, Trible reads *hā'ādām* in Genesis 1 as the equivalent of "male and female," i.e., the first stage of her double metaphor. In Genesis 2–3, *hā'ādām* is read firstly as genderless proto-humanity, secondly as the man and lastly as a generic term that keeps the man visible and renders the woman invisible. At the same time "the image of God male and female" is said, by the end of Genesis 3, to participate "in a tragedy of disobedience."[70] Trible finds support for her inclusive reading of *hā'ādām* of Genesis 1:26–27 in the similar language of Genesis 5:1b–2.[71] But here literary traditions overlap: the recall of Genesis 1:26–27 in Genesis 5 is sandwiched into the genealogy of the man, Adam. Something is lost in Trible's somewhat uneasy combination of interpretive clues which, to my mind, militates against literary discernment. This is evident in her appraisal of the creative process and also, I believe, of the judgment scene of Genesis 3.

Regarding Genesis 1, Trible writes: "On the first three days God creates the skeleton of the universe and, correspondingly, on the last three the deity fills it out."[72] In other words, Genesis 1 records a two-stage

---

68. See Trible, *Rhetoric of Sexuality*, 101–2.
69. Trible, *Rhetoric of Sexuality*, 128.
70. Trible, *Rhetoric of Sexuality*, 139.
71. Trible, *Rhetoric of Sexuality*, 18.
72. Trible, *Rhetoric of Sexuality*, 12.

process with a link between the two stages which is established through the literary structure. Regarding Genesis 2, Trible describes in depth how the earth is the source of the earth creature (episode one), the earth is the source of the plants (episode two), the earth is the source of the animals (episode three). Trible calls the second filling out stage "differentiation":

> Life began with the oneness of the earth out of which Yahweh God had formed the earth creature (2:7). Here that pattern of differentiation within earthly unity continues: out of the earth Yahweh God causes to grow every tree (2:9).[73]
>
> Humanity and zoology also unite with botany. The three share Creator and material, though not the same creative process.[74]

Trible goes so far as to detect a link between the first and second stages of creation in Genesis 2 in terms of "differentiation within earthly unity." In this context, to stress "differentiation" at the expense of "derivation" is to weaken the link between first and second stage.

Moving to scene three, Trible does not detect anything beyond the tragedy of a failed love story. She writes:

> The trial established guilt: the man ate; the woman ate; and the serpent beguiled. Three separate judgments have described the outcome of their actions: the good earth is cursed; plants give way to thorns and thistles; fulfilling work has become alienated labor; power over the animals has deteriorated to enmity with the serpent; sexuality has splintered into strife; human oppression prevails. With such consequences, a happy ending to the story is impossible; only the aftermath of disaster remains.[75]

What is missing in this interpretation is what Derek Kidner calls "the first glimmer of the gospel."[76] There is no possible happy ending in this literary unit, says Trible. The reference to the "seed of the woman" is classified as marking "the persistent consequences of disobedience."[77] There is no redemption here nor does the woman have any part to play in it.

Trible does in fact find a biblical source of redemption for the aftermath of disaster. Bypassing literary boundaries, Genesis 2–3 becomes,

---

73. Trible, *Rhetoric of Sexuality*, 83.
74. Trible, *Rhetoric of Sexuality*, 91.
75. Trible, *Rhetoric of Sexuality*, 132.
76. See Kidner, *Genesis*, 70–71.
77. Trible, *Rhetoric of Sexuality*, 125.

in her hands, a "hermeneutical key" or "clue for entering another garden of Eros, the Song of Songs." She writes: "Through expansions, omissions and reversals, this poetry recovers the love that is bone of bone and flesh of flesh. In other words, the Song of Songs redeems a love story gone awry."[78] Whatever may be said for her reading of the Song of Songs, this kind of redemption paints a darker picture of Genesis 2–3 *per se* than is common in traditional interpretation. As indicated above, Trible offers her literary reading of Genesis 2–3 in contrast with allegedly misogynistic traditional readings. But are traditional readings of Genesis 2–3 as misogynistic as Trible claims? The next section will allow Augustine to function as a spokesperson in these matters.

THE RESURRECTED BODY

Trible claims that traditional reading of Genesis 2–3 is misogynistic. She lists some alleged traditional conclusions.[79] I cite some of her stated traditions (signaled with dot points) and contrast them with observations by Augustine below:

- A male God creates first man ([Genesis] 2:7) and last woman (2:22); first means superior and last means inferior or subordinate.

  Between man and wife there was a faithful partnership based on love and mutual respect; there was a harmony and a liveliness of mind and body, and an effortless observance of the commandment.[80]

- Woman tempted man to disobey and thus she is responsible for sin in the world (3:6); she is untrustworthy, gullible and simpleminded.

- Woman is cursed by pain in childbirth (3:16); pain in childbirth is a more severe punishment than man's struggles with the soil; it signifies that woman's sin is greater than man's.

  They were alone together, two human beings, a married pair; and we cannot believe that the man was led astray to transgress God's law because he believed that the woman spoke the truth,

---

78. Trible, *Rhetoric of Sexuality*, 144.
79. Trible, *Rhetoric of Sexuality*, 73.
80. Augustine, *City of God*, XIV, 26.

but that he fell in with her suggestions because they were so closely bound in partnership. In fact, the Apostle was not off the mark when he said, 'It was not Adam, but Eve, who was seduced', for what he meant was that Eve accepted the serpent's statement as the truth, while Adam refused to be separated from his only companion, even if it involved sharing her sin. That does not mean that he was less guilty, if he sinned knowingly and deliberately. Hence the Apostle does not say, 'He did not sin,' but 'He was not seduced.' For he certainly refers to the man when he says, 'It was through one man that sin came into the world,' and when he says more explicitly, a little later, 'by reproducing the transgression of Adam.'[81]

Augustine's statement that there was "love and mutual respect" between man and wife in the Garden of Eden would appear to belie the claim that traditional interpretation supposed the primal marriage to be originally a hierarchical relationship. Augustine does not support the claim that woman is held responsible for sin in the world.[82]

In traditional Christian anthropology, says Børresen, "androcentric gender hierarchy or female subordination is established by God's creative order."[83] Bird notes, however, that the message of Genesis 2–3 "is one of mutuality, of man and woman made for each other and bound together, in joy and (in the next episode) pain."[84] Trible writes that the "relationship of this couple is one of mutuality and equality, not one of female superiority and certainly not one of female subordination."[85] Augustine writes: "Between man and wife there was a faithful partnership based on love and mutual respect; there was a harmony and a liveliness of mind and body, and an effortless observance of the commandment."[86] It seems that Bird, Trible and Augustine are at one on this point.

---

81. Augustine, *City of God*, XIV, 11. Augustine cites 1 Timothy 2:14 and Romans 5:12; 14.

82. Børresen records that, according to Augustine's exegesis of Romans 5:12, Adam has sole responsibility for humanity's collective guilt but adds that "Eve's instrumental role in the first sin is repaired by the subordinate function of Mary/ church as Christ's mother/ bride." See "Patristic Interpretation of Gen 1,27 and 1 Cor 11,7," 203–4.

83. Børresen, "Patristic Interpretation of Gen 1,27 and 1 Cor 11,7," 187.

84. Bird, *Faith, Feminism and the Forum of Scripture*, 59.

85. See Trible, *Rhetoric of Sexuality*, 101.

86. Augustine, *City of God*, XIV, 26.

Trible states that "human oppression" is the consequence of disobedience.[87] Bird agrees: "For the Yahwist, this 'given' order [i.e., male domination that characterized the world of ancient Israel] is the primary sign of disordered relationships in a creation estranged from God."[88] But if male domination is a consequence of sin, why is traditional Christian anthropology said to read female subordination into God's creative order? There may be more than one reason for this. As already seen, Soskice indicates that the puzzle of Genesis 1:27 tended to be interpreted in terms of Genesis 2 read in a hierarchical way. Further, Augustine's allegorical exegesis of the *imago Dei* decidedly favors domination by the masculine *sapientia* over the feminine *scientia*. In other words, while Augustine appears to be at one with feminist exegetes on the mutuality between man and woman prior to disobedience, his allegorical use of Adam and Eve tells a different story.

In broad terms, how misogynistic is the tradition? Børresen refers to a belief that woman was not *imago Dei* based on 1 Corinthians 11:7 and 2 Timothy 2:12, stemming from Ambrosiaster, an unidentified fourth century commentator on the Pauline corpus. This belief, later attributed to Ambrose and Augustine, "survived in medieval canon law, thereby prescribing women's inferior status in church and society."[89] In this sense "God-alien femaleness" may owe less to patristic exegesis *per se* and more to what Børresen herself calls "theological inculturation."[90]

Let us return to the theological quandary expressed by Soskice:

> We find ourselves to this very day torn between two positions which are each compelling but seem at the same time incompatible. We must say that, Christologically speaking, women and men cannot be different, for 'all will bear the image of the man of heaven'. But we must also say that sexual difference is not, or should not be, a matter of theological indifference. Genesis 1 suggests that sexual difference has something to tell us, not just about human beings, but about God in whose image they are made, male and female. The unresolved question then is: where, why and how does sexual difference make a difference?[91]

---

87. Trible, *Rhetoric of Sexuality*, 132–33.
88. Bird, *Faith, Feminism and the Forum of Scripture*, 62.
89. See Børresen, "Patristic Interpretation of Gen 1,27 and 1 Cor 11,7," 191.
90. See Børresen, "Introduction: *Imago Dei* as Inculturated Doctrine," 4.
91. Soskice, *Kindness of God*, 45.

In highlighting that "all will bear the image of the man of heaven," Soskice is referring to 1 Corinthians 15:49: "Just as we have borne the image of the man of dust, we shall also bear the image of the man of heaven." On this basis, what applies in terms of the man of heaven also applies in terms of the man of dust. To bear the image of the man of dust or of heaven refers, in this context, to what Hill calls "substance." As noted, Hill's discernment that interpersonal human relationships mirror divine relationships is premised on a *unity* of substance (or equality of nature) that is also *diversity* of priority: "as the Son is from the Father, so is the woman from the man."[92]

The introductory chapter to this book drew attention to an alleged medieval debate about whether women are human or not. An entry in *The History of the Franks* by St Gregory of Tours suggests that the question was resolved by invoking the creation texts: "'Male and female he created them,' and called their name Adam, which means earthly man; even so He called the woman Eve, yet of both He used the word 'man.'"[93] This argument alludes both to Genesis 1 (male and female he created them) and Genesis 2 (the man and the woman referred to by name). The conclusion (that women are human) hinges on the gender-inclusive nature of "man" as the male collective. Feminist theologians may take issue with a male collective term. What then is to be made of women bearing "the image of the man of heaven"?

Apart from Soskice I have not found this Christological issue addressed by any modern feminist writer. The nature of the resurrected body was, however, canvassed in the early church. "Gregory of Nyssa believed that the acquisition of genitalia was implied in the first couple's post-lapsarian 'clothing with skins' and that the resurrected body would be sexless," reports Soskice.[94] As she points out, Augustine disputed this kind of thinking:

> The Christological texts weighed heavily with the Fathers. If Jesus Christ, unquestionably male, is the image of the invisible God, and we will all bear the image of the 'man of heaven', then it seemed reasonable to some to conclude that women will be resurrected as men. Augustine to his lasting credit said 'no' to this and rejected at the same time the more orthodox view,

---

92. See Hill on Augustine, *The Trinity*, XII, 338 n. 22.

93. See Børresen, "God's Image. Is woman excluded? Medieval Interpretation of Gen. 1,27 and 1 Cor.11,7," 210.

94. Soskice: *Kindness of God*, 45 n. 15.

that the resurrected body will be 'sexless'. Those who hold the woman's sex to be a defect or something necessitated only by the Fall, he believes, are quite wrong. Women will be resurrected as women in heaven, although without inciting lust. In saying this, Augustine sought to avoid the inference that woman, on her own, could not be in the image of God.[95]

If Christian anthropology has attributed an alternative view to Augustine about the inclusive nature of the *imago Dei*, it would seem that women's inferior status in church and society rests on a false premise.

A key passage in this regard is Ephesians 4:13 about attaining "the perfection of manhood" in Christ. Augustine writes:

> If . . . this passage is to be referred to the form of the resurrected body, what is there to prevent our supposing that the mention of 'man' implies 'woman' also, *vir* being used here for *homo* ('human being')? There is a similar use in the verse, 'Blessed is the man (*vir*) who fears the Lord', which obviously includes the women who fear him.[96]

The Latin word for "man" (*vir*) can be used to imply the non-gendered inclusive term (*homo*), says Augustine. The same options are available in Greek. In Acts 17:34 the Greek word for "man" (*anēr*) is used to include a woman, Damaris. I will return to the male collective along with implications for women's identity in chapter 9.

"We must say that, Christologically speaking, women and men cannot be different, for 'all will bear the image of the man of heaven,'" says Soskice. Yet Augustine assumes that women will be resurrected as women, arguing against those who believed that everyone would be resurrected as men. His argument entails a gender-inclusive sense of *vir*.[97] While not addressing the *imago Dei* directly, it does impinge on it as Soskice indicates. Augustine's insistence that the female body continues in the resurrection is hardly compatible with the "God-alien femaleness" detected by Børresen. I stated above that I had not found a modern feminist treatment of what it means for women to bear "the image of the man of heaven." At one point, Børresen acknowledges Augustine's argument in this area but does not discuss the status of women in the resurrection.[98]

---

95. Soskice: *Kindness of God*, 44–45.
96. Augustine, *City of God* XXII, 18. See Psalm 112:1.
97. See Augustine, *City of God* XXII, 17.
98. Børresen cites Augustine's treatment of this issue in *De civitate Dei* 22, 17. See

If feminist writers omit this matter of Christology, where does this leave contemporary theological anthropology?

In terms of anthropology, Børresen states that "contemporary biblical interpretation utilises three equality strategies, all of which are inherited from patristic exegesis." Here is her rendition of these strategies:

> 1. The sexual differentiation expressed in Gen 1,27b "male and female he created them," is *disconnected* from the consecutive blessing of fertility in Gen 1,28 and *linked* to the preceding image text of Gen 1,26–27a: "Let us make Adam (collective male) in our image, according to our likeness . . . And God created Adam in his image, in the image of God he created him."
> 2. Paul's argument for men's exclusive God-likeness in 1 Cor. 11,7: "For man should not cover his head, since he is the image and glory of God, but woman is the glory of man," is *veiled*. In context, Gen 1,26–27a is here combined with God's formation of Adam from clods in the soil and blowing into his nostrils the breath of life, according to Gen 2,7. In 1 Cor 11,8–9, Paul asserts man's theomorphic precedence in terms of woman's derivative formation from Adam's rib, as "an aid fit for him," according to Gen. 2,18,21–23. 3. The *negating* citation of Gen. 1,27b in Gal 3,28: "there is not male and female, for you are all one (collective male) in Christ," is interpreted as *including* women instead of *abolishing* femaleness.[99]

In this representation of "contemporary biblical interpretation" women are said to be made in God's image due to their inclusion in the collective male (Adam). Women are also said to be included in Christ on the basis that all are one (collective male). The second point (invoking Genesis 2 and 1 Corinthians 11:8–9) outlines the terms on which women are included. These "equality strategies," says Børresen, build upon "the church Father's efforts to insert women as God-like and therefore fully human, their *sub-male* femaleness notwithstanding."[100] But what is to be made of alleged "sub-male femaleness" in relation to Augustine's insistence that women will be resurrected as women?

These are complex issues. Further complexity is introduced in the intimation that patristic exegesis was at fault (in terms of modern source theory) in assuming a link between Genesis 1:27b ("male and female

---

"Patristic Interpretation of Gen 1,27 and 1 Cor 11,7," 202–3.

99. Børresen, "Patristic Interpretation of Gen 1,27 and 1 Cor 11,7," 188. Børresen's italics.

100. Børresen, "Patristic Interpretation of Gen 1,27 and 1 Cor 11,7," 188.

Hā'ādām

he created them") and the preceding "image text." As I understand her, Børresen wishes to retain the assertion of "modern theological anthropology" that "both women and men are fully God-like in their male or female humanity" while discarding underlying "equality strategies" inherited from patristic exegesis. But does modern source theory support the assertion? Historian of religion, Anders Hultgård indicates that much work done in the field of feminist theology has projected a genderless God back into biblical times and then reinterpreted the text to include women.[101] This is to outline a feminist equality strategy. But exegetical difficulties may persist. Wholesale rejection of biblical typology disallows consideration of what it means for women to "bear the image of the man of heaven."

For Soskice, the resurrected body is a bar to sexual differentiation: "women and men cannot be different for 'all will bear the image of the man of heaven.'"[102] She goes on to say, however, that Genesis 1 indicates that "sexual difference is not, or should not be, a matter of theological indifference." We may compare these remarks with what Bird and Trible have to say about the *imago Dei*. Bird argues for a latter-day egalitarian reading of Genesis 1. Trible includes women in the *imago Dei* in terms of her hermeneutical clue of feminism but distances sexual differentiation from likeness to God in her exegesis of Genesis 1:26–27. I suggest that the abstract term "equality" plays a similar role to Augustine's *sapientia*. Augustine juxtaposes "two logically *irreconcilable* themes: androcentic typology and asexual God-likeness," with a "resulting incoherence between embodied humanity and bodiless *imago Dei*," says Børresen.[103] Equality as a touchstone for God-likeness is also asexual.

Sexual difference, says Soskice, should not be a matter of theological indifference. By theological, Soskice means that this is no mere question of anthropology: "Genesis 1 suggests that sexual difference has something to tell us, not just about human beings, but about God in whose image they are made, male and female."[104] Børresen responds differently: "When both women and men are understood to be theomorphic, God can be described by both male and female metaphors."[105] This implies

---

101. Hultgård, "God and Image of Woman in Early Jewish Religion," 29.
102. Soskice, *Kindness of God*, 45.
103. See Børresen, "Patristic Interpretation of Gen 1,27 and 1 Cor 11,7," 204.
104. Soskice, *Kindness of God*, 45.
105. Børresen, "Introduction, *Imago Dei* as Inculturated Doctrine," 4.

that theology is primarily about anthropology along the lines described by Ruether: "Feminist theology starts with anthropology rather than deducing male-female relations from an *a priori* definition of God . . . It then constructs images of God that will better manifest and promote the full realization of human potential for women and men."[106]

Børresen tracks what she calls the "gradual *humanization* of *imago Dei*."[107] But a gradual humanization may take us closer to anthropology and further away from theology proper. As represented by Børresen, innovation in this respect stems from "accommodation to post-patriarchal culture in western Europe and North America."[108] Similarly, Bird describes an ongoing cultural conversation with the ancient texts. I suspect that Trible's feminist hermeneutical clue feeds into this kind of conversation. Method aside, the result is to my mind unsatisfactory.

This chapter began by borrowing a character from *The Wizard of Oz*, the strange-looking Hammer Head with no arms and a collapsible neck. I suggested that this figure appearing on a hillside could serve to illustrate Trible's surmise about a primal "earth creature" arising from the earth. Trible does not say directly that a genderless earth creature presupposes a genderless God. The feminist method outlined by Ruether, however, opens the door to this kind of resemblance. A genderless *imago Dei*, however, does not answer the question about women's likeness to God. As indicated above, I believe the questions posed by Soskice and others are not beyond an exegetical resolution. My next chapter will address New Testament exegesis. I will enlarge on Hill's observations about 1 Corinthians 11 and attempt to answer Soskice's question about where, why and how sexual difference makes a difference.

---

106. See Ruether, "Christian Tradition and Feminist Hermeneutics," 286–87.
107. See Børresen, "Introduction, *Imago Dei* as Inculturated Doctrine," 3.
108. See Børresen, "Introduction, *Imago Dei* as Inculturated Doctrine," 3–4.

6

Gender as Metaphor

IN THE LAND MADE of china Dorothy encounters a Princess and offers to take her back to Kansas to stand as a little figurine on her aunt's mantelpiece. The Princess refuses this offer on the grounds that china figures can only talk and move around in their own country. Elsewhere their joints stiffen so that they become no more than decorative objects. Dorothy accepts that the Princess would unhappy outside her own land and bids her an amicable farewell.[1]

Earlier chapters in this book have attempted to follow the orientation of gendered language for the things of God on the understanding that such language functions as a window on the otherwise unknown. I refer to this kind of orientation as symbolic reference. One can liken this kind of reference to that of a figurine standing on a mantelpiece. A figurine of a shepherdess, for example, offers a glimpse of what a real shepherdess might once have looked like. But this is a static glimpse. The china figurine on the mantelpiece does not move or interact.

In this book I have emphasized the reality-depicting orientation of biblical imagery in order to distinguish it from the kind of illustrative projection which does not make this claim. My presentation of symbolic reference runs counter to the illustrative pictures of Sallie McFague's "metaphorical theology." I will make some further distinctions here. In standard usage "symbol" and "metaphor" are both means to offer

---

1. See Baum, *Wizard of Oz*, chapter 20.

a glimpse of the otherwise unknown. In this sense both function as a means of symbolic reference. In a narrower sense there is a difference between the two. The focus in "symbol," in its specific application, is on what can be seen, as in a figurine standing on a mantelpiece. "Metaphor" is word-oriented in a way that allows for encounter and relationship. It could be described as a means to set symbols free so that they can talk and move around. The distinction between "symbol" and "metaphor" may not always be as sharp as this but would seem applicable to the complexity of the *imago Dei*.

This brings me to a further point. Figurines made of china can be classed as symbols of flesh and blood humans. The Princess figurine and the girl (Dorothy) are both female; in this sense one functions as a symbol of the other. But flesh and blood females are not bound by the stylized representation of a figurine. This is not to say that static representation is unimportant. As creatures imaging our creator, we are in the position of the figurine. In taking the *imago Dei* seriously, we recognize our reality-depicting orientation. But there is more to be said. On a scale much larger than that of humanity to china figurine, God is not limited by the trajectory of human sexuality.

A remark by Janet Martin Soskice is noteworthy here. Chapter 3 cited Elizabeth Johnson on maternal language for the Holy Spirit in early Syriac Christianity, language subsequently redirected toward "holy mother the church" and Mary.[2] Soskice offers more detail about the role of the original language:

> Susan Ashbrook Harvey points out that Syriac Christians, in feminizing the Spirit, did not posit a female deity alongside or in distinction to a male deity. Such concrete identities were available in the pagan deities of the Syrian Orient, 'where a triad of mother, father, and son was a common configuration of divinity'. . . . Harvey highlights the wealth of bodily and gendered metaphors, but also the way in which they are layered in paradoxical and conflicting sequences: 'Roles are reversed, fused, inverted: no one is simply who they seem to be. More accurately, everyone is *more than* they seem to be—Mary is more than a woman in what she does; the Father and the Spirit are more than one gender can convey in the effort to glimpse their

---

2. Johnson, *She Who Is*, 86.

works. Gender is thus shown to be important, even crucial, to identity—but not one specific gender."[3]

"In this rhetorical excess," comments Soskice, "God is not lacking gender but exceeds gender—that to which our human experience of gender and physicality feebly but really points." We may note that Mary also has a part to play. She interacts with the divine level in a way that I will come to later.

Our human experience of gender and physicality feebly but really points to God, says Soskice. That is the orientation of symbolic reference. Perhaps, however, physicality and gendered relationships point to God in different ways. This is where my distinction between "symbol" in its narrow sense and "metaphor" comes into play. C. S. Lewis writes that "one of the ends for which sex was created was to symbolize to us the hidden things of God."[4] His focus is on the sexes as visible symbols, as they might appear on the mantelpiece. Harvey writes about flexibility of *roles*. In their own land figurines can talk and move about.

In this chapter I will consider gender as an expression of relationship. As indicated in the citation of Harvey, there are various levels to this: human, divine, also the divine-human level as is mooted in the role of Mary, mother of Jesus. I will suggest that gendered identity is not limited either to the static role of physical sex or to the more flexible role of interaction between the sexes; rather, both aspects illuminate both. In the New Testament, an addition to the *imago Dei* at the divine-human level extends the scope of gendered possibility as will be seen.

The sketch of the early Syriac tradition offered by Harvey would suggest a nuanced approach to gender in the early church. Chapter 4 indicated that this was not the only response of the early church. More recent assumptions would cast doubt on the possibility of encounter between humanity and the Godhead. This skepticism is paralleled by skepticism about the covenantal encounter of linguistic usage. Denial of such interaction and encounter impedes a nuanced reading of gender, including implications of the new covenant.

In my illustration from *The Wizard of Oz*, the Princess figurine would become no more than a decorative object if placed on the mantelpiece. Much feminist interpretation would detect this kind of attitude to

---

3. See Soskice, *Kindness of God*, 114–15, citing S. Ashbrook Harvey (1993). "Feminine Imagery for the Divine: The Holy Spirit, the Odes of Solomon, and the early Syriac Tradition." (Italics in the text as cited.)

4. Lewis, "Priestesses in the Church?," 92.

women in Christian tradition. Johnson reports the feminist response: a wish to shatter "the stranglehold on religious language of God-He."[5] She justifies this procedure on traditional grounds: "all words for God, being finite, fall short of their intended goal." This is to emphasize the negative side of the tradition in contrast with Soskice's assertion that our human experience of gender and physicality feebly but really points to God. Johnson goes on to qualify her rejection of "God-He" language, conceding that "traditional male symbols of God, key among them the image of father," could be revived in a firmament more favorable to women. Shattering is nevertheless a blunt instrument. Religious language may cease to feebly but really point to God and fail to point heavenward at all.

What is needed, I submit, is to restore the Princess to her own land. Rather than shattering a "stranglehold," this chapter explores the complexity of roles and role-reversals in the Pauline presentation of the *imago Dei*. But before entering the exegetical arena, I consider key questions, posed by psychoanalyst Luce Irigaray, in relation to her radical alternative to a sacramental universe. I then move to Lone Fatum's presentation of alleged stereotypes for women in the New Testament era.

RETHINKING SEXUAL DIFFERENCE

French feminist theorists, says Soskice, "are less likely than their Anglo-American counterparts to suppose that one can effect lasting change or achieve 'equality' while ignoring the sexed nature of texts which, historically, have informed Western intellectual culture and whose values have been exported round the world."[6] As an example, Soskice cites the question about "equality" posed by Irigaray: "equal to whom?" Soskice indicates the issues behind the question and suggests that feminist theologians would do well to take note of them: "If the answer remains 'to men', then the male is still supplying the norm around which the female or the neuter is constructed, with the further disadvantage that this andromorphism is concealed." She continues: "What we need, according to Irigaray, is to rethink sexual difference."

The quest for "equality" encompasses a broad way of thinking as well as its effect on sexual difference. Irigaray distances herself from the "norm" of Western intellectual culture in a radical way. Chapter 2 touched

---

5. See Johnson, *She Who Is*, 39–40; cf. 103.
6. See Soskice, *Kindness of God*, 107–8.

Gender as Metaphor

on her "horizon of sexual difference"[7] in which all things linguistic are abandoned, including "God—that guarantee of the meaning or non-meaning of the whole."[8] Elizabeth Johnson might not go to this extreme. She does, however, signal that the term "God" may have to be abandoned at some stage.[9] The scope of this exercise should not be underestimated.

The religious model of "God the father," states Sallie McFague, "has established a hegemony over the Western religious consciousness which it is the task of metaphorical theology to break."[10] Elsewhere she says that the ability to employ the metaphor "God the Father" (with a capital F at this point) "seems to rest on a confidence that . . . the universe is in some sense sacramental, that God is somehow the true and original father, that all things are connected among themselves because they are connected in God."[11] On this basis, the term "Father" feebly but really points to God. Other metaphors of "transference" also rely on a confidence in a sacramental universe, attests McFague. Chapter 1 considered the role of a sacramental universe in underpinning linguistic efficacy. To shatter religious language of God-He is, consequently, to shatter more than religious language. Irigaray takes the process to its extreme.

Before attempting to shatter something, it is well to be sure of one's target. The last section of chapter 5 began by contrasting a feminist perception of the patriarchal tradition, as represented by Phyllis Trible, with actual statements by Augustine. It is also well to consider what will be put in its place. Chapter 5 noted a general trend in feminist reinterpretation of key passages in which a genderless God reflects a genderless humanity, a perception understood to include women on the same footing as men. But is the male still supplying the "norm" around which this neuter is constructed?

This book has drawn attention to Rosemary Ruether's statement that feminist theology begins with anthropology. Feminism, says Ruether, "has taken its stand on an expanded unitary view of human nature, possessed fully and equally by both men and women."[12] Based on this androgynous anthropology, feminist theology "constructs images of God

---

7. *Irigaray Reader*, 164.
8. *Irigaray Reader*, 218.
9. Johnson, *She Who Is*, 44.
10. McFague, *Metaphorical Theology*, 29.
11. McFague, *Speaking in Parables*, 106.
12. See Ruether, "Christian Tradition and Feminist Hermeneutics," 286–87.

that will better manifest and promote the full realization of human potential for women and men." Soskice reports that Irigaray "is suspicious of the rush to androgyny that she detects in some feminist thought. The so-called androgynous ideal will still be male-formed."[13] In a quest to rethink sexual difference, anthropology, images of God, and broad ways of thinking intermingle in ways that may be difficult to disentangle.

"Genesis 1 suggests that sexual difference has something to tell us, not just about human beings, but about God in whose image they are made, male and female," says Soskice. She adds: "The unresolved question then is: where, why and how does sexual difference make a difference?"[14] Has the feminist movement supplied an answer? In protest against "God-alien femaleness," Kari Elisabeth Børresen advocates for both women and men being understood as "theomorphic."[15] Following on from this assumption, "God can be described by both male and female metaphors." Elizabeth Johnson writes that "the way in which a faith community shapes language about God implicitly represents what it takes to be the highest good, the profoundest truth, the most appealing beauty."[16] The shape of language is in the first instance abstract and non-gendered. While apparently gendered, SHE WHO IS follows on from this kind of language: "if being female is an excellence, if what makes women exist as women in all difference is participation in divine being . . .SHE WHO IS can be spoken as a robust, appropriate name for God."[17] The highest good, the profoundest truth, the most appealing beauty—but does such naming tell us anything about God *qua* God or about where, why and how sexual difference makes a difference?

In Irigaray's "horizon of sexual difference," reports Margaret Whitford, men and women would function as bridges between past and future, opening up "a kind of re-creation of the world."[18] Elaine Graham states that Irigaray uses female morphology as a starting-point to "rewrite Western epistemology and ontology," restoring the significance of "the body, passion, libido and the unconscious as legitimate foundations of

---

13. Soskice, *Kindness of God*, 108.
14. Soskice, *Kindness of God*, 45.
15. Børresen, "Introduction: *Imago Dei as Inculturated Doctrine*," 4.
16. Johnson, *She Who Is*, 4.
17. Johnson, *She Who Is*, 242–43.
18. *Irigaray Reader*, 164.

knowledge and selfhood."¹⁹ But an "ideal" intentionally divorced from Western epistemology and ontology becomes an exercise in projection. Graham observes further: "By placing the female body outside patriarchal culture . . . Irigaray risks rendering women's bodies immaterial and rhetorical, rather than empirical and rooted in social relations." On these terms, what becomes of sexual difference? I will return to these matters in later chapters.

In the midst of this, I question whether Christian orthodoxy, properly understood, is really conducive to what Børresen calls God-alien femaleness.[20] I find Soskice of assistance here. She draws attention to the charge, by Irigaray and others, that the legacy of Western metaphysics reduces "all others to the economy of the Same" in terms of "a masculine logic."[21] Soskice refers to the "ego's era," the "Cartesian period" (between the sixteenth and twentieth centuries).[22] The "God" of this era, she says, is viewed by secular feminism as the divine guarantor of the veracity of the insights of the [male] Cartesian subject. This "God's-eye view," continues Soskice, "separates self from other, but there is never any genuine other, always just the 'economy of the Same.'" But is this a legacy of Christian orthodoxy or of patriarchal monotheism, as in what Soskice calls "sloppy eighteenth-century rhetoric of the 'fatherhood of God and the brotherhood of man'"?[23]

As seen in my Introduction, Irigaray asks: "are the peoples of monotheism ready to assert that their God is a woman?"[24] Soskice cites Jürgen Moltmann on the connection between a patriarchal ordering of the world and a monotheistic one.[25] One might go further. If monotheism and an "economy of the Same" go together, is a feminist "ideal" exempt from this tendency? Does Irigaray's aspiration to "rewrite Western epistemology and ontology" really challenge this "norm"?

A philosophy governed by economies of One and the Same "could never be a Christian metaphysics, although it might be a particular

19. See Graham, *Making the Difference*, 136–38.

20. Børresen, "Patristic Interpretation of Gen 1,27 and 1 Cor 11,7," 187.

21. See Soskice, *Kindness of God*, 105; cf. 119, citing Irigaray, *This Sex which is not One*, 74.

22. See Soskice, *Kindness of God*, 121–22. She cites Lacan for the term "ego's era."

23. Soskice, *Kindness of God*, 83.

24. *Irigaray Reader*, 185.

25. Soskice, *Kindness of God*, 82. Soskice quotes Moltmann, "The Motherly Father: Is Trinitarian Patripassianism Replacing Theological Patriarchalism?"

Neoplatonic heresy,"[26] says Soskice. She contrasts the tendency towards monotheism with "the great efforts made by theologians and philosophers to give account of God's Being as *to-be-related*." She adds: "We may now stand at a moment of evangelical opportunity in the West, a time in which Christians not only need to hear a fully relational account of the Trinitarian life of God, but may also be receptive of it."

Why should a fully relational account of the trinitarian life constitute a moment of evangelical opportunity? Let us return to Irigaray's questions. She asks: apart from the male-formed one, what other ideal have we in which to think? She also says that we need to rethink sexual difference. If a relational account of the trinitarian life offers a clue towards rethinking the way we think, does the trinitarian Godhead also assist us to rethink sexual difference? Soskice is less optimistic about this. She writes:

> The doctrine of the Trinity tells us nothing about how men and women should relate to one another as males and females. It does not show that all men should be like the "father" and all women model themselves on a feminized Spirit. In this sense the doctrine tells us nothing about sexual difference. But it does let us glimpse what it is, most truly, to be: "to-be" most fully is "to-be-related" in difference.[27]

According to Soskice, "'to-be-related' in difference" has relevance for human nature if not for gendered human nature. But can we expect a moment of evangelical opportunity if Irigaray's second question remains unanswered?

Moltmann has something to say in this area. Whether his language about God promotes a fully relational life, either at the trinitarian or human level, is another matter. Soskice cites his perception of gendered ambivalence in the roles of God the Father:

> A father who both *begets* and *gives birth* to his son is no mere male father. He is a motherly father. He can no longer be defined as single-sexed and male, but becomes bisexual or transsexual. He is the *motherly Father* of his *only-born Son*, and at the same time the *fatherly Father* of his *only-begotten Son* . . . According to the Council of Toledo of 675 'we must believe that the Son was not made out of nothing . . . but from the womb of the

---

26. Soskice, *Kindness of God*, 119.
27. Soskice, *Kindness of God*, 124.

Father . . . that is he was begotten or born . . . from the father's own being'. Whatever this declaration may be supposed to be saying about the gynaecology of the Father, these bisexual affirmations imply a radical denial of patriarchal monotheism."[28]

Soskice comments that some feminists may be dissatisfied with a strategy of ascribing motherly attributes to the "father."

This description may offer a corrective to patriarchy. I would question whether it would challenge monotheism. Is it not more likely to favor an androgynous perception of God which, says Irigaray, will still be male-formed? Moltmann refers to God the Father as "bisexual or transsexual" and speaks of "the gynaecology of the Father." One is in danger here of an over-literalistic reading on a par with pagan religions described by Susan Ashbrook Harvey above. Simplistic equivalence supports a projection of human traits onto the divine nature.[29] However inadvertently, God is presented in the image of humanity, not the other way around. Further, such language draws attention away from the relationships *between* the Persons of the Trinity.

I return now to Dorothy's encounter with the princess figurine. In her own land, the princess can talk and move about. Elsewhere her joints stiffen. She becomes a mere decorative object on the mantelpiece. I have suggested that the *imago Dei* operates in both these ways. In their visible embodiment, the sexes function as symbols of the Godhead. In their gendered relationships, male and female interact with each other in a way that reflects trinitarian relationships. To speak of the "gynecology" of the Father would, on my view, confuse the correspondences presented by physical embodiment *per se* and gendered interaction.

If the doctrine of the Trinity tells us nothing about sexual difference what becomes of Irigaray's remark that we need to rethink sexual difference? I think Soskice misses something here. At this point I return to Edmund Hill's observations on 1 Corinthians 11:1–16. But before doing so, I will consider a feminist interpretation of this passage. Lone Fatum detects a unitary *imago Dei* on male terms in key Pauline passages, accompanied by an alleged gender-free option for women in the New Testament era. I argue that these perceptions, along with feminist reinterpretation,

---

28. Soskice, *Kindness of God*, 82–83, citing Moltmann, "The Motherly Father."

29. Cf. Soskice, *Kindness of God*, 113. Soskice points out that conceiving the Holy Spirit in terms of a feminine stereotype feeds "the unorthodox suggestion that there is sexual difference in the Trinity."

pertain to a stiffening of categories. Such categories are a far cry from an account of God's Being (and human being) as *to-be-related*.

PATRIARCHY OR PSEUDO-MASCULINITY?

A combination of asexual God-likeness and androcentric typology is logically irreconcilable, says Kari Elisabeth Børresen.[30] As seen in chapter 5, she indicates some doubt about which is the greater evil of the two. Logically, asexual God-likeness should allow full religious status for both sexes. But the asexual component of God-likeness includes women in the *imago Dei* in "man-like disguise," as Børresen puts it. This, she says, sharpens "the conflict between rational privilege and subordinate female humanity."[31] Børresen detects these tendencies in patristic interpretation, in particular in Augustine's theory of the *imago Dei*. Lone Fatum goes so far as to detect these tendencies in contrasting options for women in the Pauline churches of the New Testament.

Lone Fatum's interesting, but I think mistaken, remarks about women in the Pauline congregations highlight current confusion about the *imago Dei*. Fatum parts company with feminists who "harmonize" Galatians 3:28 and 1 Corinthians 11:2–16 in terms of theory versus practice:

> Apart from being the justification for a theological neutralization of 1 Cor 11,3–9 by means of Gal 3,28 this reduction leads to an overall distorted and diffused approach to 1 Cor 11,2–16 . . . [This passage] consists of both theory and practice and vv. 3–9 are, theologically assessed, as much fundamental theory as Gal 3,28. Only theological prejudice can decide that one theory should be accorded greater normative importance than the other, or that one fundamental saying on the relationship between man and woman . . . should take precedence of another and be accepted at face value as the eschatological idea par excellence.[32]

The charge of "theological prejudice" supplying "normative importance" to one passage in preference to another could well apply to Phyllis Trible's hermeneutical clue of feminism, as explored in chapter 5. I will return to this point.

30. Børresen, "Patristic Interpretation of Gen 1,27 and 1 Cor 11,7," 205.
31. Børresen, "Patristic Interpretation of Gen 1,27 and 1 Cor 11,7," 201.
32. Fatum, "Image of God and Glory of Man," 52–53.

Fatum argues that "Paul is not divided against himself."[33] Instead, he offers two alternatives for women, *either* annulment of sexuality in the eschatological reality of Christ (as exemplified by Galatians 3:28) *or* marriage and domination by males according to what she terms "creation theology" and "pre-christology" (as exemplified by 1 Corinthians 11:2–16):[34]

> Seeing married women in dependence of their husbands in 11,2–16 and not of Christ, Paul is merely maintaining his view from 7,32–35 in coherence with his point in 7,1–7, establishing marriage as a concession, secondary in charismatic value compared to the ideal asceticism.[35]

For Fatum, "male and female" in Galatians 3:28 refers back to Genesis 1:27b. Somewhat similarly to Phyllis Bird, Fatum sees the "man" of Genesis 1:27a as a non-inclusive term, an understanding that affects her interpretation of the redeemed model:

> The sexual characterization in male and female adding female as a secondary component to the man of creation is thus . . . not only an addition to the idea of man created in God's image, it is also a breach with the idea of man as a human entity and, as such, at one with God's creation. Thus, when Gal 3,28c speaks of the annulment of sexual differentiation, it must be taken to mean both that the addition has been annulled, and the breach healed; through Christ man has again become what he originally was, a unity and an entity in God's image.[36]

On this interpretation, a woman becomes a "son of God" by giving up her sexuality and reproductive functions and becoming male, hence joining in with the original idea of the image of God. But this freedom in Christ "does not allow Christian women any opportunity of being affirmed as women, but fixes them in a state of asexuality dependent on the androcentric concept of human normality."[37]

There are several problems for this view. Firstly, asceticism as a qualification for being a son of God only applies to women. Christian

---

33. Fatum, "Image of God and Glory of Man," 78.
34. Fatum, "Image of God and Glory of Man," 77.
35. Fatum, "Image of God and Glory of Man," 108, n. 76.
36. Fatum, "Image of God and Glory of Man," 62. The ideal of man as a unity is at odds with "the man" of Genesis 2 for whom "it was not good to be alone."
37. Fatum, "Image of God and Glory of Man," 79.

husbands still qualify as being in the image of God. This is not easily reconciled with the appeal to 1 Corinthians 7. While Paul expresses a personal preference for celibacy, his reason is specific: to focus on "affairs of the Lord," (verses 32–34) in "the impending crisis," (verse 26). There is no sense here or elsewhere in the New Testament that the purpose of asceticism is to restore the original unity, on male terms, of created humanity.[38] Additionally, it is not clear how Fatum's view of married Christian women accords with Paul's statement that all who are baptized are "one in Christ" and "heirs according to the promise," unless Christian wives were not baptized.

For Fatum, there is a dichotomy between creation theology and Christology. The references to Christ in 1 Corinthians 11 (verses 3 and 11) are judged to carry "no christological impact" and offer "no basis on which to establish an eschatological coherence" with Galatians 3:28.[39] Fatum finds 1 Corinthians 11:2–16 to be out of keeping with 1 Corinthians in general, "attesting to the presupposition that matters of gender and sexuality are in themselves a contradiction of Christ, belonging to this world of pre-christological order."[40] But if this is so, it seems odd that the passage should be introduced by verse 1 (which she omits from consideration) "be imitators of me as I am of Christ" and that 1 Corinthians 11:1–16 should be the lead passage for consideration of order in the Church.[41] The symbolic import of gender as a reflection of Christ and the Church is absent from her thinking.

Fatum concludes that both female asceticism and female sexuality were organized on "androcentric" terms. She disagrees with the feminist theory that ascetic women experienced a golden age of freedom in Pauline congregations (detected in Galatians 3:28) that was later lost (as evidenced, for example, in 1 Timothy 2) on the grounds that this was from the first

---

38. If women are included in the category of "sons of God," men are included in the category of the body or bride of Christ. These inclusive categories are not good evidence of the annulment of either sex.

39. Fatum, "Image of God and Glory of Man," 122, n. 96. Disallowing the Christological import of "Christ" in verse 3 is somewhat at odds with Fatum's insistence that vv. 3–9 are as theologically fundamental in theory as Galatians 3:28.

40. Fatum, "Image of God and Glory of Man," 119, n. 91.

41. Cf., however, Calvin's remark regarding 1 Corinthians 11:1: "This shows how badly the chapters have been divided, because this sentence has been separated from the preceding sentences, to which it belongs by right, and joined to those which follow, to which it is quite irrelevant": *Calvin's Commentaries: The First Epistle of Paul the Apostle to the Corinthians*, 226.

"a freedom on androcentrically dualistic terms."[42] Nevertheless, she appears to hold a feminist understanding in which ideal freedom is seen as freedom *from* male control rather than as freedom *for* life in Christ.

As seen above, Fatum rejects the kind of "harmonization" which would suggest that, for Paul, Galatians 3:28 was a matter of theory as opposed to his practice, expressed in 1 Corinthians 2–11. She argues against this interpretation on exegetical grounds. Her alternative proposal offers another kind of harmonization: a common thread of male control in both options allegedly offered to women. This latter kind of harmonization is also problematic, exegetically speaking. Fatum's view rests on the prior hermeneutical assumption of an original male unity, another example perhaps of "theological prejudice" at work.

Børresen writes that asexual God-likeness and androcentric typology are logically irreconcilable. Fatum's harmonization includes an androcentric component in asexual God-likeness. I disagree with Fatum's theory. Nevertheless, I believe that there is much to be said for being precise about what is at issue in Galatians 3:28 and 1 Corinthians 11:1–16. I come to this now.

FROM CREATION TO NEW COVENANT

My Introduction drew attention to Soskice's citation of Jewish writer, Tikva Frymer-Kensky:

> Whatever the precise interpretation, the plural nature of the creation of humanity applies to both the creator ("we") and the creature ("he created them male and female"). Social relationship is an indispensable part of both human nature and human purpose and there can be no utterly single human being.[43]

This is a Jewish attestation to the plural nature of both creator and creature. Social relationship is presented as intrinsic both to God the creator and to humanity. Further, the social relationship for humanity is located in sexual difference ("he created them male and female"). This observation runs counter to Lone Fatum's assumption that sexual differentiation

---

42. Fatum, "Image of God and Glory of Man," 80–81.

43. See Soskice, *Kindness of God*, 50–51 n 25, citing Frymer-Kensky, *Studies in Bible and Feminist Criticism*, 101.

is "an addition to the idea of man created in God's image" which is annulled in the new covenant.[44]

For Fatum, man created in God's image appears to reflect a monotheistic creator: the man of creation is a single entity reflecting the creator as a single entity. Edmund Hill's interpretation of I Corinthians 11:1–16 offers an alternative picture: social relationship is intrinsic to the Godhead and also to humanity made in God's image. Hill states that "the man" and "the woman" of the Corinthians passage refer back to Genesis 2. While I agree with Hill, I think there is more to be said on this point. I will come to this below.

The real challenge to the idea that women are made in the image of God comes not from the Old Testament but from the New. No New Testament author directly affirms that women are made in the image of God.[45] 1 Corinthians 11:7 states, "For a man ought not to have his head veiled, since he is the image and reflection [glory] of God; but woman is the reflection [glory] of man." Colossians teaches that Jesus "is the image of the invisible God" (1:15) and later that the new nature in Christ "is being renewed in knowledge according to the image of its creator" (Colossians 3: 10). The new nature (applying to both males and females) is in Christ, the visible risen *man* who is the image of the invisible God. Why, one may ask, is there such an emphasis on the masculine, with no apparent emphasis on the feminine in terms of the *imago Dei*?

I said above that Lone Fatum's proposal offers a kind of harmonization, based on her view that "through Christ man has again become what he originally was, a unity and an entity in God's image."[46] In Fatum's harmonization, women enter into this unity either through subordination in marriage or through ascetic renunciation of femaleness. This solution bears some resemblance to the patristic tendency to interpret Genesis 1 in the light of Genesis 2, with emphasis on the woman's role of helper. On the other hand, Fatum's harmonization does not accord with Augustine's insistence that women will be resurrected as women. John Calvin offers a further slant on these matters. Jane Dempsey Douglass writes:

> Calvin explicitly asks whether there is a contradiction between Paul's argument in 1 Cor. 11:7 and Gal 3:28. He decides that the difference is the context. The Galatians text with its insistence

---

44. Fatum, "Image of God and Glory of Man," 62.
45. James 3:9 comes close.
46. Fatum, "Image of God and Glory of Man," 62

that there is no male nor female has to do with the spiritual kingdom of God ... But he says about 1 Cor 11:7 "... both sexes were created according to the image of God, and Paul urges women, as much as men, to be re-formed according to that image. But when he [Paul] is speaking about image here, he is referring to the conjugal order. Accordingly it has to do with this present life."[47]

For Calvin, the *imago Dei* is either a non-gendered spiritual matter (as in Galatians 3:28) or gender inclusive in a temporary sense (as in the current conjugal order). Again, this leaves out Augustine's view of the resurrected body. Regarding 1 Corinthians 11:3, Calvin writes: "Here [in the civil order] the man is placed in an intermediate position between Christ and the woman, so that Christ is not the Head of the woman."[48] This would imply a subordinate position for the woman *qua* woman in the *imago Dei*.

For Calvin, there is a dichotomy between spiritual equality and gendered inequality. Fatum detects a similar dichotomy in the biblical texts but would go further in discerning its practical application for women in the New Testament era. Calvin's interpretation makes a distinction between "this present life" and "the spiritual kingdom of Christ." His emphasis on spiritual equality beyond "this present life" does not address the ongoing significance of sexual difference.

I come now to my own exegetical discussion of these matters. There is undoubtedly a shift of interest in the New Testament from being created in the image of God, to being "conformed to the image of [God's] Son" (Romans 8:29). But although the focus is different, the creational theme of plurality in unity resurfaces in a new way: instead of two becoming one, many become one in Christ. This new oneness in Christ is said to override old differentiations: "there is no longer Greek and Jew, circumcised and uncircumcised, barbarian, Scythian, slave and free, but Christ is all and in all" (Colossians 3:11). And yet old distinctions still seem to apply: "slaves obey your earthly masters" (verse 22).

The letter to the Colossians, in many ways reminiscent of that to the Galatians, offers a very strong sense of eschatological reality: "So if you have been raised with Christ, seek the things that are above" (Colossians 3:1). At this level there are apparently no distinctions. Although slaves must obey their earthly masters, the new eschatological reality gives this

---

47. Douglass, "Image of God in Women as seen by Luther and Calvin," 255.
48. Calvin, *The First Epistle of Paul to the Corinthians*. 229.

obedience a new dimension: "Whatever your task, put yourselves into it, as done for the Lord" (Colossians 3:23).[49] In the light of this eschatological reality the categories are in a sense exploded. There are no slaves, but only servants of the Lord. There are no free men either. "Masters, treat your slaves justly and fairly, for you know that you also have a Master in heaven" (Colossians 4:1). There is no sense in Colossians (or elsewhere in the New Testament) that serving has the effect of disqualifying anyone from being part of this new community in Christ: rather, serving is of the essence of being part of this new community. Status is given to all, slave and master alike. All are "called in the one body" (Colossians 3:15).

While "male and female" does not appear in the list of exploded categories in Colossians, the eschatological reality plays a part here also. Wives are told to "be subject" to husbands within a context: "as is fitting in the Lord" (Colossians 3:18). One could read this in the sense that submission *per se* is "fitting in the Lord," or in the sense that submission is qualified by what is "fitting in the Lord." Both senses probably apply. In any case there is something reciprocal about submission. Husbands are told to "love [their] wives and never treat them harshly."[50] As Charles Sherlock points out, no one is ever told to force anyone else into subjection in the New Testament.[51] Husbands are not told to ensure that wives submit to them, nor are wives told to ensure that their husbands love them. But, despite the similarity to the "master and slave" exploded category, if we did not possess the letter to the Galatians, we would probably conclude that "male and female" was not an exploded category in the same sense. But we do have Galatians. What are we to make of Galatians 3:28?

Both Galatians and Colossians make much of the oneness we have in Christ. "And let the peace of Christ rule in your hearts to which indeed you were called in the *one* body" (Colossians 3:15). "There is no longer Jew or Greek, there is no longer slave or free, there is no longer male and female; for all of you are *one* in Christ Jesus" (Galatians 3:28). Both letters make use of the image of "putting on" Christ (Galatians 3:27; Colossians 3:10). As we are clothed in Christ, we become one. And this being clothed in Christ apparently includes such things as slaves obeying

---

49. Cf. Lucas *Fullness and Freedom*, 167: "[Paul] wishes [believing slaves] to understand that, in a very real sense, *they are now not serving men at all.*" (Italics in the text.)

50. Cf. Yoder, *The Politics of Jesus*, 171. Yoder draws attention to the revolutionary innovation of Christian ethical thinking: "the subordinate person in the social order is addressed as a moral agent."

51. Sherlock, *Doctrine of Humanity*, 203.

their masters and wives obeying their husbands and the reciprocal commands to masters and husbands (although so-called "house tables" do not appear in Galatians). But does the diversity continue to exist under the clothing of oneness?

Before making a decision about "male and female" it may again be useful to look at the other categories of Galatians 3:28. The distinction between Jew and Greek did not simply stem from racial antagonism due to human divisiveness but was established by the God-given Jewish law. Christ's death and resurrection broke down the dividing wall of hostility between Jew and Gentile: in that sense "neither circumcision, nor uncircumcision is anything; but a new creation is everything" (Galatians 6:15). The old categories of slave and free, subject to God's ordering in the old covenant, are blown apart: all are servants of Christ who sets all free. In terms of male and female, there were physical reasons under the old covenant for women's exclusion from the tabernacle as there were for men (as in Leviticus 15) but these are not repeated in the New Testament. In this sense there is no distinction between male and female but all are "heirs according to the promise" (Galatians 3:29).[52] Yet the matter does not end there, because the deeper symbolic distinctions of masculine and feminine come to the fore. Once again, the categories are blown apart. The new situation in this regard is spelled out in Ephesians 5 and in 1 Corinthians 11:1–16.

A recurring image in Ephesians 5:21–33 is that of "body": "For the husband is the head of the wife just as Christ is the head of the church, the *body* of which he is the Savior" (verse 23); "In the same way, husbands should love their wives as they do their own *bodies*" (verse 28); "For no one ever hates his own *body*, but he nourishes and tenderly cares for it, just as Christ does for the Church, because we are members of his *body*"(verse 29). Genesis 2:24 is recalled in verse 31 with reference to the two becoming one *flesh,* and the notion of washing and cleansing the Church, and making the Church without "a spot or wrinkle," has a fleshly ring to it. Symbolically, the wife is one flesh with the husband (and no one ever hates his own flesh). Symbolically, the Church is one flesh with Christ. Marriage takes on a new symbolic role. "This is a great mystery, and I am applying it to Christ and the church" (verse 32). In marriage the

---

52. See Ridderbos, *Galatians*, 149: "This is not to maintain that the natural and social distinction is in no respect relevant any more . . .From the point of view of the redemption in Christ, however . . . there is no preference of Jew to Greek, master to slave, man to woman."

husband plays the typological Christ role. He is adjured to love his wife "just as Christ loved the church and gave himself up for her" (verse 25).

In 1 Corinthians 11:1–16 the dominant theme is "head" and "head covering." The topic under consideration is appropriate dress for men and women who "prophesy" (i.e., preach in contemporary terms) and "pray" (i.e., lead worship). The New Revised Standard Version translates 1 Corinthians 11:3, "But I want you to understand that Christ is the head of every man, and the husband (*anēr*) is the head of his wife, and God is the head of Christ." Otherwise *anēr* is translated as "man" in the passage. (As with the Hebrew, the Greek words for "man" and "woman" can also mean "husband" and "wife.")[53] But the topic is not marriage but ministry. Men and women have the same ministerial function (i.e., preaching and leading worship). Nevertheless, a symbolic distinction is made in the leadership roles, a distinction which reflects the fact that, in creational terms, the man is "the head" or source of the woman. The man who is already "the head" does not need a further covering. The woman who is not "the head' needs a covering on the head as her authority or badge of office (verse 10). This distinction between male and female church leadership is symbolic of the derivation of Christ from God and "the man" (new humanity or Church) from Christ.[54] But to offset the line of derivation, we are reminded that "as woman came from man, so man comes through woman, but all things are from God" (verse 12), with implications at the divine-human level as noted in chapter 4.

1 Corinthians 11:7 states: "For a man ought not to have his head veiled, since he is the image and reflection [glory] of God; but the woman is the reflection [glory] of man." The context is pivotal: the man is the image of God in the sense of symbolically representing God, the head of Christ (verse 3). In the Godhead, God (the Father) is the head or source. In humanity, "the man" is the head or source. The man as head can thus be taken here to be a type of God *the Father* in a sense that is not true of the woman. But it is already clear from verse 3 that the woman is like God in another sense: the woman plays the same role in humanity that Christ

---

53. Cf. the footnote to the texts in the New Revised Standard Version.

54. 1 Corinthians 11:3 states that Christ is the head of *every man* which could be meant inclusively as *every human being*, as in Acts 17:34 in which the phrase "some men" is said to include a woman named Damaris. In one sense it could refer to "the head of every*one*" (in the Church since the context is a letter to a church, cf. Ephesians 5:23). It is possible that the passage envisages the creative role of the pre-incarnate Word-Wisdom, or that this is in view alongside the meaning of Christ as the source of the new humanity.

plays in the Godhead.⁵⁵ (What it might mean for woman to be the glory of man is explored in the next section.)

There remains the question of why, if "male and female" is an exploded category in Christ, the Church must carefully reflect symbolic gendered distinctions in marriage and leadership. The answer is that in Galatians 3:28, as with the similar passage in Colossians, Paul is talking about "nearness-of-approach."⁵⁶ In terms of our access to God in Christ there is no distinction between male and female, Jew and Greek, slave and free. But when we come to symbolic distinctions, the issue is not "nearness-of-approach" but "nearness-by-likeness." Here the distinction remains and even gains new currency in the sense that "husband and wife" reflect "Christ and the Church." As the *imago Dei* was not lost in spite of humanity's exile from Eden, the *imago Dei* is not materially changed but given deeper significance by the restoration of "nearness-of-approach" in Christ.

"Nearness-by-likeness" has to do with what is given, not acquired. Diversity is a given, unity something to be acquired. In the creational model, the two become one, i.e., acquire unity. It may be noted that the lengthy section on order in the Church, from 1 Corinthians 11 to 14, commences with the exhortation, "be imitators of me [Paul] as I am of Christ." Imitation in terms of Christ-like behavior means acquiring a unified approach, whether in common access to the "love feast" (1 Corinthians 11:17 –33) or in the way of love itself (1 Corinthians 13). But the gifts given to the Church, while manifesting the one Spirit, allow for diversity (1 Corinthians 12, 14). Gender, which is also a given, allows for imitation of a different kind, reflecting our diversity in Christ.

In summary, this section argues that Galatians 3:28 emphasizes the unity put on or *acquired* in Christ, while 1 Corinthians 11:1–16 spells out how *given* creational unity in diversity mirrors divine-human and divine unity in diversity, with particular emphasis on the symbolic significance of diversity as it is presented in male and female church leadership. At the same time the reversal of priority in verses 11–12 can be understood to point to a similar reversal at the divine-human level.

The diagrams below attempt to illustrate and expand Edmund Hill's suggestion with regard to the interpretation of 1 Corinthians 11:3, cf. verse 8, with the addition of a further implication, outlined in chapter 4,

---

55. See Hill's suggestion in chapter 2.

56. See chapter 2 on Lewis's distinction between nearness-by-likeness and nearness-of-approach.

about the reassignment of sexual roles in terms of origin and priority at the divine-human level.

Diagram 1 – see 1 Corinthians 11:3 cf. verse 8

SOURCE		DERIVATIVE
Divine level GOD / THE FATHER	←----------→	CHRIST/WORD-WISDOM/SON
Divine–human level CHRIST	←--------→	CHURCH ("every man" i.e., new humanity)
Human level MAN (Adam)	←--------------→	WOMAN (Eve)

Diagram 2 – see 1 Corinthians 11:11-12

SOURCE		DERIVATIVE
Divine-human level WOMAN (Mary)	←-----------------→	CHRIST
Human level WOMAN	←-----------------→	MAN

UNITY IN DIVERSITY

What does the *imago Dei* mean for women? Ruether critiques Barth for making the male-female relationship analogous to the God-creature relationship.[57] She writes:

> This suggests that women by themselves do not image God. For Barth, of course, this is a false way of putting the matter, since neither man nor woman can exist by themselves, but only as the inseparable human dyad. But, within this dyad, the man images God in relation to the creature, and the woman images the creature in relation to the Creator. Barth has here re-established the patriarchal concept of corporate personality in which the male possesses the image of God for himself and for woman. She, in

---

57. See discussion of the *analogia relationis* in Ruether, "Christian Tradition and Feminist Hermeneutics," 280–83.

turn, images the creaturely in relation to God for the whole human dyad. Together the human pair images the God-man and the man-God relationship.[58]

Ruether offers the response of "most feminism today," said to favor "some version of an expanded unitary view of human nature, rejecting both a male-identified unitary anthropology and a dichotomous complementarity."[59]

Chapter 4 touched on Barth's method of retrospective anthropology in which gendered humanity as *imago Dei* is wholly dependent on the *imago Dei* realized in Christ, albeit not without the Church. Ruether comments: "Given Barth's belief in the absolute gulf between the divine and the human, this establishes the most hierarchical model imaginable as analogue for male-female relations."[60] But if Barth's understanding does not do justice to biblical nuances, an expanded unitary anthropology, said to be in the image of God, would not cast any light on the *imago Dei* question for women either. In fact, neither men nor women by themselves would image God. Ruether is not concerned about this because she regards the whole question of the *imago Dei* as a useful fiction which can be adjusted "to promote the full realization of human potential for women and men."[61] As noted in chapter 2, Ruether claims: "it is not 'man' who is made in God's image, but God who has been made in man's image."

Unitary anthropology is not a new idea. Ruether draws attention to Plato's notion of souls transmigrating from one body to another, if judged unworthy to return, as souls, to their "native star." Such souls would be without a specific sex, allowing for a male to be reincarnated as female, if unable to subdue his passions in a previous life.[62] For Plato, says Ruether, embodiment is secondary, with women associated with the lower principle of bodily life. But unitary anthropology, whether expanded or not, carries the difficulty of separating body and soul, however strongly feminists inveigh against such "dualism." It might be supposed that a construct to promote an expanded unitary anthropology would tend to reflect its asexual conception. Johnson's SHE WHO IS, however, suggests the contrary. Ruether claims to speak for most feminism today but

---

58. Ruether, "Christian Tradition and Feminist Hermeneutics," 283.
59. Ruether, "Christian Tradition and Feminist Hermeneutics," 286.
60. Ruether, "Christian Tradition and Feminist Hermeneutics," 283
61. Ruether, "Christian Tradition and Feminist Hermeneutics," 287.
62. See Ruether, "Christian Tradition and Feminist Hermeneutics," 272–73.

Johnson asserts that feminists do not speak with one voice.[63] Johnson protests (with some truth, I believe) against stereotyping "masculine" and "feminine" traits, going on to state: "This is not to say that there are no differences between women and men."[64] But if there are differences between women and men, beyond the strictly biological, what are they?

This book contends that the *sacramental* signification of difference is paramount. The key to anthropology is not unity on its own but unity in diversity reflecting unity in diversity at the divine level. I find this in both Genesis 1:26–27 and 1 Corinthians 11:1–16, the latter text offering more detail about, as well as a new depth to, the way in which humanity as male and female is in the image of the Godhead. Contrary to Calvin's interpretation outlined above, the passage from 1 Corinthians is not primarily about the conjugal order, but about church leadership. Male and female church leaders reflect the significance of creational unity in diversity taken to a new level. If women leaders are asked to play the symbolic feminine role within the Church,[65] as wives play the symbolic feminine role in marriage,[66] it is necessary to ask what this means and in what sense woman is the glory of man.

---

63. See Johnson, *She Who Is*, 10: "In the United States women of distinct racial and cultural identities expound religious wisdom in voices that criticize the dominance and racism of white liberal feminism."

64. Johnson, *She Who Is*, 49.

65. I have written elsewhere about practical implications of the symbolic "consort role" of women as church leaders. Such implications are not in conflict with female church leadership though they may apply differently in different church traditions. See "Women in Leadership."

66. For a traditional depiction of marriage as a unity in diversity, the interaction of mutual submission and male leadership is described by Theodor Fliedner (who together with his wife Friederike founded the modern deaconess movement in Kaiserswerth, Germany in the 1830s). He expresses, in his punctilious but revealing proposal of marriage to his future wife, how these two principles might work themselves out in practice:

> I am accustomed to firmly maintain the man's right to be head of the household. This sounds forbidding so I must explain more precisely. I also regard it as the Christian duty of both partners to each anticipate the other in subservience, gentleness, kindness and readiness to serve and for each to do the will of the other in preference to his own. Nevertheless, in the closeness of life together there may be cases, and such occur in those contentious earthly things, in which each partner believes to have right on his side . . . and yet only one of the two differing wills can be fulfilled . . . in such cases I lay stress on the man's right, naturally only as long as I am not convinced by something better.

See Anna Sticker, *Friederike Fliedner und die Anfänge der Frauendiakonie*, 15. My translation from the German. Stephen Seamands addresses similar questions in *Ministry in the Image of God*: "In the deep body and soul intimacy of marriage,

It can be said quite definitely what being the glory of man is not. Elaine Graham reports that the Enlightenment era tended to marginalize traditional spheres of comparative independence for women, the elevation of scientific reason along with male-dominated authority equated with the subordination of women who were portrayed in terms of nature, sexuality and domesticity.[67] Rousseau, supposedly a free thinker, wrote that education of females should be geared towards the purpose of nurturing the male.[68] This attitude drew the fire of feminist writer, Mary Wollstonecraft, who wrote fifteen pages to refute it.[69] Feminist thinking has continued to refute such an attitude. Because of this history, "the glory of man" is likely be perceived as deriving from the man and relative to the man in the sense of being his projection, an extension of himself.

This is not the picture presented in 1 Corinthians 11:1–16. In creational terms "the woman" is derived from "the man" but this is not "the man's" doing, but rather God's, as seen in verse 12: "all things come from God."[70] Something of what "the glory of man" might mean appears in the "foolishness" of 2 Corinthians 11:2: "I promised you in marriage to one husband, to present you as a chaste virgin to Christ." Here the bride is presented *to* the husband. The language of the picture in Ephesians is also the language of presenting *to*, although admittedly Christ presents the Church to himself. That Christ must first sanctify and cleanse the Church before presenting her to himself indicates that the Church is separate from Christ, not a mere extension of himself. Even in the case of Christ, though portrayed as his body, the Church is separate from him and the splendor or glory of the Church is presented *to* him.

---

we experience, as nowhere else, the mutual indwelling of human persons in each other . . . God created them for each other so that they would fit together as a unity in diversity . . ."(155); "Although roles may vary and power is not always distributed equally . . . the husband may have more power than the wife, or vice versa, depending on the particular decision being made, still there is a desire that . . . power is shared" (49).

67. See Graham, *Making the Difference*, 15. Cf. Soskice, *Kindness of God*, 121 on the secular feminist perception that "God" functions as the "divine guarantor of the veracity of the insights of the [male] Cartesian subject."

68. See de Beauvoir, *The Second Sex*, 107.

69. In chapter V of *Vindication of the Rights of Woman*, Wollstonecraft refutes the recommendations for female education in Jean-Jacques Rousseau's *Emile or a Treatise on Education*. See Todd, *Mary Wollstonecraft*, 177. Rousseau had written, "the education of women should always be relative to men."

70. Cf. Trible, *Rhetoric of Sexuality*, 102.

The distinction between a subjective projection and a true derivation or birth-giving may be made clearer if birth is considered in the ordinary biological sense. Though man is now born from woman, this does not mean that man is an extension of woman. The grammar of 1 Corinthians 11:7 could allow the "of" in the phrase "the glory of man" to be understood as intrinsic to the man, since it is a simple genitive.[71] But this would mean that the "of" referring to the man in the phrase "the image and glory of God" would also imply that man was merely an extension of God.

Some sense of Hebraic thinking behind the phrase "the glory of man" may be gained from a comparison between the description of the bride in Psalm 45 and the description of the bride in Revelations 21, 22. The future queen in the psalm comes with her own retinue and adornment:

> The princess is decked in her chamber with gold-woven robes;
> in many-colored robes she is led to the king,
> behind her the virgins, her companions, follow.
> With joy and gladness they are led along
> as they enter the palace of the king.[72]

Revelation 21:2 also depicts the bride as adorned *for* not *by* her husband: "And I saw the holy city, the new Jerusalem, coming down out of heaven from God, prepared as a bride adorned for her husband."

In both the wedding psalm and in Revelation chapters 21 and 22 the bride shares her husband's authority: "at [the king's] right hand stands the queen in gold of Ophir" (Psalm 45:9b); "and they (collectively the bride) shall reign for ever and ever" (Revelation 22:5c). As a unity, the bride and bridegroom share a joint reign; in their diversity, however, the bride bows to the bridegroom. "Since he is your lord, bow to him" (Psalm 45:11b); "his servants (collectively the bride) shall worship him (the Lamb)" (Revelation 22:3b). Yet even this hierarchy in diversity is qualified, in the New Testament, by the understanding that "whoever wishes to be first among you must be your slave" (Matthew 20:27).

Diversity in terms of source and derivation is not a one-way process. This is evident in the presentation of 1 Corinthians 11:1–16. As noted above, God [the Father] is the head (or source) of Christ. This is mirrored at the human level in two ways. In a creational sense, "the man" is

---

71. See footnote in the New Revised Standard translation for the word "glory."

72. Psalm 45:13b–15, cf. Hebrews 1:8–9 in which the bridegroom of Psalm 45:6–7 is said to be Christ.

the head (or source) of "the woman". Verses 11 and 12, however, reverse the lines of source and derivation: as God [the Father] is the head (or source) of Christ, "the woman" is the head (or source) of "the man." These two types of mirroring occur also at the divine-human level. Christ is the head (or source) of the new "man," the Church. By inference, the reversal of verses 11–12 applies to the relationship between Christ and his human mother. Understood in terms of relationship, "the man" and "the woman" explode the categories of "masculine" and "feminine." Being a woman is more than being feminine while being a man is not always being masculine. This is reminiscent of the remark by Susan Ashbrook Harvey, that everyone is *more than* they seem to be.[73] Harvey describes this kind of "more than" at the divine and divine-human levels. It applies at the human level as well.

I indicated above that an alleged unitary *imago Dei*, whether on male or androgynous terms, has led to the stiffening of categories. The modern emphasis on equality is not exempt from this. Even Calvin's interpretation of Galatians 3:28 would emphasize spiritual *equality* rather than spiritual *unity* in Christ. The other side of this is Calvin's conjugal order, extended to an extreme in Barth's Creator-creature dualism as the male-female analogue. But even the modern practice of assigning a lower case "c" to the church would imply inferiority for the "church" in relation to Christ. To speak of the divine-human level ought not to denote that Christ is divine and the Church human but that both are both.

This is not to deny the relevance of contingency, in the sense of being contingent on something else. Rather it is to affirm it. Sacramental meaning arising from a created world contingent on a transcendent creator is the only one that allows for embodiment. (Otherwise, the body risks being rendered as *disembodied*, contingent on human subjectivity). At the same time interdependent contingency between male and female allows for difference. Unlike the case of pagan deities, correspondence is not simplistic. Interdependence at the various levels as well as the crossover factor from one level to the next precludes simple correspondence. There is nothing God-alien in this. Priority and subservience are part of pattern. Partners exchange places. Failing this apprehension, we lose the sense of *perichoresis* or dance. This chapter concludes with a postscript on the relationship of delight as dance. This is based on a remark by C. S. Lewis with reference to Jane Austen's *Pride and Prejudice*:

---

73. See Soskice, *Kindness of God*, 114–15.

POSTSCRIPT: WOMEN, MEN AND THE DANCE

In likening the Church to a ballroom, Lewis questions whether gendered distinctions (in marriage and church leadership) should be ignored: "That would, of course, be eminently sensible, civilized and enlightened, but... 'not near so much like a ball.'" In Lewis' analogy, this would translate to "not near so much" like the *perichoresis* of divine-human interrelations.[74] Lewis takes his analogy from Jane Austen's *Pride and Prejudice*. Austen wrote at the dawn of feminism, with a keen satirical eye for what was going on in the society of her day. It is Caroline Bingley who declares that "it would surely be much more rational if conversation instead of dancing made the order of the day," to which her brother replies, "Much more rational... but it would not be near so much like a ball."[75] Caroline Bingley is in one sense a product of the Enlightenment, given her preference for what is rational. If conversation takes the place of dancing, everyone will be equally rational and there will be no need for distinctions of male and female.

But Caroline Bingley also supplies a startling list of qualifications for the "really accomplished" woman:

> A woman must have a thorough knowledge of music, singing, drawing, dancing, and the modern languages, to deserve the word; and besides all this, she must possess a certain something in her air and manner of walking, the tone of her voice, her address and expressions, or the word will be but half deserved.[76]

These qualifications may sound quaint today, but they have their counterpart in modern expectations and idealizations. The simultaneous demand for androgynous inclusion and "accomplishment" (or realization of human potential for women as well as men) resonate with modern feminist ideas.[77]

It might be objected, however, that it is Mr. Darcy who inspires the demand for conversation rather than dancing at balls, and who promotes the discussion about what constitutes "the accomplished woman." Unlike

---

74. Lewis, "Priestesses in the Church?," 93.

75. Austen, *Pride and Prejudice*, chapter XI, 41.

76. Austen, *Pride and Prejudice*, chapter VIII, 28. Caroline Bingley's "accomplished" woman excels at dancing, even though dancing is not required in a rational world. Austen, a meticulous writer, would not have included such contradictory detail without intent.

77. Cf. Ruether, "Christian Tradition and Feminist Hermeneutics," 287.

Rousseau, Darcy appears to want women to be educated in a way that would have been recognized by Mary Wollstonecraft. He contributes a further requirement to Caroline Bingley's list of achievements: "and to all this [the really accomplished woman] must yet add something more substantial, in the improvement of her mind by extensive reading."[78] Darcy appears to have a high view of women and even suggests that his view is higher than Elizabeth's. When Elizabeth is skeptical about the existence of a "really accomplished" woman on the required terms, Darcy remarks: "Are you so severe on your own sex as to doubt the possibility of all this?"

Elizabeth Johnson writes:

> As Rosemary Ruether astutely formulates the fundamental question: Is it not the case that the very concept of the "feminine" is a patriarchal invention, an ideal projected onto women by men and vigorously defended because it functions so well to keep men in positions of power and women in positions of service to them?[79]

But, in spite of being accused of pride, Darcy does not show much interest in keeping women in service to him. Elizabeth Bennett later observes: "you were sick of civility, of deference, of officious attention. You were disgusted with the women who were always speaking and looking and thinking for *your* approbation alone. I roused and interested you, because I was so unlike *them*."[80] On this evidence, we might conclude that Austen meant to portray Darcy as a "feminist."

But the Darcy who prefers conversation to dancing persists in asking Elizabeth to dance. The Darcy who seems to have such high expectations of women is later satisfied with a woman who makes no attempt to fulfill such credentials. The "feminist" Darcy changes by the end of the book and most people prefer the change. He does not end up with a lower opinion of women but rather a more realistic and human appreciation of Elizabeth. It would be ironic if present-day feminists allied their perceptions of women, as Caroline Bingley does, with the unreformed Darcy.

Elizabeth Bennett is a very different character from Caroline Bingley. She does not pretend to be anything she is not. She plays the piano

78. Austen, *Pride and Prejudice*, chapter VIII, 29.

79. Johnson, *She Who Is*, 49, 284 n. 20, citing Rosemary Radford Ruether, "The Female Nature of God: A Problem in Contemporary Religious Life." Johnson adds: "Much contemporary use of the concept of the feminine is related to the categories codified by Carl Jung."

80. Austen, *Pride and Prejudice*, chapter LX, 282–83.

but not particularly well. Unlike her sister Mary, Elizabeth plays for enjoyment, not in order to show off her "accomplishment." On the other hand, she is not easily intimidated, by Lady Catherine or anyone else.[81] Elizabeth is not a servile figure either to idealized expectation or to *force majeure*. It is not servility that allows her to play the consort role.

Her father, who shares the general prejudice against Darcy, advises her against marrying him:

> I know your disposition, Lizzy. I know that you could be neither happy nor respectable, unless you truly esteemed your husband; unless you looked up to him as a superior. Your lively talents would place you in the greatest danger in an unequal marriage. You could scarcely escape discredit and misery.[82]

Elizabeth does not dispute her father's idea about marriage but only his opinion of Darcy. She is a woman for whom *not* looking up to her husband as a superior would be an *unequal* marriage. This is a new slant on equality.

---

81. Cf. Johnson, *She Who Is*, 64. Johnson draws attention to fear and timidity as "women's primordial temptation." Cf. also 1 Peter 3:6b.

82. Austen, *Pride and Prejudice*, chapter LIX, 280.

7

The Swamp of Ambiguity

As they travel through the Land of Oz, Dorothy and her companions follow the Yellow Brick Road until they come to a broad, swiftly flowing river. In order to continue their journey, they must cross the river. Their raft is carried a long way downstream. To reach the Yellow Brick Road again they are obliged to walk back to it along the far bank of the river. They find themselves in a field of poppies which send Dorothy and the Lion into a drug-induced sleep.[1]

In my earlier book *The Wizard's Illusion* I compare the Yellow Brick Road to a *via analogia* by which language has the capacity to point to its referent. By contrast, I liken the Deadly Poppy Field to a "Land of the as-if" in which language does not claim to point to its referent except within the boundaries of its own construct or model. In so far as one remains within the model, language is deceptively similar to that of the Yellow Brick Road. Such is the powerful narcotic effect of the poppies that many inhabitants of the "Land of the as-if" may not be aware of the distinction. Those who retain awareness of linguistic non-reference are in a precarious position, always at risk of being swept downstream, further away from the Yellow Brick Road.

This chapter revisits linguistic matters raised in chapter 1, with a shift of emphasis towards women and women theorists in these areas. The journey in search of identity for women is also a linguistic journey.

---

1. See Baum, *The Wizard of Oz*, chapter 8.

One cannot find identity without solid ground on which to stand. More than that, one needs to be able to walk freely and to find companions to share the journey. Identity requires communication. Communication requires language. With the *via analogia* one has all of these. Without the *via analogia* these things are lacking. On these terms, one cannot stand in the Deadly Poppy Field because there is nothing substantial to stand on. But one can dream and invite others to share the dream.

In my analogy, I take the liberty of making additions to the topography of the Land of Oz. I associate the river with deconstruction, carrying travelers away from linguistic reference in the direction of a nihilistic sea. Let us now suppose that downstream from the "Land of the as-if" is a sluggish backwater, the "Swamp of Ambiguity." To lie down in a poppy field would not be conducive to journeying further. But some inhabitants retain the awareness that at best their thinking permits them to "live within the model." As such, they vacillate between living "within the model" and recognizing its limitations. Unable to return to the Yellow Brick Road, such ambivalence is the beginning of a journey downstream.

The language of the Deadly Poppy Field is deceptively similar to that of the Yellow Brick Road. The language of the Swamp makes no attempt to deceive in this respect. On the contrary, it is diametrically opposed to linguistic reference in the traditional sense. "Diametrically opposed" is Catherine Keller's phrase. She wishes to distance identity for women from identity for men on radically linguistic terms. In this endeavor she engages Karl Barth as a sparring partner.

In visiting the Swamp of Ambiguity, I will expand on some observations about Barth's theological method which I made in *The Wizard's Illusion*. I will suggest that Barth qualifies as a sparring partner for Keller because his method has a degree of similarity with Keller's method despite their radical differences. Barth's theory of the *imago Dei* in particular gives him a toehold in the Swamp. I will go further and suggest that, in interpreting the *imago Dei*, Augustine's method demonstrates some resemblance to Barth's method. It is important to be clear that this excursus on Barth's part (and even on Augustine's) is not representative of the Christian tradition in general. The actuality of the Yellow Brick Road which has underwritten that tradition is, I believe, only partially evident in key theories about the *imago Dei* and Barth's theory is particularly open to question in this respect.

POPPY FIELD IDENTITY

"Theological constructions," says Sallie McFague, "are 'houses' to live in for a while, with windows partly open and doors ajar; they become prisons when they no longer allow us to come and go, to add a room or take one away—or if necessary, to move out and build a new house."[2] This statement emphasizes the relativist nature of theological models. Such constructions produce their own reality, while they last. One can live in them, but they cannot be classed as reality-depicting in a wider sense. The style of living is too uncommitted for that.

In chapter 1 of this book, I refer to these kinds of theological constructions or models as "airy houses." Short-term housing generally offers a weaker sense of identity than is the case with more permanent accommodation. Nevertheless, McFague appears to derive identity from her constructions. She goes so far as to associate her models with a form of "sacramentalism":

> The model of God the creator as mother suggests an ontological (or cosmological) sacramentalism: the world is born from the being of God and hence will be like God. The model of God the savior as lover suggests a personal (or anthropological) sacramentalism: the world is in a responsive relationship to God as his beloved and hence will, in different ways, manifest that relationship. The first kind of sacramentalism, the sacramentalism of creation, is the more basic, for it implies that all phenomena in reality have potential for reflecting the deity. The second kind of sacramentalism is more selective, for it suggests that human beings as the *imago dei*, those with the greatest potential for responding as beloved to lover, can be revelatory of the God-world relationship in a special way.[3]

In the representation of "God the savior as lover" human beings have a special part to play. They are said to be "*imago dei*." In other words, human beings are active in their own model. McFague adds:

---

2. See McFague, *Models of God*, 26–27. McFague goes so far as to associate her versions of reality with "critical realism" (cf. 193 n. 43). But her position differs from that of Soskice who writes in *Metaphor and Religious Language*, 141: "we are saying that the theist can reasonably take his talk of God, bound as it is within a wheel of images, as being reality depicting, while at the same time acknowledging its inadequacy as description. This, we believe, is the position a critical theological realist must take."

3. McFague, *Models of God*, 135–36.

> Thus, in our models of God as mother of creation and as lover of the world, we can speak of God's incarnation in two ways: first, creation as a whole (God's body) is a sacrament or sign of the presence of God, and second, human beings, particularly those human beings especially open and responsive to God, are sacraments or signs of God the lover.

Is this really the language of a constructed "house" which can be abandoned at will?

If you live in a theological construction or "house" as if there is some truth in it, the dream-like or "as if" quality may appear solid and real. But let us compare McFague's "sacramentalism" with the description by Soskice of a reality-depicting orientation. Soskice draws attention to the empty tomb of Jesus. She indicates that the historicity of this event and God's involvement in it are likely issues for the Christian realist.[4] The claim of the empty tomb could theoretically be falsified, as Soskice points out. To use McFague's language of "houses," the Christian realist would be obliged to abandon it if the foundation was overtly unsound. To be obliged to abandon a "house" differs from having freedom to come and go. We are a long way here from a model of "God the savior as lover" which makes no historical claims.

In a general discussion of religious language, the empty tomb of Jesus is a crude example of reality depiction, says Soskice. She goes on to state:

> But where this position is not crude is with respect to the criticism customarily leveled at the theological realist, that he claims to describe God. The agnosticism of our formulations preserves us from this presumption, for we do not claim to describe God but to point through His effects, and beyond His effects, to Him. It is, hence, of the utmost importance to keep in mind the distinction, never remote in the writings of Anselm or of Aquinas, between referring to God and defining Him. This is the fine edge at which negative and positive theology meet, for the apophatic insight that we say nothing of God, but only point towards Him is the basis for the tentative and avowedly inadequate stammerings by which we attempt to speak of God and His acts. And . . . this separation of referring and defining is at the very heart of metaphorical speaking and is what makes it not only possible but necessary that in our stammering after a

---

4. Soskice, *Metaphor and Religious Language*, 140.

The Swamp of Ambiguity

transcendent God we must speak, for the most part, metaphorically or not at all.

At this point I return to Elizabeth Johnson who also cites Thomas Aquinas: "All affirmations we can make about God are not such that our minds may rest in them, nor of such sort that we may suppose God does not transcend them."[5] On the basis of this citation, Johnson draws the negative conclusion: "We have seen that God dwells in unapproachable light so that no name or image or concept that human beings use to speak of the divine mystery ever arrives at its goal: God is essentially incomprehensible."[6]

Stammering after a transcendent God? Neither Johnson nor McFague allow for the meeting between negative and positive theology, as described by Soskice. No name or image or concept that human beings use to speak of the divine mystery ever arrives at its goal, says Johnson. She states that analogical speech nevertheless "functions as a wheel on which [women] can spin out emancipatory language in fidelity to the mystery of God and their own good mystery which participates in that fire."[7] Such a "wheel" could well accommodate McFague's "sacramentalism."

For Johnson, religious language does not stammer but neither is it silent. For Johnson, even the writers of the New Testament did not point to God "through His effects, and beyond His effects to Him." As seen in chapter 3, she claims that first century Christians "in their effort to express the experience of the saving significance of Jesus, ransacked the Jewish religious tradition and the surrounding Hellenistic culture for interpretive elements."[8] Where is the empty tomb in this kind of thinking? If the tradition itself is no more than a human construction, it follows that the method can be used to benefit women:

> As women name themselves in power, responsibility, freedom and mutual relatedness, and affirm themselves as embodied, self-transcending persons broken by sin and yet renewed by amazing grace, new ownership of the gift of the female self as *imago Dei, imago Christi* is transacted. Simultaneously, it becomes obvious that the *imago* is flexible and returns to its giver,

---

5. Johnson, *She Who Is*, 115, citing Aquinas, *De Divinibus Nominibus* 1,2.
6. See Johnson, *She Who Is*, 117.
7. See Johnson, *She Who Is*, 116–17.
8. See Johnson, *She Who Is*, 94.

so that women who are genuinely in God's image in turn become suitable metaphors for the divine.⁹

In this description, "interpretive elements" from Christian tradition (*imago Dei, imago Christi*) are enlisted to further female liberation. To claim such elements, in the context of "women's experience of self interpreted as experience of God," is to herald the arrival of a "theological flashpoint."[10] Failing a meeting-point for negative and positive theology, theology as emancipation can take on a life of its own.

For Johnson and others, the method arises from a critique of "patriarchal" theology. The critique highlights (and overstates) the *via negativa* in order to expose faulty human roots in Christian tradition. It then claims the imprimatur of the tradition in order to be able to adjust it. But without the *via analogia*, tentative as it is, there is no imprimatur to claim. Lacking a solid epistemological basis, the feminist method cannot build. It can only borrow for temporary purposes. In this sense motive and method are at war. The reason for dismantling a patriarchal structure is to build anew for the benefit of women. The cost in this is often underestimated.

McFague's "sacramentalism" and Johnson's theological "flashpoint" lead, potentially at least, to what I call "poppy field identity." This kind of identity is based on a projection rather than external reality. The projection returns to the giver, as Johnson indicates. At the same time the lack of external foundation can easily be forgotten. The more attractive and empowering the projected reality the more likely this will be. The language often borrows from the tradition, in Johnson's words "ransacking" the tradition for interpretive elements. This gives a false sense of solidity to the project.

There is, however, a trajectory in this process which militates against too long a stay in the Poppy Field. Such theological constructions are fragile and temporary, open to deconstruction. Not all feminists and not all feminists all the time remain in the Poppy Field. If one follows the river downstream one comes to what I have called the Swamp of Ambiguity. Here we will meet with Catherine Keller and Luce Irigaray.

9. Johnson, *She Who Is*, 75.
10. See Johnson, *She Who Is*, 69.

EXODUS OF MEANING

In chapter 1 we encountered Luce Irigaray with her restless search for identity:

> [Women] want to seize that which already exists so as to bring it back to an invisible source—their source?—a place from whence they might create, create themselves *ex nihilo*? Has not history forced this impossibility upon them? They must continue to live, cut off from their beginning and from their end.[11]

The idea that women should create *themselves* is very different from the idea that women are created by God in the image of God. But, as will be seen, the narrative context for the *imago Dei* is, in Irigaray's judgment, inimical to women, part of the "impossibility" forced upon women that cuts them off from their alleged beginning and end.

Irigaray's impassioned statement encapsulates perceived needs of women: a need for identity, a need for difference, a need for meaning derived from a source dedicated to women (their source). It also intimates perceived obstacles to the fulfillment of these needs: lack of a place from which to establish identity coupled with a history which has impeded establishing identity. Finally, it suggests a method for rectifying these obstacles: women creating themselves *ex nihilo* from their own (invisible) source in order to reclaim their beginning and end. This search for identity begins, according to Irigaray, from "that which already exists." What is already known by women about themselves can be projected towards an (invisible) source with the result that women are able to create themselves.

Margaret Whitford, Irigaray's editor describes how Irigaray seeks identity for women through a supposed "divine dimension" in the *matriarchal* line in contrast with the "divine dimension" credited to the "man-father" of biblical story or patriarchal genealogy. Whitford writes:

> What Irigaray is concerned with is the possible alterity of "woman-for-herself", instead of woman simply as the 'other of the same' . . . The central condition would be a maternal genealogy, so that the daughter could situate herself in her identity with respect to her mother. The maternal should have a spiritual and divine dimension, and not be relegated to the merely carnal, leaving the divine to the genealogy of the father.[12]

---

11. *Irigaray Reader*, 109.
12. *Irigaray Reader*, 159.

Irigaray perceives a need for a specific female identity in contrast with an identity dependent on men (with women being regarded as "the other of the same"). The proposed method for establishing identity for women, it should be noted, is similar to that which is said to establish identity for men. The "spiritual and divine dimension" is *attributed* to the matriarchal genealogy *in order to* place such a genealogy on an equal footing with the alleged patriarchal genealogy.

Irigaray's desire to establish identity for women, independent of that bestowed by a male figure, leads her to distance herself from the biblical creation story: "But let us say that in the beginning was the end of her story, and that from now on she will have one dictated to her: by the man-father."[13] The biblical story is seen as the means that cuts woman off from her beginning and end. Does disowning the biblical creation story leave women without a narrative of origin? I will come back to this.

As described here, it may seem that there is little to differentiate Irigaray's method from Johnson's. Women's experience of self, interpreted as experience of God becomes, for Irigaray, the daughter situating herself with respect to her mother interpreted as experience of a spiritual and divine dimension. But the *via negativa* is no longer apparent. Margaret Whitford states that Irigaray's work is "marked by a tension between critique and the vision of a new order."[14] In chapter 2 we encountered Irigaray's depiction of a visionary future of "general cultural mutation" in which women would have a central role to play.[15] The vision appears in the form of human rapport at "the horizon of sexual difference":

> And so, those who renounce their own will go towards one another. Calling on one another beneath all saying [*dire*] already said, all words already uttered, all speech [*parole*] already exchanged, all rhythms already hammered out . . . Giving, receiving themselves/ one another in the as yet unfelt/ beyond reason . . . So as to be reborn of it, invested with the telling [*dire*] of a forgotten inspiration. Buried beneath all logic. Surplus to any existing language [*langue*]. The abeyance of all signification, unveiling the trade that underlies it, and venturing beyond . . . In this opacity, this night of the world, they discover traces of the gods who have fled, at the very moment when they

---

13. See Keller, *Face of the Deep*, 19, citing *Speculum of the Other Woman*, 42.

14. *Irigaray Reader*, 12.

15. *Irigaray Reader*, 11–12. Whitford cites *Sexes et parentés*, 200–201; *Le Temps de la différence: pour une révolution pacifique*, 23–24.

have given up ensuring their salvation. Their radiance comes of their consenting that nothing shall ensure their keeping. Not even being—that perimeter of man's narrative. Nor God—that guarantee of the meaning or non-meaning of the whole?[16]

Here the patriarchal "God" is not said to be incomprehensible but rather functions as the guarantee of meaning or non-meaning. This guarantee is repudiated by the new order. The divine dimension (discerned perhaps in "traces of the gods who have fled") is not prior to the new order but a product of it.

I suggested above that disowning the biblical creation story might leave women without a narrative of beginning. But Catherine Keller detects an alternative creation story in the *tehom* (deep) of Genesis 1:2. She writes approvingly of the supposition, considered and rejected by Augustine, that creation is like a sponge in an infinite divine sea.[17] In *Confessions* VII,I, Augustine describes his earlier idea of God "as a great being with dimensions extending everywhere . . . able to pass through material bodies . . . so that they were filled with [God's] presence" as "a false theory." For Keller, however, such a "divine sea" becomes a feminized locus for creation.

Instead of creation being "dictated" by the Word of the "man-father," Keller presents the Word *and* creation emerging from the formless *tehom*. This picture of the *tehom* is presented in opposition to Karl Barth's reading of Genesis 1:2:

> Could the Word of the Creator . . . only unify itself over *against* the feminized chaos . . . What if we begin instead to read the Word from the vantage point of its own fecund multiplicity, its flux into flesh, its overflow . . . Inversely to Barth's logocentric doctrine of the creation, a tehomic theology derives the incarnation from the chaosmic width of creation. A chaosmic Christ would represent the flow of a word that was always already materialized, more and less and endlessly, a flow that unblocks the hope of an incarnation, in which all flesh takes part.[18]

---

16. *Irigaray Reader*, 218.

17. Keller, *Face of the Deep*, 81–82. See *Confessions* VII, 5, cf. VII, I. Keller describes this picture of a sponge in a boundless sea as Augustine's "most tehomophilic trope."

18. See Keller, *Face of the Deep*, 18–19.

According to this description, Barth proposes a cosmology summed up in the Incarnation while Keller proposes an Incarnation summed up in the cosmology. I will return to this contradistinction below.

Keller adopts Irigaray's method of human attribution as the means of establishing the "divine presence" ("what if *we* begin instead to read the Word...?'). She suggests that the Word can be conceived as *materializing* (deriving its incarnation) from the width of potential embodiment said to be implicit in primeval (feminized) chaos. She writes:

> Only in relation to what we call *creation* can what we call *Creator* be signified, i.e. imagined to exist . . . In the reciprocity of influence, both arise as effects of the primal creativity. But Elohim then signifies the effect through whom all causes arise. The creativity is not a cause, not even a First Cause, but rather the condition that conditions all causal processes. The creativity itself does not become; *it makes becoming possible*. We imagine it therefore as the matrix of possibilities. In this tehomic matrix we are always beginning again. We decide; and we fall back into the undecidable. According to this imaginary of bottomless process, the divine decision is not made *for us* but *with and through us*.[19]

In such a context, meaning is process rather than content. The Word or God (Elohim) emerges; it does not determine. Keller claims to find support for "theologically originary indeterminacy" in the "billowing multiplicity" that she discerns in the *Confessions* of Augustine. But her "imaginary" does not allow the Word to be understood as Wisdom in Augustine's sense.[20] This impinges on women's identity in a sense already explored in chapter 6.

Grace Jantzen draws attention to a strategy of "double reading," developed, she says, by Derrida and Irigaray: "a sort of reading which on the one hand pays close attention to a text, but which, in that very attention, discloses a rupture in that text which requires a radically different reading of it, thus destabilizing it and in the undecidability thereby created opens the possibility of thinking otherwise."[21] This deconstructionist strategy would seem evident in Keller's depiction of "tehomic" theology. The text is Genesis 1:2–3. The radically different reading gives prominence to a model of feminized chaos. The consequence is a theology which "decides" (derives its "incarnation") from the "billowing multiplicity" of the

---

19. Keller, *Face of the Deep*, 181. Keller's italics.
20. See Augustine, *Confessions* VII, 18. Cf. Keller, *Face of the Deep*, 38.
21. Jantzen, *Becoming Divine*, 61.

model, but also falls back on the "undecidable," i.e., the undecidability of the method.

As noted, Keller proposes her reading of the Genesis passage in contradistinction to Barth's reading of it. She writes: "Could the Word of the Creator . . . only unify itself over *against* the feminized chaos . . . Inversely to Barth's logocentric doctrine of the creation, a tehomic theology derives the incarnation from the chaosmic width of creation." Keller describes Barth's reading as "logocentric" but admits that Barth's reading diverges from classical interpretation. She writes: "Barth never quite affirms the classic creation from nothing. He does it one better: the fathers were too soft on chaos. God would not create *from* such horror."[22] In other words, Keller's double reading begins not with classic Christian tradition but with Barth's departure from the tradition.

Keller describes a "tehomic" interpretation of Genesis 1:2 as "diametrically opposed" to Barth's perception that the Word of the Creator unifies itself over against chaos.[23] Barth writes in the *Church Dogmatics*:

> As this Word is spoken and repeated in the history of the covenant . . . it is thereby constantly decided that the *hay^{e}thah* of chaos is final—this world *was*. God will not allow the cosmos to be definitively bewitched and demonised or His creation totally destroyed, nor will He permit the actual realisation of the dark possibility of Gen. 1:2.[24]

The "dark possibility of Gen 1:2" casts doubt on the classical formula of *creation ex nihilo*. For Barth, says Keller: "This chaos, this 'glaring opposition to what is later described as God's good' (III.1.104), cannot serve as the material of creation."[25] On the other hand, the "dark possibility of Gen 1:2" never comes to actual realization. In this sense Barth rejects "the mythological acceptance of a primeval reality independent of God." This double rejection, says Keller, opens the door for "a third possibility." In other words, Barth could be said to anticipate the deconstructionist method of "double reading" which "discloses a rupture in the text" and "opens the possibility of thinking otherwise."

---

22. See Keller, *Face of the Deep*, 18–19. My italics. Keller cites Barth, *Church Dogmatics*, III/I, 105.

23. See Keller, *Face of the Deep*, 86, cf. 19.

24. Barth, *CD*, III/I, 109.

25. Keller, *Face of the Deep*, 86.

"Just as Barth suspected, the mythic intertextuality of verse 2, tucked microcosmically into a few mysterious metaphors, gives succor to those of us seeking a biblical starting-point before and beyond orthodoxy," continues Keller.[26] In opposing orthodoxy, Barth and Keller are in agreement. It is at the stage of "thinking otherwise" that the two "diametrically" diverge. Barth and Keller both present three protagonists: the Word, creation, and chaos. For Barth, the Word takes center stage while chaos is never to appear at all. Nevertheless, the drama is pitched against darkness, albeit darkness which remains off-stage. Keller retains the protagonists but locates them differently. Instead of creation being "dictated" by the Word of the "man-father" over against chaos, Keller proposes the Word *and* creation emerging from chaos, described as "this imaginary of bottomless process." In terms of diametric opposition, Word *and* creation take centre stage. The character who remains off-stage is the dictating man-father. The drama is pitched against *him*.

In producing a theology of a feminist *tehom*, Keller draws on both Augustine and Barth. I will return to Augustine and Barth in the last section of this chapter. But firstly, I will ask whether "bottomless process" is an accurate description of Keller's theology. To my mind, the supposedly bottomless *tehom* is more akin to a shallow swamp of conflicting processes.

SWAMP OR TEHOM?

"Only in relation to what we call *creation* can what we call *Creator* be . . . imagined to exist," says Keller. "In the reciprocity of influence, both arise as effects of the primal creativity." In other words, primal creativity precedes both creation and Creator. Primal creativity is said to be the prior condition giving rise to a matrix of possibilities in which divine decision (made with us and through us) is part of the process. But, says Keller, we always fall back on the "undecidable." This method of "bottomless process" is linked with the deep of Genesis 1:2. It should be remembered, however, that this is an imaginative association. It is mooted to counter the perceived masculine bias of the creative power of the Word. In "bottomless process," as with Irigaray's visionary utopia, we might detect a Romantic yearning for the infinite in which process is preferred to arrival.

26. Keller, *Face of the Deep*, 86.

On the negative side, an "imaginary of bottomless process" is reminiscent of an infinite regress of meaning. Sallie McFague writes about the charge, posed by deconstruction, that Western metaphysics is a history of "massive forgetfulness." What is forgotten is that "metaphor lies at the base of all our constructions, including that most sacred Text" (in which human words are said to truly refer to the Word itself). For deconstruction, continues McFague, that history is "but the play of words, interpretation upon interpretation, creating a shimmering surface that has no author and no referent."[27] This alleged history offers a picture of "bottomless process" but does not promise opportunity for "divine decision," made with us and through us.

Potentially, a strategy of "double reading" adds something to a shimmering surface without author or referent. But this potential derives from the tradition which the process rejects. A strategy of "double reading" is less positive about the tradition than Johnson's "ransacking." Nevertheless, Keller's third possibility which gives rise to divine decision-making retains the impetus of the tradition. Divine decision-making is more than a play of words.

In her "imaginary" of feminized chaos Keller borrows from more than one source, including Augustine's abandoned image of creation as a sponge in an infinite sea. In consequence, her picture of creation has a positive as well as a negative background. It is these conflicting influences which allow the play of words to become the condition for fecund multiplicity. The prior feminized locus, no longer supplanted by an external Word, becomes the vantage point for incarnation of the Word arising from the creative process. Some kind of meaning emerges on the windy surface of "bottomless" chaos.

Similar conflicting influences characterize the history of feminism. A feminized *tehom* would seem a promising candidate for Irigaray's invisible source for women, giving rise to their self-creation *ex nihilo*. But does this proposed self-creation really occur *ex nihilo*? Margaret Whitford sums up a feminist dilemma: on the one hand, feminists "share with postmodernist thought the radical critique of the Enlightenment inheritance; on the other hand, the emancipatory thrust of feminism is rooted in the Enlightenment."[28] Whitford continues:

---

27. McFague, *Models of God*, 24.
28. See *Irigaray Reader*, 12–13.

> Irigaray's contribution here is to point to the dangers for women of embracing postmodernism too hastily or too uncritically . . . She warns against displacing the male/female binary before the female side has acceded to identity and subjectivity.

"Deconstruction's critique makes clear the necessity of developing 'negative capability'—the ability to endure absence, uncertainty, partiality, relativity, and to hold at bay the desire for closure, coherence, identity, totality," reports Sallie McFague.[29] Irigaray, on the other hand, wishes to retain identity for women. A desire for subjectivity and identity, rooted in the Enlightenment, runs counter to deconstruction's hermeneutic of suspicion.

Far from representing the condition of all causal process, Keller's imaginary *tehom* would appear the product of many conflicting causal processes. I suggest that her "matrix of possibilities" could be more aptly imagined as vegetation, half-submerged and endlessly intertwining, lapped by the waters of deconstruction. This stretch of water is by no means bottomless. The mud that sustains the vegetation is not far to seek; even Irigaray does not want to lose sight of it. Boggy ambiguity, however, is not promising ground for women's identity.

Despite its promotion of subjectivity, modernism (as opposed to postmodernism) has not completely abandoned the sense of "presence" which has underwritten Western metaphysics. McFague's temporary theological "houses" support the feminist project in terms of the critique of "patriarchy" but undermine it in weakening the foundation for identity. In the feminist desire for identity and subjectivity on relativist terms, I detect a good deal of traffic between the "Land of the as-if" (where one lives in the theological construction as if it still retained metaphysical validity) and the Swamp of Ambiguity (in which in which the ground of being is overtly muddier). But modern feminists may not be the first visitors to the Swamp. In the history of Christian theology others may have been there before them, especially in relation to the *imago Dei*.

POTENTIAL *IMAGO DEI*?

This section returns to Augustine's doctrine of words as signs, a key source for the assumption of what George Steiner calls "presence" which allows language to have meaning. As already seen, deconstructionist thought disputes this premise. Sallie McFague reports that, at its extreme,

---

29. McFague, *Models of God*, 25–26.

deconstruction reduces language to "nothing but metaphor," ultimately said to consist in "the play of words, interpretation upon interpretation, creating a shimmering surface that has no author and no referent."[30] My earlier book, *The Wizard's Illusion*, contests a deconstructionist appraisal of "metaphor" which leaves out its origin in the literal language of the senses. It is not the purpose of this book to repeat what was said there in any depth except insofar as it impinges on the *imago Dei*. I will suggest that Augustine's theory of the *imago Dei* diverges from the method of his doctrine of signs, in a way which I find to resemble the theological method employed by Karl Barth. I ask about the effect, linguistic and otherwise, if the *imago Dei* is not understood as sign in Augustine's sense.

"Augustine's account of interpretation in the *de doctrina*," writes Rowan Williams, "is a set of variations on a single theme, the relation of *res* and *signum*, thing and sign, reality and representation." For Augustine, says Williams, "a doctrine of signs is a step towards a more general theory of language."[31] He goes on to report:

> There are things which, on one analysis, do not 'speak' of anything further or 'make known' anything other than themselves; but human beings do not live only a cognitive life. We are engaged with the world, moving through it as subjects of will and love . . . Augustine assumes that 'signifying' is a threefold, not a twofold affair, involving the subject *for* whom signs signify . . . We cannot miss the point that discussion of signification is also discussion of those beings who are involved in meaning or 'intending' or understanding.

Although the relation between sign (*signum*) and thing signified (*res*) is not the full sum of Augustine's theory of language, it is a necessary first step. I find this step less than clear in Augustine's theory of the *imago Dei*. On the other hand, his theory clearly emphasizes the third aspect of his doctrine of signs, involving the subject for whom the signs signify.

In his book on language and teaching, Augustine writes: "A human being is a major kind of thing, being made 'in the image and likeness of God [Gen. 1:26–27]' not by virtue of having a mortal body but by virtue of having a rational soul and thus a higher status than animals."[32] Augustine immediately goes on to ask whether humans should subordinate

---

30. See McFague, *Models of God*, 23–24.

31. Williams, "Language, Reality and Desire in Augustine's *De Doctrina*," 138–39. His italics.

32. See *On Christian Teaching*, Book One, XXII.

their love of neighbor to their love of God. For Augustine, the *imago Dei* as sign seems to be intrinsically connected with relationship with God. My point here is that nearness-by-likeness and nearness-of-approach are not separately considered. This is not to say that a threefold approach to the signifying capacity of language is problematic in itself. I suspect, however, that it is detrimental, in the first instance, to considering how human beings are said to be like God.

One must add to this that Augustine's location of the *imago Dei* in the rational soul has implications for the status of the soul in a doctrine of signs. A human being as a major kind of thing made in God's likeness might seem to accord with Augustine's doctrine of signs, humanity functioning as sign (*signum*) of God (supreme *res*). But, for Augustine, human beings as such are not the thing which functions as the sign (of God); it is the rational soul which functions as the sign. In other words, a human being as "thing" is the *vessel* of the "sign." As already discussed in this book, Augustine calls the rational or spiritual aspect of the soul "masculine." It is this spiritual aspect which, in contemplating God, constitutes the *imago Dei*. This is qualified by movement "either in the right or wrong direction."[33] Such factors would suggest a *potential* likeness to God. Further, the masculine attribution is allegorical. Augustine was of course no stranger to the allegorical method of interpretation. But, as he explains in *The City of God*, the allegorical method is permissible in supplementing, but not replacing, a primary reception of Scripture as it stands.[34] Is he departing from this rule in his interpretation of the *imago Dei*?

"There are things which, on one analysis, do not 'speak' of anything further or make known anything other than themselves," reports Williams. Augustine's contention that the mortal body is not relevant to the *imago Dei* would seem to place biological sexuality in this category. Augustine locates the *imago Dei* in the rational soul in order to differentiate human beings from animals. In other words, Augustine is bringing a prior concept to his reading of the scriptural *imago Dei*. On these terms, even the rational soul does not operate, in the first instance, as a sign

---

33. Edmund Hill, "Foreword to Books IX–XIV," in Augustine, *The Trinity*, 261.

34. See "The spiritual interpretation of the paradise of Eden does not conflict with its historical truth," *City of God*, XIII, 21. In support of his position, Augustine states: "It is . . . arbitrary to suppose that there could have been no material paradise; it is like the assumption that there were not two wives of Abraham, named Hagar and Sarah, who bore two sons, one a slave's son, the other the son of a free woman, just because the Apostle finds in them the prefiguration of the two covenants . . ."

pointing to God. Rather, a concept (human beings differentiated from animals) functions as a "thing" which identifies the "sign" (the rational soul). This method will be clearer in Barth's usage explored below but there is a hint of it here.

In further complication, the masculine attribution of *sapientia* derives ultimately from, and refers back to, the male human being. On the other hand, the rational soul is said to be the sign of divine likeness in a way that the embodied male is not. There is thus an ambivalence about which is pointing as "sign" to which. Does this open the door to endless interpretation upon interpretation? Not only are human beings as the vessel of the "sign" only in the image of God at one step removed, but the status that Augustine gives to an allegorical projection may cast some doubt on his theory of language.

Augustine maintains that a doctrine of signs is a step towards a more general theory of language, says Rowan Williams. But human beings as a major kind of thing, being made in the image and likeness of God, do not constitute a sign with any clarity. For Augustine, reports Williams: "God is *res*, and, in respect of him, all else is *signum*; God alone is to be enjoyed in and for himself."[35] This is nearness-of-approach. Western understanding of the *imago Dei* has tended to follow these lines, not only giving undue emphasis to the masculine but also stressing nearness-of-approach at the expense of nearness-by-likeness. I suspect that there has been a cost in clear discernment of linguistic processes. I find these emphases in Barth's approach to the *imago Dei*. But Barth has a more complicated general method which compounds the ambiguity.

As I understand him, Barth's method rests on what might be termed God's NO to chaos in the concept-model "Jesus Christ." In *The Wizard's Illusion*, I suggest a parallel between Barth's method and the situation of Dorothy's house, borne aloft in the eye of the cyclone to the Land of Oz. Outside the house is chaos and destruction; inside the house, Dorothy goes to sleep with her dog, Toto.[36] On parallel terms, the Church resides safely in the concept-model of "Jesus Christ." I hyphenate concept-model because, in Barth's usage, the term "Jesus Christ" appears to function in both senses.

---

35. Williams, "Language, Reality and Desire in Augustine's *De Doctrina*," 140.
36. See Baum, *Wizard of Oz*, chapter 1.

In order to explicate this usage, I turn to Sallie McFague, a self-styled "erstwhile Barthian."[37] While the content is quite different, the method deployed in McFague's model of "God the lover" would seem similar to Barth's method. As seen above, McFague presents a model of "God the savior as lover" in which human beings "can be revelatory of the God-world relationship in a special way."[38] Within her model, McFague classes human beings as *imago Dei* or *signs* of God the lover of the world. A model, on McFague's terms, is unashamedly of human construction. In the model "God the lover," human beings play two parts. Firstly, humans conceive the model. Secondly, they function as actors within the model, as sacraments or signs of the God of the model.

To my mind, Barth's method demonstrates a similar ambivalence between model as concept and model as cultural habitat. Barth writes, "From the fact that God is human . . . [a distinction] follows first of all . . . [that 'man'] is the being whom God willed to exalt as his covenant-partner."[39] He continues:

> We must affirm as second consequence the fact that through the humanity of God, a quite definite theme is given to *theological* culture in particular . . . Since God in His deity is human, this culture must occupy itself . . . with the man-encountering God and the God-encountering man and with their dialogue and history, in which their communion takes place and comes to its fulfilment. For this reason theology can think and speak only as it looks at Jesus Christ and from the vantage point of what He is.[40]

In this description, the "fact that God is human" functions as the *concept* which gives rise to the "second consequence" of theological culture and biblical history, the *content* of the model in other words. Rudolf Bultmann comments: "It is perfectly clear that Barth interprets the statements of scripture by means of a conceptuality that he brings with him. But what is the source and meaning of this conceptuality?"[41] Unlike McFague, Barth does not admit that his conceptuality is of human origin, a situation which leaves Bultmann's question unanswered.

---

37. See McFague, *Body of God*, 208.
38. McFague, *Models of God*, 135–36.
39. Barth, "Humanity of God," 50.
40. Barth, "Humanity of God," 52–53. Barth's italics.
41. Bultmann, *New Testament and Mythology and Other Basic Writings*, 89.

As seen in chapter 4, Barth makes a distinction between the "mystery of the Incarnation" and the "miracle of Christmas":

> The miracle of Christmas is the actual form of the mystery of the personal union of God and man, the *unio hypostatica* . . . The true Godhead and the true humanity of Jesus Christ in their unity do not depend on the fact that Christ was conceived by the Holy Spirit and born of the Virgin Mary. All that we can say is that it pleased God to let the mystery be real and become manifest in this shape and form.[42]

Barth presents the distinction in terms of "thing" and "sign":

> Why does the miracle of Christmas run parallel to the mystery of the Incarnation? . . . If in the Incarnation we have to do with the thing, here we have to do with the sign. The two should not be confused. The thing which is involved in Christmas is true in and for itself. But it is indicated, it is unveiled in the miracle of Christmas.[43]

For Barth, the "thing" (the *unio hypostatica*) is primary. The "sign" (the Virgin Birth) is secondary: it functions to "unveil" what is already "true in and for itself."

We may compare Barth's usage of "thing" and "sign" with Augustine's theory of language and teaching:

> All teaching is teaching of either things or signs, but things are learnt through signs. What I now call things in the strict sense are things such as logs, stones, sheep and so on, which are not employed to signify something; but I do not include the log which we read Moses threw into the bitter waters to make them lose their bitter taste [Exod. 15:25], or the stone which Jacob placed under his head [Gen. 28:11], or the sheep which Abraham sacrificed in place of his son [Gen. 22:13]. These are things, but they are at the same time signs of other things.[44]

Augustine classes concrete objects such as logs, stones, and sheep as "things" in themselves. Such "things" can also be "signs" of other "things." These other things, says Augustine, are learned through signs. In Barth's method, it is the other way round.

---

42. Barth, *Dogmatics in Outline*, 100.
43. Barth, *Dogmatics in Outline*, 96.
44. See *On Christian Teaching*, Book One, I-IV, 8–9.

For Barth, events, recounted in Scripture, function as signs in a secondary sense. They point back towards the primary concept ("fact" or "thing"). Augustine's theory of language does not function in this way. Augustine's reader is directed to begin with the *concrete* "thing" as a sign or means of access to other things with a deeper spiritual significance. Barth's reader is directed to begin with the *abstract* significance ("thing") before considering the concrete reality ("sign"). This is clear in his distinction between the mystery of the Incarnation and the miracle of Christmas: "where this mystery ['thing'] has been understood and men have avoided any attempt at natural theology, because they had no need of it, the miracle ['sign'] came to be thankfully and joyously recognised. It became, we might say, an inward necessity at this point."[45]

I stated above that Augustine's theory of the *imago Dei* seems to diverge in method from the terms of his general theory of language. In locating the *imago Dei* in the "masculine" *sapientia*, Augustine brings his conceptuality *to* this key sign of the Godhead. He then reads biblical statements about the *imago Dei* accordingly. In other words, Augustine could be said to anticipate Barth's method in this instance. This, however, is not Augustine's usual way of reading Scripture. By contrast, Barth openly applies this method in his general approach to Scripture.

Let us turn to Barth's approach to the *imago Dei*. Barth presents theological culture and biblical history as "second consequence" to "the fact that God is human" in covenant relationship with humanity.[46] This method of "second consequence" can be detected in his remarks on 1 Corinthians 11 about human likeness to God:

> According to 1 Corinthians 11:7 there is a man who actually *is* the *eikōn kai doxa theou* and from this standpoint the same can be said of every man. And side by side with this man there is a woman who is his *doxa* as He (the Head of the woman but not without her) is the *doxa* of God, and from the standpoint of this woman, or rather of her Husband, the same could be said of every woman. This man together with this woman is the man who is the image of God [*Dieser Mann mit dieser Frau ist der Mensch, der das Ebenbild Gottes ist*], who *is* it and does not merely indicate it or establish its physical possibility, like Adam and Seth and all the subsequent members of the genealogical tree.[47]

---

45. Barth, *Dogmatics in Outline*, 100.
46. Barth, "Humanity of God," 50.
47. Barth, *Church Dogmatics* III/I, 203.

Human likeness to God depends on the man who actually *is* the image and glory of God, says Barth. He draws the exegetical consequence:

> There is no need for us to pursue at this point the anthropological equation in respect of this relationship between man and wife as Paul develops it in 1 Corinthians 11 . . . It is obvious that all that he had to say about man and woman was seen from this angle, in the light of the relationship between Jesus Christ and His community, and therefore of His divine likeness, and that it is only in this way that it is presented as an 'order of creation'. We must be content merely to assert that the agreement of Paul's teaching with Genesis 1:26 f. must not be underestimated in this respect (where it is often overlooked).[48]

Here the "anthropological equation" of man and woman is to be seen in the light of Christ's divine likeness, extended to the Church. In other words, divine likeness at the human level is a "second consequence" of the primary "fact" at the divine-human level.

For Barth, the "man" Jesus Christ is the *imago Dei*, while the Church (as woman) is only in the image of God through Christ. This primary understanding of the *imago Dei* has a secondary application to individual men and women. (Adam and Seth and all the subsequent members of the genealogical tree only indicate it or establish its physical possibility.)[49] One must add to this that Barth extends the *imago Dei* to include gender by a sleight of hand. He states: "The true Godhead and the true humanity of Jesus Christ in their unity do not depend on the fact that Christ was conceived by the Holy Spirit and born of the Virgin Mary." But, failing the physical actuality of the *unio hypostatica*, why should divine likeness be classed as masculine? Further, failing an analogy deriving from human marriage, why should the Church be classed as feminine?

Rosemary Ruether reports that German Protestant theologians, writing after the First World War, "wanted to make a radical distinction between created and divine natures and to deny any shared 'being' between God and creatures."[50] This denial took the form of a movement away from the analogy of *being* between God and creatures (*analogia entis*). Instead, neo-orthodox theologians turned to Martin Buber's proposal of subject-subject (I-Thou relationship) between humans and God.

---

48. Barth, *Church Dogmatics*, III/I, 205.
49. Barth, *Church Dogmatics* III/I, 203.
50. See Ruether, "Christian Tradition and Feminist Hermeneutics," 281.

They replaced the analogy of being with what they termed the *analogia relationis*. "It is Karl Barth," states Ruether, "who most clearly develops the interpretation of the image of God as *analogia relationis* in such a way as to make the God-creature hierarchy the essential analogue for male-female relations."[51]

"The male-female analogy of Christ and church establishes, for Barth, gender relations as the basic image of the relationship of God to redeemed creation. Woman images the creature in relation to its Creator and Redeemer," continues Ruether. But a complete disavowal of an analogy of being would constitute a disavowal of the male-female analogy. To my mind, Barth borrows the male-female analogy for Christ and the Church from a linguistic method which he denies. One might ask what he means by Adam and Seth and all the subsequent members of the genealogical tree establishing the physical possibility of the image of God. Is there not a hint of *analogia entis* here?

There may be a further difficulty. An *analogia relationis* would suggest nearness-of-approach as the determining factor for the *imago Dei*. But Barth does not explain how language (and hence dialogue) can occur in the absence of an *analogia entis*. The sphere of operation for dialogue between God and humanity is not clear either. For Barth, says Ruether, "God as the one who addresses man is wholly other. Man cannot respond out of his present fallen nature, but only in Christ, who responds to God for us."[52] My question for Barth's method is: Does Christ's response for us occur at the conceptual level of the *unio hypostatica* or at some secondary level?

An overt distinction between "Jesus the Christ" and the historical Jesus appears in Barth's differentiation between "*in* history" and "*of* history":

> However it may be with the historical Jesus, it is certain that Jesus the Christ, the Son of the living God, belongs neither to history nor to psychology; for what is historical and psychological is as such corruptible. The resurrection of Christ, or his second coming, which is the same thing, is not a historical event . . . our concern here is with an event which, though it is the only real happening *in* history is not a real happening *of* history.[53]

---

51. See Ruether, "Christian Tradition and Feminist Hermeneutics," 282.

52. See Ruether, "Christian Tradition and Feminist Hermeneutics, 282, citing Barth, *Christ and Adam: Man and Humanity in Romans 5*.

53. Barth, *The Word of God and the Word of Man*, 90.

Bultmann asks what Barth means by "real" happening in this context: "What kind of event is it of which one can say that 'it far more certainly really happened in time than all the things that the historians as such can establish.'"[54] It is at this point that Bultmann adds the remark that Barth "interprets the statements of scripture by means of a conceptuality that he brings with him."

A distinction between the historical Jesus and Jesus the Christ, the Son of the living God impinges upon Barth's presentation of the Incarnation. Keller describes Barth's doctrine of creation as "logocentric." But what does Barth mean by the Logos? If the concept of "Jesus Christ" operates separately from the sequential nature of the biblical narrative where does this leave the pre-incarnate Logos or Wisdom? Barth describes Christ as *like* the 'wisdom' of the Old Testament:

> He to whom the New Testament ascribes participation in creation has only divine and human form, like the 'wisdom' of the Old Testament. He is not an 'intermediate being'. He is the divine person who acts, suffers and triumphs as man . . . He is the Mediator between God and man, like the 'wisdom' of the Old Testament.[55]

Wisdom, admits Barth, was in some sense acknowledged beyond Judaism at the time of Christ:

> It is now known that the writers of the New Testament found themselves on prepared ground inasmuch as the notion of a second divine being assisting in the work of creation had become general in their day. What they ascribe to Jesus Christ [e.g. in Colossians 1:17; John 1:1; Hebrews 1:2] was not only ascribed by Philo to the Logos but also to the syncretistic theosophy and cosmology of the time.[56]

But Barth distances himself from this syncretistic background. In emphasizing the divine person who acts, suffers and triumphs as man, Barth de-emphasizes the prior existence of the Logos:

> It has to be kept in mind that the whole concept of the *logos asarkos*, the 'second person' of the Trinity, as such, is an abstraction. It is true that it has shown itself necessary to the christological

---

54. See Bultmann, *New Testament & Mythology*, 89, citing *Die kirchliche Dogmatik*, 3/2 (1948): 535–36.

55. Barth, *Church Dogmatics*, III/I, 53.

56. Barth, *Church Dogmatics*, III/I, 52.

> and trinitarian reflections of the Church . . . The New Testament speaks plainly enough about the Jesus Christ who existed before the world was but . . . it does not speak of the eternal Son or Word as such, but of the Mediator, *the One who in the eternal sight of God has already taken upon Himself our human nature*, i.e., not of a formless Christ who might well be a Christ principle.[57]

On this representation, the reflections of the Church might be said, in Johnson's parlance, to have "ransacked" syncretistic sources in search of "necessary" christological and trinitarian doctrine.

Contrary to Barth, Augustine uses a syncretistic interpretation of the Logos as a basis for apologetics:

> We know what Porphyry, as a Platonist, means by 'principles'. He refers to God the Father, and God the Son, whom he calls in Greek the Intellect or Mind of the Father . . . But this Platonist failed to see that Christ [the Word 'through whom everything came into existence' . . . when 'the Word became flesh and dwelt among us'] was the 'principle'.[58]

For Augustine, the Word *becomes* flesh. Barth, however, presents Christ in terms of the eternal sight of God. On these terms Christ "has already taken upon Himself our human nature" *before* the creation of the world.[59] Once again, Barth's heavy reliance on a conceptuality that he brings with him would cast doubt on the Word becoming flesh in human history.

In terms of the *imago Dei*, I should add that Barth finds a parallel between interpersonal relationships "in the sphere of Elohim" and the human level:

> Man is created by God in correspondence with this relationship and differentiation in God Himself: *created as a Thou that can be addressed by God but also as an I responsible to God*; in the relationship of man and woman in which man is a thou to his fellow and therefore himself an I in responsibility to this claim.[60]

The above quotation has three parts to it. The *likeness factor* between God and humanity appears in the first and third parts. Likeness consists in the capacity for relationship at both divine and human levels. The middle

---

57. Barth, *Church Dogmatics*, III/I, 54. My italics. Cf. chapter 4.
58. Augustine, *City of God*, X, 23, 24.
59. Barth, *Church Dogmatics*, III/I, 54.
60. Barth, *Church Dogmatics*, III/I, 198. My italics.

part of the quotation (which I have put in italics) introduces something else: a capacity for relationship between the two levels, divine and human. Here again is a capacity for relationship between a "Thou" and an "I." But the emphasis is on difference rather than likeness. "Man" is a created being, addressed by, and responsible to, God. This would seem to preclude equality of nature at the divine-human level.

For the sake of clarity, I will glance back at the previous chapter. Chapter 6 is really the heart of this book since it outlines in detail Edmund Hill's presentation of the *imago Dei*, together with my additions to it.[61] I present the *imago Dei* as a series of analogous interpersonal relationships (at the human, divine-human and divine levels), with the understanding of equality of nature by both parties at the various levels. Despite any similarity of language, my proposal is distinct from Barth's version of the *analogia relationis*. For Barth, as I understand him, the *imago Dei* resides in the concept-model "Jesus Christ" as a bridge in an otherwise vertical relationship (if relationship it can be called) between God and humanity.

As seen above, Augustine's theory of the *imago Dei* distinguishes between humans and animals with the result that the *imago Dei* excludes sexual differentiation at the biological level. Barth makes a similar point:

> The differentiation and relationship between I and Thou in the divine being in the sphere of Elohim are not identical with the differentiation and relationship between male and female. That it takes this form in man, corresponding to bisexuality of animals too, belongs to the creatureliness of man rather than to divine likeness.[62]

The exclusion of biological sexuality precludes the possibility of horizontal analogous pairs. For Augustine, biological sexuality continues to be relevant as an allegory of the mind. For Barth, human sexuality is apparently not relevant to divine likeness (although said to establish its physical possibility).

I have stated above that the method outlined by "erstwhile Barthian" Sallie McFague appears to be an adaptation of Barth's method. McFague is not only open about the human source for her method but also about promoting new non-biblical models. In this, she differs from Barth. McFague and Barth, however, are alike in attaching a model (second consequence in Barth's terminology) to their concept. McFague's

61. See Hill in Augustine, *The Trinity*, 338 n. 22.
62. Barth, *CD*, III/I, 196.

model-metaphors disclaim confidence that "the universe is in some sense sacramental, that God is somehow the true and original father, that all things are connected among themselves because they are connected in God."[63] She goes so far as to say that it is the task of metaphorical theology to break the hegemony of the model-metaphor "God the father."[64] This does not prevent her from proposing a sacramental system. But the premise is different. In her method, the universe is constructed, rather than a received. This is not the real universe but a projected model of it. Barth denies a primary *analogia entis* and places the dialogue and history of man-encountering-God and God-encountering-man in a secondary "consequence" or model. In other words, neither Barth nor McFague seem to engage with real dialogue in the real world. This is reminiscent of what Steiner calls the break in the covenant between word and world. The loss of embodiment in this will be explored in the next chapter.

For Augustine, says Williams, "a doctrine of signs is a step to a more general theory of language." He adds: "We cannot miss the point that discussion of signification is also discussion of those beings who are involved in meaning or 'intending' or understanding."[65] I would reply that a discussion of the *imago Dei* entails a discussion of signification as well as of theology and anthropology. There are far-reaching implications here. Male dominance is not, I maintain, the only problem in key traditional interpretations of the *imago Dei*. The tendency towards linguistic ambiguity is of equal concern. Feminist forays in the Swamp of Ambiguity do nothing to correct this tendency.

---

63. McFague, *Speaking in Parables*, 106.
64. See McFague, *Metaphorical Theology*, 29.
65. See Williams, "Language, Reality and Desire in Augustine's *De Doctrina*," 139.

8

Writing the Body

WHEN THE FOUR COMPANIONS of *The Wizard of Oz* arrive at the country inhabited by china figures they encounter a high wall also made of china, too smooth to climb. The Tin Woodman makes a ladder which allows his companions to reach the top of the wall. It is a long way down and the ladder is too heavy to be lifted over the wall, so the Scarecrow falls down and lies below to make a soft landing for the others. As they jump, his companions avoid the Scarecrow's head which is full of pins, placed there by the Wizard as part of the Scarecrow's "bran new brains." The exercise flattens out the straw body of the Scarecrow which has to be patted back into shape.[1]

The last chapter traced a trajectory of thinking which departs from the solid ground of the Yellow Brick Road in favor of relativism and deconstruction. In *The Wizard of Oz*, the Deadly Poppy Field is not far from the Road in terms of distance, but the scent of the poppies produces a drug-induced sleep. I liken this situation to the deceptive potential of relativist models. As long one lives within it, a model may appear to have cogency beyond its relativist rationale. If, on the other hand, one retains awareness of the relativist nature of one's thinking, the loss of solid support behind it becomes more obvious. In her books on "metaphorical theology" Sallie McFague attempts *both* to live within her models *and* to retain awareness of their relativist nature. This approach is intrinsic to the feminist critique

---

1. See Baum, *Wizard of Oz*, chapter 20.

of "patriarchy." The critique is couched in terms of relativism. These terms govern the course. However far one travels, ambivalence and loss of reality are implicit from the beginning of the journey.

One of the negative implications is a loss of a sense of embodiment. This might seem obvious: doubt about access to the external world must entail doubt about access to one's own body. But the point is obscured by the critique: loss of embodiment is attributed to the patriarchal perspective rather than to the relativist presupposition of the critique itself. That "patriarchy" may have contributed to loss of embodiment was argued in the final section of the previous chapter. This does not alter the difficulty with the critique. Far from offering a cure, the proposed remedy looks set to aggravate the disease.

In *The Wizard of Oz*, the Scarecrow allows his companions to flatten out his body and then pat it back into shape. Feminist writers would take issue with this. That is the burden of their complaint about "patriarchy": for too long the female body has been jumped on and reshaped by the male observer. Elaine Graham draws attention to Luce Irigaray and others who wish to do some shaping of their own. A key phrase for this kind of shaping is "writing the body."[2] But the phrase itself contains a contradiction: "writing the body" implies a writer, in which case the body is determined by something else. As will be seen below, a feminist search for embodiment is played out in a context of conflicting influences. Margaret Whitford, Irigaray's editor, describes the response to conflict as the "enactment of the tension."[3]

MAXIMIZING THE DIFFERENCE

In her extensive study of feminist thinking in society and the churches, Elaine Graham draws attention to the work of "radical" feminists who seek to maximize sexual difference, in contrast with "liberal" feminists wishing to "minimize sex difference beyond reproduction."[4] In terms of my illustration from *The Wizard of Oz*, the wish to minimize sexual

---

2. Graham, *Making the Difference*, 135: "'Writing the Body' is a feminist strategy which deploys a celebration of women's bodiliness in a direct challenge to patriarchal expropriation." Whitford cautions against reducing the complexity of Irigaray's work to the simplicity of a formula "writing the body" (*Irigaray Reader*, 2–3). I take the liberty of applying the term in a sense that goes beyond a narrow formula.

3. See *Irigaray Reader*, 13.

4. Graham, *Making the Difference*, 135.

difference could be likened to flattening out the Scarecrow's body while maximizing sexual difference would entail a process of reshaping it.

Rosemary Ruether maintains that most feminism today favors an expanded unitary view of human nature.[5] Luce Irigaray, on the other hand, envisages grave consequences from minimizing sexual difference:

> Certain tendencies of the day, certain contemporary feminists, are noisily demanding the neutralization of sex . . . That neutralization, if it were possible, would correspond to the end of the human race. The human race is divided into *two genres* which ensure its production and reproduction. Trying to suppress sexual difference is to invite a genocide more radical than any destruction that has ever existed in History.[6]

Irigaray goes on to state the need for "a culture of the sexual which does not yet exist, whilst respecting both *genres*." Elsewhere she goes so far as to state:

> Something of the consummation of sexual difference has still not been articulated or transmitted. Is there not still something held in reserve within the silence of female history: an energy, morphology, growth or blossoming still to come from the female realm? Such a flowering keeps the future open. The world remains uncertain in the fact of this strange advent.[7]

Here is a positive view of what might be called "delayed ontology." One can ask how satisfactory this delay would be for women.

The neutralization of sex would spell the end of the human race, states Irigaray. This is to indicate the scope of the matter. Graham remarks that the churches have not kept pace with secular enquiry into gender as an issue:

> Critical studies of gender have shifted over the past 30 years from concern with empirical measures of 'sex differences' to a more theoretical characterization of gender as an aspect of social relations; yet debates in theology and the churches have not moved beyond a characterization of the 'sex'/'gender' distinction that has now become out-dated. It is clear that a deeper and more critical enquiry is necessary, into the nature and extent of gender difference, its origin and dynamics, as well as

---

5. Ruether, "Christian Tradition and Feminist Hermeneutics," 286.
6. *Irigaray Reader*, 32.
7. *Irigaray Reader*, 176.

the implications for policy and practice. Such an interrogation needs an interdisciplinary perspective and a sophisticated theoretical focus.[8]

Graham states that studies in the human and social sciences indicate complex understanding of "how we inhabit our bodies in and against historical and cultural contexts."[9] At the same time traditional culture is subject to critique:

> Models of action that presuppose rationality ... autonomy and freedom of self-determination have been exposed as particular and historically-conditioned accounts, dating from the Enlightenment and the Scientific Revolution. The most outstanding example of ... altered notions of agency has arisen from feminist theories which identify human action and knowledge as profoundly embodied.[10]

The implications of a "profoundly embodied" view of human nature as it impinges on sexual difference are perhaps yet to be explored.

As seen above, feminist theory does not speak with one voice in this matter. Irigaray's endorsement of sexual difference comes hard up against the effect, seen as negative, of long standing "gender dualism." Graham reports:

> Critical accounts of the portrayal of gender in Greek philosophy ... tend to characterize it as unremittingly dualistic, and responsible for all subsequent systems of Western thought in which male and female are dichotomous and polarized.[11]

This dichotomy is said to be symptomatic of a broad cultural trend. Graham continues:

> Gender dualism is only one element in a much more comprehensive system of Western thought; the male/female dichotomy must be seen as a guiding organizing category for other binary pairs which mutually reinforce each other.

Such polarities are recurring themes in feminist discourse. Frances Gray cites A. Summers:

---

8. Graham, *Making the Difference*, 6.
9. Graham, *Making the Difference*, 145.
10. Graham, *Making the Difference*, 224.
11. Graham, *Making the Difference*, 12–13.

> The system of dualism in Western philosophy as a method of organising ideas has produced numerous theories attempting to describe and validate separate and opposing sexual characteristics. The distinctions of mind/body, good/evil, Logos/Eros have at all times been utilised in the spurious quest to give male supremacy a philosophical justification. By defining women as separate and as radically different (not just in biological capacity, but, as theorists as diverse as Nietzsche and Jung have argued, in essence from men) the realities of power and exploitation and cultural apartheid have been obscured or even justified.[12]

Western thought, inherited from Greek philosophy, is said to promote a dualistic system, linked with opposing sexual characteristics. Such dualism is seen as negative in its effects on women. Psychoanalysis, whether on Jung's terms or Irigaray's, would seem at one on the two "genres" of sexual difference. Irigaray, however, rejects male supremacy and its effects, as will be seen.

Psychoanalysis may side with the wish to maximize sexual difference, but the matter does not end there. Grace Jantzen writes: "one of the basic insights of the psychoanalysts which sets them apart from the religious and philosophical tradition of Augustine and Descartes and Locke is that human subjectivity is not a simple given":

> Persons are not ready-made souls inserted into bodies by God, nor minds which could be mature and whole independent of the physical history of the individual (and which could arguably continue after bodily death). Rather, human personhood is *achieved*, and achieved at considerable cost . . . In order to become a unified subject, some of these desires have to be repressed. This repression of desires is the formation of the unconscious; and from the unconscious, repressed desires may always threaten to erupt. Therefore strategies have to be in place to control thought, feeling and behaviour, lest the fragile subject falls apart once again into fragments.[13]

Such strategies, however, may be open to question. Irigaray, one-time pupil of Jacques Lacan, dissociates herself from the "patriarchal" orientation of his Freudian school of thought. Jantzen supplies the background to Irigaray's dissent:

---

12. See Gray, *Analytical Psychology and the Question of the Feminine*, 129, citing Summers, *Damned Whores and God's Police*, 80.

13. Jantzen, *Becoming Divine*, 8–9.

> To begin to understand Irigaray's answer [to Freud and Lacan] . . . and to see what religion has to do with it, it helps to see that according to Freudian theory modified by Lacan, the achievement of subjectivity (and the repression of unacceptable desires) takes place according to what Lacan, in deliberate echo of Catholic liturgy, calls the Law or Name of the Father. This thinly disguised religious formula indicates the authoritative nature of social demand, its patriarchal character, and also its religious structure. Indeed the obverse of the boy's repression of his desire for his mother is his entry into the language and civilization and social world of the fathers, which after Lacan can be referred to as 'the symbolic'. The 'symbolic' in French thought . . . includes all of language . . . and . . . can be used to designate the broad conceptual patterns of civilization.[14]

In this description, patriarchy, Catholic liturgy and "the symbolic" of culture are classed in similar terms.

Irigaray parts company with classic psychoanalysis in some areas but not in all. She challenges the cultural suppression of the female but not the prior distinction between male and female. For Irigaray, as Graham reports, "patriarchal thought essentializes [the female body] as 'Other' and immaterial and represses the feminine into the male unconscious."[15] In this context, says Graham, the female body "has no opportunity to create for itself a coherent identity." In response, "Irigaray uses female morphology deliberately to create an alternative ontology":

> In opposition to the unitary logic of patriarchal . . . speech, the female body possesses multiple sites of pleasure . . . Thus, women gain access to *jouissance*: the polymorphous, uninhibited sensuality which characterizes the pre-Oedipal realm of pure desire. Such a celebration of female sexuality serves to prefigure the feminist Utopia in which the feminine is not repressed by the 'symbolic' or cultural realm, but released like the unconscious under analysis. A logic which conceives of one sex alone—male, with female as lack—is thus challenged by a feminist voice which appropriates the products of its own psychic imaginings (necessarily born of the body) and transforms them into concrete social relations of feminist solidarity and social change.

Beginning with "psychic imaginings," in connection with the sexual act, the feminist voice is said to be released to facilitate social innovation.

---

14. Jantzen, *Becoming Divine*, 9–10.
15. Graham, *Making the Difference*, 136–37.

This undertaking entails novel categories of thought. Graham reports: "Irigaray's radical project to rewrite Western epistemology and ontology restores the significance of the body, passion, libido and the unconscious as legitimate foundations of knowledge and selfhood."[16]

The introduction to this book drew attention to Irigaray's advocacy of an "upheaval in symbolic order" in the assertion that God is a woman.[17] Frances Gray offers the following comment on Irigaray's method:

> [Luce Irigaray's] insistence on a . . . feminine-feminine symbolic/imaginary self-consciously yet ironically mimics the stereotypical image of woman found in the Western canon. Likewise, her appropriation of 'god', even as she values Feuerbach's rewriting of the concept, deploys stereotypical elements of the Christian symbolic/imaginary . . . Women's essence is derivative *in part* from the masculine-paternal symbolic/imaginary, yet its propulsion towards and engagement with a *telos*, implicit in Aristotle's notion of a cause, which is embraced as women's own ideal horizon, is the framework for a feminine-feminine symbolic/imaginary . . . Her essence is thus fluid and mobile, unconstricted by the negative demands and limitations of the masculine symbolic.[18]

Irigaray responds to religion, along with its deployment as a "symbolic," by way of psychoanalysis. But while she appropriates "god" along with stereotypical elements of the "Christian symbolic/ imaginary," such appropriation carries its own reinterpretation. Whatever is derivative is radically reoriented. As already seen in this book, she abandons "God—that guarantee of the meaning and non-meaning of the whole."[19]

For Irigaray, the Christian symbolic/imaginary is tied to a masculine "symbolic," hence her radical project to rewrite Western epistemology and ontology. But the attempt to maintain sexual difference while abandoning a guarantee of meaning is an uneasy exercise. Margaret Whitford draws attention to a further source of conflict for modern feminists: "On the one hand, they share with postmodernist thought the radical critique of the modernist Enlightenment inheritance; on the other hand,

---

16. Graham, *Making the Difference*, 137.
17. *Irigaray Reader*, 185.
18. Gray, *Analytical Psychology and the Question of the Feminine*, 147.
19. See *Irigaray Reader*, 218.

the emancipatory thrust of feminism is rooted in the Enlightenment."[20] Whitford adds:

> Irigaray's contribution here is to point to the dangers for women of embracing postmodernism too hastily or too uncritically . . . She warns against displacing the male/female binary before the female side has acceded to identity and subjectivity . . . In its enactment of the tension, [Irigaray's work] does not provide answers; it rather appeals to the reader to begin to invent the next step(s).

Women are said to be caught between a postmodern deconstruction of the subject and an unresolved search for a sense of their own worth and meaning. In this regard, Irigaray's contribution appears both conservative and revolutionary. She wishes to appropriate the emancipist thrust of modernism, at least in the short term. In doing so, she opens the door to an unresolved plethora of "next steps."

I will consider some proposed ways forward in the next section. As noted, Irigaray warns against a hasty departure from subjectivity, inherited from the Enlightenment. On the other hand, Graham draws attention to "feminist theories which identify human action and knowledge as profoundly embodied."[21] These differing emphases have the potential to reaffirm a polarity between mind and body, assertions to the contrary notwithstanding.

NEXT STEPS

"The human race is divided into two genres," says Luce Irigaray. "Trying to suppress sexual difference is to invite a genocide more radical than any destruction that has ever existed in History."[22] Irigaray upholds the female side of sexual difference, seeking emancipation for women in terms of subjectivity and identity as well as a new social order with input from the female body in new guise. Graham indicates that models of agency presupposing rationality, autonomy and freedom of self-determination (in a word, subjectivity) have given way to feminist theories identifying "human action and knowledge as profoundly embodied."[23] If feminist

---

20. *Irigaray Reader*, 12–13.
21. Graham, *Making the Difference*, 224.
22. *Irigaray Reader*, 32.
23. Graham, *Making the Difference*, 224.

notions of agency were to go so far as to de-emphasize subjectivity, the impetus to reshape the body would be correspondingly weakened. I have not found this to be the case. On the contrary, feminist theories would appear to sustain the presupposition of autonomy and freedom of self-determination. It is on this basis, for example, that Irigaray invites the reader to invent the next steps.

This section considers various "next steps." The term "writing the body" applies to these responses in a broad sense but not all writers embrace Irigaray's configuration. In general, the relationship between body and mind, nature and culture, remains problematic. Despite the aim to restore the significance of the body, Graham's study discerns a propensity towards lack of embodiment in Irigaray's project: "By placing the female body outside patriarchal culture, the more effectively to challenge androcentric norms, Irigaray risks rendering women's bodies immaterial and rhetorical, rather than empirical and rooted in social relations."[24]

If one thinks in terms of *The Wizard of Oz*, the Enlightenment's emphasis on subjectivity at the expense of embodiment can be likened to the Scarecrow's flattened body. (The "bran new brains" are not affected by the flattening process.) Irigaray's wish to retain the female side of the male/female binary harks back to a prior stage, before the Enlightenment's flattening of the body. On the other hand, her appeal to the reader to invent the next steps (an invitation to reshape the female side) would seem to come after it. Irigaray goes so far as to state that women "want to seize that which already exists so as to bring it back to an invisible source—their source?—a place from whence they might create, create themselves *ex nihilo*?"[25] In that invisible source is there not something of a flattened body, open to creation from nothing?

There is some tension between seizing that which already exists and self-creation *ex nihilo*. Graham expresses something of this ambivalence: "For . . . Irigaray and psychoanalysis, the crucial issue is one of morphology: the body is the site of the creation of identity, and is therefore very properly the focus of critical discourse." But, continues Graham, "the risk of Irigaray's strategy is not so much due to her concentration on the body itself, but more the way in which morphology is rendered as a pre-social, fixed essence which silences rather than invites further examination."[26]

---

24. Graham, *Making the Difference*, 137–38.
25. *Irigaray Reader*, 109.
26. Graham, *Making the Difference*, 138–39.

On the whole, critical strategies of Irigaray and others are said to facilitate social change:

> Feminist strategies of writing the body . . . deliberately draw upon the psychoanalytic fusion of psyche and soma: the body as no longer passive, but always holding the potential to 'speak' and disclose new self-knowledge previously repressed and now stored in the unconscious. It also serves to harness the element within psychoanalysis that sets civilization and desire at odds, and argues that bodies are simultaneously constrained and determined by society and social pressures, but also stand beyond and outside culture, threatening to undermine the surface order both of conscious rationality and of the social order. Arguably, it is this tradition, rather than a return to determinism and essentialism, that characterizes Irigaray's work.

Graham draws attention to "the psychoanalytic fusion of psyche and soma." Whether this fusion is really the speaking agent in psychoanalysis will be considered in the next section.

While exploring feminist theory in many disciplines, Graham also presents her own "next steps." She wishes to avoid a sex/gender dichotomy along the lines of a body/mind dichotomy:

> In attempting to avoid biological determinism, the sex/gender distinction . . . risks a corresponding form of social 'categorism' by seeing learning, social roles and externally imposed norms as the sole constituents of gender identity. Yet this obscures the body as an agent in the formation of gender altogether, with two consequences. Firstly, gender is perceived as a matter of behaviour and consciousness, presupposing disembodied minds as the primary and determinant sites of gender: a perpetuation of, rather than a challenge to, Cartesian dualism. Secondly, the privileging of consciousness universalizes and abstracts the material and historical aspects of 'lived experience'.[27]

But if, as in key feminist theory, the body threatens to undermine the surface of conscious rationality and the social order, the material and historical aspects of "lived experience" become something of a melting pot.

Undermining conscious rationality raises the further question of a source of values. "The challenge," comments Graham, "is to contemplate

---

27. Graham, *Making the Difference*, 124.

human nature as contingent and contextual, but also to consider the ethical and political implications of such . . . [an] understanding."²⁸ She asks:

> Does such a dissolution of the subject, and a disavowal of any notion of personhood that is independent of human discourse lead to an anti-humanism? Or can ethical and political value-commitments be founded on some enduring notion of the person that does not collapse into metaphysics or essentialism?

In answer, she reports that "many commentators are turning to accounts of 'truth' and 'value' as grounded in the purposeful and value-directed practices and activities of human communities."²⁹ Graham offers "value-directed practice" as a positive response in relation to the postmodern critique of metaphysics and dominant rationality. For Graham, this approach is both open-ended and liberating:

> Such a perspective translated into theology would speak of the contingency and situatedness of human existence and knowledge, and the provisionality of our apprehension of the divine . . . the centrality of practice—as self-reflexively reflecting and constructing gender identity, relations and representations—is confirmed as the focus of critical attention for a theology of gender. It would . . . add a feminist critique of . . . [traditional] claims to truth and value by attending to latent aspects of domination and exclusion in the formulation of such values.

To my mind, Graham's "value-directed practice" resembles the role of the "speaking" body of Irigaray and others. I will return to Graham's "centrality of practice" in relation to theology and the *imago Dei* in chapter 10.

A quest for embodiment, along with values on relativist terms as in Graham's "centrality of practice," does not avoid ambiguity. At this point I will glance back at chapter 7. The previous chapter considered a deconstructionist strategy of double reading which detects a rupture in a text, destabilizes it and opens the possibility of thinking otherwise. This strategy is said to be developed by Derrida and Irigaray.³⁰ Insofar as it overlaps with the destabilizing aspect of Irigaray's project, Graham's "centrality of practice" is perhaps less of an alternative to, and more of a development from within deconstruction itself. In its full rigor, "deconstruction's

---

28. Graham, *Making the Difference*, 223.
29. Graham, *Making the Difference*, 226–27.
30. Jantzen, *Becoming Divine*, 61.

critique makes clear the necessity of developing "negative capability"—the ability to endure absence, uncertainty, partiality, relativity, and to hold at bay the desire for closure, coherence, identity, totality."[31] A strategy of double reading, on the other hand, would redirect this "necessity" into seemingly more palatable channels.

The following "next steps" offered by Sallie McFague, Catherine Keller and Elizabeth Johnson represent what I judge to be variations on Graham's "value-directed practice." While she does not claim to be a feminist writer, McFague admits that she is influenced by "feminist epistemology"[32] Her "metaphorical theology" also offers a template for key feminists. On these terms, "next steps" engage with embodiment in the absence of a frame of external reference. Ontology in this context is realized within a projected model. As a theatre of action, "body" takes front of stage, but mind in the guise of imagination is directing the show. The script has a value-directed orientation, the sense of becoming or overcoming never far away.

The question posed by McFague is: what if? ("What if God's promise of permanent presence to all space and time were imagined as a worldly reality, a palpable, bodily presence?")[33] Chapter 7 drew attention to her models of "God the creator as mother" and of "God the savior as lover." Such *models*, says McFague, suggest forms of "sacramentalism." In other words, McFague inserts a traditional framework into a relativist framework. (Is there an element of double-reading in this procedure, McFague's disavowal of deconstruction notwithstanding?) The method opens the door to a new kind of theological shaping. "We are trying to think in an as-if fashion about the God-world relationship, because we have no other way of thinking about it," continues McFague.

I find a similar procedure in Catherine Keller's alternative reading of Genesis 1:2–3. Theology is read as it were backwards: "What if we begin . . . to read the Word from the vantage point of its own fecund multiplicity, its flux into flesh, its overflow?"[34] This is to ask McFague's question: what if? McFague imagines God's presence as palpable and bodily to all space and time. Keller presents an "imaginary of bottomless process" representing "the flow of the word that was always already

---

31. See McFague, *Models of God*, 25–26.
32. McFague, *Super, Natural Christians*, 2.
33. See McFague, *Models of God*, 69–70.
34. See Keller, *Face of the Deep*, 18–19.

materialized . . . a flux that unblocks the hope of an incarnation, in which all flesh takes part."[35] The material and historical aspects of "lived experience" might seem the predominating factor of these presentations. It must be recalled, however, that these aspects of "lived experience" belong within the model or "imaginary."

As seen in chapter 7, Keller's reading of Genesis 1:2 identifies a feminized *tehom* as a source of creativity, along the lines of the supposition, considered and rejected by Augustine, that creation is like a sponge in an infinite divine sea.[36] I find something like this in Johnson's proposal of a panentheist cosmos. Rejecting classical theism ("isolationist and dualist") and pantheism (a "suffocating deception" that encourages women to "submerge themselves in the 'all' of a man or family or institution"), Johnson continues:

> If theism weights the scales in the direction of divine transcendence and pantheism overmuch in the direction of immanence, panentheism attempts to hold onto both in full strength. Divine transcendence is a wholeness that includes all parts, embracing the world rather than excluding it, as the etymology of panentheism, "all-in-God," suggests, while divine immanence is given as the world's inmost dynamism and goal . . . This fundamental vision of mutual coinherence in which Holy Wisdom is present throughout the universe while everything is embraced in her inclusive freedom and compassionate love is highly compatible with feminist values . . . [Holy Wisdom] is like the boundless sea encompassing a tiny island.[37]

The boundless sea encompassing a tiny island resembles Augustine's sponge image. Johnson classes her presentation of panentheism as a "working paradigm," in similar vein perhaps to the "what if" espoused by McFague and Keller.

I do not find in Johnson the openly deconstructionist flavor that characterizes Keller. But the themes are similar: feminist values, movement towards an undefined but positive future, resolution of old polarities. Johnson writes: "A theology of the Creator Spirit overcomes the dualism of spirit and matter."[38] She outlines her theology in evolutionary terms:

---

35. Keller, *Face of the Deep*, 19, 181.

36. Keller, *Face of the Deep*, 81–82. See *Confessions* VII, 5, cf. VII, I. Keller describes this picture of a sponge in a boundless sea as Augustine's "most tehomophilic trope."

37. See Johnson, *She Who Is*, 231–32.

38. Johnson, *Women, Earth and Creator Spirit*, 59–61.

> Matter, alive with energy, evolves to spirit . . . Distinct from classical theism which separates God and the world, and also different from pantheism which merges God and the world, panentheism holds that the universe, both matter and spirit, is encompassed by the Matrix of the living God in an encircling that generates freedom, self-transcendence, and the future, all in the context of the interconnected whole.[39]

Johnson traces her "interconnected whole" back to the evolutionary Big Bang.[40] She also refers to God as Creator.[41] The relation of a panentheist God to a God as Creator is unclear.

To my mind, movement towards an undefined future, while compatible with a creative process, sits awkwardly with God said to be creator. Usage of the term "*ex nihilo*" seems similarly awkward. As seen, Keller posits a creative process which generates both creator and creation. One can compare Irigaray's remark that women "want to seize that which already exists so as to bring it back to an invisible source—their source?—a place from whence they might create, create themselves *ex nihilo*?"[42] In this case the creator—woman as self-creator—is, of necessity, prior to the creative process.

Keller opposes "the logic of *ex nihilo*" insofar as it results in binary oppositions: "one is either good or evil, corporeal or incorporeal, eternal or temporal, almighty or powerless, propertied or inferior."[43] The terms, however, can be altered. She continues: "One need not argue that this grid of dualisms necessarily accompanies the *ex nihilo* argument—only that historically it has done so." One can ask, however, whether the feminist method really overcomes dualisms. Keller's wish to counter creation produced by a masculine Word with a prior feminized *tehom* introduces a new dichotomy: she refers to "tehomophilic" and "tehomophobic" symbolism.[44] For Keller, theology based on the masculine Word is dominating and single-voiced while theology based on the feminine *tehom* is potentially many voiced. An *immaterial* Creator is contrasted with a *material* creative process.[45] What this differentiation does not say is that

39. Johnson, *Women, Earth and Creator Spirit*, 37–43.
40. Johnson, *Women, Earth and Creator Spirit*, 37.
41. Johnson, *Women, Earth and Creator Spirit*, 39.
42. *Irigaray Reader*, 109.
43. Keller, *Face of the Deep*, 49.
44. See Keller, *Face of the Deep*, 25–28; 36–38.
45. See Keller, *Face of the Deep*, 49–54, citing Irenaeus, *Against Heresies* to highlight

to situate a material creative process within an "imaginary" is to render it equally "immaterial."

There is a further difficulty with this kind of thinking. McFague states that her metaphor of "the world as God's body . . . does not totally identify God with the world any more than we totally identify ourselves with our bodies."[46] Paul S. Fiddes comments that there is no dualism of spirit and body *within* the metaphor but that, for McFague, "God as spirit *and* body, or the embodied spirit of the universe is a metaphor for the final reality of God which remains totally hidden."[47] He cites Grace Jantzen who "rightly objects that this is just another form of dualism."[48] Regarding a panentheist conception, Jantzen writes:

> Insofar as this means that God could exist without the world, or that there is a 'part' or aspect of God somehow beyond or other than the world, this collapses after all into dualism, and is not analogous with the relationship between a person and her body as I sketch it. If, on the other hand, it merely means that God is not reducible to physicalism, then it does not differ from pantheism. I suspect that panentheists often shuffle rather uneasily between these two positions.[49]

Johnson's objection that pantheism is a "suffocating deception" that encourages women to "submerge themselves in the 'all' of a man or a family or institution" might have something to say here.

Like McFague, Johnson factors in the unknowable God.[50] At the same time speech about the "mystery of God" does not point to God as such. Rather, it reflects or should reflect "the full reality of women as well as men" along with "symbols from the natural world" for the purpose of "the liberation of all human beings and the whole earth."[51] As seen in chapter 3, Johnson finds "material content" for speaking in female terms of the mystery of God in the "clearly personified figure of Sophia" and the "power of the mother symbol."[52] Elsewhere she writes:

---

the distinction.

46. McFague, *Models of God*, 71.
47. Fiddes, *Participating in God*, 287, citing McFague, *The Body of God*, 150.
48. Fiddes, *Participating in God*, 288, citing Jantzen, *Becoming Divine*, 265.
49. Jantzen, *Becoming Divine*, 271 n. 5
50. Johnson, *She Who Is*, 40.
51. See Johnson, *She Who Is*, 55–56.
52. See Johnson, *She Who Is*, 103.

> How shall we speak of Creator Spirit? If we search the scriptures with our major thesis in mind, we find a small collection of cosmic and female symbols of the Spirit, most of which are marginalized by a patriarchal imagination. Remembering these texts can give us the beginnings of a vocabulary for an ecological ethic and spirituality.[53]

She quotes Ann Belford Ulanov, *The Feminine: In Jungian Psychology and in Christian Theology*:

> The figure of the dove in the gospels and in Christian art... links the Holy Spirit with the broad pre-Christian tradition of divine female power: "Iconographically the dove is a messenger of the goddess [Aphrodite] and of the Holy Spirit."[54]

Johnson distances herself from "Jung's psychological assessment of the feminine anima"[55] which I outline below. Nevertheless, she states that women's religious experience is "a generating force" for "symbols for the divine," growing from a "deep level that Tillich identifies as the collective unconscious."[56]

Many of these themes and assumptions reappear in Irigaray's alternative to classic psychoanalytic theory, as will be seen. In general, key feminist writers abandon external truth, along with "presence" in language, on the grounds of its basis in the "masculine" Word. Consequently, any wish to retain the method of Cartesian subjectivity occurs on a weakened epistemological foundation. Some form of cogency for Johnson's proposals would appear to come through symbolic motifs in the subconscious mind. In consequence, there are two potential sources of epistemology, stemming from the Cartesian and psychoanalytic legacies. If there is a link between the rational and the sub-rational legacies, it is found in the ideologically inspired projection of the imagination which relies on both. But a projection of the imagination does not link the female subject with the external world. In such "next steps" dualism is overcome, if at all, *at the expense of* embodiment.

---

53. Johnson, *Women, Earth and Creator Spirit*, 44.
54. See Johnson, *Women, Earth and Creator Spirit*, 46.
55. Johnson, *She Who Is*, 174–75.
56. Johnson, *She Who Is*, 46, citing Paul Tillich, *Dynamics of Faith*, 41–48.

THE MATRIARCHAL LINE

Elaine Graham cites the Freudian aphorism, "biology is destiny."[57] But what is meant by "biology"? Graham continues: "Freud's genius lay in the recognition of the power of the unconscious, the fusion of body and mind in the drives and the fragmented and heterogeneous self."[58] The claim is made that the unconscious mind offers access to "biology." In other words, one can know the gendered self through analysis of the unconscious.

This assumption, reports Graham, is evident in Jungian thought: femininity "is represented in the unconscious by the 'anima,' identified as 'tenderness, sensitivity, seduction, indefiniteness, feeling, receptivity, yielding and understanding'"; masculinity, is represented by the "animus," identified with the "capacity to penetrate, take charge, initiate, create, to articulate and express meaning." The distinction "is offset by traces of a 'shadow' archetype of the opposite gender in the individual's unconscious." But these distinctions, indicates Graham, do little to dispel a stereotyped perception of "masculine" and "feminine" traits.[59]

In what sense then can these stereotypes be deduced from psychoanalytic practice? In an address beginning "Gentlemen, psychoanalysts . . ." because adding "ladies" would not change "the masculine noun [which] always governs the agreement" Irigaray states:

> You refuse to admit that the unconscious—your concept of the unconscious—did not spring fully armed from Freud's head, that it was not produced *ex nihilo* at the end of the nineteenth century, emerging suddenly to reimpose its truth on the whole of history—world history at that—past, present and future. The unconscious is revealed as such, heard as such, spoken as such and interpreted as such within a tradition.[60]

Irigaray indicates that the discipline of psychoanalysis operates on a conceptual basis: the "unconscious" is accessed via presuppositions of the conscious mind. More than this, the process reflects a male bias: "the masculine noun always governs the agreement."

---

57. Graham, *Making the Difference*, 102, citing S. Freud, *The Essentials of Psychoanalysis*, 402–11.

58. Graham, *Making the Difference*, 115.

59. See discussion in Graham, *Making the Difference*, 45–46.

60. *Irigaray Reader*, 80–81.

Irigaray critiques the effect on clinical practice: "your ears are already... open or closed in the right places... even before your analysand begins to speak. His or her particular is no more than a *proof* of the cogency of your universal."[61] This, she adds, was not always the case:

> Freud and first psychoanalysts did not act quite like this, or at least not for some time. For them, every analysis was an opportunity to uncover some new facet of a practice and a theory... But once psychoanalytic 'science' begins to claim to have discovered the universal law of the workings of the unconscious, and once every analysis is no more than an application or a practical demonstration of that law, the only status the now complete 'science' can possibly have is that of an era of knowledge already over.

There is an ambiguity to psychoanalysis. Which comes first: particular or universal; embodied sexuality or gendered stereotyping; body or mind?

Graham appears to regard this kind of ambiguity as a virtue. "Freudian psychoanalysis," she says, "is a testimony to the prevalence and self-reflexivity of gender systems, imbuing not only the forces which shape our consciousness, but the structures of thought—myths, sciences, therapeutic techniques—we summon in order to analyse that same consciousness."[62] Some of the ambiguity stems from the scope of the enterprise:

> As well as being characterized by theoretical pluralism, psychoanalysis can be said to be distinguished by a diversity of disciplinary dimensions. Firstly, it can be understood as a general theory of developmental psychology, advancing various hypotheses about the human journey from infancy to adulthood... with the acquisition of socially sanctioned sexual orientations and gender roles and attributes. Secondly, psychoanalysis stands as a specific form of psychotherapeutic practice... Thirdly, psychoanalytic theories provide analytical frameworks for the interpretation of wider aspects of human culture: themes in art, religion, literature and politics.[63]

But Irigaray's remarks challenge analytical frameworks.

Some female psychoanalysts have responded to classical psychoanalysis by a theory called "object-relations," based on attachment to the mother, in which Freudian characterization of femininity as "lack"

---

61. *Irigaray Reader*, 83. Irigaray's italics.
62. Graham, *Making the Difference*, 118.
63. Graham, *Making the Difference*, 100.

is turned on its head. Object-relations theorists argue that masculinity *represses* "all qualities associated with the maternal and nurturant, constructing a psychosexual identity founded on control, objectification and detachment," reports Graham.[64] This, she says, results in a masculinity which is "fragile, insecure and unresolved." But, while reversing Freudian stereotypes, this theory still argues for a universal law. As such, it is open to critique along the lines outlined by Irigaray above. Graham indicates a possible conflict in such generalities: "there may be an unexamined contradiction here, between a brittle and threatened male subjectivity and a dominant, hegemonic cultural construction of masculinity."

The Jungian distinction between masculine and feminine stereotypes along with their shadow archetypes is accompanied by detection of the influence of ancient myths in the unconscious. Frances Gray compares Irigaray and Jung in this respect:

> Luce Irigaray explores and condemns the banishment of female genealogy from Western mythic narratives... The Demeter and Persephone (Kore) myth provides Luce Irigaray with an avenue for exploring the mother-daughter relation and the primal mother. Jung also discussed this myth... But... he speaks of the mother-daughter relation as something to be overcome.[65]

While Irigaray takes issue with classic selection and interpretation of myths, she does not query the relevance of myths: "Give or take a few additions and retractions," she says, "our imaginary still functions in accordance with the schema established through Greek mythologies and tragedies."[66]

Rival interpretations of myths along gendered lines are associated with rival interpretations of history. Margaret Whitford observes:

> In 'The bodily encounter with the mother', Irigaray puts forward the idea which is the cornerstone of her work: that western culture is founded not on parricide (as Freud hypothesized in *Totem and Taboo*), but on matricide. Irigaray's reinterpretation of the story of Clytemnestra reads the myth as an account of the installation of patriarchy, built over the sacrifice of the mother and her daughters (one daughter, Iphigenia, literally sacrificed by Agamemnon, the other one, Electra, abandoned to her madness, while Orestes, the matricidal son, is designated to found

---

64. Graham, *Making the Difference*, 108–9.
65. Gray, *Analytical Psychology and the Question of the Feminine*, 123.
66. *Irigaray Reader*, 36.

the new order). The major cultural taboo is on the relationship with the mother.[67]

Irigaray detects an ancient conflict between a matriarchal system and an alleged transition to patriarchy which "forbids the daughter to respect the ties of blood *with her mother*."[68] She adds: "Our current morality is still dependent upon these very ancient events."

As noted, Irigaray challenges the "symbolic order" or patriarchal "conceptual patterns of civilization" according to Lacan's modification of Freud, represented as the "Law or Name of the Father," in deliberate echo of Catholic liturgy.[69] Irigaray classes this male-dominated state of affairs as "murder" of the mother. "When patriarchy is established," says Irigaray, "the daughter is separated from her mother, and more generally, from her family. She is transplanted into the genealogy of her husband, must live in his house, must bear his name, and so must her children etc."[70] Elsewhere she states: "It is . . . necessary, if we are not to be accomplices in the murder of the mother, for us to assert that there is a genealogy of women . . . within our family: on our mothers' side we have mothers, grandmothers and great-grandmothers, and daughters."[71] The "murder of the mother" motif is associated with Greek mythology but also with current morality along with Christian motifs: "No Jacob's ladder for a return to the mother. Jacob's ladder always climbs up to heaven, to the Father and his kingdom."[72] Violent activity from mythical Greek protagonists is thus attributed to the "Father and his kingdom."

Let us pause here and consider the assumptions by psychoanalysts in the light of the feminist critique and response to "patriarchy." I have already argued that the feminist critique challenges a masculine bias behind conceptual thinking but does not challenge the method itself. Similarly, Irigaray rejects a masculine bias in discerning a universal law in the workings of the sub-conscious but responds by seeking an alternative universal law in a female genealogy associated with Western mythical narratives. The matter does not rest with rival universal laws according to gender. Graham reports that object-relations theory attempts to reverse

---

67. *Irigaray Reader*, 25.
68. *Irigaray Reader*, 199. Italics in the text.
69. See Jantzen, *Becoming Divine*, 9–10.
70. *Irigaray Reader*, 199.
71. *Irigaray Reader*, 44.
72. *Irigaray Reader*, 40.

Freudian assumptions about the opposite sex. In other words, universal law systems (whether Freudian or feminist) are said to apply to both sexes. There are multiple problems with these approaches and gendered identity appears to suffer in consequence.

Common to both "patriarchal" and feminist theories is the assumption that abstract universal "laws" offer the possibility of inclusion and identity. While the feminist critique questions a masculine bias in this assumption, it does not question the assumption itself. "Give or take a few additions and retractions," says Irigaray, "our imaginary still functions in accordance with the schema established through Greek mythologies and tragedies."[73] On the other hand, it would appear that "our imaginary" has some choice about which mythologies it wishes to foster, along with how such mythologies are to be interpreted.

Irigaray exhorts women to avoid complicity in the "murder of the mother." But how is this to be achieved? As seen above, Irigaray draws attention to the genealogy of women. She continues:

> Given our exile in the family of the father-husband, we tend to forget this genealogy of women, and we are often persuaded to deny it. Let us try to situate ourselves within this female genealogy so as to conquer and keep our identity. Nor let us forget that we already have a history, that certain women have, even if it was culturally difficult, left their mark on history and that all too often we do not know them.[74]

At this point the method undergoes a shift. Women are no longer seen as governed by an abstract universal law, expressed in mythological terms. Rather, they are urged to preserve their identity by active association with the women of history.

"Let us try to situate ourselves within this female genealogy so as to conquer and keep our identity," says Irigaray. To my mind, this method is demonstrated in the biblical story of Naomi and Ruth. Phyllis Trible sums up her appraisal of this story:

> In scene one, Naomi and Ruth stand alone. They are women without men. They make their own decisions; they work out their own destinies. This posture continues in scene two, though the situation is more complex, since in Boaz a strong male appears. Hence, it is all the more important to discern that the

---

73. *Irigaray Reader*, 36.
74. *Irigaray Reader*, 44.

> power of the story is not transferred to him. The women continue to shape their tale, as both structure and content confirm. Scene two is their struggle to survive physically even as scene three is their struggle to survive culturally. In both scenes Boaz is reactor to their initiative. Scene four commences with the shock of reminder. After all, it is a man's world, and concerns of women may well be subsumed, perhaps even subverted, by this patriarchal climate. Yet the women of Bethlehem do not permit this transformation to prevail. They reinterpret the language of a man's world to preserve the integrity of a woman's story.[75]

Naomi and Ruth are particular women in a historical context. Their story is identified as a woman's story by a larger group of women, the women of Bethlehem. The story begins with the particular; it ends on a note that has universal implications.

As seen above, Irigaray detects a dramatic rupture in the imposition of patriarchy: "When patriarchy is established, the daughter is separated from her mother, and more generally, from her family. She is transplanted into the genealogy of her husband, must live in his house, must bear his name, and so must her children etc."[76] The biblical story of Naomi and Ruth, however, does not associate a patriarchal system with the loss of women's identity. Naomi exhorts each of her daughters-in-law to return to her "mother's house" (Ruth 1:8). It is Orpah who makes this choice. Ruth chooses to bear a son according to the genealogy of her deceased husband. Irigaray acknowledges that "we already have a history, that certain women have, even if it was culturally difficult, left their mark on history and that all too often we do not know them."[77] But the mark left on history may transcend Irigaray's framework.

A Freudian concept of the unconscious incorrectly claims to "reimpose its truth on the whole of history—world history at that—past, present and future," asserts Irigaray.[78] She does not, however, critique the supposition that the subconscious mind functions as the voice of gendered "biology." Nor does she critique the supposition that this voice speaks the language of Greek mythology, apparently generalized to the women of world history, past, present and future. Thus far Irigaray the psychoanalyst: there are presuppositions here that a feminist approach

---

75. Trible, *Rhetoric of Sexuality*, 195–96.
76. *Irigaray Reader*, 199.
77. *Irigaray Reader*, 44.
78. *Irigaray Reader*, 80.

does not avoid. Irigaray the activist, however, seems to function differently. Here identity is *not* said to come from the supposed subconscious mind of the individual analysand. Identity comes from solidarity with historical women.

Imposing a surmised universal law in the clinical practice of psychoanalysis is detrimental to women, says Irigaray. Does this apply only if the universal law is couched in male terms? Does it apply only in psychoanalysis? Daphne Hampson refers to the "much-quoted" reply of Gregory of Nazianzus to Apollinarius: "What is not assumed, is not redeemed."[79] This reply, much-quoted in feminist circles, brings the distinction between universal and particular to a head. What exactly is assumed in the Incarnation of Christ?

WHAT IS NOT ASSUMED?

C. S. Lewis writes: "We . . . tend to slur over the risen *manhood* of Jesus, to conceive him, after death, simply returning into Deity, so that the Resurrection would be no more than a reversal or undoing of the Incarnation."[80] We may compare this tendency with the assertion of Apollinarius that Christ had a human body and soul, but the Divine Logos rather than a human spirit. This implied that Christ could redeem only the spiritual elements and not the whole of human nature. Gregory of Nazianzus replied: "What is not assumed, is not redeemed." A tendency, however, to regard the resurrection of Jesus as the undoing of his incarnation would argue a continuing leaning towards the view of Apollinarius. I will come back to this.

What is entailed in Christ assuming the whole of human nature? Daphne Hampson outlines a key feminist line of approach:

> Now if it could be said that God in Christ took on specifically 'male humanity', then women would be outside the scheme of salvation—and that has never been suggested. If it is to be held that both women and men find salvation in Christ, then it must be simply 'humanity' which is of significance as having been taken on.[81]

---

79. See discussion in Hampson, *Theology and Feminism*, 53–58.
80. Lewis, *Miracles*, 176. Lewis's italics.
81. Hampson, *Theology and Feminism*, 55.

This argument presents "humanity" as a non-gendered universal. Whether this is a valid interpretation of Gregory's reply to Apollinarius is another matter.

Hampson reports an argument that a non-gendered universal may have suited the patristic cultural milieu:

> The argument arises from the fact that patristics was developed within what was philosophically a Platonist tradition. It was therefore assumed in the culture that there were 'universals' and that it was the universal, rather than particular instances of that universal, which could be said most truly to exist . . . Now what is in fact being said in a Christology created within such a cultural framework, is that God in Christ took on 'humanity'—the universal . . . which is not to imply that he did not have particularities, which indeed one has to have to be human . . . God in Christ, through taking on a particular instance of humanity, shares with all human beings the universal, humanity, and it is that which is of significance.[82]

This is to detach the particularities of Christ's humanity from his universal significance.

Non-gendered significance, allegedly associated with the Incarnation, is said to gain support from language associated with baptism. "Christianity," says Hampson, "has always proclaimed Christ to be an inclusive concept. In him, it is said, there is no East nor West, he is the new Adam, the first-born of all humanity; there is in Christ no Jew nor Greek, no more male and female."[83] Regarding the "practice and theology" of baptism of the early church, Hampson writes: "Christians were baptized into 'Christ,' not into 'Jesus,' that is to say into a relationship to Jesus as God, not into the human Jesus. And Jesus as God, as the second person of the trinity, presumably has no sex."[84] At this point the argument shifts from a focus on a non-gendered universal to a distinction between Jesus as human and Jesus as God. This shift appears to have more in common with the position of Apollinarius than that of Gregory.

One can compare the distinction between the human Jesus and Jesus as God with the tendency, cited by Lewis above, to slur over the risen manhood of Jesus. As seen in chapter 6, Janet Martin Soskice links the "God" of male Cartesian subjectivity with a possible Neoplatonic

---

82. Hampson, *Theology and Feminism*, 56–57.
83. Hampson, *Theology and Feminism*, 51.
84. Hampson, *Theology and Feminism*, 54.

heresy.[85] The position of Apollinarius may be a common assumption in Western culture. We may note, however, that "Christ" was not a prior title of divinity, but a name earned via the Incarnation and crucifixion, as seen in Philippians 2:6–11.

Some remarks about Platonist assumptions as well as the language of baptism may be of assistance here. Apollinarius may well be echoing a Platonic aversion to the notion that the divine Logos could assume human form. The reply from Gregory of Nanzianzus is counter-cultural in this respect. To "assume" means to "put on" or "wear." What is "put on" in the Incarnation is, according to Gregory's reply, the whole of human being, body, soul and spirit. Baptism appears to follow a similar process in reverse: the redeemed community "puts on" the whole of the divine-human being. The apostle Paul states: "As many of you as were baptized into Christ have clothed yourselves with Christ" (Galatians 3:27). At this divine-human level, "There is no longer Jew or Greek, there is no longer slave or free, there is no longer male and female; for all of you are one in Christ Jesus" (Galatians 3:28). To be "in Christ" is an inclusive concept, as Hampson attests. But to "put on" Christ is not to "put on" a Platonic non-gendered universal, rather it is to "wear" the divine humanity of Christ. In this sense the divine-human masculinity is gender-inclusive. I will have more to say about this process in the next chapter.

In Latin (as in Greek) there is a word for "human being." In this respect, the Western tradition offers some support for a non-gendered concept. Hampson admits, however, that this was not the only traditional way of including women: "In other ages, the female seemed in some sense to be 'included' in the male, in a way that is no longer the case . . . Men were normally held to represent women also."[86] In this kind of inclusion, she adds, humanity as a whole could be "thought to be summed up in Christ." In other words, the argument that Christ's male humanity would exclude women in redemption relies on *recent* assumptions about inclusion. "Today men are not in the same way held to represent women," continues Hampson. "There are two sexes and women represent themselves."[87]

Hampson goes so far as to claim that a male-centred Christology originally gained credibility from the science of the day: "Mistaken biological beliefs, such that the male alone was thought to be a full human

---

85. Soskice, *Kindness of God*, 119.
86. Hampson, *Theology and Feminism*, 51.
87. Hampson, *Theology and Feminism*, 52.

being, underlay western culture, making this seem the more plausible."[88] Some remarks by Augustine on the resurrection of the body would suggest that she does less than justice to Christian tradition in this area. A key passage in this regard is Ephesians 4:13 about attaining "the perfection of manhood" in Christ. Augustine writes:

> If . . . the passage is to be referred to the form of the resurrected body, what is there to prevent our supposing that the mention of 'man' implies 'woman' also, *vir* being used here for *homo* ('human being')? There is a similar use in the verse, 'Blessed is the man (*vir*) who fears the Lord', which obviously includes the women who fear him.[89]

The Latin *vir* (male-centred inclusion) can be used to imply *homo* (non-gendered inclusion), says Augustine. But far from offering support for "mistaken biological beliefs, such that the male alone was thought to be a full human being," Augustine takes issue with such beliefs.[90]

Acknowledging differing responses to New Testament exhortations about attaining the full stature of Christ, Augustine states his own view: "Now St Paul talks of being 'predestined to be shaped into the likeness of God's son.' This can be taken as referring to the inner man."[91] He continues: "Because of these sayings, 'Until we reach the perfection of manhood, the stature of the full maturity of Christ' and 'Being shaped into the likeness of God's Son,' some people suppose that women will not keep their sex in the resurrection . . . but. . .will rise again as men." He then responds: "I feel that theirs is a more sensible option who have no doubt that there will be both sexes in the resurrection . . . For a woman's sex is not a defect; it is natural."[92]

---

88. Hampson, *Theology and Feminism*, 51–52. Cf. Soskice (*Kindness of God*, 85) who states that the *Summa Theologiae* summarizes the most common medieval arguments for a male saviour: "Because the male excels the female sex, Christ assumed a man's nature . . . So that people should not think little of the female sex, it was fitting that he should take flesh from a woman." Soskice cites J. Gibson who states that "Albert [the Great], and not Aquinas, was the first to introduce the Aristotelian argument that a woman is a defective man, and . . . since Christ ought to represent perfection, not an imperfection of nature, he should be incarnate as a man."

89. *City of God*, XXII, 18.
90. See chapter 5.
91. *City of God*, XXII, 16.
92. *City of God*, XXII, 17.

Tucked in among these observations about attaining the full stature of Christ, and woman's resurrected body, is a passage we have already met:

> Now in creating woman at the outset of the human race, by taking a rib from the side of the sleeping man, the Creator must have intended, by this act, a prophecy of Christ and his Church. The sleep of the man clearly stood for the death of Christ; and Christ's side, as he hung lifeless on the cross, was pierced by a lance. And from the wound there flowed blood and water which we recognize as the sacraments by which the Church is built up. This, in fact, is the precise word used in scripture of woman's creation; it says not that God 'formed', or 'fashioned' a woman but that 'he built it (the rib) up into a woman. Hence the Apostle also speaks of the 'building up' of the Body of Christ, which is the Church. The woman, then, is the creation of God, just as is the man; but her creation out of man emphasizes the idea of the unity between them; and in the manner of that creation there is, as I have said, a foreshadowing of Christ and his Church.[93]

The symbolic parallel between the man and the woman and Christ and the Church centers here on what holds each pair together. The woman is built up from something that is of the substance of the man, i.e., his rib. The Church is built up from something that is of the substance of Christ, i.e., the blood and water which flowed from his pierced side as he hung lifeless on the cross. The connection holding each pair together is physical: a rib in the case of the man and woman, blood and water in the case of Christ and the Church. In other words, the link itself is embodied. Edmund Hill observes, in relation to 1 Corinthians 11:3 "the woman is from the substance of the man in equality of nature."[94] He could have said a similar thing about the relationship between Christ and the Church.

Let us return to the exchange between Apollinarius and Gregory of Nazianzus. Both agree that Christ had a human body and soul but differ about the spirit. Gregory's reply indicates that what Christ assumes (or does not assume) in the Incarnation is relevant to redemption. This implies that, along with a human soul and spirit, Christ's (male) body is relevant to redemption. Augustine states that, like the man, the woman is the creation of God but that "her creation out of man emphasizes the idea of the unity between them," as in the parallel case of Christ and the Church. In other words, earlier thinking favored an embodied

93. *City of God*, XXII, 17.
94. See Hill in Augustine, *The Trinity*, XII, 338 n. 22.

inclusiveness. Hampson, on the other hand, would appear to rule out this out. In feminist thinking, Christ's "male humanity" is not relevant to redemption, she says, and men do not represent women but rather women represent themselves. In this area feminist thinking favors abstraction rather than embodiment and separation of the sexes as opposed to unity between them.

Elizabeth Johnson presents what appears to be a standard feminist appeal to a non-gendered human universal, rejecting "a naïve physicalism that collapses the totality of the Christ into the bodily form of Jesus":

> If the model of sharing in the image of Christ be one of exact duplication, similar to the making of a xerox copy, and if Christ be reduced to the historical individual Jesus of Nazareth, and if the salient feature about Jesus as the Christ be his male sex, then women are obviously excluded from sharing that image in full. But every one of those suppositions falls short and twists the central testimony of biblical and doctrinal traditions. The guiding model for the *imago Christi* is not replication of sexual features but participation in the life of Christ, which is founded on communion in the Spirit: those who live the life of Christ are icons of Christ. Furthermore, the whole Christ is a corporate personality, a relational reality, redeemed humanity that finds its way by the light of the historical narrative of Jesus' compassionate, liberating love: Christ exists only pneumatologically. Finally, what is essential to the saving good news about Jesus is not his bodily sex but the solidarity of the Wisdom of God in and through this genuine human being with all those who suffer and are lost. To make the maleness of Jesus Christ a christological principle is to deny the universality of salvation.[95]

There are numerous statements here, needing to be unpacked in terms of "biblical and doctrinal traditions." I will attempt a brief comparison between Johnson and Augustine in these matters below.

Johnson states: "The guiding model for the *imago Christi* is not the replication of sexual features but participation in the life of Christ." Augustine agrees that this kind of likeness is spiritual: "Now St Paul talks of being 'predestined to be shaped into the likeness of God's son.' This can be taken as referring to the inner man."[96] Johnson would take issue here

---

95. See Johnson, *She Who Is*, 71–72.
96. *City of God*, XXII, 16.

not with Augustine but, one might surmise, with some of his contemporaries who argued that women would be resurrected as men.

Johnson continues: "To make the maleness of Jesus Christ a christological principle is to deny the universality of salvation." Here there is a parting of the ways. For Augustine, the principle relies on the tangible link between the man and the woman, replicated in the divine-human relationship: "Now in creating woman at the outset of the human race, by taking a rib from the side of the sleeping man, the Creator must have intended, by this act, a prophecy of Christ and his Church." As he explains elsewhere, salvation is achieved via the tangible link between head and body.[97]

Johnson's Christology also differs from that of Augustine in terms of the identity of Jesus as the Wisdom of God. Johnson states: "What is essential to the saving good news about Jesus is not his bodily sex but the solidarity of the Wisdom of God in and through this genuine human being with all those who suffer and are lost." Augustine makes a distinction between the Wisdom of God *with* humanity and the Wisdom of God *incarnate in* a male body. "The Son of course is the Father's Word, which is also called his Wisdom," says Augustine.[98] He continues:

> But her being sent to be with man is one thing; that she was once sent to be man is another . . . when the fullness of time came she was sent . . . not to be with men or in men, since she had already been like this in the patriarchs as prophets; no, it was in order that the Word might become flesh, that is become man.

To rephrase Johnson's remark, what is essential about Jesus cannot be separated from his bodily sex for this is how the Wisdom of God became flesh. One could add that the seed of the *woman* is the source of his humanity. I will return to this in the next chapter.

The idea of operating in solidarity with or in people is a biblical one, as Augustine indicates. On the human level we have already met something of the sort in the solidarity of the women of Bethlehem with the story of Naomi and Ruth. The presence of Wisdom with the patriarchs and prophets is of a closer kind than human solidarity while the presence of Wisdom in the body of Christ is closer still. But these kinds of solidarity, while differing from each other in degree, are distinct in kind from an abstract idea of a human universal, espoused by Hampson above.

---

97. See *City of God*, XXIII, 23; cf. Augustine's reference to Galatians 3:27.
98. See *The Trinity* IV, 27.

A Christ who, in Johnson's words, "exists only pneumatologically" might be compatible with a non-gendered human universal but hardly with a Church nourished by the tangible reminders of Christ's death. A Christ who "exists only pneumatologically" would be a body without a head. Elsewhere Hampson states: "Religion lives through its concretion . . . the parables, the stories and the history, the images, symbols and metaphors by which it is carried. Of course it would be possible to have a religion which was largely abstract . . . But Christianity is not like that."[99] One might draw the general conclusion that a de-literalizing of the biblical narrative must surely cause a *loss* of embodiment. "The difficulty with bowdlerizing retellings of the story of Jesus is that we are left with such thin fare," says Soskice. She adds, "It is paradoxical that feminist theologies, which so often desire to stress particularity and embodiment, can result in a featureless and disembodied Christ."[100]

Apollinarius asserted that Christ had a human body and soul, but the Divine Logos rather than a human spirit. This implied that Christ could redeem only the spiritual elements and not the whole of human nature. Johnson, professed advocate of panentheism,[101] writes that "what is essential to the saving good news about Jesus is not his bodily sex but the solidarity of the Wisdom of God in and through this genuine human being with all those who suffer and are lost." Where does this leave redemption of the body?

In stark contrast to thin fare of feminist theologies, Paul Fiddes observes: "If this event, which has all the contingency of time and space, of the dusty roads of Galilee, the sweat of crowds and the blood of executions, is normative for the embodiment of God, then we can never escape the particular."[102] This has implications for redemption:

> So when we say 'Amen' to the Father as we meet God in all creation, we are leaning on the particular human response of Jesus, the Jesus of the wilderness beyond Jordan, of Gethsemane and Golgotha, interweaving inseparably with the ecstatic response of eternal sonship. Meeting God through bodies, we are always dependent upon the particular body of Christ.[103]

---

99. Hampson, *Theology and Feminism*, 81.
100. Soskice, *Kindness of God*, 86.
101. See Johnson, *She Who Is*, 231–32.
102. Fiddes, *Participating in God*, 290.
103. Fiddes, *Participating in God*, 289.

A Christ who exists only pneumatologically or constant dependence on the particular body of Christ? What is not assumed is not redeemed.

9

Inclusive Language

ON THEIR WAY TO the South Country of the Land of Oz, Dorothy and her friends encounter odd creatures with no arms but powerful expanding necks. The Scarecrow tries to climb the hill belonging to these creatures and is bowled over and sent tumbling back down again. The Lion roars in protest and receives the same treatment. In order to cross the hill Dorothy has to summon the Winged Monkeys who carry the travelers over by air. The so-called Hammer-Heads try to stop the travelers by shooting out their necks as they pass.[1]

The first Hammer-Head is described as the strangest man the travelers had ever seen, leaving open the possibility that "man" is an ambivalent term for this creature. In chapter 5, I compared the Hammer-Head to Phyllis Trible's non-gendered "earth creature." One could also compare the Hammer-Head to the patriarchal figure of the feminist critique. In this chapter I will take the further liberty of inventing another hill and another kind of Hammer-Head. On this hill the Hammer-Heads are female.

"Feminist theology starts with anthropology, rather than deducing male-female relations from an *a priori* definition of God," states Rosemary Ruether. "It assumes all our images of God are human projections."[2] This kind of theology shoots up from below, like the expanding necks in the *Wizard of Oz*. The method arises from the critique. "The definition

---

1. See Baum, *Wizard of Oz*, chapter 22.
2. See Ruether, "Christian Tradition and Feminist Hermeneutics," 286–87.

of God as patriarchal male is presumed to be a projection by patriarchal males of their own self-image and roles, in relation to women and lower nature, upon God," says Ruether. She adds that a feminist reconstruction of images of God "starts by seeking a just and truthful anthropology." But as she points out, the critique "changes fundamentally the nature of the discussion." In a method which shoots up from below, "just and truthful" may be open to interpretation. As seen in chapter 8, Elaine Graham reports that "many commentators are turning to accounts of 'truth' and 'value' as grounded in the purposeful and value-directed practices and activities of human communities."[3] Despite a claim to *inclusive* religious language, the method favors *differing* projections (or hills).

"The religions of the west with their male God(s) offer no way for women to achieve *our* subjectivity in relation to a divine horizon," writes Grace Jantzen. One could have no clearer expression of the need for a separate religious realization. Jantzen quotes Luce Irigaray:

> We have no female trinity. But as long as woman lacks a divine made in her image she cannot establish her subjectivity or achieve a goal of her own. She lacks an ideal that would be her goal or path in becoming . . . If she is to become woman, if she is to accomplish her female subjectivity, woman needs a god who is a figure for the perfection of her subjectivity.[4]

"The masculinist religious symbolic must be disrupted," continues Jantzen, "and space made for the female divine." If, as Ruether reports, "it is not 'man' who is made in God's image, but God who has been made in man's image,"[5] is it not permissible for God to be made in woman's image? On Irigaray's terms, not only permissible but necessary: otherwise, woman cannot become woman.

A key difficulty with this kind of thinking is that it promotes individualism. The "divine horizons" will multiply according to differing agendas. This is not the language of male *and* female jointly *created* in the image of God but of the *creation* of a "divine horizon" in relation to male *or* female. Phyllis Trible writes that the phrase "the image of God" stresses the difference (as well as similarity) between Creator and creation. The tenor, says Trible, is not defined by the vehicle; it is the moon that can

---

3. See Graham, *Making the Difference*, 226–27.
4. See Jantzen, *Becoming Divine*, 15, citing, *Sexes and Genealogies*, 63.
5. Ruether, "Christian Tradition and Feminist Hermeneutics," 287.

be seen but not possessed.[6] By contrast, Irigaray indicates that woman cannot become woman *unless* she possesses the moon. Woman needs a divine horizon made in her image.

A religious "symbolic" intentionally based on "possessing the moon" is a "symbolic" of conquest. However much it may purport, in Ruether's words, to "promote the full realization of human potential for women and men"[7] it will do so on the terms of the particular (gendered) "horizon." Jantzen uses the language of disruption and space-making. This implies that a space for the female divine must be a dedicated space which cannot be invaded by "a masculinist religious symbolic." It does not take a large stretch of imagination to picture so-called *inclusive* religious language as a series of hills in which the inhabitants actively guard their own air space.

MODEL AS WEAPON?

Can differing models be said to function as weapons? Hampson quotes Mary Daly:

> Sometimes black theology... resounds with a cry for vengeance and is fiercely biblical and patriarchal. It... tends to settle for religion as a gun. Tailored to fit only the situation of racial oppression, it... leaves unexplored other dimensions of liberation. It does not get beyond the sexist models internalized by the self... models that are at the root of racism... The Black God and Black Messiah apparently are merely the same patriarchs after a pigmentation operation—their behavior unaltered.[8]

But if this kind of black theology functions as a gun, the feminist response would seem a correspondingly fierce rejection of the biblical God and Messiah. Hampson cites Daly regarding a woman's realization that she "had to be a feminist": "the first act [she] performed... was to 'let God have it.' She killed off the male 'God.'"[9] There is more than a hint of weaponry here.

---

6. See Trible, *Rhetoric of Sexuality*, 20–21.

7. Ruether, "Christian Tradition and Feminist Hermeneutics," 287.

8. See Hampson, *Theology and Feminism*, 129–30, citing Daly, *Beyond God the Father*, 25.

9. See Hampson, *Theology and Feminism*, 109, citing Daly, *Pure Lust: Elemental Feminist Philosophy*, 396.

Killing off the male "God" would appear to promise beneficial outcomes. Hampson lists various feminist aspirations: "fundamental change"; "healing of relationships"; "non-dominative patterns of behaviour."[10] Such terms do not sound like linguistic weaponry. On the contrary, these benevolent-sounding ideals would seem to bear out Ruether's claim that feminist theology "constructs images of God that will better manifest and promote the full realization of human potential for women and men."[11] The other side of the process is more negative. Hampson reports of Ruether that as she "has come to pay more attention to issues of imagery and symbolism she has increasingly moved outside the Christian tradition, finding it to be inadequate."[12] Others go further. "Many a woman . . . has had to turn her back upon the religion within which she grew up. It simply became impossible," reports Hampson.[13]

If one turns one's back on traditional religion, where does one go? "It is urgently necessary for feminists to work towards a new religious symbolic focused on natality and flourishing rather than on death," states Grace Jantzen.[14] She paints a stark contrast between a life-promoting feminist "symbolic" and an alleged "masculinist" preoccupation with death:

> Western civilization, dominated by masculinist structures, has had both a fascination with and a dread of death . . . The preoccupation with death is matched by a fascination with other worlds, some other form of reality beyond the uncertainties of this present life, bound up as it is with the material body.[15]

This fascination, says Jantzen, appears "in the traditional religious form of looking towards heaven and treating this life merely as a preparation for that better one" and also in secular interest in "space flights and telescopes." The preoccupation with death and other worlds contrasts with "the actual world in which we live, and our responsibilities to it and to one another," a contrast reflecting "the desire to master and ultimately to escape from matter." Such thinking can be coupled with "the age-old linkage of the female with the material and the male with the rational spirit."[16]

10. Hampson, *Theology and Feminism*, 130.
11. Ruether, "Christian Tradition and Feminist Hermeneutics," 287.
12. See Hampson, *Theology and Feminism*, 108–9.
13. Hampson, *Theology and Feminism*, 173.
14. Jantzen, *Becoming Divine*, 254.
15. Jantzen, *Becoming Divine*, 129–30.
16. Jantzen, *Becoming Divine*, 130.

Let us pause here. Whether or not this depiction is true of the secular West, the link with the traditional religion of the West is less tenable, given that Christianity is not of Western origin. Phyllis Trible presents an alternative picture in her remarks on the Song of Solomon:

> Love is bone of bone and flesh of flesh. Thus I hear the Song of Songs. It speaks from lover to lover with whispers of intimacy, shouts of ecstasy, and silences of consummation. At the same time, its unnamed voices reach out to include the world in their symphony of eroticism. This movement between the private and the public invites all companions to enter a garden of delight.[17]

A simple association between traditional religion and a desire to escape from matter does not apply here. To my mind, a Western *departure* from the Christian tradition is likely to exacerbate unease with embodiment.

The proposed new religious symbolic may be less about promotion of embodiment as against a non-material tradition and more about a feminist desire for mastery at a level equivalent to male mastery. There are subtleties here because feminist rhetoric would suggest otherwise. Jantzen writes of "exploring the embodied, earthed, female divine as 'the perfection of our subjectivity.'"[18] While the language of "embodied" and "earthed" echoes the linkage of the female with the material, the method of "perfecting subjectivity" does not. The "female divine" is a projected figure, a material representation of feminist aspiration. Despite the rhetoric, she is no creature of flesh and blood.

In search of physicality, Irigaray goes so far as to draw on key Christian language, albeit on her own terms. Jantzen reports that Irigaray uses the masculinity of Jesus as a stepping-stone, to argue that "he was only a *partial* incarnation":

> He could not be the whole, the unique and only one, since he did not encompass all of humanity. Indeed, so far from seeing the incarnation as an endorsement of Jesus as the unique one, Irigaray argues for 'the incarnation of all bodies (men's and women's) as potentially divine; nothing more nor less than each man and each woman being virtually gods' . . . if [Jesus] was partial, then his incarnation leaves room for other incarnations, other trinities, other sexualities. The masculinist symbolic which looks above all to salvation from this mortal state is subverted from within. Because 'unto us a child is born', the door

---

17. Trible, *Rhetoric of Sexuality*, 144.
18. Jantzen, *Becoming Divine*, 275.

> is open to develop a new religious imaginary which will enable our sexuate becoming, the flourishing of our natality.[19]

"Unto us a child is born" is no longer related to the unique incarnation of God or even to a specific child, but rather to a diffuse sense of embodied becoming. One might wonder what Irigaray means by "incarnation."

The suggestion that Jesus, understood as a partial incarnation, might function as a prototype for the incarnation of all bodies is said to arise from Irigaray's response to Elisabeth Schüssler Fiorenza's *In Memory of Her*. Jantzen reports that Irigaray "delights in Schüssler Fiorenza's recovery of the hidden women of early Christendom, and sees her book as vastly preferable to the neutral/neuter renderings of the Christian message."[20] But, she continues, Irigaray is "ultimately disappointed with Schüssler Fiorenza's book; it does not sufficiently challenge or displace the traditional masculinist religious symbolic." Regarding Irigaray's proposal, Jantzen comments:

> Irigaray fails to do so, but it is easy to see how parallel points can be made with relation to 'race'. Jesus was a Jew. In this respect also he was partial, as any human must be . . . by Irigaray's reasoning, this leaves room for other incarnations, other 'racially' specific bodies becoming divine.[21]

Jantzen adds that a Black Messiah would accord with such thinking, "although typically this is not carried through to Irigaray's conclusion of 'nothing more nor less than each man and each woman being virtually gods.'" But, given the comment cited above, some Black theology might not qualify for a new religious symbolic.

If the Messiah is not the unique and only one, what becomes of the religion? To put it another way, how inclusive is "the incarnation of all bodies (men's and women's) as potentially divine"? Irigaray's claim to leave room for "other incarnations, other trinities, other sexualities" leaves no room for the unique Incarnation of the parent religion. Hampson draws attention to Sallie McFague's alternative models of God and asks whether they are Christian. In relation to the metaphor of the world as God's body, Hampson remarks: "We shall have a different religion, if, of God's relation to the world, we may say of her that she is related to the world as to her body. It is as though the cuckoo has used the nest to

---

19. Jantzen, *Becoming Divine*, 16–17. Jantzen's italics.
20. See Jantzen, *Becoming Divine*, 16.
21. See Jantzen, *Becoming Divine*, 17 n. 7.

lay its egg and ousted the previous chicks."²² The nest retained while the previous chicks are ejected? Is this not the language of a model in the guise of a weapon?

DISCOURSE IN THE CHURCHES

"Religion lives through its concretion," says Daphne Hampson. "Of course," she adds, "it would be possible to have a religion which was largely abstract . . . But Christianity is not like that."²³ She goes on to say: "In Christian worship, or through reading of the bible, this language and imagery is transported from the past into the present . . . Change to the concretion may be thought to be extraordinarily difficult, for the imagery is built into the literature and thought structure which form the basis of the religion."²⁴

Hampson quotes C. S. Lewis's defense of masculine language for God:

> Suppose the reformer stops saying that a good woman may be like God and begins saying that God is like a good woman. Suppose he says that we might as well pray to 'Our Mother which art in Heaven' . . . Suppose he suggests that the Incarnation might just as well have taken a female as well as a male form, and the Second Person of the Trinity be as well called the Daughter as the Son . . . But Christians think that God himself has taught us how to speak of Him. To say that it does not matter is to say either that all the masculine imagery is not inspired, is merely human in origin, or else that, though inspired, it is quite arbitrary and unessential. And this is surely intolerable . . . A child who had been taught to pray to a Mother in Heaven would have a religious life radically different from that of a Christian child.²⁵

"A feminist," comments Hampson, "will agree with Lewis that a child who prayed to a mother in heaven will have a fundamentally different conception of God! She might well say that she would have a different sense of herself as well had she grown up counting herself as made in God's image."

---

22. See discussion of McFague's models in Hampson, *Theology and Feminism*, 158–60.
23. Hampson, *Theology and Feminism*, 81.
24. Hampson, *Theology and Feminism*, 84.
25. See Hampson, *Theology and Feminism*, 82–83, citing Lewis, "Priestesses in the Church?," 90–91.

Hampson and Lewis are at one about the importance of symbolic language. They disagree about the status of the masculine imagery. As Lewis points out, the difference hinges on whether the masculine imagery is "inspired" or whether it is "merely human in origin." Hampson sides with the latter assumption: "Human beings chose the imagery through which they would capture their understanding of God."[26] Nevertheless, concludes Hampson, the claim that the symbolic language is merely human in origin does not facilitate change in the language. The "concretion" is too firmly embedded.

A child taught to pray to a mother in heaven might have not only a fundamentally different conception of God but also a different sense of herself, had she grown up counting herself as made in God's image, says Hampson. The key point here is the child's belief that she is made in God's image. Where does this understanding come from, if not from the religion? In this sense, a desire to change the "concretion" of Christianity gains its impetus from the tradition. If, as is claimed, human beings chose and continue to choose the imagery through which they capture their understanding of God, the *imago Dei* is turned on its head, but it is not abandoned. The cord of connection with Christianity is stretched but not severed. Even Irigaray retains this link with Christianity, albeit a barely recognizable one.

Let us be clear about what is at stake here. The feminist critique upholds the importance of symbolic language. The critique may go so far as to treat the parent religion as raw material for a new religious symbolic. This step entails a change in the linguistic reference of symbolic language with a corresponding ambiguity about what it actually means. This is what I call building one's own hill. But the demand for "inclusive language" is not always taken to this extreme. To the degree that it remains within the Christian fold, the demand is necessarily muted. Christianity is not an abstract religion, attests Hampson. It is anchored in its literature and thought structure in a way that resists change. In this context, feminist issues have tended to be less than clear. The churches have responded to the demand for inclusion without perhaps a full grasp of its scope.

I attempt a brief survey of varying responses below. A Catholic response appears in Boff's proposal of a feminine "principle" in the Godhead. Protestant writers have focused on the role of women in the churches and have avoided, or perhaps only touched lightly upon,

---

26. See Hampson, *Theology and Feminism*, 83–84.

symbolic implications. A Protestant response, which does not engage with the "concretion," or which fails to do justice to it, adds to the multiplicity of voices but does not facilitate clear thinking in this area.

Chapter 8 noted two different styles of feminist thinking: "liberal" feminism which seeks to minimize sexual difference beyond reproduction and a tradition of "writing the body" which purports to maximize sexual difference.[27] In the former the emphasis is on equality and the common humanity of men and women. The latter focuses on embodiment and identity for women. The wish to minimize sexual difference is reflected in Ruether's remark that most feminism today favors an expanded unitary view of human nature.[28] More recently, however, emphasis has shifted to the relevance of sexual difference. These emphases are echoed in a long-running Protestant debate about the role of women in the churches.

Regarding this issue Stanley Grenz wrote in the 1990s:

> Evangelicals today are divided into two clearly defined groups: those who believe that all facets of ministry ought to be open to women (egalitarians) and those who are convinced that women can properly serve only in supportive roles (complementarians). Despite a protracted discussion on the issue, the chasm between the two viewpoints seems to be widening.[29]

At the same time, the "egalitarian" position has undergone some development. Grenz states:

> In the past egalitarians tended to counter the complementarian position by denying any distinction between male and female. This position, often termed "androgyny," declares that there is only one fundamental human essence . . . Proponents of androgyny assert that apart from obvious differences in reproduction, no fundamental distinctions exist between males and females.[30]

More recently, claims Grenz, egalitarians "want the church to avail itself of the particular contributions of men *and* women in every aspect of its

---

27. Graham, *Making the Difference*, 137–39, and chapter 6: "Bodies: History, Epistemology and Practice."

28. Ruether, "Christian Tradition and Feminist Hermeneutics," 286.

29. Grenz, *Women in the Church*, 19–20.

30. Grenz, *Women in the Church*, 157–58. Cf. Graham, *Making the Difference*, 19–22.

life. The egalitarian case is . . . [that] the differences between the sexes demand the inclusion of both in leadership."[31]

Something of this journey appears in remarks by "convinced egalitarian" Kevin Giles:

> For the last forty years, the traditional way of speaking and thinking of God as man—as "he"—has been under fire in our cultural setting. Today, the prevailing view is that men and women are of the same dignity, ability and leadership potential, and most Christians now believe this is what the Bible teaches in principle.[32]

The view that men and women are of the same dignity, ability and leadership potential would appear to minimize sexual difference. On the other hand, querying the traditional way of speaking and thinking of God as "he" would suggest that sexual difference is relevant when speaking about God.

Giles canvasses developments over the last forty years but the debate about female leadership in the churches has a longer history. *The Methodist Defense of Women in Ministry* is a compilation of documents from the time of John Wesley. Earlier arguments appearing in these documents relate to permission for women to preach. Later arguments support ordination of women. There is a difference of tone in this progression, from appeal to biblical practice to a focus on equality of opportunity. In general, the symbolic aspect of church leadership is not considered.

The debate about female leadership continues, reports Grenz. Most Christians now believe that "men and women are of the same dignity, ability and leadership potential," states Giles. At the same time Giles contrasts his "egalitarian" view with that held by "complementarian" Wayne Grudem. As reported by Giles, Grudem writes:

> Just as God the Father has authority over the Son, although the two are equal in deity, so in marriage, the husband has authority over his wife, though they are equal in personhood. In this case, the man's role is like that of God the Father, and the woman's role is parallel to that of God the Son.[33]

---

31. Grenz, *Women in the Church*, 230.
32. Giles, "Is God male?," 5, 8.
33. Giles, "Is God male?," 6, citing Grudem, *Systematic Theology*, 1994, 459–60.

This view leaves out the reversal of gendered roles.[34] Grudem is said to extend the analogy:

> The gift of children within a marriage, coming from both the father and the mother, and subject to the authority of the father and the mother, is analogous to the relationship of the Holy Spirit to the Father and the Son in the Trinity.

It should be noted that surmises in which the relationship of man, woman and offspring are analogous to trinitarian relationships were present in Augustine's day. Augustine refuted them.[35] One may compare Susan Ashbrook Harvey's remark that early Syriac Christians rejected an understanding of the Trinitarian Godhead in terms parallel to "pagan deities of the Syrian Orient, 'where a triad of mother, father, and son was a common configuration of divinity.'"[36]

The "complementarian" position presents sexual difference in terms of a rigid distinction of roles, said to reflect roles in the Godhead. By contrast, Grenz espouses an "egalitarian" appeal to the "divine nature" which upholds a gender inclusive approach to leadership:

> God is not merely beyond male and female. Rather, God's relationship to creation takes on both male and female dimensions. Thereby, God forms the foundation for the distinctively male and female dimensions of human existence. As a consequence, a true perception of the divine nature requires the contribution of both men and women.[37]

The distinction here between male and female "dimensions" in human existence is said to stem from male and female "dimensions" in God's relationship to creation. I will return to this point.

Catholic writer, Leonardo Boff offers an interpretation which could be said to straddle the claims of both "egalitarians'" and "complementarians." Boff argues for a masculine and feminine principle in the Godhead, the Son representing the masculine principle and the Holy Spirit representing the feminine principle.[38] According to Boff, since masculine and feminine at the human level are both in the image of God both are

---

34. See chapter 6.
35. See Augustine, *The Trinity* XII, chapter 2.
36. See Soskice, *Kindness of God*, 114–15, citing Ashbrook Harvey, "Feminine Imagery for the Divine."
37. Grenz, *Women in the Church*, 150.
38. Boff, *Maternal Face of God*, 80–81.

equally eligible for "divinisation." He understands the Incarnation in the sense that "from the first moment of his conception [the human being Jesus of Nazareth] was assumed by the second Person of the Divine Trinity in such a way that he is not only a human being but God incarnate as well."[39] Similarly, Boff claims that Mary is assumed by the Holy Spirit, and thus elevated to the level of God.[40] Boff concludes that "the created feminine is eternally associated with the mystery of the Trinity, through Mary assumed by the Holy Spirit."[41] The method of "divinisation" tends towards an inversion of the *imago Dei*, created beings taken up to divinity and then reflecting back to the human level: "The Spirit, the eternal feminine, is united to the created feminine in order that the latter may be totally and fully what it can be—virgin and mother."[42] One sees here a possibility of discerning gendered "dimensions" in the Godhead. For women, however, the upshot is something of a stereotyped role.

Protestant "egalitarian" discourse is said to discern male and female dimensions in God's relationship to creation. Catholic writer Boff argues for a masculine and feminine principle in the Godhead. On the other hand, Elizabeth Johnson argues against God being perceived in terms of female and male dimensions:

> We must be very clear about this. Speech about God in female metaphors does not mean that God has a feminine dimension, revealed by Mary or other women. Nor does the use of male metaphors mean that God has a masculine dimension, revealed by Jesus or other men; or an animal dimension revealed by lions or great mother birds; or a mineral dimension, which corresponds with naming God a rock . . . If women are created in the image of God, then God can be spoken of in female metaphors in as full and as limited a way as God is imaged in male ones, without talk of feminine dimensions reducing the impact of this imagery.[43]

Johnson rejects the idea that God has a "feminine" dimension, realized in the Holy Spirit on the grounds that that the third person of the Trinity is amorphous and easily seen as subordinate to the other two persons.[44]

---

39. See Boff, *Maternal Face of God*, 90–94.
40. Boff, *Maternal Face of God*, 101.
41. Boff, *Maternal Face of God*, 102.
42. Boff, *Maternal Face of God*, 101.
43. Johnson, *She Who Is*, 54.
44. Johnson, *She Who Is*, 50.

In his remarks cited above about masculine imagery, Lewis asks what a change in religious language would mean for the Godhead before moving to the religious life of the child. Hampson asks the question the other way round: what does "the concretion" of religion mean for the child and her sense of self? Much current discourse about female leadership in the churches would seem to begin with the role of women rather than with the Godhead, proposals about gendered divine dimensions or principles notwithstanding. In some Protestant circles, the reason may be suspicion of symbolic ceremony, a suspicion which would leave questions about symbolism unaddressed.

AUTHORSHIP OF HEBREWS?

The last section of chapter 7 outlined a two-fold stance to the *imago Dei* detected in Augustine and Barth. In the first sense, the *imago Dei* resides in nearness-of-approach. For Augustine, *sapientia* is a mental function, possessed by both sexes, allowing access to God. For Barth, as I understand him, the *imago Dei* is realized in nearness-of-approach at the divine-human level. In this sense the *imago Dei* is non-gendered. The second sense of gendered likeness qualifies nearness-of approach on masculine terms for both Augustine and Barth. In addition, Barth has a strongly passive understanding of nearness-of-approach. Ruether draws attention to Barth's concept of the relation between male and female as the God-creature analogy. She remarks: "Given Barth's belief in the absolute gulf between the divine and the human, this establishes the most hierarchical model imaginable as analogue for male-female relations."[45] Hampson cites Barth's presentation of Mary: "this non-willing, non-achieving, non-creative, non-sovereign, merely ready, merely receptive, virgin human being."[46]

These two approaches to the *imago Dei*, non-gendered and gendered, seem to be reflected in two Protestant approaches to women's role. "Egalitarians" tend to stress the worth and dignity of each individual person. "Complementarians" emphasize gendered distinctions with masculine ascendancy. Gilbert Bilezikian appears to have a foot in both camps. He writes: "As members of the community where 'there is neither male nor

---

45. Ruether, "Christian Tradition and Feminist Hermeneutics," 283.

46. Hampson, *Theology and Feminism*, 100, citing Barth, *Church Dogmatics*, I.2, 191–92.

female for you are all one in Christ Jesus,' we should strive to exhibit to the world our 'sameness' in Christ."[47] He also states: "It is the responsibility of Christian men to realize that women do not derive their identity from men but from having been created in God's image and from being new persons in Christ."[48] But in his remarks on 1 Corinthians 11:7, woman's status as the *imago Dei* in her own right is less than clear. He writes:

> Men and women represent different realities in relation to God. By virtue of his unmediated origination, man's presence in worship emblemizes his head as his spiritual Maker. Man's head represents "the image and glory of God," somewhat like the "glory of God in the face of Christ" (2 Cor. 4:6). Man cannot represent mere humanity before God, since his physical head symbolizes Christ. Therefore, man is not permitted to use a headcovering in worship. He may not cover Christ (his head) in God's presence.[49]

The gendered distinction is said to hinge on the order of creation and also the man's symbolic likeness to Christ. These factors, says Bilezikian, disqualify the man from representing "mere humanity before God." It is otherwise for the woman:

> Woman in worship stands in a different relation before God. Because of her origination from man, she is fully qualified to represent the essence of complete, uncompounded humanhood before God. Her physical head emblemizes man as a reminder of her derivation from him. Therefore, she is humanity twice recognized, first for herself and again for man, represented by her physical head as her life-source. As such, she reflects the full "glory of man."

Ruether's critique of Barth regarding the relation between male and female seen as a God-creature analogy would seem relevant here.

Nevertheless, Bilezikian is open to the possibility that Hebrews could have been written by a woman. Ruth Hoppin takes up Adolph von Harnack's theory that Priscilla was the author of Hebrews.[50] Hoppin cites Bilezikian who writes that Priscillan authorship would explain "a number of semi-apologetic pleas for credibility found in the Epistle" and who

---

47. Bilezikian, *Beyond Sex Roles*, 210.
48. Bilezikian, *Beyond Sex Roles*, 211.
49. Bilezikian, *Beyond Sex Roles*, 141.
50. See Hoppin, *Priscilla's Letter*. Hoppin draws attention to Harnack, "Probabilia über die Adresse und den Verfasser des Hebraerbriefes."

"notes a tone of respectful deference" towards the readers' spiritual leaders. The inference is that her status as the glory of man would affect, but not exclude, Priscilla's authorship. This theory, says Bilezikian, "would explain the strange nature of the document, which is a cross between an Epistle and a treatise."[51]

If woman qua woman is not seen to be symbolically like God, in how far is she permitted to function in a leadership role, as in authorship of Hebrews? Bilezikian draws attention to a possible grammatical impediment to female authorship (the gender of the participle for "to tell," transliterated *diēgoumenon* in Hebrews 11:32). He suggests that the author may have used "an editorial masculine" as a subtle hint of "the limitations pertaining to her status" as a woman.[52]

"Complementarian" Wayne Grudem regards the grammatical usage in Hebrews 11:32 as proof of male authorship. He writes: "In Hebrews 11:32, the author says, 'And what more shall I say? For time would fail *me to tell* of Gideon, Barak, Sampson, Jephthah, of David and Samuel and the prophets.'" Grudem draws the grammatical conclusion:

> In English not much can be told about the author from this verse. But in Greek, the expression 'to tell' is a participle (*diēgoumenon*) that modifies "me," and the participle is masculine (the feminine form would be *diēgoumenēn*). So the author identifies himself as male. Someone could respond, "Well that's just part of the disguise so that people won't know she is a woman." The problem with that argument is that it involves the author in dishonesty, saying something that she *intends* all Greek readers to take as an indication that she is a man.[53]

An editorial masculine would be deceptive, says Grudem.

Grudem regards the grammatical point as decisive. Bilezikian is more hesitant about this and open to other indications of Priscillan authorship in the letter itself. Regarding the grammatical point, the original readers would have known who was writing to them; an editorial masculine would not have functioned for them as a disguise. Argument on this point between Bilezikian and Grudem leaves out the possibility that the participle

---

51. Hoppin, *Priscilla's Letter*, 31, citing Bilezikian, *Beyond Sex Roles*, 302–3.
52. Bilezikian, *Beyond Sex Roles*, 303.
53. Grudem, *Countering the Claims of Evangelical Feminism*, 152. Grudem's italics.

could be a conditional neuter for an impersonal verb in the accusative absolute: ("for time will fail me *if it come to telling in detail of.*")⁵⁴

In terms of inclusive language and the *imago Dei* it would be ironic if discussion were to hang on one Greek letter in an obscure point of grammar. This is not to say that this particular instance does not need to be addressed. But Grudem's prior position on the status of women would seem to govern his conclusion. He does not appear to be alone in this approach. What is needed, I submit, is a fresh appraisal of the biblical evidence, including Hoppin's work on Hebrews.

In the greeting in Romans 16:3, the apostle Paul goes so far as to refer to Priscilla and Aquila as working with him in Christ. Does a female author for Hebrews breach the conditions for female leadership described elsewhere in the New Testament?⁵⁵ The use of first-person plural exhortations is persistent in Hebrews, with the exception of the last chapter in which are a number of direct commands. Hebrews 13 reads like a letter, unlike the rest of Hebrews. This raises the further possibility that Hebrews 13 is a postscript, written by Aquila to Priscilla's sermon-like treatise, a theory that provides solutions to the absence of an opening greeting in Hebrews and the otherwise inaccurate statement in Hebrews 13:22: "I have written to you briefly."⁵⁶ Joint authorship of Hebrews by Priscilla and Aquila, whether sustainable or not in terms of *Quellenforschung*, is brought forward here as an illustration of a possible breadth of function for female leadership, limitations notwithstanding.

BORN OF WOMAN

"The masculinist religious symbolic must be disrupted," says Grace Jantzen, "and space made for the female divine."⁵⁷ Perhaps, however, this is to underestimate the kind of space which the *imago Dei* already offers.

---

54. Cf. Hebrews 9:5 (literally: "concerning which it is not now to speak in detail") and Goodwin, *A Greek Grammar*. Cf. also Hoppin, *Priscilla's Letter*, 49-52.

55. Cf. 1 Corinthians 14:33-36; 1 Timothy 2:11-12. I have written about these texts and their implications in my own church, the Uniting Church in Australia. See "Women in Leadership," 154-59. Cf. also Chicote, *Methodist Defense of Women in Ministry*, 57 (document 21).

56. Further evidence for joint authorship may be noted in the concluding style of Hebrews 12 followed by the inconsecutive opening of Hebrews 13 and the allusion to a shepherd theme (rather than priestly theme) in Hebrews 13:20.

57. See Jantzen, *Becoming Divine*, 15.

Priscillan authorship of Hebrews, if sustained, would exemplify this kind of space. Female leadership based on the claim of a feminine dimension in the Godhead would tend to narrow its scope. This book argues for a different kind of gender inclusiveness.

Jantzen, citing Irigaray, contrasts an alleged "masculinist" desire for "salvation from this mortal state" with the "flourishing of our natality," a feminist appropriation of "unto us a child is born." Such a flourishing is said to encompass the masculinity of Jesus, albeit as a "partial incarnation."[58] For a feminist to engage the masculinity of Jesus in a positive way is unusual to say the least, and Jantzen expresses reservations about it:

> Has not the maleness of Jesus been used endlessly in western christendom to bolster the masculinist symbolic, serving to guarantee the superiority of men, to exclude women from priesthood, to identify women with the sinfulness of Eve over against the male Christ, the second Adam?[59]

Perhaps, however, "unto us a child is born," seen in a particular "sexuate" sense to use Irigaray's word for it, offers a corrective to "masculinist" distortions in Western Christendom.

This is of course not what Irigaray has in mind. She does not seek to restore Western Christianity to its rightful form but to develop a "new religious imaginary," envisaging the "incarnation of all bodies (men's and women's) as potentially divine; nothing more nor less than each man and each woman being virtually gods."[60] But does this aspiration reflect something missing in the tradition? Lewis writes that we "tend to slur over the risen *manhood* of Jesus, to conceive him, after death, simply returning into Deity, so that the Resurrection would be no more than a reversal or undoing of the Incarnation."[61]

In terms of Christian tradition, unease with physicality would leave out the resurrection of the body. In this case tradition would be less than Christian. We may note that a feminist emphasis on Christ's humanity rather than on his masculinity would also omit Christ's risen manhood. Irigaray's emphasis on incarnation is in line with the manhood of Jesus *against* a feminist method of inclusion. This is not to say that Irigaray

---

58. See Jantzen, *Becoming Divine*, 16–17.
59. Jantzen, *Becoming Divine*, 16.
60. See Jantzen, *Becoming Divine*, 16–17.
61. Lewis, *Miracles*, 176, (Lewis's italics).

endorses Jesus as risen man. For Irigaray, as I understand her, women are the birth-givers, in the "flourishing of natality," body-givers. In such thinking there is no need for resurrection of the body and presumably no need of redemption except from the sin of "patriarchy."

Let us pause here. In search of inclusive categories, key feminists argue *both* for vocabulary for God reflecting sexual difference *and* for redemption in terms of a non-gendered Christ. By contrast, Irigaray's multiple "incarnations" take human embodiment to the divine level and do not exclude the maleness of Jesus. Setting Irigaray's agenda aside, could a fresh appraisal of "unto us a child is born," along with Jesus as risen man, have something to say about women's identity from a Christian perspective? Biblically speaking, salvation from this mortal state is not an escape from the physical *per se* but from matter's propensity to decay. The physical resurrection of Jesus has flow-on effects for his followers. In this sense, there will be multiple "incarnations," women and men sharing the divine humanity of Jesus.[62] The implication of "unto us a child is born" for women's identity will take some teasing out. In the process some traditions may need to be relinquished.

I turn now to Jantzen's reservations about Irigaray's approach. As seen above, Jantzen is dubious about invoking the masculinity of Jesus: "Has not the maleness of Jesus been used endlessly in western christendom . . . to exclude women from priesthood, to identify women with the sinfulness of Eve over against the male Christ, the second Adam?"[63] I will come to the exclusion of women from the priesthood below. Chapter 4 considered a tradition of identifying women with the sinfulness of Eve, not so much over against the second Adam but in contrast with the obedient virginity of Mary, mother of Jesus. I suggested that the tradition might go so far as to construe sexual activity as a concomitant of the sinfulness of Eve, contrary to Irigaray's endorsement of "the flourishing of our natality." Be that as it may, perhaps a tradition emphasizing Eve's sinfulness is less than biblical.

Biblically speaking, the second Adam is presented, not over against Eve but over against the first Adam. In his commentary on Romans, F. F. Bruce writes:

> To Paul, Adam was more than a historical individual, the first man; he was also what his name means in

---

62. See Romans 8:19–23; Augustine, *City of God*, XIII, 23.
63. Jantzen, *Becoming Divine*, 16.

Hebrew—'humanity' . . . Paul was apparently conversant with what is widely called the Hebrew concept of corporate personality, and his thought could readily oscillate on the one hand between the first Adam and sinful humanity, and on the other hand between Christ, 'the second man', and the community of the redeemed.[64]

The connection between sinful humanity and the first Adam relies on the Hebrew concept of corporate personality. For this reason, Eve is not held responsible for human sinfulness.

I said above that Irigaray's multiple "incarnations" might find some echo in the resurrection of the body. At this point we come to the biblical form of inclusive language. Soskice states: "We must say that, Christologically speaking, women and men cannot be different, for 'all will bear the image of the man of heaven.'"[65] Failing the Hebrew concept of corporate personality, women cannot bear the image of the man of heaven. Chapter 8 touched on the abstract inclusive language of "humanity" as opposed to the concrete universals of the first and second Adam. I will have more to say about concrete universals in the next chapter.

Regarding the Hebrew male collective, let us briefly glance back at chapter 5. Phyllis Trible contends that in Genesis, chapters 2 to 3, the term *hā-'ādām* changes meaning from sexually undifferentiated earth creature to male character to a "generic term that keeps the man visible and renders the woman invisible."[66] From the standpoint of Trible's hermeneutical clue of feminism, the sting comes in the invisibility of the woman. But is this a necessary appraisal of corporate personality? Is it possible to regard *hā-'ādām* as an all-purpose term, both specific and gender inclusive? Further, even if the third meaning of *hā-'ādām* renders the woman invisible, the first Adam is not included at all in the promise of redemption of Genesis 3:15. Unlike the first and second Adam, the mother of the second Adam is not an all-purpose term. But she can, I believe, function as a concrete universal for women.

I come now to Jantzen's objection to the exclusion of women from the priesthood. Daphne Hampson offers a useful outline of some classic arguments in this respect, along with her objections to these arguments.

---

64. Bruce, *Letter of Paul to the Romans*, 119–20.
65. Soskice, *The Kindness of God*, 45.
66. Trible, *Rhetoric of Sexuality*, 134–35.

Hampson begins with the perception of Mary and redeemed humanity in Catholicism:

> It is in Catholicism in particular, within Christian history, that there has been a construct of the 'feminine' . . . In Catholicism the feminine is at least present, either through the position given to the virgin Mary, or through a certain place being reserved for 'the feminine' as symbolized by the church and humanity. The problem is that this understanding of the 'feminine' is very different from how feminist women (and perhaps most women) see themselves.[67]

Everything else aside, a construct of "the feminine" is in itself a far cry from Irigaray's quest for embodiment.

Something of a construct of "the feminine" appears in Boff's theory of the *imago Dei*. As seen above, Boff writes: "The Spirit, the eternal feminine, is united to the created feminine in order that the latter may be totally and fully what it can be—virgin and mother."[68] Construed as virginity, purity and submission, Hampson indicates that a construct of "the feminine" is seen as desirable for humanity as a whole in relation to God. Such qualities are contrasted with unredeemed human nature: men said to be caught up with the world and worldly pride, women connected with the body and sexual temptation. Hampson adds that the isolation and celibacy of Catholic theologians and priests would appear to have something to do with these perceptions: "Indeed one may be permitted to think that in some cases a certain romance with the 'feminine' (exemplified by the virgin Mary or the church) has been a substitute for real relations with human persons of the opposite sex."[69]

In this context, Hampson reports discussion about the priesthood:

> [Mary's] fiat, her 'be it unto me according to thy word' in response to God, is seen as the perfect human response to God, which is to be modelled on the female response to male initiative. It will be said by men who want to convince women that they, equally, have a place within the Christian scheme of things, that of course we are all 'feminine' in relation to God. (Indeed it is frequently said that, if it is the case that only men can be priests, only women can be mothers.) But this is scarcely of help to women. In the first place it tends to simply fuel a certain

---

67. Hampson, *Theology and Feminism*, 99.
68. Boff, *Maternal Face of God*, 101.
69. Hampson, *Theology and Feminism*, 100.

> understanding of gender, so that the feminine has a particular place and women are supposed to be a certain way. But secondly it is no equivalent . . . The equivalent of the male taking on the 'feminine' role of humanity in relation to God, would be that women should take on the 'masculine' role of representing God to humanity as priests.[70]

As represented by Hampson, the arguments for the male priesthood offer a place for women in the Christian scheme of things. But, although presented as "equal," Hampson does not find the place offered to women a satisfactory equivalent to that offered to men.

In the Roman Catholic and Anglo-Catholic tradition, the role of representing Christ to humanity is masculine: hence the priesthood is reserved for men. "Of course," admits Hampson, "not all traditions believe that Christ is represented by the celebrant."[71] As a non-Catholic, it is not my intention to argue in favor of this practice. Nevertheless, I will examine the arguments presented above in the light of what C. S. Lewis has to say about the role of the male celebrant:

> To us the priest is primarily a representative, a double representative, who represents us to God and God to us. Our very eyes teach us this in church. Sometimes the priest turns his back on us and faces the East—he speaks to God for us: sometimes he faces us and speaks to us for God. We have no objection to a woman doing the first: the whole difficulty is about the second . . . Only one wearing the masculine uniform can (provisionally, and till the *Parousia*) represent the Lord to the Church: for we are all, corporately and individually, feminine to Him.[72]

In this scheme of things, one does not need to wear the "masculine uniform" in order to represent the Church to God. The representational function of "to God for us" is on a different footing to the representative function of "to us for God."

In the Catholic tradition, reports Hampson, "We are all 'feminine' in relation to God." Lewis shares this view: "we are all, corporately and

---

70. Hampson, *Theology and Feminism*, 100–101.

71. Hampson, *Theology and Feminism*, 55–56.

72. See Lewis, "Priestesses in the Church?," 90; 93. Irigaray's remark above that the "masculinist" symbolic looks to salvation from this mortal state can be compared with Lewis' remark that the representative function of the masculine uniform is provisional (until the *Parousia*). In other words, the "masculinist" celebrant is relevant to this mortal state, not to salvation from it.

individually, feminine to Him." Women as well as men are permitted to function as spokespersons for this corporate role, to speak to God for us, states Lewis. In other words, gender at the human level is not at issue since the representational function of "to God for us" occurs at the divine-human level of the Church in relation to Christ. By contrast, the representative function of "to us for God" occurs at the human level. The priest in his humanity (wearing the "masculine uniform") represents God in Christ to the Church, the mystical body of Christ. In relation to the Church, this symbolic function operates "from below."

In the Catholic tradition, as described by Hampson and Lewis, the celebrant wears the "masculine uniform." Janice Rees, however, draws attention to a variant on this tradition. She reports that, for Sarah Coakley, the *crossing* of the "ontological binary difference" between God and humanity in the Incarnation is in some way reflected in the liturgical act of the Eucharist: "As an ordained priest who stands *in persona Christi*, Coakley has found herself crossing from the traditionally understood 'masculine' divine side of the altar, representing Christ, to the 'feminine' side in representing the church."[73] A female priest on the "masculine" side of the altar would not operate symbolically in the way described by Lewis. I would add that, if "ontological binary difference" signifies that the "masculine" and "feminine" sides of the altar are to be seen as ontologically different, the liturgical act would not reflect equality of nature between Christ and the Church. Speaking from outside the Catholic tradition, I suggest that further clarification is needed in this area. In particular, how does the situation described by Janice Rees relate to Elizabeth Johnson's assertion that women are *imago Christi*?[74]

"The equivalent of the male taking on the 'feminine' role of humanity in relation to God, would be that women should take on the 'masculine' role of representing God to humanity as priests," argues Hampson above. But the distinctions are more complex than this. On biblical terms, both men and women are permitted to preach, as Lewis points out.[75] This still leaves the "to us for God" representative role of the male priest without female equivalent. What if, however, the reciprocal is not a female equivalent at the priestly level but humanity (qua woman) assuming the otherwise masculine priority in relation to the God-man? To

---

73. See Rees, "Sarah Coakley: Systematic Theology and the Future of Feminism," 310.

74. See Johnson, *She Who Is*, 69.

75. See Lewis, "Priestesses in the Church?," 89.

argue this reciprocal is of course to rethink the role of Mary. As Hampson points out, limiting Mary to her "be it unto me according to thy word" is not the whole story in biblical terms: "In the scriptures there is put into her mouth a powerful magnificat, which speaks of the overturning of an unjust order and the creation of social justice."[76] One might add that the Magnificat may only hint at an even greater reversal, in divinity becoming feminine in relation to humanity.

Let us now return to Irigaray's attempt, cited above, to recover a god-like function for women in appropriating "unto us a child is born." Do we need to travel outside Christianity in order to engage the godlike potential of women's physicality? For traditions in which Christ is represented by the celebrant, the priest in his masculine sex offers a sacerdotal embodiment of "to us for God." If we add that women in solidarity with Mary offer a permanent embodiment of "unto us a child is born," the god-like potential of women may become more apparent. The very fact that this is not a sacerdotal function takes this function to a new level.[77] The priest with his masculine "uniform," functions at the human level. Mary operates at the divine-human level.

In relaying arguments in relation to the male priesthood, Hampson reports: "Indeed it is frequently said that, if it is the case that only men can be priests, only women can be mothers." She objects that this argument "tends to simply fuel a certain understanding of gender, so that the feminine has a particular place and women are supposed to be a certain way." I am not proposing this kind of stereotyping. In the same way that the masculine "uniform" of the priest does not suggest that all men should become priests, women's solidarity with Mary does not suggest that all women should become mothers. In this respect Irigaray's appropriation of "unto us a child is born" comes closer to its generic application.

As Hampson describes it, Christian tradition (Catholicism in particular) has promoted a construct of "the feminine," everything relating to women including the role of Mary subsumed within it. At the same time the construct of "the feminine" is not limited to women: we are all feminine in relation to God. Hampson sees this extended approach negatively, in particular in relation to "feminine" language for God:

---

76. Hampson, *Theology and Feminism*, 100. Hampson does not capitalize "Magnificat."

77. Lewis draws attention to Mary's lack of a sacerdotal role, biblically and historically; see "Priestesses in the Church?," 89.

Inclusive Language 255

> The effect of such imagery is to enrich or enlarge our concept of the male, or what may be truly be said to be 'masculine'. God (who is basically seen as male) is portrayed as nurturing and caring, Christ as feeding and protecting. It may well be said that the patriarchal understanding of what it means to be male is abandoned. But such a move does nothing for women, or for the concept of the feminine *per se*: it expands our understanding of what it is to be considered authentically male . . . Indeed one might well say that, through this augmentation of what it is to be considered male, the male now absorbs all in himself.[78]

To counteract this enlargement of the male Hampson suggests a parallel enlargement of what is considered authentically female: "In order to change the understanding of women . . . we should have to apply what have been thought to be characteristically male attributes to the female symbol. For example, the female should be seen to embrace headship or authority."

This argument, however, does not challenge the conception that "the feminine" functions as a construct. It leaves out the traditional use of gendered language to indicate relationship: we are all feminine *in relation to* God. The way forward, I submit, is to divest "the feminine" of its dominance as a construct or *noun* and to recover its potential as an *adjective*. A similar approach then applies to "the masculine."

Male and female, says Lewis, are "live and awful shadows of realities utterly beyond our control and largely beyond our direct knowledge."[79] It is because the transcendent realities are largely beyond our direct knowledge that the indirect knowledge, supplied by gendered humanity as the *imago Dei*, is of such importance. This does not mean that "masculine" and "feminine" are to be projected as transcendent realities (or constructs). Abstract projections have the effect of producing non-interactive stereotypes (even if the list of traits is extended).

Theoretically, the list of traits could be extended to the extent of making distinctions of sex irrelevant. This tendency is apparent in much of secular life as Lewis points out:

> As the State grows more like a hive or an ant-hill it needs an increasing number of workers who can be treated as neuters . . . The factory and the political party are artificial

---

78. Hampson, *Theology and Feminism*, 94–95.
79. Lewis, "Priestesses in the Church?," 94.

creations . . . In them we are not dealing with human beings in their concrete entirety—only with 'hands' or voters.[80]

This development is not without consequences. Treating human beings as neuters leaves the question of gendered identity unaddressed. Irigaray's quest for a new religious imaginary to enable the "sexuate" becoming of women points to an alternative trajectory.

Hampson contends that "the conservative and Catholic world order is collapsing" along with an "ordering of reality" in which there is "a 'complementarity' between male and female."[81] In consequence, she says, Lewis's comparison of the Church with a ball is outmoded:

> The understanding of the feminine as complementary to the masculine which Lewis describes in this essay has, I would suggest, in a large part ceased to exist. (Within ten years of his writing, that is to say in the sixties, men and women dressed much alike to dance, and jived with one another, the women dancing together if the men were more interested in drinking beer.)[82]

In other words, there have been two responses to the decline of the conservative world order. Men and women dressing much alike to dance would accord with human beings functioning as neuters. On the other hand, women dancing together and men more interested in drinking beer would point to a separation of the sexes. (To revert to *The Wizard of Oz*, this separation could be said to parallel male and female Hammer-Heads claiming their separate hills.)

Since the nineteen sixties ballroom dancing has experienced something of a revival, although turning it into a competitive spectator sport is perhaps to make it "not near so much like a ball." In traditional ballroom dancing, the dancers can exchange places without disturbing the distinctions of sex. In other words, ordering of gendered reality does not necessarily mean a one-way interaction. In Lewis's analogy, male and female dancers (as live and awful shadows of transcendent reality) give meaning to gender as an adjective without turning it into a construct. That is the nature of this kind of dance.

---

80. Lewis, "Priestesses in the Church?," 91; 93.
81. Hampson, *Theology and Feminism*, 101.
82. See Hampson, *Theology and Feminism*, 101–2.

AN EXEGETICAL POSTSCRIPT

"Do not despise yourselves, you men: the son of God assumed manhood. Do not despise yourselves, you women: God's son is born of woman," states Augustine.[83] Lewis writes that we "tend to slur over the risen *manhood* of Jesus."[84] On the supposition that Christ's male body resumes its significance for men what is the equivalent for women?

In chapter 6, I argued that the reversal of the woman and the man in origin and priority (as in 1 Corinthians 11:11–12) can be understood to apply to the relationship of Mary and Jesus. Let us compare this with the rather obscure addendum of 1 Timothy 2:15: "Yet she will be saved through childbearing, provided they continue in faith and love and holiness, with modesty." Firstly, the verse appears to begin with "generic" woman before moving to the plural "they." Secondly, in two possible interpretations of *dia tēs teknogonias* (of childbearing in general or the birth of a specific child) both have to do with motherhood.

It is hardly likely that salvation would, in an ordinary sense, be available to women on grounds other than those previously outlined in 1 Timothy 2:5–6. But given the context of the deceiving of Eve, the reference to childbirth would be pertinent for two possible reasons: the penalty of pain in Genesis 3:16a, and the promise associated with the "seed of the woman" in Genesis 3:15.[85] It is possible that there is a double entendre in this verse. The verb translated "shall be saved" (*sōthēsetai*) could be understood in two senses: as protection during otherwise painful and dangerous childbirth, and as a reference to the role of "the woman" in salvation.

If this verse refers to the birth of a specific child, the role of Mary in giving birth to Jesus comes to the fore. In other words, this verse qualifies what is said previously, in a similar way to the qualification in 1 Corinthians 11:11–12. In fact, it spells out what I think is implied in 1 Corinthians 11:11–12, i.e., that the reversal of the woman and the man in origin and priority can be applied to the relationship of Mary and Jesus. The change of pronoun, from "she" in the first half of the sentence to "they" in the second half, would seem to indicate the relevance of "she" to all women.

---

83. See Bettenson, *The Later Christian Fathers*, 218, citing Augustine, *de agone Christiano*, 12.

84. Lewis, *Miracles*, 176. Lewis's italics.

85. See Kidner, *Genesis*, 70–71 on "the passing over Adam for *the woman* and her seed." Among New Testament references, Kidner cites 1 Timothy 2:15 as a possibility.

Let us now stand back and consider this verse in its context of the Pauline commentary on the narrative of Adam and Eve. I drew attention to Augustine's remarks on this passage in chapter 5:

> They were alone together, two human beings, a married pair; and we cannot believe that the man was led astray to transgress God's law because he believed that the woman spoke the truth, but that he fell in with her suggestions because they were so closely bound in partnership. In fact, the Apostle was not off the mark when he said, 'It was not Adam, but Eve, who was seduced', for what he meant was that Eve accepted the serpent's statement as the truth, while Adam refused to be separated from his only companion, even if it involved sharing her sin. That does not mean that he was less guilty, if he sinned knowingly and deliberately. Hence the Apostle does not say, 'He did not sin,' but 'He was not seduced.' For he certainly refers to the man when he says, 'It was through one man that sin came into the world,' and when he says more explicitly, a little later, 'by reproducing the transgression of Adam'.[86]

Several things are worthy of note. Augustine states that the woman is *not* the key figure held responsible for sin. At the same time Augustine upholds the Pauline assertion that the woman was deceived while the man was not deceived. In 1 Timothy 2:12–14 both the man's priority and woman deceived continue to affect the new order. If it refers to Genesis 3:15, the addendum of verse 15 would seem to qualify this: the woman has a counterbalancing role in the birth of the child.

In baptism, as noted in chapter 8, the redeemed community "puts on" Christ's divine-human masculinity, in accordance with the Hebrew concept of corporate personality. For the redeemed community, this unity transcends distinctions at the human level including the distinction between male and female. The redeemed community has a feminine persona in relation to Christ at the divine-human, not human, level. Christ's risen manhood spans both human and divine-human levels in way not paralleled by the Church. For women, however, "unto us a child is born" enters into both levels.

---

86. Augustine, *City of God*, XIV, 12. Augustine cites 1 Timothy 2:14 and Romans 5:12; 14.

10

Narrative Identity

AT THE END OF *The Wizard of Oz* Dorothy is informed of a power she has possessed from her arrival in the Land of Oz. A cyclone had whirled her away from Kansas, taking her across the desert to the Land of Oz. Her house landed on, and killed, the wicked Witch of the East. Dorothy inherited the Witch's silver shoes which have the power to take her home. The return journey can be made in three steps, but Dorothy does not find this out until the end of the story. Dorothy is not the only character who needs to cross the desert. The little man who pretends to be a wizard constructs a balloon for the purpose. In order to maintain his deception, the man tells the inhabitants of Oz that he is going to visit a great brother Wizard who lives in the clouds.[1]

Who is the Wizard of Oz? Briefly, one might call him a manipulator who doesn't really exist. Who is Dorothy? Briefly, one might say that she is a little girl who takes a whole narrative to discover what she already has. Dorothy and the Wizard are alike in wanting to cross the desert. They differ in how they do so. Dorothy reaches her goal. It is not certain that the Wizard ever does. Dorothy asks for advice and makes use of what she has received. The Wizard constructs his own means of travel and tells others, deceptively, what his journey is about.

1. See Baum, *Wizard of Oz*, chapters 1, 17 and 23.

We know who Dorothy and the Wizard are via the story. This means of knowing does not apply solely to fictional characters. In response to the question of identity (*Who* says I?), Paul Ricoeur writes:

> We first answer this question by naming someone, that is, by designating them with a proper name. But what is the basis for this proper name? What justifies our taking the subject of an action, so designated by his, her or its proper name, as the same throughout a life that stretches from birth to death? The answer has to be narrative. To answer the question "Who?" as Hannah Arendt has so forcefully put it, is to tell the story of a life. The story tells about the action of the 'who'. And the identity of this 'who' therefore itself must be a narrative identity.[2]

According to Ricoeur, identity comes from the story of one's life. Ricoeur calls this "a narrative identity."

Sallie McFague also appeals to narrative in relation to identity. "One of the most interesting characteristics of our contemporary culture," she says, "is its intense interest in the self, in autobiography, in life-styles."[3] She goes so far as to describe autobiography as a "metaphor of the self."[4] For McFague, however, neither the self nor "metaphor" is open to what is outside its own constructed world. "What we *know*," she states, "are the metaphors or projections of the self, the worlds it creates."[5] She continues:

> It is hard to deny where modernity has landed us—after Galileo toppled us from the center of the universe, human beings are, curiously, back there again, albeit in a somewhat different guise. In a sense we are "stuck" with our centrality: we cannot, finally, get outside of ourselves, we cannot jump out of our skins. But what many voices increasingly are saying—from the existentialist tradition to the women's movement—is, "Why should we want to?"[6]

On the assumption that one cannot jump out of one's skin what is the origin of identity? Does the life story supply identity for the self or does the self determine the story?

---

2. See Blamey, "From the ego to the self," 598, citing Ricoeur, *Time and Narrative*, vol. 3, 246.
3. McFague, *Speaking in Parables*, 146–47.
4. McFague, *Speaking in Parables*, 149.
5. McFague, *Speaking in Parables*, 147. McFague's italics.
6. McFague, *Speaking in Parables*, 148.

In *The Wizard of Oz*, one of the Wizard's deceptions consists in filling the Scarecrow's head with bran and pins and needles so that the Scarecrow happily believes he has been given "bran-new brains." I have said that the Wizard does not really exist. The Wizard is only the alter-ego of a little man who is under no illusion about the actual efficacy of the new brains. "Experience is the only thing that brings knowledge," he tells the Scarecrow, "and the longer you are on earth the more experience you are sure to get."[7] But what of those who cannot and do not want to jump out of their skins? In relation to life story, McFague too cites Hannah Arendt:

> Hannah Arendt says that the revelatory quality of speech and action comes about in "sheer human togetherness." . . . Because of its inherent tendency to disclose the agent together with the act, action needs for its full appearance the shining brightness we once called glory, and which is possible only in the public realm.[8]

How, one might ask, do those who are "stuck" in their centrality enter the public realm in the first place?

MASTER OR DISCIPLE?

I said at the beginning of this book that McFague uses the example of the Wizard's green glasses to illustrate what she means by "metaphor." Autobiography, construed as a "metaphor of the self," extends this kind of thinking: life story is known through the spectacles of the viewer. By contrast, Ricoeur describes, in his lengthy "Intellectual Autobiography," how he came to question "the transparence" of the "*Cogito*." "The subject," he writes, "does not know itself directly but only through the signs deposited in memory and imagination by the great literary traditions."[9] Here, according to Ricoeur, is a further source of identity for the self: not only personal story but story embedded in culture.

McFague's understanding of the self is in line with her understanding of metaphor. The same can be said of Ricoeur, but Ricoeur differs from McFague in both categories. The difference between them hinges on access to the public realm. Ricoeur's approach is evident in his

---

7. See Baum, *Wizard of Oz*, chapter 15.

8. See McFague, *Speaking in Parables*, 175. McFague cites Hannah Arendt, *The Human Condition*, 180.

9. See Ricoeur, "Intellectual Autobiography," 16–17.

description of his intellectual journey. He attributes a public sphere of operation to metaphor:

> Already in *The Rule of Metaphor* the suspension of the first-order reference of ordinary language opened the way for a second-order reference in which the world is manifested, no longer as an ensemble of objects to be manipulated, but as the horizon of our own life and projects, in short, as our being-in-the-world.[10]

He then goes on to apply this sphere of operation to a theory of understanding:

> I came to the conclusion that, despite the idealist thesis of the ultimate self-responsibility of the mediating subject, subjectivity did not constitute the primary category of a theory of understanding, that it has to be lost as origin if it is to be recovered in a more modest role than that of radical origin. To be sure, there is still a need for a speaking-subject to receive the matter of the text, to make it its own, to appropriate it, in order to balance the correlative moment of *distanciation* of the textualizing of experience. The proof that appropriation does not imply the surreptitious return of sovereign subjectivity lies in the necessity that one dis-appropriate oneself, a necessity imposed by the self-understanding before the text.

He concludes: "I then stated . . . I exchange the ego, master of itself, for the self, disciple of the text."

Metaphor, says Ricoeur, gives access to an order of the world beyond the manipulating subject. More broadly, the subject does not know itself directly but rather in relation to the "text" of experience and the great literary traditions. Ricoeur is alluding to a public sphere which is intrinsically sacramental, which, as McFague attests, rests on a confidence "that all things are connected among themselves because they are connected in God." She cites Ricoeur in this context: "it is an index of the situation of man at the heart of the being in which he moves, exists, and wills, that the symbol speaks to us."[11]

In *The Wizard of Oz*, the little man who pretends to be the Wizard tries to dissuade the Scarecrow from asking for "bran-new brains" on the grounds that experience is the only thing that brings knowledge.

---

10. Ricoeur, "Intellectual Autobiography," 35.

11. McFague, *Speaking in Parables*, 106. McFague cites Paul Ricoeur, *The Symbolism of Evil*, 356.

In his capacity of Wizard, however, he supplies the "brains" which the Scarecrow asks for. Let us consider the distinction between McFague and Ricoeur in these terms. "What we *know*," says McFague, "are the metaphors or projections of the self, the worlds it creates."[12] On this basis, the subject's thinking capacity is primary, "bran-new brains" or otherwise. By contrast, Ricoeur states:

> I came to the conclusion that, despite the idealist thesis of the ultimate self-responsibility of the mediating subject, subjectivity did not constitute the primary category of a theory of understanding, that it has to be lost as origin if it is to be recovered in a more modest role than that of radical origin.

Subjectivity is not "the primary category of a theory of understanding," says Ricoeur. Rather, the subject receives identity, through life experience, through "the signs deposited in memory and imagination by the great literary traditions," from the symbol which speaks *to* us. Clearly, Ricoeur's approach accords with the little man's advice to the Scarecrow while McFague inclines towards the device of the Wizard.

Ricoeur summarizes his position as follows: "I exchange the ego, master of itself, for the self, disciple of the text." Can one claim to be a "disciple of the text" while at the same time seeking to foster subjectivity? Ricoeur would suggest that these are incompatible aims: that "sovereign subjectivity" has to be lost as origin if it is to be recovered in a more modest sense of "narrative identity." Some feminist voices might dispute this. McFague includes the women's movement among those neither able nor wishing to "jump out of their skins." At the same time, she appears to endorse Hannah Arendt's location of identity in the public realm. She is not alone in this apparent contradiction. Grace Jantzen, citing Luce Irigaray, typifies the wish to promote women's subjectivity, to become "free, autonomous, sovereign."[13] Jantzen also draws on Arendt's work. She admits, however, that her reading of Arendt is "against the grain."[14]

On Ricoeur's terms, "sovereign subjectivity" must be renounced as the "primary category of a theory of understanding." On McFague's terms, this is not possible because the subject is unable to "jump out of its

12. McFague, *Speaking in Parables*, 147. McFague's italics.

13. See Jantzen, *Becoming Divine*, 12, citing Irigaray's essay "Divine Women." For Irigaray, the achievement of subjectivity is linked with the possibility of self-transcendence in terms of the "divine ideal." On Ricoeur's terms, I would class this as aspiration (not abdication) on the part of the ego.

14. Jantzen, *Becoming Divine*, 144 n. 5.

skin." In this context, Jantzen gives an indication of how Arendt might be read "against the grain." She writes:

> From the time that Arendt wrote her doctoral dissertation on Augustine, she began to see natality as a fact of our being which should be considered, along with death, as a philosophical category.[15]

Jantzen reports Arendt's conclusion:

> Human beings are not gods who can create *ex nihilo*. The new things that we can begin are begun out of our bodily and material existence; and the fact that we have the capacity for such new possibilities is because we come into the world through birth, that we are 'natals'.

Jantzen then offers her response:

> Taking the idea of natality seriously has direct and immediate consequences for a shift in the imaginary. It affirms the concreteness and embodied nature of human lives and experience, the material and discursive conditions within which subjects are formed and out of which a religious symbolic must emerge.

If human beings are not gods who can create *ex nihilo* one might ask what becomes of Luce Irigaray's statement that women "want to seize that which already exists so as to bring it back to an invisible source—their source?—a place from whence they might create, create themselves *ex nihilo*."[16]

In order to grasp what seems to be at stake in this, I will return to *The Wizard of Oz*. I have said that Dorothy takes her directions from the unfolding adventure of the story. The Wizard is inspired by the *idea* of finding identity in a magical world. This idea has "direct and immediate consequences for a shift in the imaginary," to use Jantzen's turn of phrase. It is within this "shift in the imaginary" that the Wizard's identity as subject is formed and out of which his persona is extended. His purported visit to a brother wizard is certainly an extension of his persona as the Wizard of Oz. While not precisely the emergence of a religious symbolic, a rendezvous in the clouds might offer some semblance of it. I say this, not with the intention of offering a literary interpretation of *The Wizard*

---

15. See Jantzen, *Becoming Divine*, 145–46, citing Hannah Arendt, *The Life of the Mind: Thinking and Willing* II, 84.

16. *Irigaray Reader*, 109.

of Oz, but in an attempt to trace how reading "against the grain" could function as a source of inspiration.

As noted in the introduction to this book, Jantzen states openly that external truth is not her main concern. She does not directly challenge the Freudian or Marxist conclusion that religion is an exercise in illusion. Rather, her interest centers on the moral aspirations of projected religion. She writes:

> If human characteristics are projected on to the divine, if human beings seek to *become* divine, the important question will not be so much one of truth as one of *adequacy*. Are the characteristics thus projected really the ones that will best facilitate human becoming? Do they constitute a worthy divine horizon? Or are they partial, distorting, or inimical to the flourishing of some groups of people?[17]

Such projected thinking would appear to look to Arendt's work for substance. On Jantzen's terms, the *idea* of embodied human experience offers a substratum for "the imaginary . . . within which subjects are formed and out of which a religious symbolic must emerge."

Reading "against the grain" (i.e., borrowing from a frame of reference one does not share) would seem, on the face of it, to be a fruitful activity. "Arendt emphasizes the performative," says Jantzen. She cites a summary by Joan B. Landes: "in Arendt's public sphere individuals perform deeds and narrate stories; they are not just talking heads but embodied, suffering subjects who move in the world in relation to others. Such a world is a 'web of relationships' constituted by 'enacted stories.'"[18] Jantzen extols the benefits of this environment:

> Its ideal is a community where natality is celebrated by welcoming and nourishing the new little strangers whose arrival makes for new beginnings, and thus of openness to strangers—to alterity—more broadly. In such a world mutual respect and care for one another's flourishing are standard, rooted in the gendered embodiment of natality.

One must ask, however, what kind of flourishing could happen and what openness to "alterity" if the public sphere is only transplanted linguistically into the sphere of "the imaginary."

---

17. Jantzen, *Becoming Divine*, 89. Jantzen's italics.

18. See Jantzen, *Becoming Divine*, 225–26, citing Landes, "The Public and the Private Sphere: a Feminist Reconsideration."

There are complexities here to which I will return in the third section of this chapter. The next section considers key feminist aspirations in a broad context, encompassing the social sciences and feminist theology. I draw heavily on Elaine Graham's study in these areas.

CONTINGENT, EMBODIED AND DIFFERENT

"Whilst gender is a complex and constructed phenomenon, it is not merely an incidental aspect of our experience of being human," writes Graham.[19] This observation would seem to run counter to the minimizing of sexual difference. Graham continues: "The decisive impact of gender as a form of social relations is suggestive of a model of human nature as profoundly relational, requiring the agency of culture to bring our personhood fully into being." She adds: "This resounds with other perspectives that emphasize such an identity as thoroughly compatible with a Trinitarian model of God." Here is a suggestion, albeit undeveloped, of a metaphysical component. She also states: "Authentic analysis of gender must be informed by accounts of human bodiliness."[20] Culture, relationship, identity, embodiment, a metaphysical component: how do these factors interact and what do they tell us about gendered human nature?

Graham's study draws on multiple sources in a way that I cannot replicate here but at times, as I judge, she speaks with her own voice. Her remarks on theology would seem a case in point. Theology, says Graham, "must engage with the pluralism and complexity of interdisciplinary theories of gender at a profound level."[21] This process, she adds, may result in skepticism about a "universal 'human nature' enduring throughout history and across diverse social conditions," skepticism which has ethical and philosophical consequences:

> Whatever human nature may be, it is inaccessible to our understanding beyond the medium of our own culture and agency. The challenge of this concerns the ethical and political implications of the dissolution of self-evident standards of human need and value; and whether it is possible to understand human identity as contingent and contextual but also enduring and constant.

Graham goes on to outline theological consequences. I will return to these.

19. Graham, *Making the Difference*, 223.
20. Graham, *Making the Difference*, 225.
21. See Graham, *Making the Difference*, 222–23.

Chapter 8 noted Graham's circular theory of interaction between culture, subject, and ideology modifying culture, a theory she calls "the centrality of practice."[22] "Gender is but one manifestation of human social relations," she says, and, as such, "generated and maintained by human *practice*, symbolic and material."[23] This statement may be measured against Hannah Arendt's remark, reported by McFague, that "because of its inherent tendency to disclose the agent together with the act, action needs for its full appearance the shining brightness we once called glory, and which is possible only in the public realm."[24] If, for Arendt, the public realm might be said to resemble a theatre, this is, for Graham, a theatre very much still in the making. "The challenge," she says, "is to find ways of speaking which cast bodies as the primary source and medium of our relationship to the world—as a kind of 'vantage point' for experience, whilst lending diversity and provisionality to such accounts."[25]

Diversity and "provisionality" as keynotes in the public realm are not without potential problems. There are ethical implications as Graham admits. One need not stop at ethics. Graham outlines the consequence for the sciences:

> The dilemma for feminist epistemology in seeking an alternative to androcentric science and knowledge-claims lies in its exposure of all knowledge as socially-constructed and subjective ... Yet clearly a postmodern scepticism can lead to relativism; if all we have in science are competing narratives, within which a subordinate standpoint [of] knowledge has no automatic primacy, how do we decide between rival discourses?[26]

Lack of an epistemological basis can affect human identity. Graham draws attention to postmodern perspectives which "dethrone axioms concerning the transparency of language, the unity of consciousness and reason, and the self-possession of the individual," with the result that personal identity is "contradictory and fragmented."[27]

Let us pause here. Subjectivity and selfhood, contingent upon the individual's inhabitation of culture, suffer something of a check in a

22. Graham, *Making the Difference*, 227.
23. Graham, *Making the Difference*, 217.
24. McFague, *Speaking in Parables*, 175.
25. See Graham, *Making the Difference*, 225–26.
26. Graham, *Making the Difference*, 206–7.
27. Graham, *Making the Difference*, 224.

climate which strongly critiques its own cultural roots. Feminist notions of agency are particularly affected by this climate. Appeals to the embodied nature of human action and knowledge are played out not only against a deconstructionist background but also in rejection of a "patriarchal" foreground. Feminist appeals to the body may cast classic subjectivity aside, only to reinvent themselves on Irigaray's terms. In the process of inventing an alternative ontology, Graham reports that Irigaray "risks rendering women's bodies immaterial and rhetorical, rather than empirical and rooted in social relations."[28] Here are echoes of McFague's metaphors or projections of the self. Put in terms suggested by Jantzen, this is a subjective journey governed by a "shift in the imaginary," in search of a new story-symbolic. Small wonder then if embodiment remains something of a chimera and identity becomes contradictory and fragmented.

Something more is evidently needed to accord with "a model of human nature as profoundly relational." Graham proposes bodies as "a kind of vantage point for experience."[29] Does her desire to establish the *embodied* subject, *contingent* upon the individual's inhabitation of culture, have anything in common with Ricoeur's dictum: "I exchange the ego, master of itself, for the self, disciple of the text"? Ricoeur, it should be recalled, locates text and disciple in a sacramental universe. On this basis, the individual is contingent on culture but culture itself is contingent on something else. Graham's study extends to thinking and application in the churches. In considering Graham's engagement in these areas, it is worth bearing Ricoeur's further parameter in mind.

So far, I have considered Graham's study in terms of embodiment and cultural contingency. The matter comes to a head in her treatment of sexual difference. If bodies are said to be "the primary source and medium of our relationship to the world" one might expect that male and female bodies would take front of stage. But Graham immediately goes on to state: "It may well be that there is a definitive difference between inhabiting a male body and a female one; but we must recognize the extent to which our understanding of our bodies, and of ourselves *as* bodies, is always culturally constructed and mediated."[30] As I judge, Graham is ill at ease with Irigaray's starting-point of a distinctively female pre-social essence. Without a distinctively female starting-point (or external text in

---

28. Graham, *Making the Difference*, 137–38.
29. Graham, *Making the Difference*, 226.
30. Graham, *Making the Difference*, 226. Graham's italics.

Ricoeur's parlance) it is hard to see how there could be a narrative of difference or even why one would, as Graham proposes, aspire to *make* such a narrative. On the other hand, Graham's "centrality of practice" accords with Irigaray's program for women to invent the next steps. I will come to a comparison of Ricoeur and Irigaray in the next section.

While her study is helpful in amassing interdisciplinary insights, I find that Graham's remarks in relation to gender and theology tend towards an unresolved interaction of ingredients rather than a coherent framework. She detects a positive direction in a "number of recent works" which "provide pointers towards forms of critical theological studies of gender, and suggest ways in which a theology of gender might be constructed from the vantage points of human practice." As an example of this development, she cites James Nelson's study of the male body: "The Doctrine of the Incarnation suggests for him that sexuality and physicality must affect spirituality and identity.[31] At this point, male sexuality makes a positive appearance in Christian doctrine. But, as already seen, the masculinity of Christ has tended to be problematic for feminists.[32]

If the doctrine of the Incarnation has something to say about sexuality and physicality, does it follow that sexuality and physicality have something to say about the Godhead? Graham draws back from this. As noted above, she writes: "Whatever human nature may be, it is inaccessible to our understanding beyond the medium of our own culture and agency." She continues:

> Such a rejection of essential human nature outside the relations and interactions of human culture bears significant implications for theological anthropology, and for the Christian doctrine of the *Imago Dei*. It challenges notions of an eternal, pre-existent human nature, and suggests that theological teachings concerning a God-given order of creation or Natural Law which pre-ordains separate functions for women and men may be untenable.[33]

It is at this point that she states that a "model of human nature as profoundly relational" is "thoroughly compatible with a Trinitarian model of

---

31. Graham, *Making the Difference*, 228, citing Nelson, *The Intimate Connection*, 21–28. If embodiment is important, resurrection of the body takes on renewed significance. But compare Johnson's contention that Christ exists only pneumatologically. (See *She Who Is*, 72.)

32. See also Graham, *Making the Difference*, 38–39.

33. Graham, *Making the Difference*, 223.

God." What she does not say is that the relevance of a Trinitarian model of God for human nature depends on the validity of the *imago Dei* which, on such terms, would be "profoundly relational."

"Theological traditions that have disregarded bodily experience in the articulation of spiritual and ethical verities may well need to be reformulated," states Graham.[34] In a climate of diversity and "provisionality" one might wonder what she means by spiritual and ethical verities. The matter comes to a head in the vexed question of gendered metaphors for "the holy."

> In their use of gendered metaphors for God . . . theologians are reminded that gender is an artefact of human culture, and not a metaphysical category. However, faith-communities can only use human terms and images by which to apprehend the divine. The substitution of 'feminine' terms to replace patriarchal images of Father, King and Lord in inclusive liturgies and prayers are no more 'value-free' than patriarchal language, although arguably they represent important aspirations on the part of worshipping communities to count women's experiences as equally holy, and worthy of imaging the holy, as those of men.[35]

Gender, said to be an artifact of human culture (and not a metaphysical category), does not explain the relevance of bodily experience nor does it, in itself, explain why women's experience should be a "vantage point" for language about God.

Graham admits that female images for God carry their own agenda in a similar way to "patriarchal language." She does not admit that *replacing* "patriarchal" images speaks of exclusion rather than inclusion nor does she consider how gendered metaphors illustrate trinitarian social relations. She adds: "Some of the most creative work in Christian liturgy and hymnody goes far beyond the corrective of 'God as Mother' to interpret truly inclusive language as embodying a much greater plurality of imagery." At this point the focus moves away from gender towards embodiment in a broader sense. Whether such wealth of imagery is to be counted as "holy and worthy of imaging the holy" on an equal basis with the use of human terms is not explored. One might surmise that such apprehension of "the holy" would sit comfortably with a panentheist or pantheist projection.

---

34. Graham, *Making the Difference*, 226.
35. Graham, *Making the Difference*, 224–25.

Graham proposes her "centrality of practice" as a positive response "in the wake of the dissolution of metaphysics, natural law or objective truth as 'foundational' epistemological criteria."[36] For Graham, "truth" in inverted commas is "understood as realized within and through human practice and material transformation."[37] In this context, she writes:

> The impasse of postmodernism is resolved not by turning away from its critique of metaphysics and dominant rationality, but by insisting that purposeful, coherent and binding values can be articulated from within the core of human activity and value-directed practice.

Such thinking "translated into theology would speak of the contingency and situatedness of human existence and knowledge, and the provisionality of our apprehension of the divine." Graham concludes her study by envisioning an alternative direction: practical strategies on the part of churches "to foster the values, relationships and truth-claims of a more 'gender-inclusive' community."[38] The aspiration towards "a more gender-inclusive" community would seem to function as a "binding" value unlike the provisional values and truth-claims intended to produce it.

In placing "truth" in inverted commas, Graham's study joins the company of those who depart from the Yellow Brick Road. Her emphases on cultural contingency and embodiment leave out contingency on what she calls "the holy." My final section will return to the body as vantage point from my own perspective. The next section contrasts modes of receiving identity. Where is identity to be found if "we are stuck with our centrality" as McFague contends, neither desiring nor able to "jump out of our skins"?[39]

TWO TYPES OF SELF-EMPTYING

This book asks about the origin and nature of women's identity as *imago Dei*. As seen above, Ricoeur argues for identity received from life story and, more broadly, from the signs deposited in memory and imagination by the great literary traditions. For Ricoeur, the signs or symbols speak to us in the public sphere, through the agency of metaphor. Metaphor

36. See Graham, *Making the Difference*, 226. Graham's italics.
37. Graham, *Making the Difference*, 227.
38. Graham, *Making the Difference*, 231.
39. McFague, *Speaking in Parables*, 148.

is thus a voice from the external world, a world which is imbued with meaningful signs, in short, a sacramental universe. In his "Intellectual Autobiography" Ricoeur alludes to the way in which metaphor gives access to what lies beyond the reach of ordinary language:

> Already in *The Rule of Metaphor* the suspension of the first-order reference of ordinary language opened the way for a second-order reference in which the world is manifested, no longer as an ensemble of objects to be manipulated, but as the horizon of our own life and projects, in short, as our being-in-the-world . . .[40]

In order to apprehend the "second-order" reference of metaphor, ordinary linguistic reference must be suspended. In a similar way, Ricoeur indicates that "sovereign subjectivity" must be suspended in order to gain access to what he calls narrative identity.

McFague, who sometimes claims to follow Ricoeur's theory of metaphor, argues in fact for something quite different. She presents autobiography as a "metaphor" of the self. "What we *know*," she says, "are the metaphors or projections of the self, the worlds it creates."[41] This is "sovereign subjectivity" in its full rigor. In order to understand McFague, and the debt she claims to owe to Ricoeur, one must enter the projection of the self and the world it creates.

For ease of reference, I liken the public sphere in which Ricoeur's understanding of metaphor operates to the Yellow Brick Road in *The Wizard of Oz*. By contrast, I suggest that McFague's idea of autobiography as a "metaphor" of the self operates in the nearby Poppy Field. In this section, I will compare McFague's theory of metaphor with the "courage" offered by the Wizard to the Cowardly Lion. As noted in the introduction to this chapter, the Scarecrow is pleased to receive his "bran-new brains." Similarly, the Cowardly Lion is convinced that he owes his courage to a drink from a square green bottle. This conviction is based on belief in the magic power of the Wizard. The magic power belongs to a projection, the world created by the Wizard. I will come to the reason for choosing this illustration below.

40. Ricoeur "Intellectual Autobiography," 35.

41. McFague, *Speaking in Parables*, 147. McFague's italics. But cf. her remark for example in *Models of God*, 197 n. 16: "The relationship between image and concept which I support is articulated by Ricoeur, whose well-known phrase 'The symbol gives rise to thought' is balanced by an equal emphasis on thought's need to return to its rich base in symbol. See esp. 'Biblical Hermeneutics,' *Semeia* 4 (1975); and *The Rule of Metaphor*, study 8."

Ricoeur casts doubt on the primacy and transparency of the thinking self. As seen, his voice is not the only one in this area. "Models of action that presuppose rationality . . . autonomy and freedom of self-determination have been exposed as particular and historically-conditioned accounts, dating from the Enlightenment and the Scientific Revolution," reports Elaine Graham.[42] She draws attention to feminist theories "which identify human action and knowledge as profoundly embodied." One must ask, however, whether these theories operate in the public sphere or only in deceptively similar territory.

Chapter 8 drew attention to Irigaray's critique of classic psychoanalytic theory on the grounds that the classic theory rests on "patriarchal" presuppositions and archetypes. Far from representing the unconscious mind, says her critique, such presuppositions represent the continuing dominance of "sovereign subjectivity" to use Ricoeur's phrase. But Irigaray's wish to substitute alternative archetypes in relation to women does not alter the *method* of classic psychoanalytic theory. Irigaray's project may sound like a radical departure from "sovereign subjectivity," given that it seeks to restore "the significance of the body, passion, libido and the unconscious as legitimate foundations of knowledge and selfhood."[43] But neither the method employed by Irigaray nor the result of her radical project would confirm this departure. Graham indicates that Irigaray develops femininity as an immaterial metaphysical category in which the unconscious mind is said to play a part. On Irigaray's own showing, classic appeals to the unconscious mind entail conscious presuppositions. Recent feminist appeals to the unconscious mind entail a similar conscious projection.

This section is entitled "Two types of self-emptying." To explore these matters, I will sketch differing responses to metaphysical categories. We will recall that Grace Jantzen acknowledges the Freudian or Marxist claim that religion is an exercise in illusion. Ricoeur reports in this regard: "Feuerbach, the common master of all atheism, tells us: let us return to man what he has given to God, so that man reappropriates what he has poured into the sacred by emptying himself."[44] Atheism, as represented here, locates the realm of the sacred in the sphere of projection. Jantzen does not query this. To this degree, she aligns herself with atheism. But

---

42. Graham, *Making the Difference*, 224.
43. Graham, *Making the Difference*, 137.
44. Reagan and Stewart, *Philosophy of Paul Ricoeur*, 237.

this does not deter her from pouring feminist aspirations into the realm of the sacred. Her question is: which aspirations will "best facilitate human becoming."[45] Jantzen's projected aspirations take her into the kind of territory described by McFague: "What we *know* are the metaphors or projections of the self, the worlds it creates."[46]

I said above that I would compare McFague's theory of metaphor with the "courage" offered by the Wizard of Oz to the Cowardly Lion. The Wizard takes a square green bottle and pours out the supposed courage into a beautifully carved green-gold dish. One may liken this activity to pouring out aspirations into the realm of the sacred. As part of the Wizard's stock in trade, the contents of the green bottle have nothing to do with external truth. Nevertheless, what is poured out would appear to facilitate leonine becoming.

In the story, the Cowardly Lion does not really owe his courage to the contents of the green bottle. In one sense it functions as a placebo for him. It is his belief in the efficacy of the drink which has the desired effect. In another sense, the Cowardly Lion is not cowardly at all. A lion is a symbol for courage and this particular lion has already demonstrated courage. This latter sense belongs to the sphere of the Yellow Brick Road, the sphere of Ricoeur's understanding of metaphor, not McFague's.

Let us attempt to pull these various threads together. Here, at more length, is what Ricoeur has to say in these matters:

> Feuerbach, the common master of all atheism, tells us: let us return to man what he has given to God, so that man reappropriates what he has poured into the sacred by emptying himself. But I think that our question—and we understand it better after Marx, Nietzsche and Freud—is: what is man? Do we know man better than we know God? In the end, I do not know what man is. My confession to myself is that man is instituted by the word, that is by a language which is less spoken *by* man than spoken *to* man.[47]

The view of "man" as the agent of self-determination, says Graham, has been exposed as a "historically conditioned" account.[48] Classic psychoanalytic theory to some degree questions the transparency of "sovereign

---

45. Jantzen, *Becoming Divine*, 89. Jantzen's italics.
46. McFague, *Speaking in Parables*, 147. McFague's italics.
47. Reagan and Stewart, *Philosophy of Paul Ricoeur*, 237.
48. Graham, *Making the Difference*, 224.

subjectivity." Ricoeur puts it this way: "But I think that our question—and we understand it better after Marx, Nietzsche and Freud—is: what is man?" If human self-determination is open to doubt, how does one respond? Ricoeur invokes the sacramental universe: "My confession to myself is that man is instituted by the word, that is by a language which is less spoken *by* man than spoken *to* man."

Before moving on, it is important to consider some parameters. Ricoeur questions the validity of "sovereign subjectivity" in the name of what I have called the Yellow Brick Road. On the other hand, subjectivity in its historically conditioned sense retains some connection with the Yellow Brick Road, as in, for example, the male/female binary. It is not the Enlightenment but deconstruction which questions this binary along with the linguistic efficacy which sustains it. Key feminists are caught somewhere in the middle, questioning and promoting "sovereign subjectivity" as they question and promote religion. Much of this has to do with the critique of "patriarchy," seen to be in league with the male/female binary among other things. In the process there is a change of ground. The scene of action moves from the Yellow Brick Road to the Deadly Poppy Field and beyond.

"My confession to myself is that man is instituted by the word, that is by a language which is less spoken *by* man than spoken *to* man," says Ricoeur. This is to reiterate what he says elsewhere: "I exchange the ego, master of itself, for the self, disciple of the text."[49] But how does one become what he calls a "disciple of the text"? Ricoeur describes this process:

> To be sure, there is still a need for a speaking-subject to receive the matter of the text, to make it its own, to appropriate it, in order to balance the correlative moment of *distanciation* of the textualizing of experience. The proof that appropriation does not imply the surreptitious return of sovereign subjectivity lies in the necessity that one dis-appropriate oneself, a necessity imposed by the self-understanding before the text.

In order to receive the word spoken *to* man, one must dis-appropriate oneself before the text. This is one kind of self-emptying.

The other kind of self-emptying may be inferred from Ricoeur's citation of Feuerbach: "let us return to man what he has given to God, so that man reappropriates what he has poured into the sacred by emptying

---

49. Ricoeur, "Intellectual Autobiography," 35.

himself."⁵⁰ I submit that key feminists fulfill this exhortation, albeit in a spirit unintended by the common master of all atheism. Jantzen writes:

> If human characteristics are projected on to the divine, if human beings seek to *become* divine, the important question will not be so much one of truth as one of *adequacy*. Are the characteristics thus projected really the ones that will best facilitate human becoming?'⁵¹

To rephrase Feuerbach, Jantzen's approach might be expressed in these terms: "Let us empty ourselves into the sacred in order to reappropriate what we have poured out so that what we have poured out will facilitate human becoming." This kind of self-emptying accords with the "courage" poured into the green-gold dish and drunk by the Cowardly Lion.

I stated above that in order to understand McFague and the debt she claims to owe to Ricoeur, one must enter the projection of the self and the world it creates. I also stated that Jantzen's approach might be expressed in these terms: "Let us empty ourselves into the sacred in order to re-appropriate what we have poured out so that what we have poured out will facilitate human becoming." It is this kind of entering into one's own projection or outpouring which seems to come to fruition in a feminist search for a new "symbolic." Elizabeth Johnson writes: "The symbol gives rise to thought. With this axiom Paul Ricoeur points to the dynamism inherent in a true symbol that participates in the reality it signifies."⁵² But what kind of reality is at issue? One must bear in mind that, for Ricoeur, the symbol points to and participates in the reality of the Yellow Brick Road. In order to appropriate the symbol, thought must dis-appropriate itself before this text. That this is far from Johnson's kind of thinking was demonstrated in chapter 2.

I have said that key feminists both question and promote "sovereign subjectivity" as they question and promote religion. As seen in chapter 8, the questioning of subjectivity owes something to psychoanalysis as a discipline as well as to a feminist critique of classic psychoanalysis. If one takes all this and pours it into a green-gold bowl, where does one arrive? As I judge, Johnson's method does not dis-appropriate itself before an external text but reaffirms itself before its own outpourings or "symbols" said to derive from a level "that Tillich identifies as the

---

50. Reagan and Stewart, *Philosophy of Paul Ricoeur*, 237.
51. Jantzen, *Becoming Divine*, 89. Jantzen's italics.
52. Johnson, *She Who Is*, 47.

collective unconscious."⁵³ That the unconscious mind is not independent of "sovereign subjectivity" is the burden of Irigaray's critique of classic psychoanalysis

Johnson's kind of outpouring and response is demonstrated in her description of religious experience:

> Women's religious experience is a generating force . . . a clear instance of how great symbols of the divine always come into being not simply as a projection of the imagination, but as an awakening from the deep abyss of human existence in real encounter with divine being . . . So it is, when the concrete, historical reality of women, affirmed as blessed by God, functions as symbol in speech about the mystery of God.⁵⁴

To my mind, Johnson's description of women's religious experience has much in common with Jantzen's appropriation of Hannah Arendt's work seen above:

> Taking the idea of natality seriously has direct and immediate consequences for a shift in the imaginary. It affirms the concreteness and embodied nature of human lives and experience, the material and discursive conditions within which subjects are formed and out of which a religious symbolic must emerge.⁵⁵

Johnson's description of the deep abyss of human existence might be rephrased as follows: "The idea of women's encounter with the mystery of God has direct and immediate consequences for a shift in the imaginary. It affirms the concrete historical reality of women within which subjects are formed and out of which a religious symbolic must emerge."

For Johnson, the goal of facilitating women's becoming finds some biblical support. She writes:

> Feminist theologians love the vision of wholeness, equality and freedom celebrated in an early baptismal hymn: in the oneness of Christ Jesus "there is neither Jew nor Greek, neither slave nor free, neither male nor female" (Gal 3:28).⁵⁶

> If the image of God is the ultimate reference point for the values of a community, then the structure of the triune symbol stands

---

53. See Johnson, *She Who Is*, 46.
54. Johnson, *She Who Is*, 46–47, citing Ricoeur's *Symbolism of Evil*.
55. See Jantzen, *Becoming Divine*, 146.
56. Johnson, *She Who Is*, 31.

as a profound critique, however little noticed, of patriarchal domination in church and society. The power of an interpersonal communion characterized by equality and mutuality, which it signifies, still flashes like a beacon through a dark night, rather than shining like a daytime sun.[57]

At the same time Johnson claims that the criterion "for testing the truth and falsity, the adequacy and inadequacy, the coherence and incoherence of theological statements and religious structures . . . is the emancipation of women toward human flourishing."[58] This is, finally, to place "symbol" under the governance of human aspiration.

To link the image of God with "an interpersonal communion" in the "structure of the triune symbol" has some features in common with the understanding of the *imago Dei* argued in this book. But the frame of reference has moved away from the Yellow Brick Road. Here is the beginning of a journey downstream. The emancipation of women stems from an era which valued some absolutes. To place religious "symbol" and ethics under the governance of human aspiration is to disturb their foundations. It is deconstruction which counts the cost of this process. Graham reports that, according to deconstructionist philosophies, "equality" and "difference" are not absolutes but are themselves constructs.[59] McFague notes that "deconstruction's critique makes clear the necessity of developing 'negative capability'—the ability to endure absence, uncertainty, partiality, relativity, and to hold at bay the desire for closure, coherence, identity, totality."[60]

Deconstructionist philosophies pose a challenge within the feminist movement. Graham goes on to state:

> Indeed, one of the main criticisms of the poststructuralist impetus within feminism is that it deprives the woman's movement of a clear identity upon which to build a political programme; it is thus seen as a withdrawal from engagement, a theory devoid of practice, and a collapse into the very metaphysics which it claims to deconstruct.[61]

---

57. Johnson, *She Who Is*, 223.
58. Johnson, *She Who Is*, 30.
59. See Graham, *Making the Difference*, 185.
60. McFague, *Models of God*, 25–26.
61. Graham, *Making the Difference*, 186.

Narrative Identity

In holding at bay a desire for closure and coherence, "negative capability" would seem at odds with a political program. Does it offer a kind of metaphysics, denials notwithstanding?

As seen, Irigaray seeks to retain women's identity on radically new grounds. If one cannot dis-appropriate oneself before a "text," seen to belong overwhelmingly to patriarchal discourse, is there another kind of dis-appropriation? Irigaray objects to the "sovereign" self of the male gaze, seeing only a reflection of itself in the concave speculum used in vaginal examinations. But what lies beyond the male gaze? For Irigaray, reports Graham, women's difference, rendered invisible, constitutes a space outside representation:

> To find the authentic woman requires stepping into non-identity, and perceiving woman as non-being, absence, loss of self in an almost 'mystical' experience of surrender of self-identity . . . in the space to which patriarchal discourse cannot penetrate because there is no longer anything to reflect, women can discover a purposeful and autonomous self-determination.[62]

The green bottle is emptied out to its last dregs. To rephrase Feuerbach afresh, Irigaray's approach might be expressed in these terms: "Let us empty out all 'text' about ourselves in order to reinvent ourselves and the sacred, out of an empty green bottle."

Despite her cautionary advice against too easy acceptance of postmodern theory, Derrida's notion of *différance* (the "simultaneous assertion and negation of meaning") would seem to figure largely in Irigaray's search to find the authentic woman. At the same time the aim for women to "discover a purposeful and autonomous self-determination" signals the return to "sovereign" subjectivity. How this might be achieved from an empty bottle is what Graham attributes to the "mystical" component. Chapter 2 of this book noted the extent to which Irigaray is prepared to go in entering into the "is not" facet of the imagination. Her description of "the horizon of sexual difference" outlines an existence beyond all signification, all meaning and even being. This is the stuff of revolutionary Romanticism, a visionary future of a "general cultural mutation" in which women would have a central role to play.[63]

---

62. Graham, *Making the Difference*, 176–77.
63. See *Irigaray Reader*, 11–12.

Such a "beyond" would in Keats' phrase "tease us out of thought."[64] Or would it? Irigaray's visionary future has a program to it as well as the poetry of non-definition. This would appear to belie the claim that the poststructuralist impetus within feminism lacks a political program. But if *différance* is the substance of the program (which in itself is beyond all substance), where, it can be asked, does the signification for pursuing it come from? This is perhaps the feminist dilemma *par excellence*. The further one travels in search of a new "symbolic," the farther one gets from theoretical cogency as well as practical engagement. As one moves downstream from the Yellow Brick Road, the returns from a process of self-emptying appear to diminish.

CONCRETE UNIVERSALS

"The subject," says Ricoeur, "does not know itself directly but only through the signs deposited in memory and imagination by the great literary traditions."[65] These traditions supply access to "signs" or "symbols" embedded in the universe. The "*Cogito*" or thinking self knows itself *through* this access. Ricoeur's confession to himself is: "man is instituted by the word, that is by a language which is less spoken *by* man than spoken *to* man."

The word spoken *to* humanity manifests itself, according to Ricoeur, in the early chapters of Genesis:

> These great narratives which . . . put into play space, time and characters woven into story form, have in fact an irreducible function. It is a threefold one. First, they place the whole of mankind and its drama under the sign of an exemplary man, an *Anthropos*, an Adam, who symbolically stands for the concrete universal of human experience. Secondly, they give to this history an élan, an allure, an orientation, by unfolding it between a beginning and an end; they thus introduce a historical tension into human experience, starting from the double horizon of a genesis and an apocalypse. Finally . . . they recount how man, originally good, has become what he is in the present.[66]

---

64. See *Irigaray Reader*, 218. Cf. Keats "Ode on a Grecian Urn."
65. See Ricoeur, "Intellectual Autobiography," 16.
66. Reagan and Stewart, *Philosophy of Paul Ricoeur*, 41.

Ricoeur writes of an exemplary man (an *Anthropos*, an Adam), evidently a key source for what he terms "narrative identity." But the exemplary man, said by Ricoeur to stand for "the concrete universal of human experience," is a primary source for the "patriarchal" discourse which Irigaray and others wish to discard.

The suggestion that an exemplary man might stand for the concrete universal of human experience is subject to question in Phyllis Trible's interpretation of Genesis 3:22–24:

> If the word *hā-'ādām* in these closing verses ... is read not as a generic term but as an exclusively male reference, then the story never says that the woman was driven out of the garden ... Though this interpretation may be tempting, the interlocking structures and motifs of the story do not validate it.[67]

Whatever the temptation for Trible's feminist hermeneutical clue, her literary exegesis does not permit a reading that says that the woman was never driven out of the garden. Trible describes *hā-'ādām* in these verses as "generic man and invisible woman."[68] On these terms, the whole of mankind and its drama would seem hardly to include women although Irigaray goes so far as to offer a new gloss on "invisible woman." Other feminist writers might be tempted to discard or at least radically reinterpret these great narratives. On the other hand, the notion that women are created in God's image tends to persist.

In her editorial introduction to a series of essays outlining a history of biblical interpretation, Kari Elisabeth Børresen refers to the *imago Dei* as "inculturated" doctrine.[69] The adverse effects of this are generally attributed to "patriarchy" but perhaps residual Neoplatonism would be a more accurate term. While I disagree with her conclusions, Børresen's overview offers some useful clues. Similarly helpful is Elaine Graham's multi-disciplinary study which points to gender as a form of social relations in the context of embodied identity. In general Graham's study rejects a sex/gender distinction hovering between biological determinism and social "categorism."[70] Social "categorism" and "inculturated" doctrine would seem to go hand in hand. If neither biology nor culture determine

---

67. Trible, *Rhetoric of Sexuality*, 143, n. 54.
68. Trible, *Rhetoric of Sexuality*, 144.
69. See Børresen, "*Introduction: Imago Dei* as Inculturated Doctrine."
70. Graham, *Making the Difference*, 124; cf. 226.

human nature, does it not follow that human nature is determined by what is outside either.

While she calls Augustine's efforts to include women "feminist," Børresen observes that the "man-like disguise" for "women's *imago Dei*" sharpens "the conflict between rational privilege and subordinate female humanity."[71] The inclusion of women in the *imago Dei* runs counter to subordinate female humanity on Neoplatonic terms. On the other hand, Augustine's means of including women reflects the vertical Neoplatonic hierarchy between "masculine" and "feminine," hence the need (in women's case) for a "man-like disguise." The premise of a God-like *sapientia* is an "inculturated" idea. In other words, reliance on an abstract idea (and corresponding projections) has done women a disservice.

Nevertheless, an abstract idea remains a keynote in feminist thinking, the assertion of God-like privilege extended to include women. Børresen advocates describing God by male and female metaphors on the grounds that both women and men are understood to be "theomorphic."[72] Graham refers to "important aspirations on the part of worshipping communities to count women's experiences as equally holy, and worthy of imaging the holy, as those of men."[73] In a way similar to Augustine's usage of *sapientia*, women's experiences are presented as "theomorphic" on the grounds of being "holy" or "worthy." It is not then embodied femaleness *per se* but the alleged worthiness of women's experience which is said to be *imago Dei*. One then arrives at Elizabeth Johnson's SHE WHO IS.

Despite his "feminist" intention, Augustine's use of allegory signals a wrong turning in the history of interpreting the *imago Dei*, as Børresen attests. But the allegorical turn, as it might be called, is not limited to Augustine. Allegory was only one exegetical device available to him. By contrast, key feminists employ a form of allegorical projection in a much more wholesale way. Feminist theology constructs images of God from the basis of a "just and truthful anthropology" in order to promote human potential, reports Rosemary Ruether.[74] Grace Jantzen goes so far as to assert that this is a way for humans to become divine. In the previous section I depicted Jantzen's approach in these terms: "Let us empty ourselves into the sacred in order to re-appropriate what we have poured out

---

71. Børresen, "Patristic Interpretation of Gen. 1,27 and 1 Cor. 11,7," 201.
72. Børresen, "Introduction: *Imago Dei* As Inculturated Doctrine," 4.
73. Graham, *Making the Difference*, 225.
74. Ruether, "Christian Tradition and Feminist Hermeneutics," 287.

so that what we have poured out will facilitate human becoming." To my mind, Irigaray takes this further: what is poured out is too "patriarchal" to be re-appropriated, except perhaps ironically. The empty vessel itself plays a key role (from the perspective of *ex nihilo* or non-being where there is no longer anything to reflect) in a "mystical" facilitation of human becoming.

This chapter argues for a descent from rarefied abstractions to what Ricoeur calls "narrative identity." The feminist wish to discard or radically reinterpret the biblical narrative is paradoxically accompanied by what I have called a thin thread of attachment to *hā-'ādām*, supplied by the *imago Dei*. If Augustine's foray into allegory has resulted in a distortion of the narrative, the way forward will evidently entail reappraisal of the narrative. At the same time reappraisal of the method which distorted the narrative in the first place would be timely. With this in mind, I turn to some remarks by Sandra Schneiders. In doing so, I will look more closely at some logical implications of Augustine's allegory.

Like Augustine, Schneiders makes use of more than one method in matters impinging on the *imago Dei*. She outlines her perception of the operation of religious metaphor, critiquing Augustine in the process:

> We create the metaphor to say something about God; but then God seems to be saying something about the vehicle of the metaphor. Thus, if God is king, there is a tendency to see kings as divine. If God is male, then males are divine and masculinity becomes normative of humanity, the true image of God as St. Augustine maintained in an infamous passage.[75]

What she does not say is that in this instance Augustine is using an allegory, the focus unavoidably on the allegorical figure.

I have said that an allegorical method in relation to the *imago Dei* has historically done women a disservice. Schneiders sounds a parallel warning here: "As theologian Sallie McFague explains, a metaphor can only function as a metaphor and thereby give us access to the mysterious if the "is," i.e., the affirmation, and the "is not," i.e., the negative qualifier, are held on tension."[76] One needs to step back at this point. For Schneiders, metaphors are apparently intended to give access to the mysterious.

---

75. Schneiders, *Women and the Word*, 28, referring to Augustine, *On the Trinity*, XII, 7, 10. Cf. chapter 2.

76. Schneiders, *Women and the Word*, 27, citing McFague, *Metaphorical Theology*, 32–42.

This is not the case for McFague who states: "I do not *know* who God is, but I find some models better than others for constructing an image of God commensurate with my trust in a God as on the side of life. God is and remains a mystery."[77] In other words, McFague does not profess to offer access to the mysterious. As in Augustine's allegory, the focus is on the projected image or vehicle. If the supposed or notional tenor is God, the sinful connotation of the literal vehicle comes to the fore. Instead of a deeper meaning qualifying the sinful vehicle, the projected meaning (the "is") is seen to inappropriately glorify the sinful vehicle unless the projection undergoes a simultaneous negation (the "is not").

"We create the metaphor to say something about God," says Schneiders. This is to signal that "metaphor" is a human creation, apparently no more than a projection of human experience. Such "metaphors" are to be consciously affirmed *and* consciously disowned. Schneiders, applies the method to God addressed as father: "It is equally and simultaneously true that God is, and is not, our father."[78] She adds: "If the denial is repressed the metaphor succumbs to literalism, i.e., it dies. But the literalized metaphor, like an unburied body, is not harmless to its environment, the imagination." In other words, language for God should not go very far. This mental caveat does not sit easily with Jantzen's program for projecting human characteristics onto the divine in order for humans to become divine. Neither does it reflect Johnson's focus on women's religious experience as a generating force for great symbols of the divine. In general, concern about the danger of literalized metaphor is reserved for the feminist critique of "patriarchy."

I stated above that Schneiders demonstrates more than one method in matters impinging on the *imago Dei*. Elsewhere she departs from her reservation about the metaphor of God as father. She observes:

> Jesus' metaphorical attribution of fatherhood to God . . . laid the foundation for his creation of a new family. Those who called no man on earth father (Mt 23:9), that is, who were subject to no human patriarch, could freely associate themselves in a new community of disciples bound together by faith in Jesus. Even Jesus' mother had to make the transition from blood relationship to faith relationship in order to become a member of this new community . . . And those who followed him became brother and

---

77. McFague, *Models of God*, 192 n. 37.
78. Schneiders, *Women and the Word*, 27.

sister and mother to him (Mk 3:31–35), i.e., his new family who, by his invitation, could also call God "Abba" (cf. Mt 6:9).[79]

In order to safeguard the tension between the affirmation and the negative qualifier, it would be necessary to add that those who called God "Abba" became and did not become brother and sister and mother to Jesus and were and were not his new family. But Schneiders indicates that God's fatherhood supplants earthly parenting. In this latter case she appears to express a sacramental approach to the literal and familiar. She describes Jesus's healing use of literal vehicles:

> By his use of "Abba" for God and by his presentation of God as father of the prodigal, Jesus was able to transform totally the patriarchal God-image. He healed the father metaphor which had been patriarchalized in the image of human power structures and restored it to the original meaning of divine origination in and through love.[80]

This is a sacramental understanding, with meaning deriving from the divine origination, a source which McFague disowns.[81]

The new family of Jesus, depicted by Schneiders, reflects the description by Ricoeur of "the concrete universal of human experience" placed "under the sign of an exemplary man." In Schneiders' example, the exemplary man is of course the second Adam who reverses the wrong turning of humanity. Even Jesus's mother, attests Schneiders, "had to make the transition from blood relationship to faith relationship in order to become a member of this new community." Schneiders takes this further. She goes so far as to place this concrete universal of human experience under the sign of an exemplary man *and* woman. Chapter 4 considered Schneider's proposal that Mary Magdalene could function as the figure symbolically representing "the Johannine community, the church, the new people of God."[82] If one argues, as I do, that Mary mother of Jesus retains her specific role as God-bearer, one arrives not

---

79. Schneiders, *Women and the Word*, 48.

80. Schneiders, *Women and the Word*, 48.

81. See McFague, *Models of God*, 192, n. 37. McFague writes: "it seems to me that to be a Christian is to be persuaded that there is a personal, gracious power who is on the side of life and its fulfillment, a power whom the paradigmatic figure Jesus of Nazareth expresses and illuminates; but when we try to say something more, we turn, necessarily, to the 'loves' we know (unless one is a Barthian and believes that God defines love and that all human love only conforms to the divine pattern)."

82. Schneiders, *Written That You May Believe*, 217.

with invisible woman but two visible women. Visibility is the nature of concrete universals.

In her "exegetically based reflection on the women in John's Gospel," Schneiders declares her intention to provide "resources for the imagination of contemporary Christians as they deal with the issue of women in the church today."[83] Resources for the imagination would suggest a wide scope, especially in relation to the issue of women in the church today. Elsewhere, as seen, she maintains that imagination is in danger of "literalized metaphor" which operates "like an unburied body . . . not harmless to its environment."[84] Imagination, unconstrained by exegesis, raises the specter of allegory. In effect, literalized metaphor functions as allegory if it is sustained as a lived-in projection.

The possibility of specters and unburied bodies brings us back to the history of what I have called the allegorical turn in relation to the *imago Dei* and the imagination of Augustine's day. In his theory of the *imago Dei*, Augustine turns away from narrative encounter between Adam and Eve to a surmised inner man (*sapientia*) and inner woman (*scientia*), with a vertical relationship between the two. For Augustine, the God-like nature of the (masculine) *sapientia* is offset, not by a simultaneous disowning of this assertion but by the inclusion of women in the *imago Dei*. Nevertheless, *sapientia* draws on nearness-of-approach in a way that is denied to *scientia*. As Elaine Graham indicates, holiness or worthiness is at issue here. Taken on its own, the allegory suggests a logical progression: one sees not only why "man" (*sapientia*) is superior to "woman" (*scientia*) but also why "woman" (*scientia*) is closer to falling into sin, a short step to claiming that the woman of the narrative is responsible for sin. One can take this further still. If the "man" (*sapientia*) is already worthy of imaging "the holy," what logical need is there for a second Adam? Logically, the need is for some kind of atonement on the part of *scientia*. If obedient submission on the part of the new Eve is classed as atonement, and if the mother of Christ is understood to fulfill that role, it is the mother of the descendant (rather than the descendant himself) who crushes the serpent's head. Specters and unburied bodies indeed!

This cautionary tale may serve to warn against departing from strict exegesis. Let us confine ourselves to the biblical narrative along with commentary on the narrative from biblical sources. In her study of John's

---

83. Schneiders, *Written That You May Believe*, 95.
84. Schneiders, *Women and the Word*, 27.

Gospel, Schneiders states: "John does seem to imply that the mother of Jesus had some special role in relation to the salvific work of Jesus."[85] In my exegetical postscript to chapter 9, I suggested that Timothy 2:15 qualifies the legacy of Eve, with verse 15 outlining the special role of the mother of Jesus in the salvific work of Jesus, along with to its relevance to women today.

Chapter 4 drew attention to the two-fold role of the woman. This twin heritage comes to fulfillment and is reasserted in the new covenant. The role of the woman as spouse is realized, as Schneiders points out, in "the Johannine community, the church, the new people of God." She goes so far as to associate this role with the symbolic figure of Mary Magdalene: in the garden setting of the tomb, Jesus ("both the promised liberator of the new creation and the spouse of the new Israel") encounters the woman (who symbolizes the new Israel).[86] To view the encounter between Jesus and Mary Magdalene in this light is to place the new order under the sign of an exemplary man *and* woman, as seen above. One might go further. Woman, apparently prone to deception, is also the one most ready to believe.

To take up Schneiders' suggested figure of Mary Magdalene as exemplary woman does not necessitate disowning the mother of Jesus. Rather, the two-fold role of the woman is then realized in terms of two exemplary women. That there is a hierarchy of priority in the relationship between the new Adam and the new Israel cannot be denied. This is not, however, the vertical hierarchy of *sapientia* and *scientia* but a horizontal hierarchy. That it is horizontal and not vertical is underlined by the counterbalancing role of the mother of Christ.

If it is permissible to see the twofold role of the woman fulfilled in two exemplary New Testament women (bluntly that there are two new Eves in the new covenant), one must ask how women in general associate themselves with these figures. If Mary Magdalene symbolically represents the new people of God, both men and women are placed under the sign of an exemplary *woman* in relationship with the exemplary man. Women's participation in the role of Mary, mother of Christ, functions, I believe, somewhat differently. In my postscript to chapter 9, I drew attention to my suspicion that the change of pronoun, from "she" in the first half of 1 Timothy 2:15 to "they" in the second half, indicates that "she"

---

85. Schneiders, *Written That You May Believe*, 97.
86. Schneiders, *Written That You May Believe*, 217.

has embracing significance for all women. In other words, the birth of the child applies to generic woman (and does not imply any obligation on the part of women to become mothers). Further, this concrete universal is specific to women. A history of allegory associated with Mary has, I believe, deprived women of this specific source of narrative identity.

"The challenge," says Elaine Graham, "is to find ways of speaking which cast bodies as the primary source and medium of our relationship to the world—as a kind of 'vantage point' for experience, whilst lending diversity and provisionality to such accounts."[87] To suggest that two historical women function as "vantage points" for the concrete universal of women's experience is to offer a way of speaking which casts embodiment as a primary source and medium of our relationship to the world. These women's roles are different, which might address Graham's criterion of "diversity." I suggest further that "provisionality" is supplied in the flexible nature of the gendered *imago Dei*.

This book contends that embodiment, difference and gender rooted in social relations are realized in the *imago Dei*. At issue is neither irrevocable biological essentialism nor human consciousness nor culture as the source of personhood. Far from removing the order of creation from the contingent and contextual, the God-given order of the creation stories undergoes God-given historical modification. The functions of human nature are subject to change (as for instance in the resurrection). Personhood is molded, not only by human but also by divine discourse. This is the enduring but also not un-modifiable personhood that Graham would appear to seek.

It is suggested here not that external factors be denied in their interrelation with the conscious subject but that this context be broadened to include what has tended to be excluded since the Enlightenment. As the concept of the *imago Dei* assumes a sacramental epistemology, the concepts of creation, covenant and Incarnation assume a spatiotemporal world that is not closed to the transcendent but rather is open to interaction. This is to enter into the framework of Ricoeur's narrative identity and his confession: "that man is instituted by the word, that is by a language which is less spoken *by* man than spoken *to* man."

---

87. Graham, *Making the Difference*, 226.

POSTSCRIPT: THE MYTHIC WAY

I will not conclude this chapter without a remark about imagination. McFague reports that imagination is now understood to be a function of the right brain.[88] For some feminists, the subconscious mind in connection with the imagination nevertheless figures prominently in generating a religious symbolic congenial to women. Graham draws attention to "Irigaray's radical project to rewrite Western epistemology and ontology" by means of a "feminist voice which appropriates the products of its own psychic imaginings (necessarily born of the body) and transforms them into concrete social relations of feminist solidarity and social change."[89] Irigaray invites "the authentic woman" to invent the next steps towards self-determination[90] but her project takes her into deconstructionist territory in what Graham describes as an almost "mystical" experience of surrender of self-identity. Is invention or imagination likely to be nourished in this environment?

In this book, as with its forerunner *The Wizard's Illusion*, I have drawn on *The Wizard of Oz* in an attempt to explore the kinds of ground occupied by Irigaray and others. I turn at this point to another fantasy, *The Lord of the Rings*. Here is what C. S. Lewis has to say about its author's capacity for invention:

> Probably no book yet written in the world is quite such a radical instance of what its author has elsewhere called 'sub-creation'. The direct debt (there are of course subtler kinds of debt) which every author must owe to the actual universe is here deliberately reduced to the minimum. Not content to create his own story, he creates, with an almost insolent prodigality, the whole world in which it is to move, with its own theology, myths, geography, history, palaeography, languages, and order of beings—a world 'full of strange creatures beyond count'.[91]

88. See McFague, *Metaphorical Theology*, 195 n. 3. McFague cites Lucy Bregman "Religious Imagination: Polytheistic Psychology Confronts Calvin": "Bregman suggests an intriguing list that includes 'left' and 'right' brains," says McFague. The lists (which McFague supplies) associate "Imaginative; Art; Symbolic; Myth; Eastern, primitive; Feminine; Renaissance; Liberating; Spontaneous Pleasure" with the right brain as opposed to various apparently "masculine" left brain functions. I find similarities here with the Jungian distinction between the animus and anima, with this difference, that these lists do not apply to the unconscious mind.

89. Graham, *Making the Difference*, 137.

90. See Graham, *Making the Difference*, 176–77. See also *Irigaray Reader*, 12–13.

91. Lewis, *Of This and Other Worlds*, 113—14, citing "Prologue," *The Fellowship of*

Is an ambition to rewrite Western epistemology and ontology to be achieved by anything less?

Once she enters her newly envisaged world, Irigaray seems to hope that "the authentic woman" will continue to live there. But this is not Tolkien's aim for his readers. McFague describes the "mythic" aim of Tolkien's trilogy:

> For what the mythic pattern, the heightened renditions of good and evil . . . allow for is what Tolkien elsewhere has called "recovery," seeing things as we are meant to see them . . . The way to the recovery of perception is accomplished here through the *heightening* of things, making the familiar more alive, more potent, more splendid than it is in the "Primary World." The unfamiliar, the sight of things in their singularity, is accomplished by the deformation of the familiar in the direction of the larger than life: this is the mythic way, to stretch reality, to open the cracks into it.[92]

"Recovery," seeing things as we are meant to see them, stretching the familiar to open the cracks into reality: there is a radical difference between this procedure and that of stepping into the milieu of non-being for the purpose of self-determination.

Elsewhere McFague describes her proposed process of "remythologization":

> What this sort of enterprise makes very clear is that theology is *mostly* fiction: it is the elaboration of a few key metaphors and models. It insists that we do not know very much and that we should not camouflage our ignorance by either petrifying our metaphors or forgetting that our concepts derive from metaphors. We must not forget the crack in the foundation beneath all our imaginings and the conceptual schemes we build upon them. That crack is exemplified in the "is not" of metaphor which denies any identity in its assertions . . . That is, metaphorical theology is a post-modern, highly skeptical, heuristic enterprise, which claims that . . . we must try out new pictures that will bring the reality of God's love into the imaginations of the women and men of today.[93]

---

the Ring.

92. McFague, *Speaking in Parables*, 134–35. McFague's italics.

93. McFague, *Models of God*, xi–xii. McFague's italics.

This is McFague in skeptical mode. The negative qualifier or "is not," cited by Schneiders above, has a decisive role even in pictures of the reality of God's love.

We may note that that McFague uses the word "crack" to describe both Tolkien's "mythic way" and her own way of "remythologization." But what is revealed through the crack differs from one to the other. Tolkien stretches reality in order to reveal what is there. McFague's "crack in the foundation beneath all our imaginings and the conceptual schemes we build on them" reveals not what is there but what is not there: "the 'is not' of metaphor which denies any identity in its assertions." While Irigaray attempts to move beyond skepticism she does not move beyond the "is not" aspect. Rather, it would seem, she attempts to build in the notional space of McFague's crack.

This, however, is not Irigaray's only method. Chapter 8 noted Irigaray's response to the "murder of the mother." The phrase comes from a supposed female archetype in the unconscious mind: the story of Clytemnestra, read by Irigaray, as an account of the installation of patriarchy, built over the sacrifice of the mother and her daughters.[94] Rejecting the "murder" does not, in this instance, entail rewriting of Western epistemology and ontology. It does not presage descent into "the crack in the foundation beneath all our imaginings and the conceptual schemes we build on them" in order to conduct the unimaginable and inconceivable. Rather, Irigaray's response is positive. She exhorts women not to forget their specifically female heritage. "Let us try to situate ourselves within this female genealogy," she says, "so as to conquer and keep our identity." To "situate ourselves" in a shared history is reminiscent of Ricoeur's confession to himself. To rephrase it: "Our confession to ourselves is that women are instituted by the word, that is by a language that is less spoken *by* women than spoken *to* women." I find echoes here of a journey by companions, walking together along a Yellow Brick Road.

---

94. See *Irigaray Reader*, 25, 44.

Conclusion

Aunt Em had just come out of the house to water the cabbages when she looked up and saw Dorothy running towards her.

'My darling child!' she cried, folding the little girl in her arms and covering her face with kisses. 'Where in the world did you come from?'

'From the Land of Oz,' said Dorothy gravely. 'And here is Toto, too. And oh, Aunt Em! I'm so glad to be home again.'[1]

This is the homecoming scene of *The Wizard of Oz*, a very short chapter, comprising one narrative sentence and two speeches. We have already been told that Dorothy is an orphan. The woman she calls aunt is not a biological relation. The country is grey and flat. The old house that plays such a pivotal role in the story is a one-roomed shanty. The new farm house built by Uncle Henry is presumably no more impressive. But home is home and Dorothy is glad to be there at last.

Homecoming is about belonging. There is something outside the self to belong *to*. That something speaks to us. We respond. It is not, in the first instance, the other way round. The speaking-self, as Paul Ricoeur calls it, is not primary. Ricoeur writes of the necessity that one dis-appropriate oneself before the text. By "text" he means personal life

---

1. Baum, *Wizard of Oz*, chapter 24. See also chapters 1 and 23.

story which speaks to the self from the outside. More broadly he writes that "the subject does not know itself directly but only through the signs deposited in memory and imagination by the great literary traditions."[2] This is a homecoming to something that speaks through culture from beyond culture. If the self cannot dis-appropriate itself before this text, what does this say about the search for belonging and identity?

"We *are* relational beings, and if this is not obvious to us, then it only shows how deeply we are prey to that most insidious of modern myths, the myth of the self-constituting subject of so much modern thought," states Janet Martin Soskice.[3] But, for many feminists, there is a difficulty in dis-appropriating the self. If Western culture speaks to the self at all, it speaks the language of "patriarchy." Luce Irigaray goes so far as to say that women should recreate themselves *ex nihilo*, in which case women, as speaking selves, would owe nothing to the great literary traditions. The price of such divestment is, as I have said, rarely considered.

Homecoming is about belonging to something outside the self. If there is nothing (*nihilo*) outside the self, there is nothing to belong *to*. Some in our postmodern world would go so far as to repudiate the desire to belong. Sallie McFague reports that "deconstruction's critique makes clear the necessity of developing 'negative capability'—the ability to endure absence, uncertainty, partiality, relativity, and to hold at bay the desire for closure, coherence, identity, totality."[4] Even the self-constituting subject is at risk here. Irigaray's version of *ex nihilo* stops short, I believe, of this extreme. She writes of a place of rebirth beyond all "signification."[5] But Utopia is not home.

Faced with postmodern "negative capability," Irigaray clings to subjectivity as the way forward for women. At the same time, she wishes to discard "all signification" along with "God—that guarantee of the meaning or non-meaning of the whole." She is not alone in this. McFague disassociates herself from the "Christian symbolic universe," the signs, discerned by Ricoeur, embedded in the universe and bearing witness that "all things [are] connected among themselves because they are connected in God."[6] If this sort of connection is disowned along with the external

---

2. See Ricoeur "Intellectual Autobiography," 16, 35.
3. Soskice, *Kindness of God*, 121.
4. McFague, *Models of God*, 25–26.
5. *Irigaray Reader*, 218.
6. See McFague, *Speaking in Parables*, 106.

God, what does this say about the *imago Dei*? Can the *imago Dei* be recreated *ex nihilo*? If that were possible, and some believe it is, one may still ask why it should be desirable. Does not the desire itself owe something to the tradition?

"The idea of *imago Dei*," says Kari Elisabeth Børresen, "is fundamental in theological anthropology, being a primary example of interaction between the concept of God and the definition of humanity."[7] It is the idea of the *imago Dei* that many feminist writers find so appealing. This is perhaps as good an indication as any of the feminist quest for identity. To begin with an idea is to begin with the self-constituting subject, an endorsement of, rather than a departure from, much modern thought. In short, key feminists adopt a modern, otherwise "patriarchal," method while distancing themselves from the biblical roots on which the *imago Dei* rests. The method retains some vestige of its Neoplatonic (if not biblical) foundation, a foundation commonly rejected by feminists. Yet if "all signification" is abandoned, where does identity come from?

In this book I have tried to put forward two key points. Firstly, the *imago Dei* belongs to Ricoeur's scenario of a role more modest than self-constitution for the speaking-subject. Secondly, the "patriarchal" flavour, so readily discerned by the feminist critique, owes more to non-biblical than to biblical aspects of Western culture. The way forward, I suggest, is a cool appraisal of Western culture with the aim of divesting it of anti-biblical accretions. Chief among these are the primacy of the speaking-subject and some Hellenic assumptions about the male-female binary. This does not mean abandoning everything in the tradition or, to be more accurate, our twin heritage of Hellenic and Judeo-Christian traditions. If one does, there is nothing left.

This book is about a change of method as well as an enquiry into the nature of the *imago Dei*, in particular as this affects women. In the companion book, *The Wizard's Illusion*, I began the journey of uncovering a subjective, ultimately nihilistic, trajectory in postmodern thinking, along with the feminist response to it. McFague's comparison of metaphor with the green glasses which made the Emerald City appear green indicates her endorsement of a subjective approach. Her contention about the non-efficacy of metaphor is linked with her hermeneutic of suspicion towards a traditional symbolic universe. By contrast, metaphor as the means of access to "our being-in-the-world" is linked with what Ricoeur calls

---

7. Børresen, "Introduction; *Imago Dei* as Inculturated Doctrine," 1.

"narrative identity." In short, if McFague's method can be summed up as a Green Glasses approach, Ricoeur's method can be summed up as a Green Fingers approach. I make use of such illustrations in an attempt to elucidate complex matters. As with McFague's example, such illustrations are generally borrowed from the Land of Oz. For my purposes I have added a few topographical details as will appear in the following review.

Broadly speaking, chapter 1 supplies a map of the terrain. The Yellow Brick Road offers a known way of meaning and identity, based on a broad, not exclusively Christian, tradition of a symbolic universe. But the known way suffers a check. Western culture arrives at the River of Deconstruction. One has a choice then. Crossing the river requires some rethinking. On the far side, the Poppy Field promises a semblance of meaning as long as one lives within one's own model (as illustrated by the otherwise illusory Green Glasses). Downstream, and even more equivocal, lies the Swamp of Ambiguity. Both the Poppy Field and the Swamp of Ambiguity stop short of "negative capability" in its full rigor, where the waters of deconstruction empty into a nihilistic sea.

Chapter 2 sketches the allegorical method, linked with the historical demythologizing of Hellenic divinities as well as an impetus towards fresh constructions. Philosophically, a symbolic universe *and* an allegorical tendency run side by side in Western history. Both these elements appear in Augustine's theory of the *imago Dei*. In a modern feminist variant, Elizabeth Johnson demythologizes the Thomist "He Who Is" and, on this conceptual ground, projects the symbolic model, SHE WHO IS. It is at this point that I introduce the distinction between a Green Glasses and Green Fingers approach. Johnson endorses McFague's theory of metaphor with its demythologizing and re-mythologizing method, the Green Glasses approach as I term it.[8] Ricoeur calls philosophy's demythologizing tendency philosophical *hubris*.

Chapters 3 and 4 explore biblical parallels between divinity and humanity as expressed in gendered terms. This is a literary appraisal which seeks signs embedded in the tradition as a starting-point for enquiry. This journey runs counter to a feminist hermeneutic of suspicion towards the tradition and may yield some surprises. In her adventures, Dorothy does not realize that she is empowered and protected by the Silver Shoes and the Kiss on the Forehead. There is more to be discovered.

8. See *Women, Earth and Creator Spirit*, 72 n. 5 which lists McFague, *Models of God* "among the pioneers in religious thinking." See also Johnson's endorsement on the back cover of McFague, *Super, Natural Christians*.

Chapters 5 and 6 take an exegetical turn. Feminist exegetes detect God-alien femaleness in the biblical tradition. The concept of God and the definition of humanity are at stake. We encounter *hā-'ādām*, functioning in the guise of a genderless Hammer-Head, in a feminist rereading of the creation stories. But this kind of rereading does not engage with the nature of sexual difference. In New Testament churches, Lone Fatum detects a genderless option for women who are otherwise subjected to male-centered dominance. I indicate that gendered stereotypes have a Hellenistic rather than a biblical origin. Chapter 6 supplies my exegetical theory of the *imago Dei*, based on the interaction between embodiment and gendered relationships. The Son has a feminine persona towards the Father but a masculine persona towards humanity. Such relations are paralleled and counter-paralleled in a complex interweaving of masculine and feminine, not least in the relationship between Mary and Jesus.

Later chapters consider gender and women's identity. Chapter 7 engages with the philosophical background to much feminist thinking. This is the domain of the Poppy Field and the Swamp of Ambiguity, the River of Deconstruction never far away. Feminist theologians are not quite alone in this. I detect forays in the field by Augustine and Karl Barth. The remaining chapters canvas identity from the viewpoints of embodiment, inclusive language, and the subject in relation to "the text," as Ricoeur terms it.

For Ricoeur, identity comes from the outside. He calls this "narrative identity." There is letting go in this, a self-emptying which is quite different from the narrative-emptying strategy recommended by Irigaray. To let go on Ricoeur's terms entails some prior confidence in the story as it stands. This is why the Kiss on the Forehead is so important. One needs to discern whether God-alien femaleness is really part of the story or whether various fellow travelers on the Yellow Brick Road have distorted the narrative.

To return to the narrative as it stands requires some literary sensitivity. The *imago Dei* is part of the narrative and cannot, on literary terms, be separated from it. Jewish writer, Tikva Frymer-Kensky observes:

> Whatever the precise interpretation, the plural nature of the creation of humanity applies to both the creator ('we') and the creature ('he created them male and female'). Social relationship

is an indispensable part of both human nature and human purpose and there can be no utterly single human being.[9]

There are social consequences in the story. It is all about relationship. "We *are* relational beings, and if this is not obvious to us, then it only shows how deeply we are prey to that most insidious of modern myths, the myth of the self-constituting subject of so much modern thought," says Soskice.

The biblical narrative is about a relational humanity reflecting a relational creator. By contrast, the modern world favors self-creation. "What we *know* are the metaphors or projections of the self, the worlds it creates. The relativity of knowledge demands such a perspective," says McFague. "We cannot finally, get outside of ourselves, we cannot jump out of our skins."[10] She adds that many voices, including voices from the women's movement, are increasingly saying, "Why should we want to?" In urging women to create themselves *ex nihilo*, Luce Irigaray wholly endorses the myth of the self-constituting subject. At the same time, she objects to the male view of women, the "specular economy," in which the woman's bodily surface becomes a mere mirror reflecting the male back to himself.[11] But if self-creation and relativism are the order of the day, on what basis can the male view of women jump out of its skin? On what basis can a world created by the self (male or otherwise) become *more than* a mirror reflecting the self? For such a basis, is the women's movement, even at its radical extreme, radical enough?

A "specular economy" centered on its own self-projection resembles what Ricoeur calls the "temptation of gnosis."[12] He states: "And yet we must not simply stop with the failure of successive gnoses . . . The challenge has to be taken up as a provocation to think more and to think anew."[13] There are two steps to this: the method must be abandoned; a new kind of thinking must ensue. In saying this, Ricoeur argues for a dis-appropriation of the world-creating self in order to receive what is outside the self. By contrast, Irigaray and others want to think anew without abandoning the method. But can the self think anew in terms of its

9. Soskice, *Kindness of God*, 50–51 n. 25 citing *Studies in Bible*, 101.
10. McFague, *Speaking in Parables*, 147–48.
11. See McFague, *Super, Natural Christians*, 189 n. 22.
12. Reagan and Stewart, *Philosophy of Paul Ricoeur*, 46. See also Ricoeur, "Reply to Stephen T. Tyman," 473.
13. Ricoeur, "Reply to Stephen T. Tyman," 475.

own creation? Taken to its extreme, does not Romantic aspiration "tease us out of thought"?[14] Jung writes:

> Significantly enough, it is Kant's doctrine of categories, more than anything else, that destroys in embryo any attempt to revive metaphysics in the old sense of the word but at the same time paves the way for a revival of the Platonic spirit.[15]

There is a Romantic as well as psychoanalytic trajectory here. More than anything else old certainties are adrift. Significantly enough, the way may be paved for the "abeyance of all signification" as outlined by Irigaray.[16]

One of the difficulties in the debate about gender—a key potential source of disunity—is the history of the metaphysical component. The history is complex: trajectories overlap and compete with each other. To follow Jung's sketched history more closely: a demythologizing tendency, originally applied to Hellenic divinities, has resurfaced in the rise of subjectivity and consequent weakening of the metaphysics adopted by the West. The effect can be observed in what Soskice, citing Lacan, refers to as the "ego's era," the "Cartesian period" (between the sixteenth and twentieth centuries), in which metaphysics increasingly enters the domain of sovereign subjectivity, the "God's eye view" demythologized to the realm of human ideas. Soskice writes that the "God" of the (male) self-constituting subject is a philosophical fiction in which "there is never any genuine other, always just the 'economy of the Same.'"[17] Far from rejecting such thinking, Jantzen responds on this new demythologized footing: "the religions of the west with their male God(s) offer no way for women to achieve *our* subjectivity in relation to a divine horizon."[18] The Platonic spirit, premised on the new metaphysics, promotes an "economy of the Same" on its own terms. On such gendered metaphysical terms, one might wonder if we will continue to be relational beings.

The self creates its own world, says McFague. The self can go so far as to posit a "divine horizon" in order to perfect its subjectivity. Key feminists assume that this is the religious method. Jantzen reports that Irigaray extends the method, with all bodies (men's and women's) envisaged

---

14. See Keats, "Ode on a Grecian Urn".
15. See Jung, *Aspects of the Feminine*, 119; 122.
16. *Irigaray Reader*, 218.
17. See Soskice, *Kindness of God*, 121–22.
18. See Jantzen, *Becoming Divine*, 15.

as potentially divine.[19] I have likened these multiple "divine horizons" to a series of hills inhabited by varying types of Hammer-Head. To take the illustration further, what is to prevent the eruption of a mountain range of divinities? Should this occur, Olympus will be reborn.

The original Olympus was a hotbed of disunity and moral degradation, tendencies pivotal to its historical demythologizing.[20] Nonetheless, Jung detects its continuing existence in the "living dispositions" of the subconscious mind.[21] Elizabeth Johnson discerns "symbols for divine mystery" at the "deep level that Tillich identifies as the collective unconscious."[22] Irigaray claims that Western culture is built on matricide, in terms of the myth of Clytemnestra and her daughters.[23] The "murder of the mother motif" along with her proposed rebirth might well be a source of disunity in Olympus.

A "Cartesian" trajectory along with revival of the Platonic spirit would appear alive and well in the women's movement. On the one hand, key feminists endorse the self-constituting subject. On the other hand, the female subject is urged to project a "divine horizon" to counter the male God(s). The impetus towards self-creation represents a demythologizing tendency, with loss of input from the external world. The projection of "divine horizons" represents a re-mythologizing tendency. In terms of women's identity, the trajectory seems to vacillate between minimizing sexual difference—a demythologizing approach to the body—and maximizing sexual difference, associated with the projection of "divine horizons." Minimizing sexual difference would lead to a loss of gendered identity. Maximizing sexual difference risks a separation of the sexes.

In the concluding chapter of her study on gender and theology, Elaine Graham writes that "gender as a form of social relations is suggestive of a model of human nature as profoundly relational, requiring the agency of culture to bring our personhood fully into being."[24] One sees echoes here of Soskice's remark that we are relational beings, even of Ricoeur's description of narrative identity. Graham adds: "This resounds with other perspectives that emphasize such an identity as thoroughly

19. Jantzen, *Becoming Divine*, 16–17. Jantzen's italics.
20. See Lewis, *Allegory of Love*, 61–62; cf. Augustine, *City of God*, IV, 27.
21. See Jung, *Aspects of the Feminine*, 119.
22. Johnson, *She Who Is*, 46.
23. *Irigaray Reader*, 25.
24. Graham, *Making the Difference*, 223.

compatible with a Trinitarian model of God." There are hints here of the way forward suggested in this book. Graham stops short of a sacramental universe, offering the alternative of "truth" grounded in the "purposeful and value-directed practices and activities of human communities."[25] But is this development not likely to lead to polarities between communities?

In this book (and also in *The Wizard's Illusion*) I have likened metaphysics in the old sacramental sense to a Yellow Brick Road. Historically, the "God" of the Cartesian subject does not depart from the Road, at least not at first. Even Cartesian self-consciousness must ultimately affirm the linguistic "presence" of the traditional God, says Steiner.[26] Feminist "images of God" or "divine horizons" take a different path. The reason for this divergence is a rejection of the male "God" and all his works. But leaving the Yellow Brick Road has consequences. The feminist "God's eye view" lacks the cogency of the patriarchal "God's eye view" with a further effect on the cogency of identity. This is not to say that the "God" of the male Cartesian subject is the living God of the Christian faith. "The theologian might object—should object—that this 'God' is not the God of Jesus Christ," says Soskice.[27] She states that a philosophy of "the One and the Same" could "never be a Christian metaphysics, although it might be a particular Neoplatonic heresy."[28]

A Neoplatonic heresy might look deceptively like Christian metaphysics. In my parlance it is a fellow traveller on the Yellow Brick Road. But let us return to relational human beings reflecting a relational God. In this book I have likened gendered relations at the human level to the mobility of china figurines in their own land. There they can talk and move around. It is only when they are taken away and placed on a mantelpiece that their joints stiffen so that can only stand straight and look pretty. One might suspect that those with the male "God's eye view" described by Soskice have a mantelpiece somewhere in their luggage. But even standing straight might be beyond those with nothing solid underfoot.

What our postmodern world has come to would seem not so much a loss of religion as a loss of the "other," supplied by metaphysics in the old sacramental sense. This is not to say that all belief in the guise of religion has offered access to the "other." Soskice draws attention to a tradition of

---

25. See Graham, *Making the Difference*, 226–27.
26. Steiner, *Real Presences*, 121.
27. Soskice, *Kindness of God*, 122.
28. Soskice, *Kindness of God*, 119.

Western metaphysics in which only males are truly generative and the Logos, as seed of generation, is symbolically male.[29] In response, Irigaray wishes to rewrite Western epistemology and ontology, in a space beyond the bounds of traditional male preserves.[30] In doing so, I have argued, she takes the female figurine on a journey to foreign lands.

To restore her to her own land is to return to the Yellow Brick Road. This may well be a sticking point for many feminist theologians. On the other hand, the Yellow Brick Road, however it may have been colonized by Western philosophy, owes much to the Middle East. From Christianity, the West inherits not an economy of One and the Same but an economy of the One who is also Three. If meaning, identity and genuine interaction between the sexes are the desideratum, where should we look? Soskice observes, "We may now stand at a moment of evangelical opportunity in the West, a time in which Christians not only need to hear a fully relational account of the Trinitarian life of God, but may also be receptive to it."[31]

This is not to say that openness to God is, in itself, divine likeness in a gendered sense. A Green Fingers orientation is neither male nor female. But the orientation is a prelude, I believe, to discerning the nature of the gendered *imago Dei*. To be receptive of a fully relational account of the Trinitarian life of God and a correspondingly relational account of gendered human nature is, as Ricoeur puts it, to lose subjectivity as origin in order to recover it in a more modest role. If the ego's era persists in the West, and even proliferates in multiple guises, this step will be counter-intuitive for us all. Is it *hubris* that would hold us back or fear?

A proposed loss of sovereign subjectivity for women might well invoke the specter of "invisible woman" and "God-alien femaleness." The other side of this is Irigaray's invisible woman, set free to recreate herself in a space beyond the gaze of a "specular economy." But Irigaray also draws attention to the matriarchal line and wishes to give it greater visibility. Before irrevocably crediting the matriarchal line with a self-created "divine horizon," can we not give the biblical narrative a hearing? What if the matriarchal line is already God-bearer? There is one blessed among women because of the fruit of her womb. This is not a "divine horizon" but divinity itself, born of woman.

---

29. Soskice, *Kindness of God*, 110.
30. Graham. *Making The Difference*, 137.
31. Soskice, *Kindness of God*, 119.

Where is women's identity to be found? In this book and my previous one, *The Wizard's Illusion*, I have taken readers on a journey in the Land of Oz. One does not need to be a Christian to walk the Yellow Brick Road. As Jewish writer, Tikva Frymer-Kensky attests, one does not need to be a Christian to begin to appreciate the *imago Dei*. One does need the Christian story to contemplate *theotokos* as she really is.

Christianity, says Daphne Hampson, lives in its concretion.[32] G. K. Chesterton's poem "A Song of Gifts to God" speculates about what the relationship to a human mother might have meant to Wisdom incarnate. The poem describes the attitude of Christ to the earthly gifts of the wise men: such gifts will be received with "the high gratitude of God" from the One "Who had a Father for all time, yet thanks him for a Mother."[33]

---

32. Hampson, *Theology and Feminism*, 81.
33. See Chesterton, *Spirit of Christmas*, 38.

Bibliography

Abetz, Katherine. *The Wizard's Illusion: A Conversation from Oz with Sallie McFague and Others*. Eugene, Oregon: Resource, 2022.

———. "Women in Leadership." In *Swimming between the Flags: Reflections on the Basis of Union*, edited by W. and K. Abetz, 154–59. Bendigo, Victoria: Middle Earth, 2002.

Abrams, M. H. *A Glossary of Literary Terms*. New York: Holt, Rinehart and Winston, 1966.

Allen, Sister Prudence. *The Concept of Woman: The Aristotelian Revolution, 750 BC–AD 1250*. Grand Rapids, Michigan: William B. Eerdmans, 1985.

Anglican-Roman Catholic International Commission (ARCIC), *Mary: Grace and Hope in Christ*. London: Morehouse, 2005.

Augustine. *The City of God*. Translated by Henry Bettenson. London: Penguin, 1984.

———. *Confessions*. Translated by R. S. Pine-Coffin. Harmondsworth, Middlesex: Penguin, 1987.

———. *On Christian Teaching*. Translated by R. P. H. Green. Oxford: Oxford University Press, 2008.

———. *The Trinity*. Translated by Edmund Hill. New York: New City, 1991.

Austen, Jane. *Pride and Prejudice*. London: Pan, 1968.

Azkoul, Michael. *The Influence of Augustine of Hippo on the Orthodox Church*. Lewiston, NY: Edwin Mellon, 1990.

Barth, Karl. *Church Dogmatics*, III/I: *The Doctrine of Creation*. Translated by J. W. Edwards. Edinburgh: T. & T. Clark, 1958.

———. *Dogmatics in Outline*. Translated by G. T. Thomson. London: SCM, 1966.

———. "The Humanity of God." Translated by John Newton Thomas. In *The Humanity of God*, 33–64. London: Fontana, 1967.

———. *The Word of God and the Word of Man*. Translated by Douglas Horton. New York: Harper, 1957.

Baum, L. Frank. *The Wizard of Oz*. Reprint, London: Penguin, 2012.

Beattie, Tina. *Rediscovering Mary: Insights from the Gospels*. Liguori, Missouri: Triumph, 1995.

Bettenson, Henry, ed. *The Later Christian Fathers: A Selection from the Writings of the Fathers from St. Cyril of Jerusalem to St. Leo the Great*. Oxford: Oxford University Press, 1970.

Bilezikian, Gilbert. *Beyond Sex Roles: What the Bible Says About a Woman's Place in Church and Family*. Second Edition. Grand Rapids, Michigan: Baker, 1985.

Bird, Phyllis A. *Faith, Feminism and the Forum of Scripture: Essays on Biblical Theology and Hermeneutics*. Eugene, Origen: Cascade, 2015.

———. "Sexual Differentiation and Divine Image in the Genesis Creation Texts." In *The Image of God: Gender Models in Judaeo-Christian Tradition*, edited by Kari Elisabeth Børresen, 5–28. Minneapolis: Fortress, 1995.

Blamey, Kathleen. "From the Ego to the Self: A Philosophical Itinerary." In *The Philosophy of Paul Ricoeur*, edited by Lewis Edwin Hahn, 571–603. Chicago and La Salle, Illinois: Open Court, 1995.

Boff, Leonardo. *The Maternal Face of God, The Feminine and Its Religious Expressions*. Translated by Robert R. Barr and John W. Diercksmeier. San Francisco: Harper & Row, 1987.

Børresen, Kari Elisabeth. "God's Image. Is Woman Excluded?: Medieval Interpretation of Gen 1,27 and 1 Cor 11,7." In *The Image of God: Gender Models in Judaeo-Christian Tradition*, edited by Kari Elisabeth Børresen, 210–35. Minneapolis: Fortress, 1995.

———. "God's Image, Man's Image, Patristic Interpretation of Gen 1,27 and 1 Cor 11,7." In *The Image of God: Gender Models in Judaeo-Christian Tradition*, edited by Kari Elisabeth Børresen, 187–209. Minneapolis: Fortress, 1995.

———. "Introduction; *Imago Dei* as Inculturated Doctrine." In *The Image of God: Gender Models in Judaeo-Christian Tradition*, edited by Kari Elisabeth Børresen, 1–4. Minneapolis: Fortress, 1995.

Brown, Peter R. L., *Augustine of Hippo: A Biography*. London: Faber and Faber, 1967.

Bruce, F. F. *The Letter of Paul to the Romans: An Introduction and Commentary*. Leicester: Inter-Varsity, 1989.

Bultmann, Rudolf. *New Testament and Mythology and Other Basic Writings*. Translated by Schubert M. Ogden. Philadelphia: Fortress, 1989.

Bunyan, John. *The Pilgrim's Progress*, edited by Roger Sharrock. Harmondsworth, Middlesex: Penguin, 1968.

Calvin, John. *Calvin's Commentaries: The First Epistle of Paul the Apostle to the Corinthians*. Translated by John F. Fraser. Edinburgh: Oliver and Boyd, 1960.

Carr, G. Lloyd. *The Song of Solomon: An Introduction and Commentary*. Leicester: Inter-Varsity, 1984.

Chesterton, G. K. *The Spirit of Christmas*. London: Xanadu, 1984.

Chicote, Paul W. *The Methodist Defense of Women in Ministry: A Documentary History*. Eugene, Oregon: Cascade, 2017.

Christensen, Michael J. *C. S. Lewis on Scripture: His Thoughts on the Nature of Biblical Inspiration, the Role of Revelation and the Question of Inerrancy*, 57–59. Nashville: Abingdon, 1989.

Clark, Elizabeth A. *Women in the Early Church, Message of the Fathers of the Church 13*. Collegeville, Minnesota: Michael Glazier, 1983.

Cole, Alan. *The Epistle of Paul to the Galatians*. Grand Rapids, Michigan: William. B. Eerdmans, 1965.
de Beauvoir, Simone. *The Second Sex*. Translated and edited by H. M Parshley. New York: Vintage, 1989.
Douglass, Jane Dempsey. "The Image of God in Women as seen by Luther and Calvin." In *The Image of God: Gender Models in Judaeo-Christian Tradition*, edited by Kari Elisabeth Børresen, 236–66. Minneapolis: Fortress, 1995.
Doyle, James A. and Michele A. Paludi. *Sex and Gender: The Human Experience*. Madison, Wisconsin: Brown and Benchmark, 1995.
Fatum, Lone. "Image of God and Glory of Man: Women in the Pauline Congregations." In *The Image of God: Gender Models in Judaeo-Christian Tradition*, edited by Kari Elisabeth Børresen, 50–133. Minneapolis: Fortress, 1995.
Fiddes, Paul S. *Participating in God: A Pastoral Doctrine of the Trinity*. London: Darton, Longman and Todd, 2000.
Flexner, Elinor. *Mary Wollstonecraft*. New York: Coward, McCann & Geoghegan, 1972.
Giles, Kevin. "Is God male?" *Zadok Perspectives* 142 (2019) 5–8.
Goodwin, William W. *A Greek Grammar*. London: Macmillan, 1974.
Graham, Elaine. *Making the Difference: Gender, Personhood and Theology*. Minneapolis: Fortress, 1996.
Grant, Robert M. *A Short History of the Interpretation of the Bible*. Philadelphia: Fortress, 1984.
Gray, Frances. *Jung, Irigaray, Individuation, Philosophy, Analytical Psychology and the Question of the Feminine*. London: Routledge, 2008.
Grenz, Stanley J. *Women in the Church: A Biblical Theology of Women in Ministry*. Downers Grove, Illinois: InterVarsity, 1995.
Gruber, Mayer I. "The Motherhood of God," *The Motherhood of God and Other Studies*. Atlanta, Georgia: Scholars, 1992.
Grudem, Wayne. *Countering the Claims of Evangelical Feminism*. Colorado Springs, Colorado: Multnomah, 2006.
Hampson, Daphne. *Theology and Feminism*. Oxford: Basil Blackwell, 1990.
Hayter, Mary. *The New Eve in Christ: The Use and Abuse of the Bible in the Debate about Women in the Church*. London: SPCK, 1987.
Holladay, William L. *Jeremiah 2: A Commentary on the Book of the Prophet Jeremiah, chapters 26–52*. Minneapolis: Fortress, 1989.
Hoppin, Ruth. *Priscilla's Letter: Finding the Author of the Epistle to the Hebrews*. Fort Bragg, CA: Lost Coast, 1997.
Hultgård, Anders. "God and Image of Woman in Early Jewish Religion." In *The Image of God: Gender Models in Judaeo-Christian Tradition*, edited by Kari Elisabeth Børresen, 29–49. Minneapolis: Fortress, 1995.
Jantzen, Grace M. *Becoming Divine, Towards a Feminist Philosophy of Religion*. Manchester: Manchester University Press, 1998.
Jaspers, Bernd and Geoffrey W. Bromiley, eds. *Karl Barth–Rudolf Bultmann Letters 1922–1966*. Grand Rapids, Michigan: Eerdmanns, 1981.
Johnson, Elizabeth A. "Mary and the Image of God." In *Mary, Woman of Nazareth: Biblical and Theological Perspectives*, edited by Doris Donnelly, 25–68. New York: Paulist, 1989.
———. *She Who Is: The Mystery of God in Feminist Theological Discourse*. New York: Crossroad, 2007.

———. *Women, Earth and Creator Spirit*. New York: Paulist, 1993.
Jung, Carl Gustav. *Aspects of the Feminine*. Translated by R. F. C. Hull. London: Routledge, 2003.
Keats, John. "Ode on a Grecian Urn." In *A Book of Poetry*, edited by W. M. Smyth, 177–79. London: Edward Arnold, 1963.
Keller, Catherine. *Face of the Deep: A Theology of Becoming*. London: Routledge, 2007.
Keown, Gerald L. *Jeremiah 26–52*. Dallas, Texas: Word, 1995.
Kidner, Derek. *Genesis: An Introduction and Commentary*. Leicester: Inter-Varsity, 1967.
———. *Love to the Loveless: The story and message of Hosea*. Leicester: Inter-Varsity, 1983.
Knight, George A. F. *Hosea: Introduction and Commentary*. London: SCM, 1960
Lewis, C. S. *The Allegory of Love: A Study in Medieval Tradition*. Oxford: Oxford University Press, 1958.
———. "Bluspels and Flalansferes." In *The Importance of Language*, edited by Max Black, 36–50. Englewood Cliffs, N.J.: Prentice-Hall, 1962.
———. "Christianity and Literature." In *Christian Reflections*, edited by Walter Hooper, 15–26. Glasgow: Fount, 1983,
———. *The Four Loves*. Glasgow: Fount, 1998.
———. "The Language of Religion." In *Christian Reflections*, edited by Walter Hooper, 164–79. London: Fount, 1983.
———. *Miracles: A Preliminary Study*. London: Geoffrey Bles, 1947.
———. "Priestesses in the Church?" In *God in The Dock*, edited by Walter Hooper, 87–94. London: Fount, 1984.
———. "Tolkien's *The Lord of the Rings*." In *Of This and Other Worlds*, edited by Walter Hooper, 112–21. London: Fount, 1985.
Lucas, R. C. *Fullness and Freedom*. Leicester: Inter-Varsity, 1980.
Martis, John. "The Self Found Elsewhere: Phenomenological Faith meets Deconstructive Doubt." *Pacifica* 22, no. 2 (2009) 198–214.
Mascall, E. L. *Existence and Analogy*. London: Darton, Longman & Todd, 1966.
McFague, Sallie. *The Body of God: An Ecological Theology*. Minneapolis: Fortress, 1993.
———. *Metaphorical Theology: Models of God in Religious Language*. Philadelphia: Fortress, 1982.
———. *Models of God: Theology for an Ecological Nuclear Age*. Philadelphia, PA: Fortress, 1987.
———. *Speaking in Parables: A Study in Metaphor and Theology*. Minneapolis: Fortress, 2007.
———. *Super, Natural Christians: How We Should Love Nature*. Minneapolis: Fortress, 1997.
McKane, William. *Proverbs: A New Approach*. London: SCM, 1970
Mounce, Robert H. *The Book of Revelation*. Grand Rapids, Michigan: William B. Eerdmans, 1987.
Neumann, Erich. *The Great Mother: An Analysis of the Archetype*. Translated by Ralph Mannheim. Princeton, N. J.: Princeton University Press, 1974.
Newsom, Carol A. "Woman and the Discourse of Patriarchal Wisdom: A Study of Proverbs 1–9." In *Gender and Difference in Ancient Israel*, edited by Peggy L. Day, 142–60. Minneapolis: Fortress, 1989.

Origen. "Genesis Homily 1 13." In *Homilies on Genesis and Exodus*. Translated by Ronald E. Heine. Washington, DC: The Catholic University of America Press, 1981.

Parmée, Douglas, ed. *Twelve French Poets 1820–1900: An Anthology of 19th Century French Poetry*. London: Longmans, Green & Co, 1966.

Power, Kim. *Veiled Desire: Augustine on Women*. New York: Continuum, 1996.

Ranke-Heinemann, Uta, *Eunuchs For the Kingdom Of Heaven: Women, Sexuality and the Catholic Church*. Translated by Peter Heinegg. New York: Doubleday. 1990.

Reagan, Charles E. and David Stewart, eds. *The Philosophy of Paul Ricoeur: An Anthology of His Work*. Boston: Beacon, 1978.

Rees, Janice. "Sarah Coakley: Systematic Theology and the Future of Feminism." *Pacifica: Australasian Theological Studies* 24, no. 3 (2011) 300–314.

Ricoeur, Paul. "Intellectual Autobiography." In *The Philosophy of Paul Ricoeur*, edited by Lewis Edwin Hahn, 3–53. Chicago: Open Court, 1995.

———. "Reply to Stephen T. Tyman." In *The Philosophy of Paul Ricoeur*, edited by Lewis Edwin Hahn, 472–76. Chicago: Open Court, 1995.

Ridderbos, Hermann N. *The Epistle of Paul to the Churches of Galatia*. Grand Rapids, Michigan: William B. Eerdmans, 1984.

Ruether, Rosemary Radford. "*Imago Dei*, Christian Tradition and Feminist Hermeneutics." In *The Image of God: Gender Models in Judaeo-Christian Tradition*, edited by Kari Elisabeth Børresen, 267–91. Minneapolis: Fortress, 1995.

Sayers, Dorothy L. *Are Women Human?* Grand Rapids: William B. Eerdman, 1974.

Schneiders, Sandra M. *Women and the Word: The Gender of God in the New Testament and the Spirituality of Women*. New York: Paulist, 1986.

———. *Written That You May Believe: Encountering Jesus in the Fourth Gospel*. New York: Crossroad, 2003.

Schüssler Fiorenza, Elisabeth. "Feminist Remappings in Times of Neoliberalism." In *The Bible and Feminism, Remapping the Field*, edited by Yvonne Sherwood, 170–85. Oxford: Oxford University Press, 2017.

Seamands, Stephen. *Ministry in the Image of God: The Trinitarian Shape of Christian Service*. Downers Grove, Illinois: Intervarsity, 2005.

Sherlock, Charles. *The Doctrine of Humanity*. Downers Grove, Illinois: Intervarsity, 1996.

Soskice, Janet Martin. *The Kindness of God: Metaphor, Gender and Religious Language*. Oxford: Oxford University Press, 2008.

———. *Metaphor and Religious Language*. Oxford: Clarendon, 1985.

Steiner, George. *Real Presences*. London: Faber and Faber, 1991.

Sticker, Anna. *Friederike Fliedner und die Anfänge der Frauendiakonie*. Frankfurt am Main: Neukirchener, 1963.

Swartley, Willard M. *Slavery, Sabbath, War and Women: Case Issues in Biblical Interpretation*. Scottdale, Pennsylvania: Herald, 1983.

Swidler, Leonard. *Women in Judaism: The Status of Women in Formative Judaism*. Metuchen, NJ: Scarecrow, 1976.

Tasker, R. V. G. *The Gospel According to St. John, An Introduction and Commentary*. Grand Rapids, Michigan: William B. Eerdmans, 1972.

Todd, Janet. *Mary Wollstonecraft: A Revolutionary Life*. London: Weidenfeld & Nicholson, 2000.

Trible, Phyllis. *God and the Rhetoric of Sexuality*. Philadelphia: Fortress, 1989.

Whitford, Margaret, ed. *The Irigaray Reader, Luce Irigaray*. Oxford: Blackwell, 1992.

Williams, Rowan. "Language, Reality and Desire in Augustine's *De Doctrina*." *Journal of Literature & Theology* 3, no. 2 (1989) 138–50.

Yoder, John Howard. *The Politics of Jesus*. Grand Rapids, Michigan: William B. Eerdmans, 1994.

Index

Abrams, M. H., 2, 2n6, 11, 11n3
allegory, description of, 11, tenor and
    projected vehicle in, 41–42, 68
  as literary device (Hagar and Sarah),
    11, 88, 99–101, 107–8
  attributed to *imago Dei* idea,
    feminist history of, 3–4, 6, 43;
    Johnson's usage of, 54–59, 62,
    68; McFague's approach, 70, 72;
    women's eligibility for the
    priesthood, Ruether's argument
    for, 43–44, 282–83
  counter-allegory (Hill on
    Augustine's *imago Dei* theory),
    90, 92
  demythologized, 40, fresh allegorical
    construction, history of; in
    academia (philosophical
    approach), 40, 43, 88, 295,
    literature, 41, theology, 87–93
  in interpretation of Mary, 51,
    102, 109–14, 288; Song of
    Solomon, 83
  in the *imago Dei*, Augustine's theory,
    43, 46–52, 141, 190–91, 199,
    282–86; Augustine's position on
    allegorical usage, 40–41, 89
Allen, Sister Prudence,
  influences on Augustine, 47
ambiguity
  as step towards nihilism, 175–200,
    effect on language, 200, loss
    of coherence, identity in,
    188; in Keller's opposition to
    "logocentrism," Barth's version
    of, 183–85, 191, 197
  in feminist use of symbolic
    language, 239
  in Graham's "centrality of practice,"
    211–12
  in history of *imago* doctrine, 90–92
  in psychoanalysis, 218
Anglican-Roman Catholic International
    Commission (ARCIC)
    statement.
  See under *Mary: Grace and Hope in
    Christ*
androgyny,
  as denoting sexuality, genderless
    earth creature without sexuality
    (Trible), 116
  early "egalitarian" position, 240;
    in feminist aspiration, Irigaray
    suspicious of, still male-formed
    ideal, 152
  imago Dei not indicative of
    androgynous God (Soskice), 128
  mixture of gendered language for
    God not indicative of (Hayter),
    77
  Moltmann on "gynecology of the
    Father," 155
Apostles' Creed. *See under* Barth, Karl

Index

Apollinarius. *See* Gregory of Nazianzus versus Apollinarius

Aquinas, Thomas
- Aristotelian belief in woman's inferiority, 45; introduced by Albert the Great, 55n57; biblical alternative, 46
- doctrine of analogy, presuppositions of, 55, role of imagination in, 57; God as self-existing "He who is," 54, Johnson on, 56–57, 57n63, 179n5
- on participation in divine perfection, 55, 58
- on women not eligible for priesthood, 45
- speech about God tentative but reality-depicting, *via negativa* and *via analogia*, 69, 87, meeting-point for, 178–79

Aristotelianism
- Aristotelian essence as source behind linguistic meaning (Steiner), 23–24
- McFague on, 45, 47, 56
- Johnson on, 45
- Soskice on, 55n57, 226n88

archetype
- as seen in copy (Lewis), 42, 68, 76
- Wisdom as archetype of *Ishah* (Swidler), 79, 83
- *See also under* Jung, Carl

Arendt, Hannah. *See under* McFague, Sallie; Jantzen, Grace; Ricoeur, Paul

Augustine (of Hippo)
- Eve deceived, Adam responsible for sin, 139–40, 140n82, 258
- ideal *scientia*, Mary as meta-symbol of, 102
- moral depravity of old gods, 40n5
- on language: doctrine of signs and things in, 189, 190–91, 200, world perceived as sign, Wisdom's role in, 33–34
- on Wisdom as "she," 34, 82–83, 82n45, 184; difference between solidarity with humanity and incarnate as man, 229–30
- resurrected body, sexual difference sustained in, 142–44
- "sponge" theory of creation in infinite divine sea rejected, 183, 183n17, 187, 213, 213n36
- use of allegory by, 40–41, 89; in theory of the *imago Dei*, 46–53, consequences of, for women, 286, for language, 188–91
- women's identity (as in Christ born of woman), 53, 53n52; women's sex not a defect, 142–43, 226

autobiography
- as metaphor of the self, 260–61, 272, philosophy, theology, physics and art seen as, 21

Austen, Jane, 172–74

Azkoul, Michael, 47–48

baptism
- Christians baptized into Christ, not Jesus (Hampson), 224
- genderless identity in, "backdated" in patristic exegesis to include women (Børresen), 118, 121
- loss of female identity in (Fatum), 157–58
- *See also under* nearness-of-approach

Barth, Karl,
- admits departure from orthodox approach, method retrospective, 98–100, 167
- *analogia relationis*, against *analogia entis*, 166n57, 196 (*see also under* nearness-of-approach)
- Apostles' Creed read from second article, mystery of Incarnation (thing) prior to miracle of Christmas (sign), 97–100 (*see also* Augustine, on language, doctrine of signs and things in)
- departs from classic *ex nihilo*, creation against chaos, primeval chaos never realized actuality for, 185–86, 191 (*see also under* Keller, Catherine)

Jesus Christ, already human at creation (in God's sight), 98; as concept-model, 99, 112, 191–93, detached from world history, 197–200 (*see also* Bultmann, Rudolph, on Barth's method)
   on the *imago Dei*, 100, 195, "most hierarchical model imaginable" (Ruether), 166n57, 167, 244
Beattie, Tina
   on Mary as rebuke to female sexual desires, 113
better
   short-term "as if true" model-metaphors ("houses") open to "better" alternatives, 26, for our time, 31, 44–45; detachment of relativism lost in feminist aspiration, 26–27
   See also deconstruction: constructs rejected, notion of "better"
Bilezikian, Gilbert
   on authorship of Hebrews, 245–47
   on Hebrews 11:32, grammar of, 246–47 (*see also under* Grudem, Wayne)
   on the *imago Dei*, 244–45
Bird, Phyllis
   method of conversation with culturally captive texts, *imago Dei* as male, but open to reinterpretation, 130–32
   man of creation, 116n3, 157, as *imago Dei*, 126–27, sexual difference secondary to, 126–28
   on disordered creation as cause of male domination, 130
   source theory for creation texts, 126, Wortbericht and Tatbericht in Genesis 1, 126–27
Boff, Leonardo, on feminine "principle" in the Godhead, 242–43, 251
Børresen, Kari Elisabeth,
   on God-alien femaleness, 120, 124, 132, 152, 296, 301
   on *imago Dei*, as idea, 118, 294, women's inclusion in backdated patristic exegesis, 121; Augustine's theory of, 121–22, 156, 282; enculturated doctrine in, 124, 281, modern "equality strategies" in, 125, 144–45
Brown, Peter, 46n26
Bruce, F. F. *See under* "man" as a collective term
Bultmann, Rudolph
   on Barth's method, 98, 192, 196–97
Bunyan, John, 11, 41

Calvin, John
   on spiritual equality/inequality in marriage, 160–61
Carr, G. Lloyd
   typology from Old to New Testament compared with free-floating allegorical method, 88–89
Cartesian legacy
   as original axiom of "logocentrism," 23–24, 30, 300, epistemology based on, 216 (*see also* logocentrism, *Logos*-order)
   Cartesian thinking self, 210, period of, 153, 298; Rimbaud's alternative to, 23
   subjectivity of the (male) self, God and women seen through male eyes, 30, 32, 224–25, 298–99
Chesterton, G. K., 302
Christensen, Michael,
   on "myth" as solution to propositional dilemma (Lewis), 69–70
   on *via analogia/ via negativa* (Aquinas), 69, 87
churches
   capital C for Church Catholic, reason for, 171
   on demand for women's inclusion, 35, response to, 8, 238–44
   scope of secular gender studies, churches not keeping pace with, 203–4
   See also female church leadership
Cole, Alan, 107–8
Council of Mâcon, 4–5, 5n12

covenant
- between word and world, 30, 35, covenantal/ non-covenantal language, 24–25, 30, 62, 149
- encounter, two-party relationship in, 60, 86; lost in interpretation, 54, process of "mining" traditions, 93, 112
- old/new, relationship between, 34, 107 (see also *theotokos*, Mary as; Schneiders, Sandra)
- on divine-human level in new covenant, 105–6, 149, 159–66

critical realism
- espoused by Soskice, compared with McFague, 3, 177n2
- *See also* reality-depicting frame of reference

dead metaphor. *See under* metaphor
de Beauvoir, Simone, 169n68
deconstruction
- "break in covenant between word and world," loss of God-concept in (Derrida), 24–25; everything is interpretation, 33, infinite regress of meaning, 187, origin of metaphor in literal language of senses left out by, 189
- constructs rejected: notion of "better," 26, equality, 278, male/female binary, 275, 278
- nihilistic trajectory ("negative capability"), loss of meaning in, 180, 187, 189, lack of identity in, 208
- yearning in, 64
- *See also* double reading

demythologizing/remythologizing process
- described, 26; concept retained (unlike deconstruction), 26
- "God the father" demythologized, 20, 44, loss of epistemology in, 298
- Greco-Roman gods demythologized, 43
- Platonic spirit reborn, 64; feminist reappropriation of "what is sacred," 273–74, 276

Derrida, Jacques. *See under* deconstruction; double reading
Descartes, Réné. *See* Cartesian legacy
"divine horizon" for women. *See under* Grace, Jantzen
doctrine of analogy
- *See under* Aquinas, Thomas; Augustine, doctrine of signs and things in,

double reading
- developed by Derrida and Irigaray, 184, 211; more positive than "negative capability," 187, 211–12
- in Barth, 185; in Keller, 184–85; in Graham's "centrality of practice," 211; in McFague's "sacramentalism," 212

Douglass, Jane Dempsey, 160–61
Doyle, James (and Michele A. Paludi), 49n34
dualism
- Creator/creature (Barth), 171
- Johnson on, 90, 213
- Keller on, 214, further dualistic pairs for, 214–15
- male/female and other binary pairs as in Greek legacy, 90. 204–5
- mind/body, 52, 59, 210; in unitary anthropology, 167
- panentheist/ unknowable God, 215

economy of the same. *See under* subjectivity
embodiment
- as in Song of Solomon (Trible), 83, 236
- as in the resurrected body, 142–43, 226–27, in relation to typology (Soskice), 145, (*see also under* Lewis, C. S., on Jesus's risen manhood, slurred over)
- as rooted in historical and cultural context, not subjectivity, 268; contingent on sacramental universe, 171
- body as "vantage point," 230– 31, 267–68, 288

feminist emphasis on, in
"imaginary," 183–84, 212,
265; loss of in Enlightenment,
"patriarchy" held responsible
for, 202
lack of, in Irigaray's project, 153,
209, 212–16; in feminist
approach to redemption,
227–30; *imago Dei* not found in
biological sexuality (Augustine),
189–90; (Barth), 199
minimizing/maximimzing, 202–8,
266, 299,
See also under sexual difference
Enlightenment, the
female education to nurture men
(Rousseau), 169n69, Mary
Wollstonecraft's response to,
169, 169n69, 172–73
rational conversation, Caroline
Bingley's espousal of, 172
sacramental universe weakened by,
288
subjectivity promoted, loss of
embodiment in, 204, 273, 208,
male domination in, 169
women's emancipation stemming
from, 187–88, 207–8
epistemology
Barthian: "thing" (divine institution)
prior to "sign" (creaturely
reality), 192–95, McFague's
models based on, 192
Cartesian legacy, originally retaining
tradition, 24, subjective
development from, 30
psychoanalytic source for, 57–58,
216, 298–99
traditional, 12–13, 16, 23–24,
20; Thomist, 24, 57; Johnson
stepping back from, 57
equality
equality strategies from patristic
legacy (Børresen), 144–45
equal to whom (Irigaray), 150
of nature (at divine, divine-human,
human levels), 52–53, 117, 134,
142, 199, 227, 253; capital C for
Church, 171
evolution. *See under* Johnson, Elizabeth
evil, concept of, symbols of,
Augustine on (Ricoeur), 32, 38
in feminist view of "patriarchy," 156,
binary oppositions in, 204–5,
214
in mythic pattern, 290
Wisdom as "good and evil,"
knowledge of, 79, parallelled in
Eden story, 119
ex nihilo
Barth's divergence from classic *ex
nihilo* (Keller), 185
in self-creation of women (Irigaray),
28, 181, 187, 209, 214, 293, as
non-being, 283; feminized chaos
as, 214, human beings as not
godlike creators *ex nihilo*, 264
psychoanalytic categories not *ex
nihilo* (Irigaray), 217

Fatum, Lone
imago Dei on male terms, women
not included *per se*, 155, 159
on theological prejudice in feminist
interpretation, 156
on two options for women in early
church, 156–57; sexuality,
marriage as pre-christological,
158
femaleness
as God-alien, 78, 118, 120–24, 132,
141, 143–44, 152–53, 296, 301
ascetic renouncing of (Fatum), 160
in relationship of delight, 120
female church leadership,
arguments for, 164–65, 168n65;
Methodist history of, 241,
247n55; "concretion" of
Christianity against women
priests, 238–39, 250–56
reflecting gendered dimensions of
God's relationship to creation
(Grenz), 242

feminist theology
  critique of "patriarchy," 4, 6, 20, 44, 46, 62, 132, 180, 182, 187, 204, 207, 211, 277–78, 284
  emancipist projection, 13, 27, Ricoeur's use of "symbol" reinterpreted in, 31–32
  epistemology weakened, 188, 201–2, 220—21, 232–33 267, 275
  resurrected body not addressed, 142
feminist egalitarian anthropology
  in structure rather than content of Genesis 1 (Bird), 131
  male norm persisting in (French theorists), 15
  nature of resurrected body omitted in, 145
feminine, the
  as construct, Mary associated with, 251–56
  as negative of balanced pair, 65–66
  codified by Jung, 173n79, 216; repressed in male unconscious, 206; product of *jouissance* (Irigaray), 206
Feuerbach, Ludwig. *See under* Ricoeur, Paul
fiction
  allegory as, 42
  meaningful language of, in children's story (Lewis), 18
  model-metaphors as *mostly* fiction (McFague), 3, 70, 73–75, 290
  See also "useful fiction" frame of reference
Fiddes, Paul
  on embodiment, 230–31
  on McFague, dualism between "metaphor" and unknowable God in, 215
Flexner, Elinor. *See under* Mary Wollstonecraft
Freudian theory,
fusion of body and mind in unconscious, 217
  modified by Jacques Lacan, 28, 206
  object-relations theory countering, 218–19

religion as exercise in illusion, 6, 265, 273
  See also under psychoanalysis
gendered language for God
  as means to "see the moon," 79, 87, 147; biblical pointers, 80–82, relational tenor of, 255
  divine inspiration for (Lewis)/ human origin of (Hampson), 238–39
  feminine language for the Holy Spirit, early Syriac history of, 91, 148–49, 242
  feminist approach to, Gruber on, 77–78
  "of little consequence" (Hayter), 77, 88
  See also women's experience/identity
gendered stereotypes
  abstract projections, 255, Hellenistic origin for, 65, 66; complementary dualism in (Johnson), 92
  dimensions of God, 242, Johnson on, 243; principles (Boff), 242–43
  New Testament options for women (Fatum), 150
  Schneiders on, 110–11
  universal law attributed to, 217, 219, Jungian archetypes, 217
Giles, Kevin, 241
glory of man, woman as, 47, 160
  as not image of man, 53, but derivative from the man, 164, 168–71
  humanity twice recognized (Bilezikian), 245–46
  in modern equality strategies (Børresen), 144
  See also sexual difference: sacramental unity-in-diversity, offset factor
God
  as genderless Western concept, 118, reinterpreted in feminist theology, 145

as masculine in early Judaism, 118;
  Yahweh modelled on male
  peasant farmer (Bird), 129
as present, in linguistic transfer,
  22–24, 188, 300; source for
  Western theology, metaphysics,
  epistemology (Steiner), 24, 35;
  creation uttered and meant by
  (Augustine), 33–35 (see also
  under epistemology, traditional)
as Trinitarian, to-be-related
  (Soskice), 14, 154, as opposed
  to patriarchal monotheism
  (Moltmann), 154–55; man,
  woman, child analogy
  (Grudem), 242; also in early
  pagan divinity, 242, refuted by
  Augustine, 242
as unknowable, 215
"God the father," as in "fatherhood
  of God, brotherhood of
  man," 14, 153; as patriarchal
  model, feminist hermeneutic
  of suspicion towards, 5, 12,
  13; hegemony to be broken
  (McFague), 13, 20, 25, 30, 151,
  200, stranglehold of God-He to
  be shattered (Johnson), 62, 150;
  relativist consequences of, 151
Jesus's relationship with God the
  father seen as distinct from
  patriarchal model (Schneiders),
  285
"world as God's body" as model, 73;
  in touch model (McFague), 61;
  panentheism (all things in God),
  213–14, 230
gods (Hellenic), fate of,
  demythologized as projections of
  concepts, 40; "re-mythologized,"
  60, allegorized, as Gnostic
  projections, 31–32, as
  personified passions, as purely
  literary figures, 40–41
Jungian archetypes, 41, 64; rebirth
  of Platonic spirit, 62–63,
  182–83; human beings as gods,
  236–37

Graham, Elaine
  feminist emphasis on embodiment,
    208, 273; social sciences on,
    204; Enlightenment subjectivity,
    historically conditioned, 274,
    attitude to women, 169
  language for God, women's
    experience as worthy of imaging
    "the holy," 270, 282, 286
  on deconstruction, equality, male/
    female binary rejected as
    constructs, 278; postmodern
    identity contradictory and
    fragmented, 267
  on Irigaray, 202: female body as
    immaterial projection, 152–53,
    206, 268, as fixed gendered
    essence, 209, but agent for social
    change, 206–7, 210, Western
    epistemology, ontology rewritten,
    152, 207, 289; non-identity
    beyond patriarchal gaze, 279
  on psychoanalysis, 217–20
  on sex/gender distinction, gender
    socially constructed, but
    "essentialism" and "social
    categorism" rejected, 210,
    268, imago Dei as, 269; gender
    profoundly relational, 266, 299
  on the Trinity, imago Dei, 266,
    269–70
  "vantage point," body as, 267,
    Incarnation as, 269, 288;
    "centrality of practice," as source
    of values, 211, 233, 271; loss
    of sacramental universe in,
    300, ethics if human nature
    contextual, 210–11, 266
  See also churches; dualism;
    minimizing/ maximizing the
    body
Grant, Robert (on allegorical biblical
  interpretation,), 40, 89
Gray, Frances,
  on Hellenic dualisms in Western
    culture, 204–5
  on Irigaray, 207, Jung compared
    with, 219

Grenz, Stanley,
  on "egalitarians" and
    "complementarians," 240–42
Gregory of Nazianzus against
  Apollinarius, 223–25, 227, 230
Gregory of Nyssa. *See under* Soskice,
  Janet Martin
Gruber, Mayer
  maternal expressions for God in
    Isaiah, 77–78
  on Trible, Phyllis, women's identity
    for, 78
Grudem, Wayne
  on Hebrews, 11:32, grammar of,
    246–47
  on the Trinity (*imago Dei*), 241–42

Hagar
  as allegorical figure of Old
    Testament law, 11, 88, 100, Jesus
    born under, 108
  allegorical usage distinct from
    historical figure, 190n34
Hampson, Daphne
  feminist aspirations, 235
  on Barth's presentation of Mary, 244
  on baptismal language, baptized into
    Christ, not Jesus, 224
  on "concretion" of Christianity,
    230, 235, 237, 238, 244, 302, of
    human origin, compared with
    Lewis, 238–39; on exclusion of
    women from priesthood, 250–
    54, argument against, 251–53
  on construct of the feminine,
    254–55, conservative order
    collapsing, 256
  on sexism in theology, 234
  two kinds of inclusive language,
    225, earlier inclusive language
    excluded, 227–28
  "What is not assumed," 223;
    (abstract) universals, 229, in
    patristic culture, 224
Hayter, Mary, 77, 83
head/body language
  body without head, 230

head/body relationship between
  Christ and the Church, salvation
  through, 229
headship (Johnson), 90, for women
  (Hampson), 255
on the man as head, woman glory of
  the man: 160, 163–64, 164n54;
  (Augustine), 48, 51; (Barth)
  100, 194; Bilezikian, 244–45;
  (Børresen) 144; (Calvin) 160–
  61; (Hill), 52–53; (Lewis), 53
in marriage, 168n66, typological
  Christ role for the man, 163–64,
  reversal of roles in, 170–71
Hill, Edmund
  on Augustine's theory of the
    imago Dei, diagram of, 89–90,
    use of allegorical figures in,
    role of Mary alleged, 49, 51,
    89–90; meaning of "mind" for
    Augustine, 49n35
  on 1 Corinthians 11:1–16
    (interpersonal relationships
    at divine and human levels),
    correspondences between,
    67, equality of nature for both
    parties in, 38, 52–53, 117, 134,
    142, 160, 227
  on Wisdom, 81n43, changes of
    gender with Wisdom become
    flesh, 82–83
Holladay, William
  on reassignment of sexual roles, 106
  See also under *theotokos*, Mary as
Hoppin, Ruth. *See under* Bilezikian,
  Gilbert, on authorship of
  Hebrews
Hultgård, Anders
  on divine inspiration assumed in
    creation stories, 117
  on Western genderless
    reinterpretation of Yahweh, 118
  feminist reinterpretation of, 145

identity
  as narrative, 260, 263, 272, 281,
    283, 288, 296, 293, 299 (*see also
    under* Ricoeur, Paul)

Index

in deconstruction, rejection of, 278
in redemption, 249
search for, viii, 35, 175–76, 181, 208, 249, 279
"unto us a child is born," 249–56
(*see also* universals: concrete, *theotokos*)

illusion
in remythologizing, 35, 71–72, 87
(*see also* "useful fiction" frame of reference)
religion as (Marx; Freud), truth framework not main concern (Jantzen), 6–7, 265, 275
truth as (Nietzsche), 17–18, 26, linguistic reference as (Mallarmé), 22–23

imagination
as function of "right" brain, 289, 289n88
attributed to sub-rational mind, 23, 216, in psychoanalysis, 289, linked with projected "symbols," 277, 58, 277, generating "symbolic," 289
appealing to contemporary imagination, fostering women's identity, 286
in mythopoeia, 289–90, contrasted with remythologizing; danger of "is not" aspect of metaphor, 284, but viewed positively in Irigaray's utopia, 279,
in narrative identity, 261, 263, 271, 280, 293
in Romantic reappropriation of Greco-Roman gods, 41 62; in reappropriation of Christianity, 41, 62–65, in reappropriation of the *via negativa*, 62
in traditional sacramentalism (Aquinas), 57, 75
in "world as God's body" and other constructs, 212, method attributed to Paul's letters and John's gospel (McFague), 57

imago Dei
as copy to original, 255, created in God's image, 59, 150; incorrect surmise about, 67, 82n49, 88, 121–20, 124, 171; literary sources for, 70, 72, 76, 117, 141, 165–66, narrative inimical to women (Keller), 181
as idea, premise in theological anthropology, 118–20, 239, 294, persisting in feminist theology; humanization of, 146; models for (McFague), 177–78, 192,; women's theomorphic status asserted, 59, 91–92, 124, 179–80, 282 (see also *imago Christi*, women as)
Barth on, 97, 100–101, 194–200, as "most hierarchical model imaginable" (Ruether), 167, 171, 176 (*see also* Bilezikian, Gilbert)
complexity of roles, 149, role-reversals in, 161–66, 171, 199; embodiment, social relationship in, 288, 296; metaphor as means to apprehend, 148
epistemology in, 61, 288; fate of if sacramental universe demythologized, 20, 44
legacy of interpretation, 123–24, 161; inculturated doctrine, 281; linguistic ambiguity in, 199–200; Maçon on, 4–5; modern, 240–45
originally male, women originally excluded from (Børresen), 125; (Bird), 126–28, (Fatum), 155, 160; subordinate typology in, 122–23, 145, 156; sexual difference/fertility excluded from (Augustine),189–90, 199, 244; (Barth), 199, 244; (Bird), 126–28, reinterpreted to include women, 145
two-stage metaphor in (Trible), 116, 133–37, 145
See also under allegory; Augustine's theory of; embodiment; nearness-by-likeness (*imago Dei*), nearness-of-approach

imago Christi, women as, 91–92, 179–80, 253
Incarnation, 35, 82, 288
    as concept-model (Barth), 191–92, 193–94, 196–97
    as model (McFague), 177–78, 192; (Keller), 183–87, 213
    as partial (Irigaray), multiple incarnations, 236–37, 248–50
    implications for masculine imagery (Lewis), 238–39, for redemption, 223–25, 227–31
    in maleness not undone in Jesus's risen manhood (Lewis), 223
    See also Boff, Leonardo; Graham, Elaine
inclusion
    methods of, 117–18, 122, 144, 172, 221, 225–26, 248–50, 286
    scope of, 239, 241, 270, 280,
    See also "man" as collective term
infinite regress
    of metaphor, deconstructionist argument for, but leaves out literal language of senses as origin for, 189
Irigaray, Luce
    search for women's identity in, in matriarchal line, 181–82, 301, by association with women of history, 221, 291
    "horizon of sexual difference", 63–64, vision for new order, 63–65, 186, 206–7, 293; need to rethink sexual difference, equal to whom, 150
    jouissance as means to social change, 206–7, delayed advent for, 203
    male "symbolic," with Christian attribution and (male) narrative, rejected, 182; women not "the other of the same," 181–82, against "specular economy," 65, 297, 301; Western epistemology and ontology to be rewritten, 152–53, 206–7, 289–91, 301
    on classic psychoanalytic stereotypes, 217–18, 277, mythic narratives reinterpreted, 219, Christian motifs attributed to, 219–20
    See also under Incarnation
"is not"
    applied to (patriarchal) God, 283–84, but not to feminist emancipatory language, 179
    projection/bit of nonsense/placebo, 73–74, 274; crack in foundation of conceptual truth, 290–91
"is" projected as "what if," 73–74, 183–84, 212

Jantzen, Grace
    explanation of "symbolic," religious attribution in, 205–6; alternative proposal, 6, 247, 268, 298, connection between women and material in, flourishing of "natality," 235, Hannah Arendt read "against the grain," 263–65
    on Derrida, 24, "double reading," 184
    on "divine horizon" for women, 87, 233–36, 282, 298–99, women's subjectivity in, 263, 263n14; Irigaray's support of Jesus's maleness (as partial incarnation), 236–37, Jantzen's reservations about, 248–49
    on panentheist "shuffle," feminist panentheism reducing to pantheism, 215
    on psychoanalysis, 28, 205, Irigaray's dissent from Lacan, 205–6
    process theology, rejection of ontological realism in, 94,
    religion as ethical aspiration (Marxian and Freudian illusion theory not challenged), 6–7, 71—72, 276, truth not main concern, 7, 71–72, 273–74, doctrine of analogy rejected, 75
Johnson, Elizabeth
    emancipatory language, 152, espoused for women as *imago Dei*, *imago Christi* (whole Christ only pneumatological), 228; women's experience key to

imago Dei, 67, "the feminine" rejected, 173, 173n79
evolutionary origin of "creator" God, 213–14, on panentheism, 213 (*see also under* dualism)
migration of language for God, 109: early Syriac, 90–91, 148; Mary as mother figure, 91, 112; Wisdom, 91–92; on "ransacking" traditions, 93, 180, Christian and pre-Christian, 93, gnostic, 91n78, to continue as method in feminist project, 92–93
on "symbol," collective unconscious as source for, 299; Ricoeur's use of "symbol" reinterpreted, 58, 276
on unknowable God, 179, against male/female dimensions in, 243; word "God" patriarchal, but method similar to alleged patriarchal, 60
SHE WHO IS based on Thomist He Who Is, without Thomist epistemology, 151, 295, yet Thomist method of imagination claimed, 57

Jung, Carl
archetypes, 41, 64, 217, 219, shadow 217, 219, as mythic narratives, 219, source for "the feminine," 173n79, 204–5, compared with Irigaray, 219
subconscious as source of epistemology, rebirth of Platonic spirit in, 64, 298–99

Keats, John, 62–63, 280
Keller, Catherine
Barth viewed as "logocentric," 197, but unorthodox on chaos, 186
cosmology "diametrically opposed" to Barth's, 183–86, but some similarity with, 176, 186, Augustine's rejected "sponge" image reclaimed, 184, 186–87, 213, 213n36
dualism opposed, 214, but new dualisms proposed, 213n36, 214–15
"imaginary" of bottomless feminized chaos in Genesis 1:2 (*tehom*), 183–84, 186–87, 212–13, prior to 36 "man-father" narrative, 183; sense of becoming in, 184, 214
method of double reading (text of Genesis 1:2 destabilized, redirected),185–87, detected in Barth's reading of text, 185–86

Keown, Gerald, 105n23
Kidner, Derek.
on seed of the woman, Adam passed over in, 97, 98, 113, 138, 257n85,
on "wilderness" for Israel, different experiences of, 85

Lewis, C. S.
allegory and symbol differentiated, 41–42, 68; history of allegory, 40–41: Greco-Roman gods demythologized, 40; fresh allegorical constructions, 40–41; in Romantic period, 41, 62
on Jesus's risen manhood, slurred over, 223, 224, 248, 257
on metaphor, access to truth via, 17, 19, 29, 30; compared with Nietzsche on status of dead metaphor, 17–18; meaningful use of language, 18–19, 27
mythopoeia (Tolkien's sub-creation), 289
on priesthood, 44, women not eligible, reason for, 171–72, 252–53; women may preach, 253; divine source of biblical imagery, compared with Hampson, 238–39, 244
on religious language, 14, 15n41, "myth" as, 69, 70; archetype seen in copy (sacramentalism), 42, 60, 68, 76; on glory of man, woman as, 53, 53n51 (*see also* nearness-by-likeness, *imago Dei*)

Lewis, C. S. (*cont.*)
  on symbol, metaphor, definition, method of, examples, 15n42; male and female as shadows (symbols) of transcendent reality, 6, 10, 149, 255–56, compared with Irigaray, 10
  via negativa, Johnson on, 61
literal/ symbolic meaning
  method of living in/ being drawn beyond (Ricoeur), 71, 75, 87–88
logocentrism (*Logos*-order)
  Logos as Ground of Being for something in what we say, "presence" in, many avenues to but one ultimate source (Steiner), 23–24, 30; onto-theological unity in (Jantzen), 24
  Ricoeur's presentation of cosmic "symbol," *Logos*-history insufficiently attentive to, 30
  Barth's method described as (Keller), 183, 185, 197, but method excludes pre-incarnate Logos, 197–98
  Logos, 197–98, 223, 225, 230, ancient tradition as male, 31n47 (*see also under* Wisdom)
  Logos-order, 24, feminist opposition to, 25, 204–5; broken, 22, 25, to be broken (McFague), 19–20, 25, 30
Lucas, R. C., 162n49

Mallarmé, Stéphane
  "purity" within language itself as liberation, 22–23, reference to external world rejected, 22
"man" as collective term, 123
  means to include women, 142–43, invisible woman (Trible), 250
  "man of heaven" as collective term, 125, 141–43, 145; "man of dust," 142
  women included in Latin term for "man" (*vir*), Greek term (*anēr*) 143, 225

male/female relationship
  as ruler/consort, relationship of delight, 80, 80n41, 81, 84–86, 95–96, 113, 120, 171–74
  offset by reversal of priority, 113, 165–66
Mascall, E. L.
  doctrine of analogy, presuppositions of, 55–56
Mary, Grace and Hope in Christ,
  typology, 8n24, Mary-Eve typology, 101–2; 109–10
  Mary born under the law, 108; change in new covenant, 109n37
  on the *imago Dei*, 60; covenant relationship, 60, as male/female love affair, 86
  on mistranslation of Genesis 3:15, 96n4
Mary, mother of Jesus
  as allegory/model, 88, 109, 249, 288, as ideal *scientia*, 102; Johnson on history of, 91–93
  as illustration of faith in Hill's diagram, 51, 89–90 (*see also under* Hill, Edmund)
  Barth on, 97–101, 112, 193, 195, 244
  Børresen on, 122, 140n82
  Schneiders on, 110–11
  Soskice on, citing Susan Ashbrook Harvey, 148–49
  under the old covenant, 103, 107–8, 113; new covenant, 103, 104, 108; active role at wedding but not as bride, 108–9, possible other roles, 112–13
  See also *theotokos*, Mary as; Beattie, Tina, Boff, Leonardo, "feminine, the"
Mary Magdalene, Schneiders on, 111, 285, 287
McFague, Sallie
  as "erstwhile" Barthian, 192, 199; values dependent on God described as "Barthian," 285n81; unknowable God, except through human models, 62, 72–74, dualism in. 215; claims

to be influenced by Ricoeur, 29–31, 75
influenced by feminist epistemology, 19, 212; on patriarchal model, 5; feminist/ existentialist reluctance to "jump out of one's skin," 260, 263, 271, 297, 298
imagination as function of right brain, 289
on "contemporary crisis of language," 9, usage of model-metaphor, 12, metaphor of juxtaposition, 20, anthropomorphisms, 20 (*see also* Schneiders, Sandra, on metaphor, McFague's theory in; better; "useful fiction" frame of reference)
on deconstruction, 187– 89, 278, 292, 293
on imaginative pictures for theological concepts, 31, for re-mythologizing Christian faith, 20, 72, contrasted with clinical approach, 72; as short-term "houses", 26, 88, contemporary, 93; new projected footing for, 29, 31–32, 44, 71, method attributed to Paul's letters, John's Gospel, 44–45, Augustine's Neoplatonism, Thomas's Aristotelianism, 45, 47, 56, 57, 61, Bible as poetic classic, 72
on "in touch" model of being and knowing, 61; metaphor "the world as God's body," 72–73; on sacred world order, 73–74, 73n19, sacramentalism, humans as *imago Dei* within model, 177, 192, 212–13; on dead metaphor, Lewis classed with Nietzsche, 17, 22
on metaphor (classical), sacramental universe, 12–13, 16, 151, 262, Ricoeur's endorsement of, 12, McFague's distance from sacramental universe, 13, 17, 19, 25, 27, 39–40, 44, 293; "metaphorical theology" to break hegemony of, 13, 25
on "metaphor" of self (autobiography), 21, 260–61, 263, 272, 274 (Hannah Arendt appealed to, 261, 267)
on relativism, 201, aware of while living in model, 201
on Tolkien's mythopoeia, 290, remythologizing contrasted with, 290, "is not" factor in, 291
McKane, William
on Proverbs 8, 80n41
metaphor,
all truth beyond language of senses dependent on, 17–19; in "classical" metaphor, "God the father" as source of connection with external world, 12–13, 16, 21, 39, 151, psycho-physical parallelism, 19
definition, 11, vehicle and tenor (Richards), finger pointing to moon (Trible), 116, 147–49; meaning of dead metaphor preserved (Lewis), 18
in the *imago Dei*, gendered relationships as, 10, 19–20, reading archetype in copy, 76–87
McFague's usage (model-metaphor), 12, 295, Schneiders on, 283–84 , in relation to unknowable God, 215, as anthropomorphism, 20— 21, as "metaphorical" theology, 29; hegemony of "God the father" to be broken, 13, 19–20, 25, 27, 30, 44, 200, 294; loss of truth in, 20–21, 40; bit of nonsense, 73, 75–74, 290—91; "contemporary crisis of language," 9–10
prevalence of metaphor, McFague on, 17, 21, but Nietzsche classed with Lewis, 17 (see Nietzsche, Friedrich; Mallarmé, Stéphane; deconstruction)
Ricoeur's usage, 262, 271–72, 274, 294–95; McFague's appeal to Ricoeur in, 29–31, 272n41

mind/body dualism. *See under* dualism, mind/body
minimizing/ maximizing the body, 202–8
   demythologizing/remythologizing tendency in, 299
   neutralization of sexual difference, danger of (Irigaray), 203, loss of gendered identity in, 299, gendered relations counteracting, 266
   maximizing difference, possible separation of sexes in, 299, "writing the body," 202n2
misogyny
   Augustine viewed as misogynist, 46, but endorsed *theotokos*, women's identification with, 53
   in traditional interpretation of creation texts (Trible), 132, 139
   women not *imago Dei* (Børresen on Ambrosiaster), 141
modernism
   promoting subjectivity but not abandoning sacramental "presence," 185
   Irigaray's caution against abandoning male/female binary, 208
Mounce, Robert
   on woman giving birth to male child in Revelation 12, 103n20
myth
   as narrative about transcendent reality, 69–71, 71n9, 76, 79, 83; demythologized, 43, 73 (*see also* demythologizing/ remythologizing process)
   associated with right brain, 289n88
   modern "myth" of self-constituting subject, 293, 297
   in psychoanalysis, 219, 299,

nakedness/clothing
   clothed in good deeds, 86, in being baptized in Christ, 162–63, 225
   nakedness as relationship of delight, 83, 84, as shame and misery, 84, 86n61

Soskice on Gregory of Nyssa's view, post-lapsarian "clothing with skins" as genitalia, 110,
nearness-by-likeness (*imago Dei*), 52, 60
   in early Genesis, diversity, created (given) nature of, 165; still intact after eviction from Garden, 119
   in marriage, ministry, symbolic roles in, 165
   reversal of priority in, diagram of, 166
nearness-of-approach, 52, 60
   as non-gendered, as unity in Christ, acquired in baptism, 165
   loss of, 119
   in Augustine's interpretation of the *imago Dei*, 190, doctrine of signs, 191, 244
   in Barth's interpretation of the *imago Dei*, in *analogia relationis* 196, 244
   in Thomist participation in God, 59, SHE WHO IS, 59
   scientia as, 65–66
Neoplatonism
   influence on Augustine, 47; in Augustine's theory of the *imago Dei*, 47, McFague on Augustine, 45, 47, 56; Børresen on, 124, 282
   Soskice on, philosophy of "the One and the Same" as Neoplatonic heresy,153–54, 300, God of (male) Cartesian subjectivity, 224
   role in "patriarchy," 281
   See also Plato
Newsom, Carol
   on Wisdom, parallels between divine and human levels in Proverbs, 81–82, 81n44
Nietzsche, Friedrich,
   compared with Irigaray, 204–5
   on metaphor as illusory source of truth (rubbed coin image),17, compared with Lewis, 17–19, 26, compared with McFague, 27, 31
   What is man, post Nietzsche, Ricoeur on, 274–75

Origen
    as influence for Augustine: Christian allegorization principles, 40, 89; ancient model of masculine and feminine, 48; disembodied *imago Dei*, 49n37, 51n44
    allegorical interpretation of Old Testament systematized, 88, critiqued by Augustine, 40, 88–89

panentheism. *See under* Jantzen, Grace; Johnson, Elizabeth
Parmée, Douglas, 23
patriarchal model. *See under* God
patriarchal monotheism
    in late antiquity, 40
    Irigaray on, 5–6, 14, 128, 53
    Soskice on, 153—54; citing Moltmann, 14, 153, 154–55
perichoresis (dance), 171–72
Philo, 40, 48, 50 197
Plato
    abstract universals, 225
    influence in Augustine's theory of the *imago Dei*, 47–48
    Ruether on reincarnation for Plato, lower principle for women, 167
    source behind linguistic meaning (Steiner), 23–24, 35; Williams on, 33
    symbolism in Plato's dialogues, 42, Jung on Platonic spirit, 298
philosophical *hubris*
    demythologizing/ remythologizing tendency in Western philosophy, 31, 38, 59, 65, 295, 301
    in Augustine (Ricoeur), 32
    in remythologizing, 31–32
postmodernism, 188, 208, 271,
Power, Kim
    on Council of Mâcon, 4–5
    on Augustine's inclusion of women in the *imago Dei*, 5, 49
    on ancient model of masculine/ feminine as superior/inferior, 48
    on Mary as ideal *scientia*

process theology. *See* Jantzen, Grace: process theology, rejection of ontological realism in
projection theories of religion, 6–7, 71–72
projected universe
    symbolic "Catholic" sensibility promoting "sacred world order"/ "Protestant" skepticism, as functional cosmology (McFague), 73–74, 88
    distinction between symbol and allegory lost in, 11, 41
psychoanalysis
    cultural suppression of female, 206, repressed in male unconscious mind, Irigaray's alternative to, 207, 209–10
    Freudian aphorism, fusion of psyche and soma as "speaking agent," 10, 210; universal law in, 222–23, queried by Irigaray, 217–18, 277
    levels of operation in, 218
    object-relations theory, 218–19
    sexual difference, 205
    subjectivity achieved by repression, method of as source of culture (*see under* "symbolic, the"), 13, 28–29, 32, 276

Rees, Janice on Sarah Coakley, 253
    on liturgical act, 253
    doctrine of creaturehood, *imago Dei* starting point for enquiry, 7n23
Ranke-Heinemann, Uta
    on Augustine, 46
    on Mary, 113n54
reality-depicting frame of reference, 148
    empty tomb, 178
    as "theology stammering after a transcendent God," 178–79
relativism, 3, 21, 26, 61, 177, 188, 201, 202, 211, 212, 267, 278, 293, 297
remythologizing. *See* demythologizing/ remythologizing process

resurrected body
    all bearing image of man of heaven (Soskice), 145, 250
    omission of in Calvin's theory of the *imago Dei*, 160–61
    Jesus's risen manhood, 249, slurred over (Lewis), 223, 248
    Augustine on, 47–48, 143, 226–27, against Gregory of Nyssa, 110, 142
Richards, I. A., metaphor, definition of, 2, 11n31
Ricoeur, Paul
    hermeneutics of restoration, 75, on allegorical relation of Old to New Testament, 88; Origen's systematizing, 88
    identity as narrative, 260, 263, 283, 285, 296, on Hannah Arendt, 260, great literary traditions, 271, 280, 291–92, exemplary man, 280–81
    "is" and "is not" (meaning beyond literal "is not"), on symbol, 71, contrasted with analogy, 71, 75, 87–88, metaphor as, 262, 272
    on Feuerbach's wish to reclaim "sacred" for "man," 273, 274; on "what is man?" (Freud, Marx, Nietzsche), 274
    "symbol gives rise to thought," 272n41, symbol speaks to us, 12, 16, 29, 34, 262, 268, 275, 293, 294, as "other," 57; *Logos*-history insufficiently attentive to, 30, as in Augustine on original sin, 32, 33; as philosophical *hubris*, 38, 295, as gnosis, 33, 35, 297, to be renounced, 60, 65, 67
    transparence of "Cogito" questioned, self as disciple of "text," 261–63, 273, 275, 276, 297, 301
Ridderbos, Hermann, 107, 163n52
Rimbaud, Arthur,
    "I" as "other" in sub-rational frame, 22–23, ethical vision (social responsibility) in, 23, 29

Romantic movement, 41, 62, 64, 186, 279, 298,
Ruether, Rosemary Radford
    Hampson on, 235
    on Augustine, 49n34
    on Barth, 166, 195–96, 244
    on feminist theology, 20–21, 232–33, 282, thought comes first, 31; expanded unitary anthropology, 151, 167, 203, 240; "the feminine," 173, female "bridegrooms," 43–44; papal statement on women, 82n49
    on *imago Dei* idea, 32, 167, change in frame of reference in, 3–4, 6, 20, 39, 43–44, 146, 167
    on reincarnation (Plato), 167

sacramentalism, traditional, 42, 68, 71, 76,
sacramental universe, 13, 21, 44, 60–61, 65, 150, 151, 268, 272, 300
    sexual difference as sacramental (*see under* sexual difference, as sacramental unity in diversity)
sacramentalism reborn as model, 73–74, 88, 177–78, 179–80, 212
    See also Jung: rebirth of Platonic spirit; projected universe
sapientia /scientia
    as (masculine) nearness-of-approach/ (feminine) as not nearness-of-approach: Azkoul on, 47, Power on, 50; Augustine's usage of, 48—49, 50n42, 59, 65, 141, 145, 191, 194, 244, 282, 286–87; Hill's diagram of, 51
Sayers, Dorothy, 1–2, 4, 12
Schneiders, Sandra
    on exemplary woman, Mary Magdalene as, 111, 285, 287
    on Mary, mother of Jesus, 110–11, 113, 286–87, 113, blood-relationship to faith relationship, 284–85
    on metaphor, McFague's theory in, 283–84, 290–91; Jesus's healing use of "abba" in, 284–85, 286

Schüssler Fiorenza, Elisabeth,
Irigaray's response to, 237
recent publishing trends excluding feminist voice, vii
Seamands, Stephen, 168n66
sexual difference
assumed in psychoanalysis, 205; culture does not yet exist (Irigaray), horizon of, 63, 182, 203, 279, need to rethink, 65, 153–54
as embodiment, 204, lack of detail on nature of (Graham), 268
addition to "man" of creation (Bird), 127–28
corresponding to Trinitarian relationship, as mystical, 6, sacramental unity-in-diversity, 159–74, offset factor, 164–66 (*see also under* Hill; Soskice on divine correspondence, Jewish attestation)
feminist challenge in (Whitford), 207, 208; "egalitarian" response to, 240
marital hierarchy compared with spiritual unity (Calvin), "most hierarchical model imaginable" (Ruether on Barth); "complementarian" position on, 242
not matter of theological indifference, 125, 141, 145, 146, 152
Sherlock, Charles, 162
Soskice, Janet Martin, viii
on Aquinas, 55n57, 178–79, 55n57, 226n88
on gendered language for God (early Syriac), 148–49; "fatherhood of God, brotherhood of man," 14, 153, Trinity as to-be-related, 154, 155n29, Moltmann on, 14n37, 153–55
on Irigaray, 150, 152–53; lack of embodiment in feminist theology, 230
on (male) Cartesian subjectivity, divine guarantor for, 30, 225, 298, 300, female as negative, 65–66; modern myth of self-constituting subject, 293, 297
on patristic approach to creation texts, 122–24, 123n21, 126, 141; Gregory of Nyssa's theory that first couple originally sexless, 110, 134n60
on the *imago Dei*, humans as relational beings, 128, Jewish attestation, 2, 159; exegetical conflict between *imago Dei* and resurrected body, 125, 141–43, 145, 250
on reality-depicting frame of reference, 26, 177n2, 178–79; metaphor, 2; useful fictions, 3
Steiner, George
on deconstruction anti-God as Father of meaning, 24–25
on Mallarmé, 22–23, Rimbaud, 22, 23
on meaning, "presence" in language, 22, 23–24, 27, 30, 35, 188, 300; break in covenant between word and world, 22, 25, 200
See also under logocentrism (*Logos*-order),
stereotypes for women, Johnson on, 168
subjectivity, as sovereign
as (male) Cartesian, 224–25, "economy of the same," 153, 298
female subjectivity, 187–88, 208, 263, 263n13, 273, 275, 276, 279, 293, 298, cultural critique in, 267–68, 276; "divine horizon" for women in, 233, 236, 298
mind/body dualism in, 171, 209
in psychoanalysis, 28, 205–6, 219, Irigaray's critique of, 277
to be lost as origin (Ricoeur), 262–63, 272, 275, 301
submission
as not God-alien, 171
in connection with Mary, 251, 286

submission (*cont.*)
   in relationship with God, 50;
      new dimension in under new covenant, 162, 168n66
symbol
   description of, 11, 71; "symbol gives rise to thought" 272n14
"symbolic, the"
   in Freudian theory, Catholic liturgy echoed, 28, 206
   symbolic order, upheaval in, if God declared a woman (Irigaray), 10, 28–29
Swartley, Willard
   on theological interpretation as mirror, window, 8, 8n25, 50, 59
   liberationist writers, 9, 9n28
Swidler, Leonard, 79, 83

Tasker, R. V. G., 109n36
tehom imagined as bottomless process. *See under* Keller, Catherine
theotokos, Mary as.
   Mary as, 10, 48, 104, 302
   revolutionary nature of, 106, 165–66, male not involved in, 97, 98
   "unto us a child is born," 254, 257–58, 285, 296
   See also under Mary, mother of Jesus
Todd, Janet. *See* Wollstonecraft, Mary
Trible, Phyllis
   exegetical method, 78, 94, 132, 135–39; metaphor as moon to be seen but not possessed, 78–79, 83, 87, 233–34
   genderless proto-humanity, 115–16
   on *imago Dei*, 79, 82, 132, 145, 146, double metaphor in, 116; differentiation, 133, on primal couple, 140–41; judgment, 96n5, 136–37; invisible woman, 133, 137, 250, 281,
   on Jeremiah 33:22b, 105–6,
   on Ruth, Naomi and the women of Bethlehem, 221, 233–22
   on Song of Solomon, 83, 236
   (*See also* misogyny)

trinitarian Godhead (as to-be-related), 10, 14, 154, 155, 301,
typology, 8, 8n24, 88, 89, 145
   as in Eve/Mary, complex, 97–98, 109, 145

unity
   in Christ (baptismal), 171, 258
   in equality of nature, 103, 117, 142, 227, as gendered unity in diversity, 119–20, 133, 228
   original humanity/ proto-humanity (Bird, Børresen, Fatum, Trible on), 133, 135, 157, 157n36, 158–60
"useful fiction" frame of reference, 3–5, 7, 10, 12, 13, 39, 167
universals
   abstract, 218–21, 223, 224, 225, 228, 229, 230,
   concrete, 250, 280, 281, 286: exemplary man (Adam); 280, 281 (second Adam), 285; exemplary woman, *theotokos*, 250, 288,
   See also under Schneiders, Mary Magdalene as

via analogia, 69, 75–76, 79, 87, 92, 175, 176
   projected version, 74, 75, 180
via negativa, 69, 71, 74, 77, 78, 87, 92
   projected version, 62, 74, absent for Irigaray, 182

Whitford, Margaret
   on dilemma for feminist critique of Enlightenment, 187–88, 202, 207–8
   on Irigaray's matriarchal line, 181; "murder of the mother," 219–20; utopia, 63–64, 152, 182
   writing the body, 202n2
Wisdom
   as Word of God (Logos), 34–35, 50, 51, 76, 79–83, 80n41, 80n42, 81n43, 82n45, 86, 106, 112, 164n54, 184, 197, 229, 302

as homeland, road (Wisdom incarnate) to homeland(Augustine), 34

Mary as mother of Wisdom, 113

parallel of ideal wife in Proverbs, 112

See also *sapientia*; Johnson, Elizabeth

wisdom tradition

in apocryphal literature; in John's gospel, 84

in Old Testament, 86; Proverbs, 81–82; Song of Songs (Trible), 83

Wizard of Oz, The, illustrations based on:

balloon flight, destination uncertain, 259

Dorothy's house in cyclone, ecclesiastical model (Barth), 191, 259

Dresden China Country, as traditional sacramentalism, 67, 68

green glasses, metaphor as starting point of subjectivist quest, 59, 60, 61, 68, 69, 74, 261, 268, 295, as means of pretense/illusion, 3

Hammer-Heads as genderless proto-humanity, 115, 146, 296, figure of projection, aggressive space-claiming, 232, 256, 299

Lion's placebo courage, as projected "sacramentalism," not necessary for lion in traditional sacramentalism, 274

Oz the Great and Terrible, as patriarchal figure, 1, 4, 37, 60, 61, 65, 68, 113, 114

Poppy Field, as living within model ("as if"), 27, 175, 176, 180, 201, 272, 275, 295, 296

River, Deconstructionist, trajectory towards nihilism of, 27, 175, 176, 180, 295, 296

Yellow Brick Road, as traditional epistemology, sacramental approach in, 27, 29, 30, 35, 61, 95, 175, 176, 201, 271, 272, 274–76, 278, 280, 291, 295–96, 300–302

Wollstonecraft, Mary opposing Rousseau, 169, 169n69, 173

women's experience/identity

ambiguity not basis for, 188

worthiness of, for the *imago Dei*, gendered language for God, 282, 286

women in ordained ministry/lay ministry, 168n65

Methodist history of, 241, deaconesses, 168n66

www.ingramcontent.com/pod-product-compliance
Lightning Source LLC
Chambersburg PA
CBHW050837230426
43667CB00012B/2031